Activities Handbook for the Teaching of Psychology

Volume 3

■

Vivian Parker Makosky
Chi Chi Sileo
Linda Genevieve Whittemore
Christine P. Landry
Mary Lynn Skutley
Editors

AMERICAN PSYCHOLOGICAL ASSOCIATION
Washington, DC 20002

Library of Congress Cataloging-in-Publication Data
(Revised for vol. 3)

Activities handbook for the teaching of psychology.

Vols. 2–3 edited by: Vivian Parker Makosky . . .
[et al.].
Includes bibliographies and index.
1. Psychology—Problems, exercises, etc.   I. Benjamin,
Ludy T., 1945–   . II. Lowman, Kathleen D., 1948–
BF78.A28   1981   150′.7   81-1648
ISBN 0-912704-34-9   (v. 1)
ISBN Volume 2: 1-55798-030-6
ISBN Volume 3: 1-55798-081-0 (acid-free paper)

Copies may be ordered from
American Psychological Association
Order Department
P.O. Box 92984
Washington, DC 20090-2984

In the United Kingdom and Europe, copies may be ordered from
American Psychological Association
3 Henrietta Street
Covent Garden, London
WC2E 8LU England

Published by
American Psychological Association
750 First Street, NE
Washington, DC 20002

First Printing, July 2001
Second Printing, February 2006
Third Printing, July 2007

Printed in the United States of America

TABLE OF CONTENTS

FOREWORD

Five hundred years after Johannes Gutenberg devised a method of printing from movable type, the lecture continues to thrive as a teaching technique in the United States. Teachers lecture to their students because their teachers lectured to them when they were students. Indeed, lecturing can be an effective way of teaching, or, perhaps more accurately, of prompting students to learn what the lecturer wants them to know. Lecturing ensures a steady flow of information from the teacher's mouth to the student's notebook, but research findings suggest that more active approaches can increase motivation, learning, and retention. Even masterful lecturers recognize that a variety of classroom activities, if used appropriately, can be informative, engaging, provocative, and memorable.

To provide a readily available compendium of such activities, the American Psychological Association (APA) published Volume 1 of the *Activities Handbook for the Teaching of Psychology* in 1981 and Volume 2 in 1987. The large number of copies sold reveals that the first two volumes are widely used to enliven psychology classes for countless students and teachers. Reasons for their popularity are easy to understand. First, they cover most of the main areas of the discipline and offer something of value for teachers of almost all psychology courses. Second, the majority of the activities require little or no elaborate equipment. Third, the activities have been tested and found to be effective by experienced teachers.

This third volume in the series includes a diversity of demonstrations, assignments, and experiments to complement any psychology textbook or teaching approach. Similar in format to the previous volumes, this one contains chapters covering methodology; sensory processes and perception; learning and memory; developmental psychology; social psychology; personality, abnormal, and clinical psychology; statistics; and special topics. Chapters on ethics and on gender roles and stereotyping are unique to Volume 3. The appendixes contain a potpourri of useful information.

Almost all of the activities are new; Volume 3 is intended to supplement rather than supplant the first two volumes. Some of the activities in this volume were originally published in APA's newsletter, *High School Psychology Teacher*, or in *Teaching of Psychology*, the quarterly journal of APA's Division 2 (Division on the Teaching of Psychology). Volume 3 is a splendid addition to a distinguished series; together the three volumes provide a trove of teaching treasures. Regardless of their persuasion and approach, teachers at all levels should own and use all three volumes of the *Activities Handbook*.

Like many other teachers, I am personally indebted to the dedicated scholars who agreed to share their work and to the editors of this important series. They help us to make our teaching of the fundamental facts, concepts, and principles of psychology more stimulating and captivating. As teachers, we should try to remember how difficult it was for us to learn some of the things that we routinely expect our students to know. We should also often remind ourselves of Meyer's Law, which states that it is a simple task to make things complex but a complex task to make them simple. The activities in this volume will help to simplify and improve our teaching of psychology at all levels. Three years from now, my copy of Volume 3 will be as dog-eared as my copies of the first two volumes—a convincing indication of this volume's pedagogical value.

Charles Brewer
Professor of Psychology
Furman University

PREFACE

The first volume of *Activities Handbook for the Teaching of Psychology* was published by the American Psychological Association in 1981, in an attempt to promote excellence in the teaching of psychology by the dissemination of "recipes" for successful demonstrations, exercises, and assignments. The positive response to that volume made it clear that there was a great demand for knowledge about effective teaching techniques. Over the years, it became clear that the first volume could not satisfy the demand for concrete guidance from experienced teachers, and the second volume was published in 1987. The goals for both volumes were similar: to provide assistance and guidance to teachers through the clear presentation of an array of alternatives to the traditional lecture approach, to reach out to teachers of psychology at both the high school and undergraduate college level, and to serve as a source of inspiration to both new and experienced teachers. This third volume is another step on the road to those same goals.

Those of you familiar with the first two volumes will recognize that several topics are comparable across publications: chapters on methodology; on sensory processes and perception; on learning and memory; on developmental and social psychology; on personality, abnormal, and clinical psychology; and on special topics. The relevance of these basic topics endures. Volumes 2 and 3 also include chapters on statistics. Whereas the chapters on motivation and emotion and on computers in teaching were unique to Volume 2, the present volume includes chapters on ethics and on gender roles and stereotyping. If you have used Volume 2, you will find Volume 3 familiar: The activities have been edited into the same standard format, with an emphasis on organization and convenience. Each activity begins with an editor's note and provides information in Concept, Materials Needed, Instructions, and Discussion sections.

The overall characteristics and philosophy of all three volumes are consistent. There are demonstrations, assignments, and research projects included that can be used in conjunction with virtually any text or course plan. Some require a few minutes and some require a whole class period. Some extend over days or weeks. We have tried to provide for flexibility through variety. Although some activities require that students have prior knowledge of specific material, this is most often knowledge that may have been gained earlier in the same course. Thus, most activities can be used with students in introductory level classes as well as in upper-level undergraduate courses. Most of the activities in this volume require little or no special equipment. In cases in which special equipment is needed, the authors have either given clear instructions on how to construct the materials or provided a source for supply. There are appendixes of references to articles on how to construct inexpensive equipment.

Two features of the volume will provide for ease and efficiency in sorting through activities. Each chapter begins with a brief summary of the activities included in that chapter. In addition, the editor's notes (in italics) at the beginning of each activity alert the instructor to the complexity of the activity, the amount of advance preparation needed for the activity, the prior knowledge students need for the activity, or exceptional time requirements of the activity.

Two features of the volume provide for additional flexibility in the use of the activities. The index of descriptive key words initiated in Volume 2 has proven very useful, and such an index is provided in Volume 3 as well. This cross-listing will allow the user to search for activities relevant to specific concepts that may be located in more than one chapter. Second, the editor's note at the beginning of each activity may suggest modifications or additional uses for the ideas contained in the activity.

Seven appendixes appear in this book. Appendix A contains all the chapter summaries and titles of appendixes from Volumes 1 and 2 of the *Activities Handbook*. Appendix B provides information on the basic statistics used in psychological research. Bibliographic material on the construction of inexpensive classroom and laboratory equipment is provided in Appendix C, and the simple approach is further outlined in Appendix D, which describes the use of invertebrates as a sample population. Appendix E lists selected computer resources, and Appendix F suggests topical readings on ethical principles. Finally, Appendix G directs the reader to APA offices where more information may be obtained.

Classroom activities and assignments can be varied infinitely, and when a topic is particularly intriguing, instructors may choose to customize an exercise to their own needs. This customization has occurred in an activity focusing on the experience of inverting or reversing lenses, which was incarnated as Activity 22 in Volume 1, reincarnated as Activity 10 in Volume 2, and reincarnated again as Activity 20 in Volume 3. There are other examples as well. Sometimes teachers may create variations on the same basic activity or may create activities independently that are quite similar. In all volumes in this series, efforts have been made to give appropriate credit to the originators of activities, and if there have been any oversights or inaccuracies, we ask that you let us know.

This series would not have been possible without the many teachers who donated their time, experience, and creativity. We wish to thank each and every one of them, not only for their ideas but also for their cooperation in making revisions and answering questions. The names and addresses of all contributors are listed at the back of the book should readers wish to write directly to an author about an activity.

A number of people deserve special thanks for their contributions to this volume. First of these is Charles Brewer, who agreed to write the introduction to the volume in spite of being up to his elbows in coursework and up to his eyebrows in manuscripts. He is not only an example to us all in his teaching but also the editor of the APA Division 2 journal, *Teaching of Psychology*. We greatly appreciate his willingness to give of his time and of himself. In addition, several Educational Affairs people and Patricia Harding-Clark contributed invaluable secretarial support. Finally, we wish to acknowledge the expertise of Christine P. Landry, Carlotta Ribar, Stephanie Selice, and Mary Lynn Skutley, whose technical editing ensured that this volume would meet the same high standards as previous volumes in the series.

Vivian Parker Makosky
Educational and Public Affairs

Chi Chi Sileo
Linda Genevieve Whittemore
Office of Educational Affairs
American Psychological Association

CHAPTER 1
METHODOLOGY

The activities in this chapter offer a wide variety of approaches to teaching methodology, at varying levels of difficulty. Most of them require little or no special equipment. Activities 1 and 3 are quick, simple, and straightforward demonstrations requiring no prior knowledge of psychology on the part of the students. Activity 2, while also fairly fast and easy, requires more preparation and materials. It introduces students to the observational study of live animals; the instructor should make sure that the animals are handled in a humane manner. Activity 6 is an interesting demonstration of the illusory correlation effect and is easily adaptable to a statistics course.

Activity 4 is an out-of-class assignment that teaches students to develop and use their own experimental design, and the activities that follow provide interesting corollaries to this: Activity 5 stresses research and writing skills in self-experimentation; Activity 8 teaches students to select the most appropriate research methods; and Activity 9 encourages students to take a critical approach to their analysis of research findings.

For those who wish to provide a real challenge to themselves and their students, Activity 7 presents a rigorous exercise in construct validation, suitable for advanced undergraduates. Activity 10, which teaches the concepts of taxonomy, is also best suited to more advanced students who have had some exposure to methodology and statistics. Activity 11 is a long-term project that will help students develop new ways of thinking and of learning and will help them gain a deeper understanding of the scientific method.

1 A Neat Little Demonstration of the Benefits of Random Assignment of Subjects in an Experiment

David L. Watson
University of Hawaii at Manoa

This activity is a simple and fast way to illustrate the uses of random assignment. No prior knowledge and no advance preparation is necessary. It can be used with medium-to-large classes. You can emphasize the point even more strongly by repeating the activity, drawing again from the same pool of subjects!

CONCEPT

The major advantage of randomly assigning people to conditions in an experiment is that any variables that might affect the outcome of the experiment that are not controlled will be randomly divided between the conditions of the experiment. The experimenter first pools the names of all subjects, then uses a random procedure such as flipping a coin to assign people to different conditions of the experiment. For example, suppose the experiment presents an intellectual challenge to the subjects. Their intelligence might affect how well they perform, quite independently of how they are treated by the experimental conditions. If more intelligent people are assigned to one condition than another, it will seem that the condition leads to better performance, but in fact it will be the personal characteristic (intelligence) of the subjects that makes the difference. To avoid this possibility, researchers can randomly assign subjects to conditions. Thus, some intelligent people and some relatively unintelligent people will be assigned to each of the various conditions of the experiment. If there are still differences in how well the subject groups perform, the experimenter can be more confident that the results are due to the treatment of the conditions rather than to the personal characteristics of the subjects.

Some students have difficulty understanding the procedures and advantages of this random assignment of subjects to conditions. The purpose of this demonstration is to make it clear to them.

INSTRUCTIONS

Tell the class that you think you have invented a way of coaching basketball that will lead to greatly superior results. The teams you train are going to be winners. But you want to test this idea: Is it really the way you train your teams that makes the difference? You propose to run an experiment. One team will be trained by your new method, and the other will be trained by the traditional methods. Each team will then play in a tournament. If your training method is really superior, the team coached by it should do better in the tournament.

However, you are worried about one thing over which you have no control: the height of the players. Everyone knows that height makes a big difference in basketball. Suppose the team you train has mostly average or short people on it, while the team trained the traditional way has a lot of tall people on it. The taller team will have a real advantage in the tournament, even if your training method really is superior. How to solve the problem?

Random assignment of subjects! Start with a pool of all the potential players. Half of them will go on the traditionally coached team, and the other half will go on your new method team. You can now demonstrate that random assignment will allocate tall, average, and short players to each team and will thus eliminate height as a possible confounding variable in your experiment.

In this demonstration, I use only one sex to avoid too much variation in height. I usually use only female students because they comprise about two thirds of my class.

Tell the class that you are going to randomly assign female students to the two teams by flipping a coin. Pick students at random to put on one of the two teams. If the coin comes up *heads*, the student goes on Team A. If it comes up *tails*, the student goes on Team B. Then begin flipping coins. Ask the students to stand on different sides of the room as they are assigned to one of the two teams. After you have assigned 10 players to each team, line up Team A in front of the class, arranged from tallest to shortest. Then line up Team B behind them, arranged the same way. The randomization will assure that the two teams are now clearly equal in height, and that variable may be eliminated from your hypothetical experiment.

DISCUSSION Do the students now see that the procedure for assigning subjects is random and that the height advantage has been eliminated from consideration in your hypothetical experiment?

SUGGESTED READING Watson, D. L., deBortali-Tregerthan, G., & Frank, J. (1984). *Social psychology: Science and application.* Glenview, IL: Scott, Foresman.

2 OBSERVATIONAL RECORDING OF RODENT BEHAVIOR: BEHAVIOR PROFILE OR ETHOGRAM

Ellen P. Reese
Mount Holyoke College

This is an observational study of animal behavior in a laboratory setting. As written, it includes rats, gerbils, cages, and so forth, but it could be adapted for other animals or settings. This activity is appropriate for introductory students, but the time involved may make it an upper-level activity. Students work in teams, and the concepts explicated include operational definitions of variables and interobserver reliability.

CONCEPT A behavior profile, or ethogram, shows the frequency or duration of an animal's engagement in various activities. The data can be plotted as a function of age: In puppies, sleeping and nursing decrease with age as various kinds of play increase. Or we can look for changes over time: After a period of sleep, an animal may first eat and may then engage in exploration, play, or other activities that the setting allows. We can look for sex differences or for distributions of behavior in different kinds of environments. We can see how an animal distributes its time in the presence and absence of one or more conspecifics. Other variables may include the time of day or an early history in an enriched compared with a relatively barren environment.

The most difficult task in recording ongoing behavior is often defining the behavior to be observed. The test of an acceptable definition is that two people observe the animal independently, but at the same time, and that their records agree as to when each activity occurred. It can take anywhere from several minutes to several days before two observers develop and revise a definition so that they agree on at least 90% of the observations that they record.

Behavioral definitions are described in Reese (1978, pp. 40–43) and Sulzer-Azaroff and Reese (1982, pp. 67–68). A workable definition includes the following components:

> *Behavior*—that which must be seen, heard, felt, or otherwise observed;
> *the context or situation*—when, where, and with whom the behavior must occur if it is to be recorded as an instance falling within the definition;
> *criteria*—any restrictions on rate, intensity, duration, latency, accuracy, neatness, or other properties of a response; and
> *measurement*—If you are going to use interval recording or momentary time sampling, your data will report the percentage of intervals or time samples in which the behavior occurred, not the actual frequency or duration. To interpret data obtained from observational recording, we need to know the recording procedure that was used as well as how the behavior was defined.

Procedures for observational recording are also described in Reese (1978) and Sulzer-Azaroff and Reese (1982). Different procedures are appropriate for different classes of behavior and for different situations. We will use interval recording to collect the data for the behavior profiles.

In this lab, you will observe and record the behavior of (a) a female rat with 3 female offspring, selecting 1 baby to observe, and (b) a litter of gerbils and their dam.

1. Observe in pairs (or trios) so that you can measure interobserver agreement, or the reliability of your observations.

2. Adapt the data sheet (see sample) for the situation you will observe, providing the information requested at the top and adding categories for the columns we have left blank. For this exercise, you might select from the following categories of social behavior: proximity (within 2 inches of) dam or sibling (you can write *D* for dam and *S* for sibling), investigate (sniff) dam or sibling, and spar or fight dam or

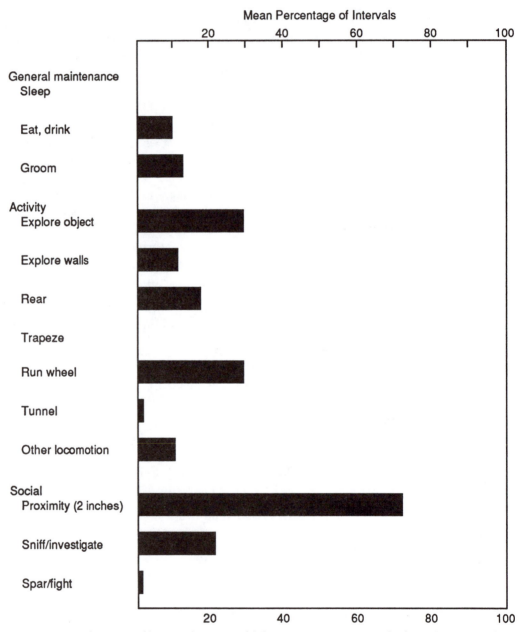

Figure 2-1. *Behavior profile, or ethogram, of laboratory rat in an enriched environment. (Three female rats, 47 days old, reared with their dam. Data based on thirteen 10-minute samples.)*

sibling. Label the last column *Other* and write down any other significant behavior that may occur.

3. Select a group to observe, and watch them for 5 minutes, discussing the behavior with your partner to see if you are defining the behavior the same way.

4. When you feel relatively confident that you agree on the different classes of behavior, select an animal, and be sure you agree to observe the same one!

5. Start the timer and observe for 5 minutes, recording any occurrence of any activity in 15-second time intervals.

Not all of the categories are mutually exclusive; for example, an animal could be both rearing and exploring the walls of the tank. In that case, record both activities as occurring in the same interval. Remember that with interval recording, you do not record each occurrence of the behavior within an interval; rather, you record whether the behavior occurred at all during that interval.

6. After 5 minutes, stop the clock and take a break.

7. After the break, record another 5-minute sample.

For each activity, perform the following analysis:

1. Sum the number of intervals in which the behavior occurred.

2. Calculate the *percentage of intervals*, dividing the total by the 40 intervals you observed.

3. Enter your percentages for each category on the group data sheet.

4. Calculate the group mean percentage of intervals the animals engaged in each of the activities you recorded and draw the behavior profile as shown in Figure 1. If you observed two species, plot their data side by side to make comparisons easier.

Calculate interobserver agreement for scored intervals only, using the formula: no. agree ÷ no. agree + disagree × 100 = percent interobserver agreement.

DISCUSSION

Figure 2-1 shows a behavior profile for three 47-day-old rat pups that were housed in a large, 50 gallon fish tank with several objects to manipulate and explore. The pups spent 71% of the intervals in close proximity to one another, and they ran in the running wheel during 30% of the intervals. Most of the rest of their behavior consisted of exploring each other (21%) or the walls and various objects in the enclosure.

Older rats are generally less active, and gerbils are generally more active than rats of the same age. Comparisons between rats and gerbils also depend on the time of day the observations are made. Rats are nocturnal animals and are more active at night, whereas gerbils are diurnal and are more active during the day.

REFERENCES

Reese, E. P. (1978). *Human behavior: Analysis and application.* Dubuque, IA: Wm. C. Brown.

Sulzer-Azaroff, B., & Reese, E. P. (1982). *Applying behavioral analysis: A program for developing professional competence.* New York: Holt, Rinehart & Winston.

Data Sheet

Observer _____ Day _____ Date _____ Time _____
Species _____ Identification _____ Age _____ Weight _____ Ad lib (%) _____
Setting _____ Other present _____ Other _____

Time interval	Sleep	Explore		Rear	Locomotion	Groom	Eat or drink	Running wheel	Tunnel	Other
		Object	Walls							
0–15										
30										
45										
1:00										
15										
30										
45										
2:00										
15										
30										
45										
3:00										
15										
30										
45										
4:00										
15										
30										
45										
5:00										

3 A FIELD EXPERIMENT IN HELPING

David L. Watson

University of Hawaii at Manoa

These are detailed instructions for a field experiment in helping, written in clear language that students in high school or introductory psychology classes will easily understand. No prior knowledge is necessary, but the assignment extends over class periods. The instructor needs to reproduce the instructions. The assignment could be modified for a written report rather than a class discussion.

CONCEPT

Whether a person who needs help receives it from bystanders is affected by several variables. In this exercise, students are told how to carry out a field experiment in helping. Teams of students drop books. The instructions to the students fully detail how to carry out the experiment, but the students choose the independent variables to manipulate. For example, they could manipulate the sex of the person dropping the books: Do men help women more than they do men? Students give the exercise very high ratings. It is fun dropping books around town to see how people react.

MATERIALS NEEDED

Duplicate for each student a copy of the Instructions section on the accompanying pages.

INSTRUCTIONS

Set up 3- or 4-person teams. Give out the instructions to the student. The teams should read them and begin discussing how to carry out their field experiment. Allow a bit of time for their planning. Some will be able to do their field experiment in class time, but others will require trips away from school. Check to be sure that they know how to do their experiment and that it can be done easily. After they have run their experiments, you can ask for reports in class, which is educational as well as a lot of fun.

Help! There are many ways a person can ask for help, and there are many projects you can carry out to study helping behavior. In one of the original research projects, students in New York City asked passersby for help. "Could you give me a dime? My wallet was stolen." Carrying out a field study like this requires some planning and practice. Here is a description of a project in which you drop some books near a potential helper. Using the same basic technique, you can study many things, called *variables*, that affect helping behavior.

The idea is simply to drop some books as a person approaches you. Use people who are walking right toward you. Don't drop them right in the person's path, because that forces the subject to stop. But don't wait till the person is beside you or walking away, either. Drop the books about 5 ft before the person comes abreast of you, slightly to the side. The number of books you drop affects the chances that the person will stop to help, so if you want to encourage helping, drop several.

The number of other people around when you drop the books has an effect. Choose a spot where there is a trickle of individual walkers. That way you can target an individual walking toward you. If you drop your books just as one person approaches you, there is no question of who should help you pick them up. Wait till the previous subject is out of sight before you choose another.

Record whether the person helps or not. To be counted as an instance of helping, the subjects must actually pick up at least one book or paper. Practice a few times to make things seem natural. Try to act the same for all subjects. This study is fun to do, but obviously you can't laugh in front of the subjects.

If you work with others, several people can take turns dropping the books. One person can be in charge of selecting the subjects who fit the needs of the research design, another can record whether help was offered or not, and two or more can be the droppers. Be sure the extra people stand far enough away from the scene of the accident. They shouldn't distract the subjects.

When people do stop to help, thank them, but if they do not stop, say nothing. It is not necessary to debrief the people in this experiment because they are not subjected to any stress and are not deceived, except in their belief that you dropped the books innocently. If someone asks, explain the experiment to them.

But what is the experiment? It is up to you to decide which variables to manipulate. You could vary the sex of the person dropping the books to see how this interacts with the sex of the subject. Do people help women more than men? Do men help women more than women help women? You could vary the age of the person dropping the books, the race of the person, how the book dropper is dressed (e.g., as a hippie or conservatively) and so on. You could vary the place where the books are dropped (e.g., on a crowded street vs. an uncrowded one, in a shopping mall vs. a suburban street) and so on.

Compare two or more groups. In a two-group comparison, drop the books with subjects in two different conditions, for example, subjects walking alone or in a group. In a three-group comparison, drop the books with subjects in three conditions, for example, children, teenagers, and adults. A four-group comparison might investigate the sex of both subject and dropper.

In this design, male droppers perform for both male and female subjects, as do female droppers. This allows you to ask if the sex of the dropper and the sex of the subject each make a difference.

Because you will have at least two conditions, you must decide on the condition of each subject. Do this randomly, by flipping a coin. If a male subject is approaching, for example, flip a coin to decide if he will have a male or female dropper.

The question is, what percentage of subjects offer to help? For example, suppose you used male and female subjects with a male dropper and ran 10 male subjects. If 3 of them helped, you would report that 30% of the male subjects helped. Whatever experiment you run, you can report the percentage of subjects who helped in each experimental condition.

DISCUSSION   Discussing how to carry out the experiment teaches the importance of controlled variables in an experiment. You can point out that if the book dropper acts one way one time but another way another time, it will affect the results. Using the actual act of picking up a book by the subject gives a clear definition of what help means in this study. How were the subjects selected? Did they pick people who looked friendly, or did they use some systematic method for picking subjects? What might happen if they were not systematic? Did they vary the person who dropped the books? Was there any danger, for example, that a pretty student dropped books for one condition of the study while a tough-looking person dropped books in another? In my experience, a number of variables affect whether help is offered or not, and the students become aware of this as they carry out the experiment.

SUGGESTED READING Rushton, J. P., & Sorrentino, R. (Eds.). (1981). *Altruism and helping behavior: Social, personality and developmental perspectives.* Hillsdale, NJ: Erlbaum.

4 A COMPUTER-BASED EXERCISE IN EXPERIMENTAL METHODOLOGY

Thomas Brothen
University of Minnesota

This is an activity whose subject matter—interpersonal attraction—will fascinate students while they learn the rigors of experimental design. It is an out-of-class assignment that can be used with classes of any size, although it is dependent on the availability of IBM or IBM-compatible computers. Students should read the text assignment on experimental design before doing the assignment. The instructor can have a copy of the programmed disc for minimal expense, although it should be requested well in advance of the assignment.

CONCEPT

This article describes an active learning exercise that uses the computer to help students understand the experimental method. It gives them practice dealing with difficult concepts by requiring them to analyze a hypothetical experiment while the computer asks them questions about it. The exercise is designed for use with the methodology unit in introductory psychology courses but can also be used as a review of basic concepts before a laboratory project in experimental design or to familiarize students with computer-based work.

MATERIALS NEEDED

The computer program is written in the Pilot language for IBM and IBM-compatible computers using the MS-DOS operating system. Users may obtain the program by sending a formatted disk in a returnable mailer with sufficient return postage to the author. In addition, a statement stipulating that the program will be used only for educational purposes must accompany the disk. The reading assignment for students is reproduced in the Experiment section.

INSTRUCTIONS

Experiment. A social psychologist studying interpersonal attraction was interested in factors that affect the amount of liking people show for each other. He wanted to find out why people might like one person more than another and what kinds of things cause the differences. The psychologist believed the widely accepted idea that people like people who are nice to them but he also felt that perhaps there is a complex relation between the degree of niceness one person shows toward another and the amount of liking the second person feels toward the first. That is, perhaps it is not just a matter of how nice person *a* is to person *b* that influences *b*'s liking of *a*. The psychologist felt that liking for someone has something to do with the sequence of that person's behavior, and he predicted that a person who changes from bad to good will be liked better than a person who has been good all along. That is, the psychologist guessed that changing from bad to good would have a positive effect on liking. His next task was to back up his guess.

The psychologist thought about the biblical story of the prodigal son who returned home after having run away. He remembered that the father was so glad to see his son return that he ended up liking him more than his other son who had stayed home and had been faithful all along. In his instance, it seemed important to discover that someone who had been bad in the past changed and became very good. The psychologist called this process *gain in esteem:* One person (the prodigal son) became nicer, so the other person (the father) gained something (esteem) from his son, and this caused the father to like his son more than ever. The psychologist realized, of course, that many things affect how much one person likes another besides a gain in esteem. Nevertheless, he felt that this variable was important and that studying it would lead to a better understanding of what makes people like each other.

The psychologist also realized that there are many ways in which people can be kind and unkind toward others. His task, then, involved seeing how a person would respond toward someone who was saying things about him or her, and the psychologist predicted that a person would like someone who changed from being nasty to being nice more than someone who had been nice all along. This prediction was a hypothesis or an educated guess, that the psychologist made about human behavior.

Once the psychologist decided what he was going to study, he had to figure out a way to study it. He felt that it would be very difficult to find and study real-life situations in which someone had changed from unkind to kind. Even if he were lucky and found enough situations, he still might not be able to say anything with accuracy about the way people act in general. The psychologist certainly did not want to base what he had to say about people in general on the information gained from what might be a few odd cases. For example, the sort of thing he wanted to study might be occurring all the time and might hardly be noticed. When it was noticed, it might be because something very unusual had occurred to make it notice-able. Observing only unusual situations would make it difficult for the psychologist to say that these situations represented the way things normally happen, like study-ing the kinds of things married couples say to one another by listening to their occasional fights. The psychologist also wanted to be able to say that the increase in liking was caused by the change in niceness instead of by something else he might not have noticed. He was being careful because he was aware of how difficult it is to keep track of causes and effects in real-life situations.

The psychologist decided to use the experimental method as a way of studying changes in niceness. With this method, he could take a group of people and expose them to a planned situation much like situations he was pretty sure they had en-countered before and would encounter again in their lives. Once they had been exposed to it, he could record their reactions and compare them with the reactions of people who had not been exposed to the situation.

Comparing reactions to two or more situations created by an experimenter is the essence of the experiment. The experimenter designs situations to determine the effects they will produce, and if different situations result in different effects, the experimenter can claim to know what the causes are. The major advantage of the experiment is that it provides information on cause-and-effect relations. Of course, when designing the situation, the experimenter must use methods that ensure an objective and unbiased investigation. If the experimenter has done this, he or she can make a reasonable claim that a cause-and-effect relation has been discovered. In our example, the psychologist can take a group of people, expose them to a carefully designed situation, study their behavior, and subsequently say that something has been learned about how people behave. He can do this only if he gets one reaction from people to one situation and a different reaction to the other.

The experimenter also has to be sure that people in the experiment are reacting honestly to the situation—that they are not acting or faking. There is the possibility that they may get a hint as to how they should act, and because most people want to do the right thing, they may feel that they are supposed to act in a certain way. To avoid this, the experimenter tries to make sure people in the experiment have no preconceived notions about how they should act. To do this, the experimenter tries to set up a situation in which the people involved have no idea about exactly what is going to happen until it does. Thus, the experimenter catches them by surprise and then finds out what they do.

To get back to the psychologist—he wanted to see who is liked better—a critic who is always nice, or a critic who is not nice at first and then becomes nice later. To do this, he had to set up a situation in which people are confronted with either of the two types of critic and had to record the people's behavior to see which of the two types is liked more. If some people are confronted with one type and other people are confronted with the other, and if one group shows more liking for their type than the other group does for their type, there is a difference in behavior to explain. The psychologist had to be sure that this difference was caused by the way the "critic" acted and nothing else. He had to take great pains to make sure that the only real difference between the situations was the behavior of the critic being kind or unkind.

The following is a brief description of how the psychologist set up his experiment. He first decided that he had to get an actor to play the part of the critic who would say kind or unkind things. Then he decided to divide the people (or *subjects*) into two groups. One group was to hear the actor say nice things the whole time, and the other group was to hear the actor say unkind things at first and nice things later. The psychologist decided to randomly select 15 people for each condition to be reasonably sure he got a good sample of normal people. If he had used only 1 person per group, his results might have reflected only differences between those 2 individuals. By using more people, he got a better idea of how most people would react. He used random selection to choose people because he wanted to make reasonably sure that both groups were similar. He flipped a coin as people came in until he had 15 people in each group. In this way, no single type of person would be in one group more than another, and he would be able to make the claim that both groups were similar in all important respects (he would like to have both groups exactly alike, but that would not be possible).

Because it would have seemed very unusual to have the subjects hear someone saying things about them for no reason, the psychologist had to make up a story and find a situation that would make it seem reasonable. To do this, he convinced the owner of an employment agency to allow him to use the agency's clients as subjects. He found that people coming into the employment agency were normally assigned to a job counselor. The psychologist simply replaced the job counselor with the actor he had hired. The actor then "interviewed" the clients/subjects individually. He mentioned that some "new techniques" were being tried by the agency and asked the clients if they were willing to take part (they all said yes). He also asked clients a series of questions about the kinds of work they had done, the kind of work they wanted, and the qualifications they had. When the subject answered each of the questions, the actor responded in one of two ways. For one group, the actor was always positive; he said nice things like "that's good" or "I'm sure you'll do fine." Because this was what normally happened in the agency, this group was labeled the control group. For the other group, the actor started off unkindly and then began behaving nicely. For the first half of the interview, he said things like "that's not very good" or "that's pretty unimpressive." For the second half, he said things like "that's a good quality you have." Because this was different from normal—the method the psychologist hypothesized would cause more liking—this group was labeled the experimental group.

After the interview, the subject was taken by the actor to the "supervisor," who in reality was the psychologist. (Because he was playing the major role in the experiment, the psychologist was called the experimenter.) The actor kept a record of which group the subject had been in but did not tell this to the experimenter. (The psychologist decided to use this double-blind technique so he wouldn't inadvertently "coach" the subjects.) The experimenter then told the subjects that the employment agency wanted to make sure that they got the best service possible. He asked the clients how things were going and how much they liked the "job counselor." In doing this, the experimenter made as sure as possible that the subjects thought the situation was real and would give their true reactions. After obtaining the subjects' reactions, the experimenter explained that they had been in a psychological experiment. He then gave the subjects each $10 for participating, answered any questions they had, and thanked them. All of the subjects thought the experiment was interesting and were happy that they could earn $10 for an hour of their time. All subjects then saw a real job counselor.

After matching the subjects' reactions to the actor's records on group membership, the psychologist found that those in the group exposed to the actor when he changed for the better (experimental group) liked him more than those in the other group (control group) liked him when he had been totally nice. From the results of this experiment, the psychologist concluded that people like someone who becomes nicer toward them. That is, an increase in niceness causes greater liking to occur. The psychologist went on to say that perhaps, if you want someone to like you, you should be rather cool at first, then should warm up and be nicer later on. This was not the end, however. The psychologist realized that people coming into an employment agency might not be like the average person in some way or that several other things could have gone wrong to invalidate his findings. He had to look for other ways to test his hypothesis. He, or other psychologists, must repeat (or replicate) the experiment and if, after several experiments, the results hold, he might even develop a theory about human behavior and become famous (even psychologists can dream).

Student participation. First, it is important that students read or review an introductory psychology textbook discussion of the experimental method before they do the exercise. I am currently using Gerow (1989), which covers the necessary concepts very well.

Second, students must then read the previous description of the experiment. The hypothetical experiment is based on the gain/loss model of attraction originally stated by Aronson and Linder (1965). It was written to demonstrate experimental design concepts in a "real-life" setting that students might have some familiarity with or understanding of.

Third, students must spend an average of 45 min on the computer-based portion of the exercise. It is intended to review the experiment as a means of remediating students' misconceptions about experimental design. It begins with a brief tutorial on how to use the computer. (Students merely have to know how to "boot up" the computer, insert the disk, type *cpi exp*, and press the *return* key to begin; the rest of the program is menu driven.) The computer then begins asking questions about the experiment. Questions are programmed in a branching design, which asks simpler questions if more difficult ones are not answered correctly. For most questions, students answer by filling in the blank with the correct term. Because the answers are terms such as *hypothesis*, *variable*, and so forth, correct spellings are required. Close approximations of spellings are flagged by the computer with a message that students should check their spelling.

If a question cannot be answered correctly, the program branches to consecutively simpler questions that restate principles and eventually require yes/no confirmation of their veracity. For example, if students have difficulty identifying the independent variable, the program might eventually branch to a question such as the following: "The independent variable is manipulated by the experimenter—yes or no?" A "no" answer would result in a statement that the answer was incorrect and that the student should try again. A "yes" answer would result in an affirming statement and a branch back to the next most difficult question missed, eventually continuing back through the independent variable section for which 100% mastery of all questions attempted is required.

Third, the computer prints a "verification of completion" when the student is finished. It includes the student's name and class identification number, a code number that differs each time to deter students from submitting false copy, and a tally of correct and incorrect answers given by the student as an indication of how well the experiment was understood. It is designed to be turned in to the instructor as proof that the exercise was completed.

DISCUSSION

The exercise is currently used as preparation for three computer-based exercises (Brothen, 1984) and other research-based projects in an introductory psychology class that utilizes learning groups and active learning (Brothen, 1986). It was originally available to students on the main-frame computer but was programmed for the microcomputer in 1986. It has been used successfully for over 10 years, and students receive a modest amount of credit (5 of 304 total course points) simply for completing it. The rationale for this is that the computer will not let them finish until they have correctly answered all questions. In this sense, the computer functions as a testing device, and the instructor has some confidence that each student has a basic knowledge of experimental method. I have also used the exercise to begin an applied psychology class for which students designed and conducted an experiment. The exercise described here served to re-acquaint students with the basics of experimental method. It can also serve as a launching point for class discussion on experiments, with students critiquing the design and designing their own improvements.

The hypothetical experiment for the exercise is based on the gain/loss model of attraction (Aronson, 1970; Aronson & Linder, 1965; Berscheid, Brothen, & Graziano, 1976; Brothen, 1977). The extensions of this model relate it to romantic love and to how people evaluate others. Work with the model has been done in the field of social psychology, but some of its rationale stems from the concept of contrast effects in perception.

REFERENCES

Aronson, E. (1970, August). Who likes whom and why. *Psychology Today*, pp. 48–50.

Aronson, E., & Linder, D. (1965). Gain and loss of esteem as determinants of interpersonal attraction. *Journal of Experimental Social Psychology*, *1*, 156–172.

Berscheid, E., Brothen, T., & Graziano, W. (1976). Gain/loss theory and "law of infidelity": Mr. Doting vs. the admiring stranger. *Journal of Personality and Social Psychology, 33,* 709–718.

Brothen, T. (1977). The gain/loss concept and the evaluator: First some good news then some bad. *Journal of Personality and Social Psychology, 35,* 430–436.

Brothen, T. (1984). Three computer-assisted laboratory exercises for introductory psychology. *Teaching of Psychology, 11,* 105–107.

Brothen, T. (1986, Spring). Using learning groups in introductory psychology. *Network, 3,* 1. (ERIC Document Reproduction Service No. ED 268 913)

Gerow, J. (1989). *Psychology: An introduction* (2nd ed.). Chicago: Scott, Foresman.

5 SELF-EXPERIMENTATION AS A TOOL FOR TEACHING ABOUT PSYCHOLOGY

Blaine F. Peden and Allen H. Keniston
University of Wisconsin—Eau Claire

This activity is an assignment that extends over several class sessions and involves both research and writing. There is little advance preparation required. Although the authors have used this assignment with introductory classes, it is more likely to be appropriate for a course in methodology. For large classes, the authors include a student peer-evaluation component to alleviate the burden on the instructor. Self-experiments involving drugs, alcohol, or other dangerous or illegal behaviors should be excluded, even if they are part of the students' normal activities.

CONCEPT

A self-experiment allows an individual to serve both as an experimenter and as a subject and provides an excellent vehicle to teach about methodology in both introductory and experimental psychology courses. Self-experimentation requires students to ground abstract methodological concepts by confronting them with the problems faced by all researchers while engaging students' desires to understand themselves. This confrontation promotes active learning and provides a concrete understanding of research methods (see also, Henderson, 1987).

Through this self-experimentation activity, students can learn to formulate scientific questions and alternative hypotheses, to operationally define independent and dependent variables, to identify and control extraneous variables, to present and interpret data, and to prepare a report in American Psychological Association (APA) style.

In our introductory psychology and introductory methods courses, each of our students performs a self-experiment that investigates a question relevant to his or her life. To enable us to carry out this activity with large enrollments, we use a process of peer-critiquing that actively involves students in collaborative learning (McKeachie, 1987) and greatly eases the workload of the instructor.

MATERIALS NEEDED

You will need to make copies of the self-experiment instructions and the form for the self-experiment proposal. When making the assignment, distribute a blank proposal to each student and present the instructions on an overhead projector.

Inform the students that they are responsible for supplying or producing the materials or equipment for their own self-experiments. The materials and equipment for each self-experiment will vary. Solving problems with materials and equipment is an important part of the learning process.

INSTRUCTIONS

Class preparation. First, lecture to the class about research methods. Subsequently, you may require the class to read Neuringer's (1981) article to learn about self-experimentation or Barlow and Hersen's (1973) article to learn about single-case experimental designs. In the next class, define the concept of a self-experiment and present examples. When doing this activity for the first time, you may want to use specific examples cited in the reading resources at the end of this article. Once you have done this activity, you may present examples from previous semesters.

Have each student generate at least three different ideas for a self-experiment as a homework assignment. Then have the students select the most promising idea of the three and write a proposal on the form that you have provided. Ask them to complete the initial proposal to the best of their ability and to bring it to the next class meeting.

Writing the proposal. The proposal form requires each student to formulate a question about the effects of some variable on his or her own behavior. For example, a student might ask whether a drug such as caffeine affects tenseness, the ability to concentrate, and sleep. After specifying a problem in the form of a question, each student proposes an experimental hypothesis and also identifies alternative hypotheses about the outcome of the experiment. That is, a student might hypothesize that caffeine increases tenseness, even though he or she also recognizes that it might not affect (or might even decrease) tenseness.

Next, students operationally define the independent and dependent variables. For example, a student might manipulate caffeine intake by consuming either a caffeinated or a decaffeinated soft drink at the same time each day. Each student must measure at least two dependent variables or one variable in at least two different ways. Thus, the student might measure the tenseness variable by how long it takes to relax, the concentration variable by the number of times that he or she looks up while studying, and the sleep variable in terms of quality and quantity.

Instruct the students to specify control procedures in their proposals. To illustrate, mention that the effects of caffeine intake could be confounded by consuming soft drinks containing different quantities of sugar. To help ensure relatively independent observations, have students record their measures on a notecard and place it in a drawer each day. Students complete their proposals by summarizing how they will conduct the self-experiment on a day-to-day basis, by suggesting ways to analyze and present the data, and by briefly considering possible outcomes and conclusions.

Learning to collaborate. The next step in the assignment entails formative (ungraded) evaluation. This phase is important because a portion of the class always fails to understand (a) that the student functions as both the experimenter and the subject, (b) that she or he must manipulate one independent variable and measure at least two dependent variables, and (c) that he or she must use appropriate control procedures. If there are few students in the class, the instructor may discuss proposals with students on an individual basis. If there are many students, as in typical introductory or methodology courses, we suggest that the instructor use a process of peer critiquing in which students exchange and critique proposals and ask and answer questions during an interactive discussion with the instructor. There are numerous advantages to this process: Students learn about a wider range of methodological problems and solutions by critiquing the proposals of other students. They also learn how to edit.

On the basis of peer comments and suggestions and the class discussion, students can make revisions and submit a second proposal for peer evaluation and class discussion during the next class meeting. After writing a proposal, revising it, commenting on other students' proposals, and participating in discussions, almost all students in research methods courses are ready to conduct their self-experiments. Introductory students sometimes need to prepare a third proposal.

Self-experimentation. During the 2–3-week period of self-experimentation, use class time to illustrate ways to present data in the form of tables and figures and to suggest ways to analyze and interpret the results. In addition, provide instruction about writing and preparing a laboratory report in APA format. If you are using the peer-critiquing process, students can exchange drafts of their papers for peer critiquing. After editing by two or three students, each paper is returned to the author, who responds in writing to the editors' comments before submitting the paper for grading. Finally, have the students submit the papers for a summative (graded) evaluation.

DISCUSSION   Engaging in this process explicitly teaches critical thinking, careful observation, and writing skills. It also provides an opportunity to assess the role of science in daily life for students who argue that science is irrelevant to their lives. Self-experiments provide an opportunity for students to test the alternative hypothesis that science and its methods are relevant to them.

Self-experiments help students master the concept of controlling an independent variable and varying it systematically. For example, many students want to know how their sleep/wake cycle affects the quality of their lives. Initial proposals often contain questions asking whether going to bed late interferes with performance the next day or whether performing an activity is easier in the afternoon than in the morning. Through discussion, students come to understand that they do not control times of the day. This leads them to manipulate the number of hours of sleep or the amount of time intervening between waking and performing an activity.

Applying the concept of an operational definition challenges all students. Consider the case of a student who wanted to define operationally the concept of *psychological tension*. Simply reporting whether she was tense was not a very good operational definition because it did not produce much variability and it left open the question of objective measurement. In discussion, the student realized that *tense* meant a noticeable stiffness in her neck, and she eventually suggested that the "time required to relax neck muscles" was a clear indication of degree of tension. The student also remembered that neck tension occurred earlier on tense than on relaxed days. Simply recording the time that had elapsed from waking to the onset of neck muscle tension provided a second measure. The contrasting measures assessed tension in opposite ways: In the first, greater tension produced a longer time to relax; in the second, greater tension produced a shorter time to onset. The valuable lesson was that there are alternative ways to specify the hypothetical relation between a construct and its operational definition. This kind of understanding sets the stage for subsequent discoveries about reliability and validity.

Specifying control procedures poses an important challenge for all researchers. One might apply the concept of counterbalancing by systematically varying the days of the week on which a decaffeinated soft drink is consumed across a period of two weeks. One may introduce the concept of holding variables constant by suggesting that students make observations at the same time each day. A clever student might implement single- or double-blind procedures.

The peer-critiquing process prompts many questions that the instructor can answer by discussing the question or the issue with the entire class. Discussion helps students clarify misunderstandings about the assignment. Having students evaluate one another's papers and respond to the editorial comments closely simulates the review process through which professional manuscripts must pass. The student editors often identify problems and write appropriate comments on the papers, thereby providing relatively immediate feedback indicative of the final grade. As the students learn the skill of editing, their comments often resemble those of the instructor, facilitating the grading process and reducing the instructor's workload.

Examples of self-experiments. In contrast to classes in which all members perform a standardized experiment, this assignment generates studies on many different topics. Each self-experiment presents unique opportunities for teaching and learning about research methods, whether the source of inspiration is personal experience or a psychological theory or principle.

The majority of our students' self-experiments are derived from personal experience. Each semester, a number of students examine the effects of food-related variables such as type of food (good vs. junk), breakfast consumption or abstention, and food temperature on measures of activity, consumption, dreaming, or sleeping. Other students assess the effects of music on reading ability, running speed, quality of sleep, or studying. Some investigate the effects of exercise on appetite, sleeping, stress reduction, or studying and test performance. Several test the impact of different study methods or environments on their learning course content. Some manipulate the intake of caffeine and measure quality of sleep or study, whereas others examine the effects of sleep deprivation on alertness, memory, or other aspects of daily life. One student measured the effects of amino acid supplements on weight-lifting ability.

A few of the self-experiments performed by students derive from a psychological theory or principle. One student measured the effects of punishment on smoking. Another asked whether there was a relation between hemispheric and visual dominance by manipulating the source of visual input (left, right, or both eyes) and measuring skills such as reading, word analysis, math, and visual perception. One student who was impressed by principles of cognitive–behavioral modification manipulated her "self-talk" and measured aspects of her social and emotional life both at home and at work.

Some research topics such as proposals to determine the effects of alcohol on a motor skill or perceptual motor impairment may raise ethical questions. In general, students choose topics relevant to their personal interests. We advise students against self-experiments that involve manipulations and measures that are not normal activities in their lives.

This self-experiment assignment challenges students to learn difficult methodological concepts in order to answer questions regarding their daily lives. Furthermore, this assignment engages the students in active rather than passive learning. From semester to semester, our students report that self-experiments help them to understand both themselves, which is important to each of them, and the content and methods of psychology, which is important to us.

REFERENCES

Barlow, D. H., & Hersen, M. (1973). Single-case experimental designs. *Archives of General Psychiatry, 29,* 319–325.

Henderson, R. W. (1987, Spring). Psychology through self-discovery. *Perspectives in Computing,* pp. 52–56.

McKeachie, W. J. (1987). Teaching, teaching teaching, and research on teaching. *Teaching of Psychology, 14,* 135–139.

Neuringer, A. (1981). Self-experimentation: A call for change. *Behaviorism, 9,* 79–94.

Altman, L. K. (1987). *Who goes first? The story of self-experimentation in medicine.* New York: Random House.

Boice, R., & Hertli, P. (1982). Do psychologists practice what they teach? *Teaching of Psychology, 9,* 86–88.

Camplese, D. A., & Mayo, J. A. (1982). How to improve the quality of student writing: The colleague swap. *Teaching of Psychology, 9,* 122–123.

Ebbinghaus, H. (1913). *Memory: A contribution to experimental psychology* (H. A. Ruger & C. E. Bussenius, Trans.). New York: Columbia University, Teachers College.

Ericsson, K. A., Chase, W. G., & Falcoon, S. (1980). Acquisition of a memory skill. *Science, 208,* 1181–1183.

Howard, G. S., & Engelhardt, J. L. (1984). Teaching rival hypotheses in experimental psychology. *Teaching of Psychology, 11,* 44–45.

Mayfield, M. (1987, September 21). In medicine, who plays guinea pig? *USA Today,* p. 2D.

Neuringer, A. (1984). Melioration and self-experimentation. *Journal of the Experimental Analysis of Behavior, 42,* 397–406.

Peden, B. F. (1982). Ungraded feedback during the drafting stages of the experimental psychology laboratory report. In W. A. Clark (Ed.), *Writing to learn across the curriculum: A manual of methods* (pp. 187–201). Eau Claire: University of Wisconsin.

Platt, J. R. (1964). Strong inference. *Science, 146,* 347–353.

Stevens, V. J. (1978). Increasing professional productivity while teaching full time: A case study in self-control. *Teaching of Psychology, 5,* 203–205.

Stratton, G. M. (1897). Vision without inversion of the retinal image. *Psychological Review, 4,* 341–360.

Underwood, B. J. (1975). The first course in experimental psychology: Goals and methods. *Teaching of Psychology, 2,* 163–165.

To expose you to the problems of experimental design and analysis, we ask that you propose and perform a self-experiment. Proceed in the following manner:

1. Formulate three questions about your own behavior. Use the one that you like best for your proposal.

2. Indicate possible answers to your question in the form of alternative hypotheses.

3. Operationally define the independent variable.

4. Operationally define two or more dependent variables.

5. Describe appropriate control procedures.

6. Conduct your self-experiment.

7. Analyze your results.

8. Present the entire enterprise in official APA format in a paper of no more than eight pages. Page 1 will be the title page. Page 2 will be the abstract page. Pages 3–6 will hold the body of the paper. Page 7 will be a reference page. Page 8 will be a figure or table page.

Self-Experiment Proposal

1. Indicate the problem in the form of a question.

2. Indicate your alternative hypotheses, including (a) experimental and (b) null.

3. Operationally define the independent variable.

4. Operationally define at least two dependent variables.

5. Specify procedures for controlling extraneous variables.

6. Briefly describe your methods, discuss (a) subject, (b) apparatus, and (c) procedure.

7. How will you analyze and present the data?

8. Briefly consider possible outcomes and conclusions.

Center for Behavioral Studies
North Texas State University
P.O. Box 13438, Denton, TX 76203
(817) 565-3460

Encouraged by the changes in student behavior resulting from their participation in self-management classes taught at the Center for Behavioral Studies and inspired by Allen Neuringer's papers and graphs on melioration and self-experimentation and by what B. F. Skinner has to say about self-control, we at the Center for Behavioral Studies propose a Self-Management and Self-Experimentation Newsletter: (1) to share data; (2) to encourage an experimental approach to increasing our understanding of our own behavior; (3) to let people know that behavior analysis is not the science of "the other one."

Behavioral and cultural selection need lots of raw material: self-management and self-experimentation can increase variability and give us a way to assess the outcome of the "mutations."

We invite behavior analysts and students of the discipline to share their own data in this bi-annual newsletter. To interest those unfamiliar with behavior analysis, please keep format, language and graphs as basic and as simple as possible.

To receive the first issue, fill out the form below and return it to the Center for Behavioral Studies at the above address.

PLEASE PASS COPIES OF THIS NEWSLETTER TO YOUR COLLEAGUES, STUDENTS, FACULTY, AND FRIENDS.

Please cut off and send to: Center for Behavioral Studies, NTSU, P.O. Box 13438, Denton, TX 76203. Thank you!

SELF-MANAGEMENT AND SELF-EXPERIMENTATION NEWSLETTER
I would like to receive the first issue of the bi-annual newsletter.

Last Name: _____ First Name: _____

Address: _____

Phone: (___) _____

Affiliation: _____

6 A Demonstration of the Illusory Correlation Effect

Thomas Rocklin
University of Iowa

You will need 20 nonprofessionally drawn pictures to show to students with overhead transparencies, slides, or an opaque projector. Twenty pictures are provided, although you may produce your own if you choose. No other materials or preparation are needed for this in-class activity, which is suitable for introductory, cognitive, social, or testing courses. Although the effect of expectations on what students believe they have observed is emphasized, the activity could easily be modified to quantify errors.

CONCEPT

There are a variety of situations in which people are quite poor at judging the degree of covariation between two variables (Crocker, 1981). This activity demonstrates one in particular, namely, an "illusory correlation" (Chapman & Chapman, 1967). In general, once two events, characteristics, or concepts become strong associates of one another, there is a bias toward remembering them as having co-occurred in a new series of exposures. For example, drawing pictures of people with big or emphasized eyes is associated with suspiciousness in the minds of both naive subjects and professional users of the Draw A Person test (Chapman & Chapman, 1967). The demonstration I describe replicates a portion of the Chapman and Chapman experiment.

MATERIALS NEEDED

The demonstration requires approximately 20 nonprofessionally drawn pictures, each depicting a person. The pictures included here were drawn by 10 people. Each person was instructed to draw one picture of a person with atypical eyes and ears and one of a person with an emphasized mouth and passive posture, characterized by outstretched arms. These are the characteristics associated with the drawing of a suspicious person and the drawing of a person concerned with being fed and cared for, respectively. Half of the drawings with atypical eyes and ears were labeled, "This person is suspicious of other people," and half were labeled, "This person is concerned with being fed and taken care of." Similarly, half of the drawings with an emphasized mouth and passive posture were given each label. An equivalent set of drawings can be created by any 10 volunteer artists. These drawings were reproduced four to a sheet on overhead transparencies, and I made a mask that allowed me to project one at a time. They could be reproduced on slides or projected with an opaque projector equally well.

INSTRUCTIONS

In introducing the activity, I describe the pictures to be viewed as having been culled from clinical files of two types of patients, patients suspicious of others and patients concerned with being fed and taken care of. I tell the students that I will show them a series of 20 pictures and that their task is to figure out how the Draw A Person test could be used to diagnose these two types of patients. I ask them to concentrate on viewing the pictures and not to take notes, because the exposures are going to be relatively brief. I then project each picture for approximately ten seconds.

After showing all 20 pictures, I ask the students to list the characteristics of the pictures that identify suspicious patients and then to do the same for characteristics of the pictures that identify patients concerned with being fed and taken care of. I then ask for suggestions from those lists to write on the board. After writing each characteristic on the board, I ask how many students had that characteristic on their list and note that number on the board. Each time I've used this activity, the list for suspicious patients has included atypical eyes and ears, and the list for patients concerned with being fed and taken care of has included a passive posture and an emphasized mouth. A substantial number of students have endorsed those characteristics.

I then explain that the labels and pictures were randomly paired. Because half of the pictures labeled as having been drawn by suspicious patients had atypical eyes and ears and half did not, students who listed these characteristics as typical of the drawings of suspicious patients had gone beyond the data and had "observed" an illusory correlation. The same is true for those who listed an emphasized mouth or outstretched arms as characteristic of the drawings produced by patients concerned with being fed and taken care of. The basis of these illusory correlations is an overestimate of the frequency of co-occurrence of the expected symptoms and the appropriate diagnostic label.

It is important at this point to clearly explain that the illusory correlation observed by most of the class is normal and is a frequently replicated finding and to discuss it in terms of the limitations of human information processing. Without a careful debriefing along these lines, some students may leave the class feeling rather foolish.

DISCUSSION

I have discussed the illusory correlation phenomenon and have used this demonstration in relation to several topics in introductory and other psychology classes. In discussing methodology, I find it important to point out that unsystematic observation, even by careful observers with high integrity, can fall victim to limitations of the human information processing system. The demonstration can be used in the "thinking" or cognitive section of an introductory psychology class or in a cognitive psychology class. It can be related to the development and maintenance of stereotypes in the social section of an introductory psychology class or in a social psychology class. It can be used in a discussion of unstandardized projective tests in a course on testing. The illusory correlation phenomenon is a pervasive one, and the demonstration can no doubt be used in settings other than these.

The demonstration has been successful each time I have used it. At the same time, in each class, I have had one or two skeptics who have maintained from the beginning that no differential diagnosis was possible. Each class was large enough (30–100 students) that simply asking for other opinions generated a list of diagnostic signs.

REFERENCES

Chapman, L. J., & Chapman, J. (1967). Genesis of popular but erroneous psychodiagnostic observations. *Journal of Abnormal Psychology, 74*, 193–204.

Crocker, J. (1981). Judgment of covariation by social perceivers. *Psychological Bulletin, 90*, 272–292.

SUGGESTED READING

Chapman, L. J. (1967). Illusory correlation in observational report. *Journal of Verbal Learning and Verbal Behavior, 6*, 151–155.

7 AN EXERCISE IN CONSTRUCT VALIDATION

George S. Howard, Paul K. Dunay, and Michael T. Crovello
University of Notre Dame

This activity is for the teacher who seeks a challenge; as the authors say, it is "not for the faint of heart." The students need to have studied validation and statistics. For the teacher who wishes to do the brief edition, the authors offer suggestions in the Discussion section. This activity can be used with classes of up to 45 or 50 students. The idea of validating one's midterm exam is inherently interesting to students at all levels, but the activity is probably unsuitable for high school or introductory psychology students.

CONCEPT   Construct validity is considered the most important type of validity in measurement theory. Other types of measurement validity include content validity, face validity, and criterion validity (whether concurrent or predictive). The definitions and test procedures for these three types of measurement validity are straightforward and fairly well-delineated.

Whenever researchers attempt to characterize situations, persons, or responses, they are interested in *constructs*. For most of the constructs of interest to psychologists (e.g., motivation, intelligence, self-concept, frustration, depression, etc.), there simply is no single criterion that measures the construct of interest perfectly. Thus, the potential for a serious conceptual problem exists. Whenever one attempts to assess the criterion validity of a test, low validity coefficients may represent either the poor validity of the test being validated (as one would hope) or the poor validity of the measure being used as the criterion.

Several studies (Cole, Howard, & Maxwell, 1981; Gabbard, Howard, & Dunfee, 1986; Howard, Conway, & Maxwell, 1985; Howard, Maxwell, Wiener, Boynton, & Rooney, 1980) have recently demonstrated that problems of *mono-operation bias* (i.e., using single-operationalized criterion measures) have served to invalidate a number of criterion validation studies in a wide array of content domains (clinical, educational, personality, and counseling psychology). In view of these problems, how can one properly assess the construct validity of any measure?

Many of these problems of construct validation can be allayed by using multiple operationalizations (or multiple methods) of the target construct in order to triangulate on the referent construct. Cook and Campbell (1979) noted that "we cannot in reality achieve widely accepted definitions of most constructs. This is because propositions about constructs are more reliable if they have been successfully tested, not only across many overlapping operational representations of a single definition of a construct, but also across representations of many overlapping definitions of the *same* construct" (pp. 62–63). The recommended alternative is to combine as many independent measures of the construct of interest as possible in order to obtain a multiple-operationalized index of the target construct. This criterion can control for the measurement irrelevancies unique to each measurement method by averaging over the irrelevancies and can assess the validity of each of the measures originally used to construct the criterion.

For this activity, we asked students to think of tests they have taken that had important implications for their lives, the construct validity of which can be assumed rather than demonstrated empirically. An immediate example was the midterm examination in their research methodology course.

INSTRUCTIONS Six methods of assessing students' knowledge of research design were used.

First, we used an objective test: The class was given a 25-item multiple-choice test on research methods. Second, we collected peer ratings. Each student was provided with a list of all the students in class and was instructed to rate as many of his or her classmates as possible on their knowledge of research methods. The percent of students rating any particular member of the class ranged from 21% to 100%. The ratings ranged from 1 (*student knows almost nothing about research methods*) to 10 (*student knows virtually everything about research methods*). Third, we used instructor ratings. The instructor rated each student, also using the 1–10-point peer rating scale. Fourth, self-ratings were collected when students rated themselves using the same scale. Fifth, an assistant conducted a 15-minute structured interview with each student, having the student respond orally to three essay-type questions on the course material. The interviewer rated the answer to each question separately, and the total rating was the average of these four ratings. And sixth, knowledge claims were assessed. Students were given three 1-page descriptions of hypothetical studies to critique for methodological shortcomings. These knowledge claims are modeled after Huck and Sandler's (1979) *Rival Hypotheses*. Each knowledge claim was rated separately by three other students, who rated it on a scale of 1 (*poor critique*) to 8 (*outstanding critique*). Each student's score was the average of the three ratings.

The multiple-operationalized approach, suggested previously, seeks evidence of convergent validity across the six target methods. But construct validity also implies evidence of discriminant validity, and "assessing construct validity depends on two processes: first, testing, for a *convergence* across *different* measures or manipulations of the same 'thing' and, second, testing for a *divergence* between measures and manipulations of related but conceptually distinct 'things' " (Cook & Campbell, 1979, p. 61). Therefore, each measurement was also used to assess a possibly related but conceptually distinct construct: knowledge of sports trivia. This additional evidence was gathered to obtain evidence of the discriminant validity of the various methods of measuring knowledge of research methodology. Thus, self-ratings, peer ratings, and instructor ratings of students' knowledge of sports trivia were also obtained using a 1 (*knows almost nothing about sports trivia*) to 10 (*knows an enormous amount about sports trivia*) scale. Students also took a 15-item objective test, and a sports trivia knowledge claims test was developed, administered, and scored by the raters in the manner described previously, as was a structured interview. Complete data were obtained from 52 students enrolled in a Research Methodology course.

Data Analysis

Mono-operationalized validation approach. The simplest level on which the data were analyzed was the mono-operational validation approach, in which each method of measuring the knowledge of research methodology was used to validate every other measure. For example, the objective test scores were validated by the knowledge claims, self-ratings, peer ratings, instructor ratings, and structured interviews. The average validity coefficients were then computed for each of the six methods of measuring knowledge of research methodology and knowledge of sports trivia.

Multiple-operationalized validation approach. Each method of measuring knowledge of research methods was correlated with a composite criterion, which was a linear combination of the standardized scores for the remaining five methods of measuring knowledge of research methodology. In other words, the objective test measure was validated against a composite criterion composed of the Z score for knowledge claims plus the Z score for peer ratings plus the Z score for instructor ratings plus the Z score for structured interview plus the Z score for the self-rating. Standard scores were used to calculate the composite criterion to insure the equal weighting of each measure. These multiple-operationalized coefficients were calculated for each of the six methods of measuring knowledge of research methodology and of sports trivia.

Confirmatory factor analytic approach (COFAMM). Pearson correlation coefficients were calculated among the objective tests, self-ratings, peer ratings, instructor ratings, structured interviews, and knowledge claims for both knowledge of research methodology and sports trivia. The intercorrelation matrix of these variables appears in Table 1. Two one-factor models were tested for goodness of fit using Jöreskog and Sörbom's (1981) LISREL V confirmatory factor analysis program.

Convergent Validity

Convergent validity is demonstrated when different methods of measuring the same trait are correlated with one another. Several approaches were used to demonstrate convergent validity.

Mono-operationalized validation approach. The average validity coefficient for each method of measurement was computed for both knowledge of research methodology and knowledge of sports trivia. These values are summarized in Figure 7-1.

Table 1. *Intercorrelations Among the Six Measures of Knowledge of Research Methods and Sports Trivia*

Variable	1	2	3	4	5	6	7	8	9	10	11
Research methods											
1. Self-ratings											
2. Peer-ratings	.36										
3. Instructor ratings	.36	.61									
4. Objective tests	.31	.09	.17								
5. Knowledge claims	.41	.46	.22	.06							
6. Structured interviews	.41	.66	.61	.37	.27						
Sports trivia											
7. Self-ratings	−.12	.00	−.04	−.10	−.10						
8. Peer-ratings	−.04	−.16	−.06	.06	−.13	−.13	.70				
9. Instructor ratings	.18	.01	.11	.16	.00	−.03	.57	.83			
10. Objective tests	.15	.00	.07	.03	−.14	−.08	.77	.75	.62		
11. Knowledge claims	.14	.19	.24	.18	.00	.26	.73	.56	.60	.61	
12. Structured interviews	.00	.02	.11	.18	−.09	.01	.81	.80	.70	.78	.71

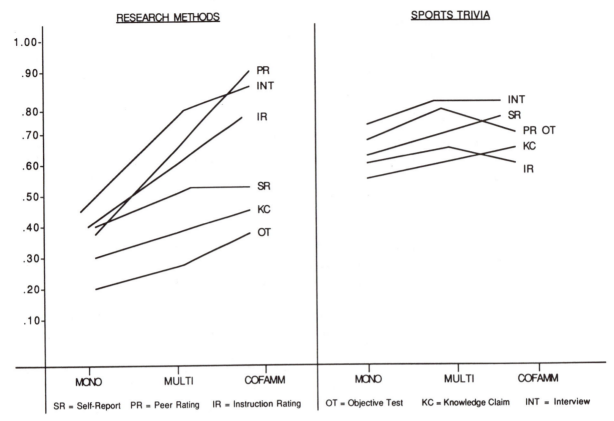

Figure 7-1. *Average validity coefficient for each method of measurement.*

Moderately high mono-operational validity coefficients of knowledge of research methodology were found for the structured interview (r = .46), peer rating (r = .43), instructor rating (r = .39), and self-rating (r = .37). Validity coefficients for ratings of knowledge of sports trivia were uniformly higher and fell within a narrow range (rs = .64–.76).

Multiple-operationalized validation approach. Correlation coefficients were computed between each measure and a linear combination of the standardized scores for the other five measures of that trait. This procedure was followed for both knowledge of research methodology and sports trivia measures. On the knowledge of research methodology dimension, structured interviews, peer ratings, instructor ratings, and self-ratings all correlated highly with their respective criteria, demonstrating their convergent validity. The correlations for the sports trivia dimension were all quite large, indicating convergence across measures.

The criteria used in this approach averaged across method irrelevancies and random error irrelevancies that were present in the criteria used in the mono-operational approach. The effects of method variance and random error variance were thus somewhat cancelled out in this criterion, allowing the effects of trait variance to be more apparent. Therefore, these coefficients were, as expected, greater than the average mono-operationalized validity coefficients.

Confirmatory factor analytic approach (Jöreskog & Sörbom, 1981). Whereas the multioperational procedure bases its criterion on a linear combination of observed variables, confirmatory factor analysis involves a latent, hypothetical construct that determines the observed variables. The measured variables are assumed to be a linear combination of the unmeasured or latent variables, and the latent variables are assumed to have caused the observed variables to appear as they do. This reveals an important relation between the latent and observed variables—one in which the choice of variables characterizes the constructs, and the constructs determine the values of the observed variables (Kenny, 1979).

This analysis determines the degree of relation between the latent variables (in this case knowledge of research methodology and sports trivia) and the observed variables (the six methods of measuring each trait). This was achieved by testing the fit of the hypothesized model (i.e., that knowledge of research methodology caused the six measures obtained) with the data. We used the maximum likelihood factor analysis (Jöreskog, 1971).

These tests were done on the LISREL V computer package. A single-factor model provided an adequate fit to the data, both for knowledge of research methodology, $x^2(8, N = 52) = 12.65, p > .12$, and for sports trivia, $x^2(7, N = 52) = 7.22, p > .40$. Almost all of the validity coefficients for both constructs showed increments over the mono- and multioperational approaches. These results were not surprising given the fact that the criterion used in the confirmatory factor analysis procedure contains no error of measurement. As long as the methods used were not highly correlated, as was the case in the present study, the information added to the analysis with the inclusion of each additional measure was unique. Furthermore, to the extent that this unique information was not merely method or error variance, the additional measures help to define the trait more completely. Consequently, when a single measure was validated against this more compelling criterion, the validity coefficients were not spuriously deflated due to poor measurement of the construct. In comparison, because the criteria used in the mono- and multioperational validation procedures were less adequately defined, the validity coefficients obtained using these approaches underestimated a given method's measurement of the trait in question.

The validity estimates of all measures do not increase uniformly as one progresses from the mono-operational through the multioperational to the COFAMM approaches. Five switches in the rank ordering of methods of measuring knowledge of sports trivia occurred from the mono-operational to the COFAMM approaches. Furthermore, while the range of estimated validity coefficients of measures of sports trivia increased somewhat from mono-operational ($rs = .64–.76$) to COFAMM ($rs = .78–.92$), the increase was dramatic for the measures of research methods from mono-operational ($rs = .20–.46$) to COFAMM ($rs = .39–.83$). Finally, using the standard tests of discriminant validity suggested by Campbell and Fiske (1959), evidence of discriminant validity was found for all methods of measuring both traits (knowledge of research methods and sports trivia).

DISCUSSION

This demonstration is not for the faint of heart. The two components of the course midterm examination (objective test and knowledge claims) received the lowest estimated validity coefficients of all measures of students' knowledge. Although psychometricians have long known that measurement techniques that rely on making assessments based on small samples of subjects' behavior can have serious validity problems, educators and students are rarely confronted with evidence suggesting the invalidity of standard educational testing practices. It is one thing to quote Cook and Campbell's (1979) statement that researchers should acknowledge methodological fallibility (i.e., there are no perfect methods), but it is quite another to see exactly how imperfect are our methods.

Complete data were presented here in order to show students how data would appear in an actual study. For an actual in-class demonstration, you might collect only self-ratings, peer ratings, objective tests, instructor ratings, and knowledge claims and perform only the mono- and multioperationalized validation approaches. These data can easily be obtained in class, and the analysis can easily be conducted with a pocket calculator.

REFERENCES

Campbell, D. T., & Fiske, D. W. (1959). Convergent and discriminant validation by the multitrait–multimethod matrix. *Psychological Bulletin, 56,* 81–105.

Cole, D. A., Howard, G. S., & Maxwell, S. E. (1981). The effects of mono versus multiple operationalization in construct validation efforts. *Journal of Consulting and Clinical Psychology, 49,* 395–405.

Cook, T. D., & Campbell, D. T. (1979). *Quasi-experimentation: Design and analysis issues for field settings.* Chicago: Rand McNally.

Gabbard, C. E., Howard, G. S., & Dunfee, E. J. (1986). Reliability, sensitivity to measuring change, and construct validity of therapist adaptability. *Journal of Counseling Psychology, 33,* 377–386.

Howard, G. S., Conway, C. G., & Maxwell, S. E. (1985). Construct validity of measures of college teaching effectiveness. *Journal of Educational Psychology, 77,* 187–196.

Howard, G. S., Maxwell, S. E., Wiener, R. L., Boynton, K. S., & Rooney, W. M. (1980). Is a behavioral measure the best estimate of behavioral parameters? Perhaps not. *Applied Psychological Measurement, 4,* 293–311.

Huck, S. W., & Sandler, H. M. (1979). *Rival hypotheses: Alternative interpretations of data based conclusions.* New York: Harper & Row.

Jöreskog, K. G. (1971). Statistical analysis of sets of congeneric tests. *Psychometrika, 36,* 109–133.

Jöreskog, K. G., & Sörbom, D. S. (1981). *LISREL V—Estimation of linear structural relationships by the method of maximum likelihood.* Chicago: National Educational Resources.

Kenny, D. A. (1979). *Correlation and causality.* New York: Wiley.

SUGGESTED READING

Cronbach, L. J. (1971). Test validation. In R. L. Thorndike (Ed.), *Educational measurement* (2nd ed.). Washington, DC: American Council on Education.

8 SELECTING APPROPRIATE RESEARCH METHODS

Peter S. Fernald
University of New Hampshire

L. Dodge Fernald
Harvard University

This activity is appealing because of the diversity of the hypotheses considered. Students need to be familiar with the text section on research methods prior to the discussion. Teachers need to copy the handouts. The activity is appropriate for classes of virtually any size, although for large classes, the instructor may need to adapt the activity for individual, written responses rather than small group discussion.

CONCEPT

This demonstration considers four research strategies: naturalistic observation, surveys, clinical procedures, and the experimental approach. Ten statements about human nature are listed on the chalkboard. Students select the research strategy most appropriate for testing each statement, and reasons for their selections are then discussed. The purpose is to help students identify appropriate research strategies for different problems and to identify problems that cannot be studied by any research method.

MATERIALS NEEDED

Provide each student with a handout of the ten statements (optional).

INSTRUCTIONS

This activity requires that students have some prior familiarity with the four research strategies. A single lecture or reading of the relevant sections of a standard introductory text will suffice.

List the ten statements on the chalkboard or hand out copies of the statements to the class. Instruct the students to place either a ?, N, C, S, or E beside each statement. The ? indicates that it is impossible to study the problem scientifically; the letter N means that naturalistic observation is the appropriate method; and the letters C, S, and E suggest that the clinical, survey, and experimental approach, respectively, are most appropriate. Tell the students that when a problem can be studied by both naturalistic observation and the experimental approach, they should indicate the latter, because it permits greater precision.

Ten Statements

1. Jogging increases lung capacity.
2. The soul remains after death.
3. When administered the Rorschach Inkblot Test, young children and regressed psychotics perceive more animals than they do humans.

Adapted from the *Instructor's Manual* of *Introduction to Psychology* (5th ed.), by L. Dodge Fernald and Peter S. Fernald. Copyright 1985, Wm C. Brown. Used by permission.

4. Individuals having one or more significant hobbies report more job satisfaction than individuals having no hobbies.
5. Unmarried cab drivers talk more with their customers than do married cab drivers.
6. Newborn infants have an innate conception of sin.
7. The purchase of tranquilizers increases during monetary crises.
8. Alcoholics with a history of poor nutrition show more signs of brain damage than alcoholics with a history of good nutrition.
9. More men than women report fantasies of making large sums of money.
10. Work productivity increases when workers are allowed flexible hours.

Divide the class into groups of 3–5 students and instruct each group to arrive at the single preferred method of study for each statement. Tell the students they will have 20 minutes, or approximately 2 minutes for each statement. At the end of 10 minutes, inform the students that there are only 10 minutes remaining, and urge them to select an answer for each statement, even if they are not sure that some of their answers are correct.

DISCUSSION Have one of the groups explain to the rest of the class which research method they considered most appropriate for the first problem. Allow other students to both agree and disagree, and try to elicit from the group members their reasons for selecting a particular research method. Once the discussion has come to a reasonable conclusion, ask another group to present their answer to the second problem. Continue in this manner until all ten statements have been discussed.

The questions and research strategies for answering these questions generate a full and spirited discussion that addresses both the merits and limitations of each research strategy. As the discussion unfolds, students should be informed of the correct answers, which are as follows: 1. *E*, 2. *?*, 3. *C*, 4. *S*, 5. *N*, 6. *?*, 7. *N*, 8. *C*, 9. *S*, 10. *E*. Both Statements 1 and 10 could be studied through naturalistic observation, but the experimental approach puts these statements to a more rigorous test.

SUGGESTED READING Fernald, L. D., & Fernald, P. S. (1985). *Introduction to psychology* (5th ed., Chapter 2). Dubuque, IA: Wm C. Brown.

9 TEACHING RIVAL HYPOTHESES IN EXPERIMENTAL PSYCHOLOGY

George S. Howard and Jean L. Englehardt
University of Notre Dame

This is both a teaching device and an actual experiment that allows students to conduct their own study of rival hypotheses and increases their ability to critique research. It requires seven lab sessions and a lecture session. The instructor will need to be well-prepared before beginning this activity. It can be used on classes of any size and is suitable for an introductory level class.

CONCEPT

Many instructors of research methods and experimental psychology courses believe that scientific rationality consists of an elaboration and refinement of disciplined inquiry. All people are capable of some degree of commonsense rationality. If students can view scientific reasoning as a natural extension and refinement of their own critical inquiries, their motivation to learn the methods and techniques of experimental psychology might be enhanced. Huck and Sandler (1979) wrote a book entitled *Rival Hypotheses* that describes a number of instances in which empirical support is claimed as a result of "research." These studies deal with knowledge claims of practical importance (such as the "Pepsi challenge" or evidence that saccharine causes cancer), and students find them very interesting to critique.

This activity explains how *Rival Hypotheses* can be used as both a teaching device and an actual experiment whereby students obtain practice performing data analysis, interpreting findings, and writing reports.

MATERIALS NEEDED

You will need at least one copy of Huck and Sandler's (1979) *Rival Hypotheses*.

INSTRUCTIONS

Begin the first day of class by pretesting all students on their ability to critique research, and then randomly assign students to one of two groups (Groups A and B). The sequence of activities in the study is presented in the following list:

> Lab Session 1: Pretest and assignment to groups
> Lab Session 2: Group A, rival hypotheses; Group B, off
> Lab Session 3: Group A, rival hypotheses; Group B, off
> Lab Session 4: Group A, rival hypotheses; Group B, off
> Lecture Session: Posttest 1 to Groups A and B
> Lab Session 5: Group A, off; Group B, rival hypotheses
> Lab Session 6: Group A, off; Group B, rival hypotheses
> Lab Session 7: Group A, off; Group B, rival hypotheses
> Lecture Session: Posttest 2 to Groups A and B

Administer Posttests 1 and 2 at the end of lecture classes at the appropriate points in time. Lectures continue throughout the course of the experiment, which has implications for the interpretation of within-group changes over time. Instruct students who have "off" lab days to use the time to complete other lab assignments such as reading material on how to write a research report.

Pretest, Posttest 1, and Posttest 2 are constructed by selecting 12 problems from *Rival Hypotheses* and randomly assigning 4 problems to each of the three tests. From the remaining problems in *Rival Hypotheses*, the lab instructor selects 12 of the most interesting and arranges them in increasing order of difficulty. Students are presented these 12 problems over the three lab periods that constitute the training intervention being evaluated.

After students individually critique each problem, the group pools its critiques and discusses the points made, and the instructor adds any additional points that were not made by the students. (Huck and Sandler provide their critiques of each problem in the book.)

The lab immediately following Posttest 2 is devoted to describing the design of the study and discussing the strengths and liabilities of the design. Encourage students to take copious notes because they will each have to write a research report of the project.

Immediately after administering Posttest 2, begin judging the test problems. Ratings are obtained from two students in the class who do not take part in the study. Raters should be trained by an instructor and should achieve an acceptable level of agreement before the actual rating of test problems begins. A student's critique is scored by rating each comment made on a 3-point scale consisting of 1 (*weak criticism*), 2 (*good criticism*) and 0 (*wrong or irrelevant criticism*). Subjects' scores are totaled across the four problems on each test and are then averaged across judges and problems.

Now give the students data on all subjects for each of the three test periods and tell them to analyze the data and to write a research report on the study (our students had already taken a semester-long course in statistics and the use of the computer for data analysis). Student papers are then critiqued by the lab instructor, marked, and returned to the students.

The project serves as a basis for several lab and lecture activities throughout the course. Perhaps the most substantial activity is consideration of the array of statistical analyses that might have been performed on the data. It is instructive for the students to realize that many different (potentially acceptable) analyses are possible and that each analysis considers a slightly different research question. In our case, although we advocated an analysis of Posttest 1 scores covaried by pretest scores as the most powerful and appropriate test of treatment effects, the value of additional analyses in affording other insights was highlighted. Furthermore, students were apprised of the conceptual difficulties involved in interpreting other seemingly plausible analyses. For example, one might naively think that a comparison of pretest scores with Posttest 2 scores for all subjects would yield an estimate of the effectiveness of the *Rival Hypotheses* lab exercises. Of course, rival hypotheses such as testing and history effects are present and uncontrolled. Furthermore, students are introduced to the subtleties of integrating design considerations (four rival hypothesis problems were randomly assigned to the pretest and four to each of the posttests) with statistical considerations (how much confidence does one have that these two tests are equally difficult, since only four problems were assigned to each test?).

Students should also be apprised of the difficulties in interpreting subjects' increases in critiquing skill due to contaminants such as nonspecific treatment effects. Finally, for the remainder of the course, ask students to consider how each new topic being considered did or did not relate to the *Rival Hypotheses* study.

DISCUSSION   As mentioned earlier, the analysis of Posttest 1 scores covaried by pretest scores was the most appropriate estimate of treatment (the *Rival Hypotheses* lab exercises) effectiveness. Group A subjects $(n = 13)$ scored significantly higher on adjusted Posttest 1 scores than did their control group $(n = 15)$ counterparts, $F(1, 25) = 24.62$, $p < .001$. Treatment subjects' scores increased 4.26 points (pretest = 5.16, Posttest 1 = 9.52) but control subjects' scores actually decreased by 1.28 points (pretest = 5.68, Posttest 1 = 4.40).

Students find it instructive to consider why analyses of Posttest 2 scores are fraught with difficulties of interpretation. For example, because both groups have studied the rival hypotheses problems, a comparison of Posttest 2 scores for the two groups would be expected to show no differences. If, on the other hand, one were to consider pretest to Posttest 2 change scores for all subjects as a measure of treatment effectiveness, interpretation would be flawed because no control group exists against which to contrast these changes. Finally, one may believe that differences between Groups A and B on Posttest 1 to Posttest 2 change scores might reflect a valid treatment effect. Such a comparison is inappropriate, inasmuch as differences between the two groups existed on Posttest 1 precisely because Group A had already received the intervention, whereas Group B had not yet experienced it. Consequently, group differences in change scores would be expected even if the treatment had been totally ineffectual, which renders interpretation of any findings problematic. By explicating the problems inherent in any consideration of Posttest 2 findings, students are once again reminded of the importance of proper design in obtaining unconfounded results.

In sum, the study accomplishes several important goals in a cost-effective manner. Students are encouraged to see the topics of research design as an elaboration of their natural critical-thinking abilities. The actual practice of analyzing and writing this study gives students some exposure to topics such as judgment techniques, nonspecific treatment effects, and so on, that can be considered more thoroughly later in the course. In addition, students are encouraged to apply their statistics backgrounds and skills to problems presented in a methods course. Finally, students receive practice in critiquing studies, which is an important part of a psychology course.

REFERENCES   Huck, S. W., & Sandler, H. M. (1979). *Rival hypotheses: Alternative interpretations of data based conclusions.* New York: Harper & Row.

10 Research Methodology Taxonomy and Interpreting Research Studies

Peter H. Bohling
Bloomsburg University

G. Alfred Forsyth
Millersville University

Richard B. May
University of Victoria

Many students do not receive this kind of exposure until a graduate statistics course. The activity is appropriate for advanced undergraduates in virtually any size class. The instructor needs to provide copies of the handouts. The activity is equally appropriate for sections on methodology or on statistics. Students need to understand the basics of both.

CONCEPT   The purpose of this activity is to help students decide when a particular type of statistical analysis should be used and what conclusions are appropriate for any research study. Selecting the correct test for significance, determining the appropriate approach for going beyond significance (e.g., parameter estimation), and determining whether cause-and-effect conclusions can be drawn are more likely to be carried out correctly if a taxonomy of research methodologies is available. This activity introduces a basic research methodology taxonomy and focuses on two aspects of research methodology that lead to confusion in the analysis and interpretation of data.

The first factor in the taxonomy is whether the researcher used an available group of subjects or a group randomly sampled from a larger population. As Edgington (1987) pointed out, statistics and research methodology books perpetuate the fiction that random sampling is usually used in experimental studies. The random-sampling model for statistical analysis developed by Fisher (1935) is appropriate when a random-sampling methodology has been used. The permutation tests developed by Pitman (1938) and updated by Edgington (1987) to apply computer technology are appropriate when an available-subjects methodology is used. Parameter estimation techniques such as confidence intervals are appropriate only with random sampling.

The second factor in the taxonomy is the distinction between experimental and classificatory studies. In experimental studies, the researcher randomly assigns subjects to different treatment groups. Classificatory studies are those in which subjects are classified into groups based on information about the subjects (e.g., gender, age). Random assignment is the critical concern in determining whether cause-and-effect statements are appropriate.

Research terminology has led to confusing these two taxonomy factors such that students become more confident in the generalization of results or in cause-and-effect interpretations when either random assignment or random sampling is used. Kempthorne (1979, 1980) pointed out the confusion in the research literature about what constitutes an experiment, the need for differentiating kinds of studies, and each study's unique interpretation implications.

MATERIALS NEEDED

You will need a copy of the handouts for each student.

INSTRUCTIONS

First, review the 2×2 taxonomy table and the definitions of the two taxonomy factors provided in Handout 1. It is usually best to do this with examples similar to those provided in Handout 2.

Next, instruct the students to read the studies in Handout 2 and to determine the appropriate interpretation of the results. This should be an open-ended assignment in which your students describe what they would be willing to conclude from the information provided.

After students have completed the open-ended responses, instruct them to answer the seven questions in Handout 3 for each of the four studies. In reviewing the students' answers to these questions, ask them how the study could be redesigned or how the results could be reported differently to increase their confidence whenever low confidence ratings are given (or should have been given).

The four studies in Handout 2 are alike in having an independent variable with an underlying continuum even though only two levels are used. They are also alike in that the dependent variable is always assumed to be on an interval or ratio scale of measurement. An extension of this activity would be to have students answer the Handout 3 questions for studies in which the independent variable is on a nominal scale (e.g., a comparison of entry-level wages in unionized and nonunionized firms) or the dependent variable is on an ordinal scale of measurement.

DISCUSSION

This activity requires students to distinguish between random-sampling and available-subjects methodologies and between random-assignment and classified-subjects methodologies. In addition, it should increase the students' understanding of the implications of using any of the four research methodologies for selecting the appropriate test of significance, for going beyond statistical significance, and for making cause-and-effect conclusions. Experience in carrying out statistical analyses with both the permutation and the random-sampling models is an important complement to this activity. Most basic statistics books provide good exercises using the random-sampling model for statistical analyses (e.g., t tests or F tests of significance). Exercises for using the permutation model for statistical analyses have been presented by Bohling and Forsyth (1987) and by Edgington (1987).

The 2×2 taxonomy presented in Handout 1 could be extended by including the scale of measurement of the dependent variable as a third factor and the scale of measurement of the independent variable as a fourth factor. Permutation is the appropriate model with an ordinal scale of measurement dependent variable. The fourth factor in the taxonomy is important in determining the nature of analyses and conclusions about trends following overall tests of significance. Question 5 in Handout 3 is of greatest interest when the studies evaluated have more than two levels.

An appropriate follow-up project to this activity is to have students critique journal articles by classifying studies according to the research methodology taxonomy. They could also note the appropriateness of the statistical analysis used, the generalizations made, and the cause-and-effect conclusions. One goal of the taxonomy and of this activity is to help students become better consumers of psychological research. This follow-up project with journal studies is an important test of the value of the activity. Students and their professors may find it interesting to note the degree to which the distinctions in the taxonomy are not recognized by researchers.[1]

REFERENCES

Bohling, P. H., & Forsyth, G. A. (1987). Statistical significance: Concrete operational activities. In V. P. Makosky, L. G. Whittemore, & A. M. Rogers (Eds.), *Activities handbook for the teaching of psychology* (Vol. 2, pp. 213–221). Washington, DC: American Psychological Association.

Edgington, E. S. (1987). *Randomization tests* (2nd ed.). New York: Dekker.

Fisher, R. A. (1935). *The design and analysis of experiments.* Edinburgh, Scotland: Oliver & Boyd.

Kempthorne, O. (1979). Sampling inference, experimental inference, and observational inference. *Indian Journal of Statistics, 40,* 115–145.

Kempthorne, O. (1980). The teaching of statistics: Content versus form. *American Statistician, 34,* 17–21.

Pitman, E. J. G. (1938). Significance tests which may be applied to samples from any populations: III. The analysis of variance tests. *Biometrika, 29,* 322–335.

---

[1] The four Handout 2 studies can be classified into the four cells of the Handout 1 taxonomy as follows: Study A = 3, Study B = 4, Study C = 2, and Study D = 1.

Handout 1: Basic Research Methodology Taxonomy

Taxonomy Factors Table

Subject assignment	Subject selection	
	Random	Available
Random	1	2
Classified	3	4

Note. Numbers indicate the four types of studies possible given these selection and assignment factors.

Taxonomy Factors Defined

Subject Selection Factor

This refers to the two major ways in which subjects can be obtained for a study. The first method is called *random sampling*. This requires the researcher to identify a population of subjects and to then select samples randomly from that population. In random sampling, every case in the population has an equal opportunity of being selected into a sample. The second method is the use of subjects who are conveniently available to the researcher. There is no systematic sampling from the population of interest with available selection. The random-sampling statistical model is used for studies in which subjects are randomly sampled from the population of interest. Permutation tests of statistical significance are appropriate for available-subject studies. Statistical inference to population parameters is limited to random-sampling studies.

Subject Grouping Factor

This refers to the two major ways subjects in the study are put into groups. First, the subjects in the study may be *randomly assigned* to experimental groups. This method gives each subject an equal opportunity of being placed in any particular experimental group. In the second method, the subjects are already *classified* as members of a particular group based on specific characteristics (e.g., gender, age). Cause-and-effect conclusions are appropriate when subjects are randomly assigned to groups but not when subjects are classified into groups.

Study A

A university was interested in using a new test to determine which applicants should be admitted. The new test was given to all college-bound high school seniors interested in attending the university. The university researcher randomly selected 30 of the approximately 750 applicants who scored between the 30th and 40th percentile ranks on the test and admitted them to the university. She also randomly selected 30 students of the approximately 750 students who scored between the 70th and 80th percentile ranks on the test and admitted them to the university. The cumulative grade point average for each of the 60 individuals in the study was obtained at the end of the first academic year. The researcher reported that, on the average, students scoring between the 70th and 80th percentile ranks on the new admissions test earned higher cumulative grade point averages than the students scoring between the 30th and 40th percentile ranks on the new admissions test ($p < .02$).

Study B

A developmental psychologist was interested in the relation between how much children are read to and their language arts abilities. She asked parents of an available group of 4-year olds to keep a daily record of the amount of time they spent reading to their children. At the end of 3 years, she found that 30 children had been read to an average of zero to one hour per week and that 30 children had been read to an average of six to seven hours per week. She gave these 60 children a comprehensive test of language arts abilities. The researcher reported that, on the average, the language arts scores of those who were read to six to seven hours per week were greater than those who were read to zero to one hour per week ($p < .02$).

Study C

A researcher was interested in the relation between alcohol consumption and reaction time in a simulated driving situation. Sixty members of the Kiwanis, Lions, and Rotary civic organizations volunteered to serve as subjects in the study. Thirty of these 60 individuals were randomly assigned to the alcohol group and the other 30 to the no-alcohol group. The individuals did not know to which group they had been assigned. Two hours before entering the simulated driving apparatus, each of the 60 persons had five drinks. While the drinks for all subjects tasted and smelled alike, there was one ounce of alcohol in each drink for the alcohol group and no alcohol in the drinks served to the no-alcohol group. The researcher reported that, on the average, the reaction time was slower for the alcohol group than for the no-alcohol group ($p < .02$).

Study D

A fast-food chain of 1,500 franchises was having difficulty with employee absenteeism. The firm decided to carry out a study to determine if adding a profit-sharing plan would reduce absenteeism. The company researcher randomly selected 60 of their franchises for the study. Thirty of those were randomly assigned to a profit-sharing plan that involved distributing 5% of the individual franchise profits each month to employees at that franchise. The employees at the other 30 franchises continued to receive their same hourly pay without the profit-sharing plan supplement. Each of the 60 franchises kept a record of the number of absences by their employees during the year-long study. The researcher reported that, on the average, the absences were lower at the profit-sharing franchises ($p < .02$).

Answer the following questions for each of the studies described in Handout 2.
1. Indicate which of the four types of studies this represents.
   ( ) 1 ( ) 2 ( ) 3 ( ) 4
2. How confident would you be in the use of the p value in this study if it were based on a random-sample model t test or F test of significance?
   Not at all ( ) 1 ( ) 2 ( ) 3 ( ) 4 ( ) 5 Extremely
3. How confident would you be if this researcher reported going beyond testing for statistical significance by computing confidence intervals?
   Not at all ( ) 1 ( ) 2 ( ) 3 ( ) 4 ( ) 5 Extremely
4. How confident would you be if this researcher concluded that there is a linear relation between the independent and dependent variable?
   Not at all ( ) 1 ( ) 2 ( ) 3 ( ) 4 ( ) 5 Extremely
5. How confident would you be if this researcher concluded that there is a cause-and-effect relation between the independent and dependent variable?
   Not at all ( ) 1 ( ) 2 ( ) 3 ( ) 4 ( ) 5 Extremely
6. How confident are you that another researcher replicating this study will obtain similar results?
   Not at all ( ) 1 ( ) 2 ( ) 3 ( ) 4 ( ) 5 Extremely
7. How confident are you that the result of this study is meaningful?
   Not at all ( ) 1 ( ) 2 ( ) 3 ( ) 4 ( ) 5 Extremely

11 TEACHING THE PROCESS OF SCIENCE IN THE INTRODUCTORY METHODS COURSE

Alan R. P. Journet
Southeast Missouri State University

This activity is actually a unit in an introductory methods course, taking up approximately six to eight class sessions. The unit encourages students to develop a way of learning that goes beyond rote memorization and helps them to apply a scientific manner of thinking to various kinds of problem solving. The assignments require the students to work together in pairs and groups, and students eventually design and test their own hypotheses. The unit gives students a thorough grounding in all aspects of the experimental method and covers topics such as pseudoscience and creationism. In addition, it can be used with any size class; no prior knowledge is necessary.

CONCEPT

As Sagan (1974) underlined, science is less a body of knowledge than it is a way of thinking. When confronted with the abstract ideas that are found in textbook discussions of the process of science, students who are concrete, operational thinkers will resort to memorization (Lawson & Renner, 1975). Because 50% or more of our students think in this way (Inhelder & Piaget, 1958; McKinnon, 1971; Journet, Young, Stanley, & Scheibe, 1987), I devised a unit to teach science in a way that allows students to apply the process to everyday problem-solving situations. This unit is part of a general education introductory science course I teach, and it takes approximately six to eight 50-minute lectures to complete. It is based on the Popperian view of science as conjecture and refutation, with the falsifiable hypothesis as the key (Popper, 1968a, 1968b), and involves a series of homework and classroom assignments that are graded at intervals.

INSTRUCTIONS

How Do We Know What We Know?

Assignment 1. Students list five things that they know. Each student then gives the list to a neighbor in class, who asks, "How do you know that?" and then writes the answers. Examples of these answers are listed on the board, with common themes developed and organized as a graph (Table 1) that shows (a) much that we "know" comes from instruction rather than analysis, (b) no one develops all their "truths" one way, (c) some ideas are not amenable to investigation all ways, and (d) science is not the only or even a superior means of exploration; rather, it is merely one of many means and one with advantages for dealing with certain kinds of questions.

Assignment 2. Students provide five statements that they associate with science, scientists, or the scientific method. First in pairs, then in groups, students reduce these to the five overall best statements, which are then written on the board for discussion. Themes commonly identified include hypotheses, observations, predic-

Table 1. *Possible Means by Which We Explore Our Universe*

	Nature of the statement	
Response to the statement	Objective	Subjective
Analysis	Experiment logic	Persuasion
Acceptance	Instruction	Predilection
	Regulation	Personal preference

tions, repeatability, testability, and so on, with emphasis on science as a process, not as information.

What is the Scientific Method?

The model (Table 2), which is also used in our investigative laboratory course for nonmajors (Journet, 1985), could easily be modified to suit different scientific terminology.

Assignment 3. After I have defined observation and generalization, students identify five observations that they have made recently on any topic they choose. Several of these are then collected for class discussion. During the rest of the unit, we use two or three examples for class discussion while students concurrently work through one or more of their own. On most occasions, the initial observations are generalizations, such as, "Students always bring books to class," "Basketball players are over 6 feet tall," or "My heart rate goes up after aerobics class." In their search for patterns, students jump over observations so rapidly that such observations are easily overlooked in analysis. This is a point that should be clarified through classroom discussion of the student examples.

The generalizations are assigned to one of two categories: simple descriptive patterns (e.g., basketball players), or an explanatory cause-and-effect relation (e.g., aerobics and heart rate) where cause and effect are both observed.

Assignment 4. Because science seeks powerful predictive patterns, the key question is always "How large should the universe be?" The larger the universe, the more predictive the generalization, but the harder it is also to test. Identifying and justify-

Table 2. *Model of the Scientific Method*

Step	Description
1	Prior knowledge, experience, and interest
2	Observation: A single perceived event
3	Generalization: A pattern discerned among observations
4	Research hypothesis: A predictive statement about the universe drawn from the generalization
5	Prediction: A testable consequence of the research hypothesis
6	Experiment: The test of the prediction
7	Experimental hypotheses (alternate and null): The expected result and the basis for comparison
8	Results: The data collected from the experiment
9	Analysis: Analysis (statistical) of the data
10	Conclusion: Re-evaluation of the research hypothesis

ing the universe for each generalization leads to the recognition that the process, so often called inductive logic, is not logical at all (Medawar, 1969). It is intuitive. Through the creative application of insight gained from prior knowledge and experience, a reasonable, defensible, and testable universe will be developed. Discussions of justification for the universe reveal the subjectivity in science, but students should not get the impression that "it's just what you think."

In the basketball player example, the universe might include all basketball players, only men, only Americans, only Missourians, and so forth. Similarly, in the aerobics example, the age and geographic source of people included in the universe must be decided.

What are Hypotheses and Where Do They Come From?

Students commonly think that their hypotheses must be correct. Such a view of hypothetical formulation may be widespread, because only the results of the process are reported in the media (and even in journals), usually only when the hypothesis has been supported. Such reporting distorts the essence of the process of science in which, as Medawar (1969) noted, we are wrong much more often than we are right. The students' erroneous views in this regard explain their frequent indications of a universe that includes only the observations and no more; after all, we can be certain of them. But science, as conjecture and refutation, simply requires that the hypothesis be a clear statement of the generalization in predictive, testable terms.

Hypotheses are derived from these generalizations; the basketball player example leads to a descriptive hypothesis about the height of players never seen, and the aerobics example produces a cause-and-effect hypothesis about the influence of exercise on heart rate. Generally, descriptive hypotheses address the question, "What is the pattern?", whereas the explanatory conjectures ask the question, "Why is the pattern?"

But we must also allow the even more intuitive conjecture of hypotheses for which explanations come not from observations but from prior knowledge. Thus, in one discussion about the pattern of cold temperatures in a classroom, the purely descriptive hypothesis that the cold pattern would continue led also to the intuitive explanatory hypothesis that the cold was caused by an incorrectly set thermostat. Although testing either hypothesis would be a legitimate application of science, the latter involves a leap to conjectured cause-and-effect relations not yet observed. Because there is much more opportunity for error in such hypotheses, the importance of the rule of reason should be stressed. Neither scientists nor nonscientists waste their time testing frivolous or unreasonable hypotheses. Given a choice among hypotheses, we make subjective decisions in favor of the most valuable and reasonable. Again, the subjectivity of science is apparent.

Much current medical research follows the purely descriptive process. Often, through the use of surveys, correlations are discerned between disease and aspects of life-style (e.g., smoking and cancer). After tests are done in which laboratory animals are used, medical treatment may be indicated, although an explanation for the correlation remains undiscovered. Tobacco companies make much of the absence of explanations, implying falsely that predictive patterns are thus less scientific.

Other medical studies, of course, address cause and effect. A conjecture about the role of fatty acids in heart disease may be that the acids are transformed into cholesterol, which is deposited in and blocks arteries. Such a conjecture can be tested by examining the arteries of individuals who die from heart disease compared with those of individuals who die from other causes.

Assignment 5. Students are now required to derive research hypotheses for their generalizations and present them for class evaluation.

How Do We Design a Test of the Hypothesis?

The first step is to develop a testable prediction from the research hypothesis. When the hypothesis itself cannot be tested directly, a testable logical consequence of it is required. In some student hypotheses, the prediction may be merely a narrowing of the universe of the research hypothesis to a testable subset or sample.

Frequently students begin an experiment immediately, without realizing the implied prediction that their experiment contains. One prediction about basketball players might define a testable subset of the universe of players to be measured, whereas a prediction about aerobics might define the aerobics activities as well as a subset of individuals that could be tested.

Assignment 6. Students are now required to identify and offer for class evaluation testable predictions from their own research hypotheses.

Assignment 7. Again, after discussion of the class examples, each student develops a test of his or her own prediction. In pairs or small groups of students, these experimental designs are then critically evaluated and discussed. Several experimental principles are illustrated: means of measurement, replication, repeatability, control of variables, objectivity in data collection, bias in sampling and test design, and so on. Students are required to identify the results they might obtain: that is, what they expect to happen and what else might happen. They are then asked if there could be any other explanation for the results they expect.

When students have determined all possible experimental outcomes, the experimental hypotheses are introduced: the null hypothesis, which is "no difference" among experimental treatments, and the alternate hypotheses, which include the expected outcome and all unwanted results. However, on those occasions when the research hypothesis defines no difference between treatments, the null becomes the expected result.

When hypotheses contain "all" rather than "most," discussion of statistics is not necessary. But hypotheses that predict "most" or predict specific differences between treatments require some introduction to statistics to illustrate two principles: (a) Tests of an alternate hypothesis are really tests of the null hypothesis of no difference, in which we hope to reject the null, and (b) statistical analysis is designed to show whether two data sets from different treatments are really different.

Assignment 8. Students conduct the test and collect data for both the class and their individual tests. If time or hypotheses dictate, you can fabricate data to analyze.

Why Can't Science Prove Anything?

If the results are as expected, the first student response is that this proves the research hypothesis is true. But because we tested only a small subset of the universe, the best we can say is that these data are consistent with the research hypothesis. As we conduct more and more tests that fail to disprove it, we will become more and more confident about our research hypothesis. But there can be no proof without testing every basketball player or measuring the influence of aerobic exercise on every individual's heart rate. Only with trivial hypotheses (e.g., all the chairs in this room are made of wood) can we test the entire universe, and in such cases we have reduced the universe to the observable, leaving no predictive power in our study. Such triviality is not science.

But what if the result is not as predicted? If the results contradict our expectation, the research hypothesis at worst must be totally wrong and at best must require modification. Seeing science as a constant struggle from falsification to falsification as we stutter toward unfalsified hypotheses severely challenges students. They have grown up in a world in which science is a way of finding facts, determining truth, and proving theories. Suddenly they have no facts, no truth, and no proof.

One illustration of the second problem of proof might involve the repair of mechanical equipment. Suppose I come home to find that my television doesn't work. I see frayed loose wires in the back of the set and reasonably hypothesize that the wiring is the problem. I predict that if I fix the wires, the television will work. So my test consists of fixing the wires and turning on the set. The alternate hypothesis predicts that the television will work, the null hypothesis predicts no difference—the set still will not work. So I fix the wires, and it works. In triumph I congratulate myself on having proven my hypothesis. But just then my younger sister walks in and says, "Hi! I didn't know you were home. I was repairing the fuse. You could have helped me."

Certainly, I got the result I predicted, but it was for the wrong reason entirely; the hypothesis I formulated had nothing to do with the problem. The correct explanation for the television's not working was something I hadn't even considered. I got the "right result for the wrong reasons." The truth table (Table 3) illustrates this dilemma in science; of course, we design our experiments carefully so that this problem is minimized, but we are never completely sure we have eliminated all other possible explanations.

Assignment 9. In relation to both the class examples and their individual examples, students then interpret the test results in terms of the experimental hypotheses and the research hypotheses.

At this point, a review of the process can be undertaken in which some commonly held misconceptions phrased as testable hypotheses are subjected to analysis. For example, the suggestion that women have one more rib than men can be tested, as can the hypothesis that mosquitoes attack men (or women) more frequently. Another useful exercise is to ask students to evaluate and appropriately amend commercial claims that rest on apparent scientific evidence.

What is Pseudoscience?

With reference again to Table 1 and the rigorous logical process of science, we now address those phenomena that are not amenable to scientific investigation but pur-

Table 3. *The Truth Table*

Result	Meaning
If I get the result that I predicted	. . . . .the research hypothesis may or may not be correct
If I get a result different from what I predicted.	the research hypothesis must be false

port to be scientific. Telltale signs of pseudoscience are phenomena that are not measurable, observable, predictable, or repeatable; do not exist in the material world; have no pattern or regularity; or involve unreasoned hypotheses formulated without a basis in experience or observation. "Hypotheses" that are unfalsifiable and therefore irrefutable illustrate the problem: A good example would be an exploration of the predictions of flood geology (as a consequence of the Noah period), one of many claims developed by creationists to satisfy the dogmatic assertions required of a literal interpretation of the Bible (Kitcher, 1982; Morris, 1974).

DISCUSSION Through the approach outlined here, students are shown that science is a means of analyzing everyday events. Unit tests consisting of analytical short answers rather than multiple-choice questions refer to everyday problems and examples in students' lives. The emphasis in testing is on comprehension and application, not memorization of terms. My evaluation of the success of the unit is based on students' ability to answer questions demanding the application of science, questions they could not answer through conventional textbook treatments.

REFERENCES
Inhelder, B., & Piaget, J. (1958). *The growth of logical thinking from childhood to adolescence.* New York: Basic Books.

Journet, A. R. P. (1985). *The science in biology: A manual for general biology laboratory.* Cape Girardeau, MO: Southeast Missouri State University.

Journet, A. R. P., Young, C. C., Stanley, C. M., & Scheibe, J. S. (1987, April). *Studies on cognitive development in a non-majors investigative general biology laboratory.* Paper presented at the annual conference of the National Association for Research in Science Teaching, Washington, D.C.

Kitcher, P. (1982). *Abusing science: The case against creationism.* Cambridge: Massachusetts Institute of Technology Press.

Lawson, A. E., & Renner, J. W. (1975). Relationship of science subject matter and developmental level of learners. *Journal of Research in Science Teaching, 12,* 347–358.

McKinnon, J. W. (1971). Earth science, density and the college freshman. *Journal of Geological Education, 19,* 218–220.

Medawar, P. B. (1969). Induction and deduction in scientific thought. In *Jayne Lectures for 1968.* Philadelphia, PA: American Philological Society.

Morris, H. M. (1974). *Scientific creationism.* San Diego, CA: Creation Life Publishers.

Popper, K. (1968a). *Conjectures and refutations: The growth of scientific knowledge.* New York: Harper & Row.

Popper, K. (1968b). *The logic of scientific discovery* (2nd ed.). New York: Harper & Row.

Sagan, C. (1974). *Broca's brain.* New York: Bantam Books.

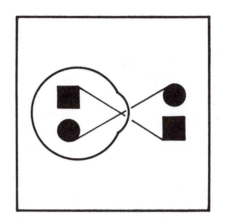

CHAPTER II
SENSORY PROCESSES
AND PERCEPTION

Because they are demonstrations of direct sensory stimulation, the activities in Chapter 2 engage the students' participation in an immediate and often dramatic way. In Activity 12, for example, students construct their own stereograms, whereas in Activity 14 students design and use reversing goggles in a demonstration that allows for firsthand experience of distorted perception and its psychological effects. The activities cover the range of sensory processes, from vision to hearing, and none require any prior knowledge or study by the students. For the most part, these activities can be quickly and easily prepared by the instructor; a few may need to be practiced before being presented to the class.

Activity 17 uses the domino theory to illustrate neural transmission, often a complicated topic for introductory psychology students. In Activity 13, students conduct an experiment on the relative size illusion. Activity 15 requires a little more preparation and materials than do the others, which need almost none; it is a detailed and enjoyable examination of visual illusions and can be incorporated, if the instructor wishes, into a lesson on descriptive statistics. Activity 18 focuses on sensory interdependencies, especially the idea of synesthesia, which is always fascinating to students, particularly if they happen to experience this phenomenon themselves. Activity 16 is a demonstration of the traveling sound wave that allows students to see this as an observable motion.

All of these activities can be used with classes of any size.

$\square$ 12 STUDENT-GENERATED STEREOGRAMS

J. R. Corey
C. W. Post College

In this activity students get hands-on experience constructing stereograms and immediate feedback enabling comprehension of the principles of stereoscopic vision. Except for ordering supplies in advance, there is little preparation that the instructor must do. This activity is suitable for small to medium classes. Students do not need prior knowledge.

CONCEPT

Students may better understand the basic principles of stereoscopic vision if they construct their own stereograms. The role of retinal disparity in depth perception, the relation between apparent distance and apparent size, and other effects can then be tested experimentally.

MATERIALS NEEDED

Students will need a Taylor–Merchant Stereopticon 707,[1] paper, drawing pens, various stencils and press-on symbols, and a metric ruler.

INSTRUCTIONS

Students may prepare stereograms to be viewed through the stereopticon by centering two fields 63 mm (2.5 in.) apart. For example, each stereogram in Figure 12-1 was prepared by first placing two dots 63 mm apart, then drawing a 50-mm (1.95 in.) circle around each. These circles define the fields. The elements of each display are composed of press-on symbols that are identical except for horizontal displacement. Avoid vertical displacement of the elements.

Elements that are separated by less than 63 mm are perceived to be closer. For good depth perception with these stereograms, students must have normal or corrected vision in both eyes.

After the students experiment with various effects, the instructor may wish to have them construct stimuli in which disparity is systematically varied and size or distance estimates are collected. If time does not permit this activity, the stimuli in Figure 12-1 may be used for the following experiments:

1. Figure 12-1a is viewed according to the directions on the stereopticon: Half of the students view it upright and the other half view it inverted. After students report that the figures are fused (i.e., they report seeing two dots inside one circle), they are asked, "Which dot appears nearer? Which dot appears larger?" If the students have difficulty in judging, they are instructed to guess. The answers ("the top one" or "the bottom one") are then sorted into 2×2 contingency tables (see Table 1a, 1b, and 1c), and the results are analyzed by using either Fisher's exact probability test or chi-square. A step-by-step procedure for calculating Fisher's test is on page 56.

---

[1] Available from the Taylor–Merchant Corp., 212 W. 35th Street, New York, New York 10001. As of this writing, the cost is $40 for 25 stereopticons. Thanks to the people at Copernicus, Huntington, New York, for helping to locate the supplier.

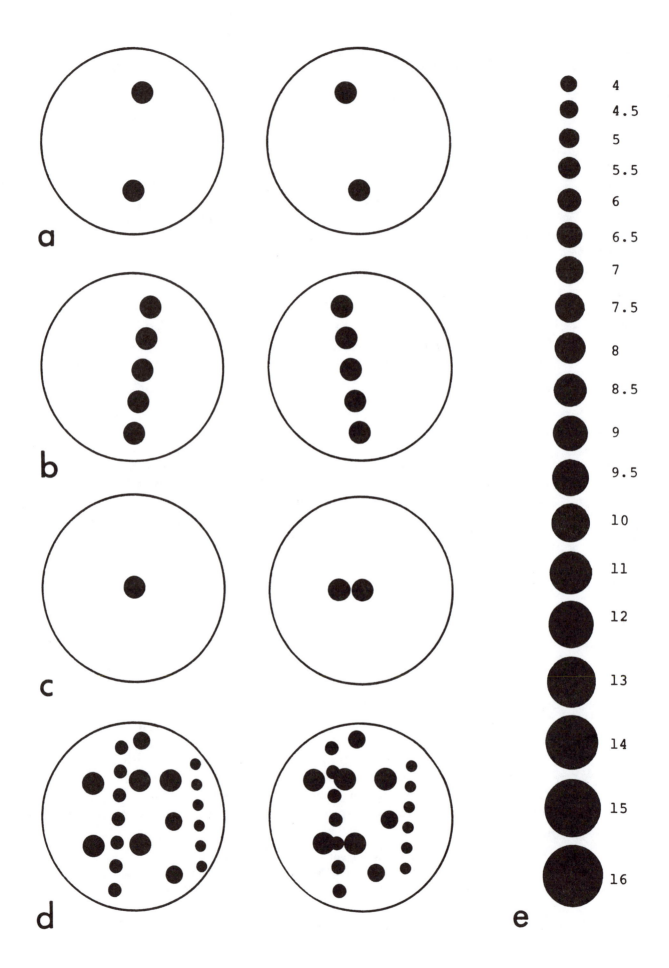

Table 1. *Contingency Tables for Responses to Figure 12-1a Under Two Viewing Conditions*

a.

		VIEWING CONDITION	
		Upright	Inverted
NEARER DOT	Top		
	Bottom		

b.

		VIEWING CONDITION	
		Upright	Inverted
SMALLER DOT	Top		
	Bottom		

c.

		NEARER DOT	
		Top	Bottom
SMALLER DOT	Top		
	Bottom		

Note. Table 1a deals with distance effects, 1b with size effects, and 1c with the relation between apparent size and distance regardless of viewing condition.

2. The stimuli in Figure 12-1b are fused and students are asked to tell which of the stimuli in Figure 12-1e appear to match each one in apparent size. The stimuli in Figure 12-1e are not to be viewed through the stereopticon. Both individual and group data showing apparent size as a function of retinal disparity may be plotted.

3. Other phenomena such as Panum's limiting case (Figure 12-1c) and complex figures (Figure 12-1d) may be demonstrated and serve as models for the construction of student stereograms.

DISCUSSION

When students generate their own stereograms, they get immediate feedback about the effects of binocular disparity of depth perception, the importance of fusion of the images, the limits of disparity, and the relation between size and depth. The optics of this situation, covered in depth in the books listed in the Suggested Reading section, may be explained by the instructor.

SUGGESTED READING

Gulick, W. L., & Lawson, R. B. (1976). *Human stereopsis: A psychophysical analysis.* New York: Oxford University Press.

Kauffman, L. (1974). *Sight and mind: An introduction to visual perception.* New York: Oxford University Press.

Figures 12-1a–12-1e (opposite page). Figures 12-1a and 12-1b are stereograms for studying size and distance effects. Figure 12-1c shows Panum's limiting case, in which one element is presented to one eye and two identical elements are presented to the other eye. This typically results in the impression of depth. Figure 12-1d is a complex stereogram constructed with press-on dots. Figure 12-1e consists of stimuli used to match the apparent size of the dots in Figure 12-1b. The number to the right of each dot is the approximate diameter of the dot in millimeters.

1. Fill in the appropriate contingency table. For example, 10 observers viewed the stimuli in Figure 12-1a and 5 reported that the top dot was nearer and smaller. Five reported that the bottom dot was nearer; 4 of these said it was smaller, and 1 said it was larger. Table 1c would look like the following:

| | | NEARER DOT | |
		Top	Bottom
	Top	a 5	b 1
SMALLER DOT			
	Bottom	c 0	d 4

2. Fisher's exact probability is computed by the following formula:

$$p = \frac{(a + b)!\ (c + d)!\ (a + c)!\ (b + d)!}{(a!)(b!)(c!)(d!)(n!)} =$$

$$\frac{6!\ 4!\ 5!\ 5!}{5!\ 1!\ 0!\ 4!\ 10!} = \frac{6!\ 5!}{10!} = \frac{1}{35} = .028$$

13 THE RELATIVE SIZE ILLUSION

Thomas J. Thieman
The College of St. Catherine

The materials needed for this activity are inexpensive and easy to prepare. Any size class can participate in this visual perception demonstration, which is likely to generate further discussion. Students do not need prior knowledge. Calculating and plotting responses to the illusions make this activity suitable for use in conjunction with a discussion of statistics.

CONCEPT

This exercise demonstrates the basic Gestalt notion of perceiving environmental events as whole units. Individual elements may lose their identity and be merged into a single, unified impression. Thus, the same event may be perceived or interpreted quite differently in different contexts. This phenomenon forms the basis of many perceptual illusions, including the relative size illusion studied here. The exercise also provides a test of Helson's (1964) adaptation-level theory.

MATERIALS NEEDED

The materials consist of 1 standard line, 1 in. long, centered and drawn horizontally on a $5\frac{1}{2}$ in. $\times$ $8\frac{1}{2}$ in. sheet of white paper, and 15 comparison lines also drawn on the same-sized sheets. The comparison lines are of 5 lengths: $\frac{10}{16}$, $\frac{13}{16}$, $\frac{16}{16}$, $\frac{19}{16}$, and $\frac{22}{16}$ of an inch, with pairs of boxes at the ends that are $\frac{5}{16}$, $\frac{15}{16}$, or $\frac{25}{16}$ of an inch on a side. The lines are horizontal and bisect the inner vertical lines of the boxes. Thus, there are 15 combinations of 5 line lengths (hereafter referred to as 1, 2, 3, 4, and 5) and three box sizes (hereafter referred to as *S*, *M*, and *L*). This coding system (e.g., S1, S2, L4, L5, etc.) should be printed lightly on the back of the comparison stimuli.

INSTRUCTIONS

Students are paired and take turns being the subject and the experimenter. They are told that their task is to judge the lengths of the lines between the boxes, relative to the standard line length, using a 7-point judgment scale ranging from 1 (*very much shorter*) to 7 (*very much longer*). Students are further instructed to use the entire scale. The standard line is present (placed to one side of each comparison stimulus) at all times.

Each subject completes five trials, each of which consists of making a judgment for each of the 15 comparison lines. The comparison stimuli are initially shuffled

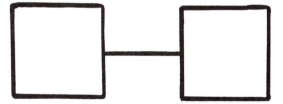

Figure 13-1. An example of the box–line display. (If the boxes are $\frac{15}{16}$ of an inch on a side, and the center line is $\frac{13}{16}$ of an inch long, this display would be labeled M2).

and reordered before every trial. Judgments are recorded on the data sheet by the experimenter without comment or feedback, and following the fifth trial the two participants exchange roles and repeat the procedure.

The analysis involves computing the mean judgment for each of the 15 comparison stimuli across the last 4 trials. Trial 1 is for practice and to establish the adaptation levels for the boxes. The means are then graphed, with the five line lengths on the abscissa, mean judgments on the ordinate, and separate curves for the three box sizes.

DISCUSSION

Helson's (1964) adaptation-level (AL) theory states that the size of an object is judged relative to the sizes of other objects in the immediate visual field. For example, a line of fixed length will appear to be relatively smaller when it is surrounded by larger objects (in contrast to a large AL) and relatively larger in the presence of small objects (in contrast to a small AL). Size judgments involve an automatic comparison process that is so natural it occurs without our conscious awareness and may be beyond our ability to consciously control or override.

The extent of the illusion is seen by the distances between the curves for the three box sizes, with the lines between the small boxes judged to be longer than those between the large boxes. One way to account for this illusion is to consider the box–line drawings as two-dimensional or flat pictures of objects in three-dimensional space (i.e., the boxes and lines may be close to or far away from the viewer). If this is the way the brain interprets these displays, then small boxes must indicate that the box–line combination is far away from the viewer and that the line is actually longer than it looks (i.e., it looks shorter because of its distance from the viewer). On the other hand, large boxes must indicate that the objects are close to the viewer, and a line between these boxes is relatively shorter than it looks (i.e., it looks as long as it does only because it is so close to the viewer). This explanation has been offered for the Müller-Lyer illusion as well (Gregory, 1978). Some questions for further discussion are as follows: (a) What are some everyday examples of this illusion in which objects are judged relatively smaller when they are surrounded by large objects and relatively larger when they are surrounded by small objects? (b) How is this principle used in advertising?

REFERENCES

Gregory, R. L. (1978). *Eye and brain: The psychology of seeing* (3rd ed.). New York: McGraw-Hill.

Helson, H. (1964). *Adaptation-level theory*. New York: Harper & Row.

SUGGESTED READING

Restle, F., & Merryman, C. T. (1968). An adaptation-level theory account of a relative-size illusion. *Psychonomic Science, 12,* 229–230.

Data Sheet for the Relative Size Illusion

Your name _____ Date of experiment _____

Your partner's name _____

Your partner's (subject's) data:

Box–line combination	Trials 1	2	3	4	5	Sum of 2–5	Mean	Mean of your own data
S1								
S2								
S3								
S4								
S5								
M1								
M2								
M3								
M4								
M5								
L1								
L2								
L3								
L4								
L5								

Judgment scale (to be placed before the subject for her or his reference). Criteria are considered in comparison to the standard. 1 = much shorter, 2 = somewhat shorter, 3 = slightly shorter, 4 = same, 5 = slightly longer, 6 = somewhat longer, and 7 = much longer.

14 A SIMPLE METHOD FOR CONSTRUCTING UPSIDE-DOWN AND LEFT–RIGHT REVERSING SPECTACLES

Fred L. Yaffe
Washburn University

In this activity, the extra effort of constructing goggles and ordering prisms required is rewarded by an engaging and dramatic demonstration. It is recommended that one or two volunteers demonstrate the effects of wearing the goggles. In smaller classes, all could participate. Students need no prior knowledge.

Upside-down or left–right reversing spectacles give students a unique opportunity to experience an area of perceptual research that has received much attention. When a student has the opportunity to wear a pair of goggles that creates a perceptual distortion, the experience creates a lasting impact. I have found that students spontaneously devise a wide variety of tasks and "experiments" when presented with these spectacles and actually enjoy watching the attempts of others and themselves to adjust to the perceptual rearrangement.

CONCEPT

It has been known for some time that the image formed by the lens of the eye is inverted and reversed left and right. Psychologists have wondered whether this inverted image is necessary for upright vision. If the image were made upright on the retina by use of a lens system, would the world appear upside down? Yes! More important, could people learn to adjust to this upside-down world and would the world eventually right itself? Most researchers agree that although the world looks normal with the spectacles on, the world never reinverts or looks upright. An analogy might be that of speaking two languages. If one can speak both Spanish and English, both of them are correct but not identical. In the same way, subjects see both the upside-down (or left–right) reversed world as normal and correct but not in the same orientation. This adaptation takes weeks to occur. Little adaptation occurs while wearing the goggles during a class demonstration.

MATERIALS NEEDED

The lens systems for upside-down or left–right reversing spectacles are easy to construct. Welder's goggles, made of plastic and available at welding supply shops or hardware stores, are easy to work with. The lenses required to make both upside-down and left–right changes are right-angle prisms, which are available through the *Edmund Catalogue.*[1] The best size is a prism that has a base of 50 mm and the other

---

[1] Request the *Edmund Catalogue* from Edmund Scientific Co., 101 E. Gloucester Pike, Barrington, New Jersey 08007.

faces measuring around 40 mm. The cost is $5–7 each. Because much of the prism face must be masked with tape to achieve the effect, I recommend that the goggles be built with a lens for each eye, although a monocular system will provide an acceptable viewing area. When constructing a binocular left–right reversing goggle, the nature of the lenses will not allow for complete elimination of binocular disparity up close. To about arm's length, subjects should see double. Most subjects report this to be a minor inconvenience when compared with the overall disruption.

The area near the base of each prism is where the image is inverted. Use electrical tape to mask the remaining part of each lens (or you could use a latex paint for a more permanent mask). For the inverting goggles the prisms are mounted base up; for the left–right reversing goggles the lenses are mounted with the base to the left. Cut the eye pieces in the welder's goggles so that the lenses will fit snugly and then glue the lenses in place. Minor adjustments while looking through the goggles are required to correctly position the prisms. Cover any other areas with tape so that subjects can only see through the exposed part of the prism.

INSTRUCTIONS It is best to ask for one volunteer from the class to wear both sets of goggles so that the students in the class can observe the relative amount of disorientation caused by each pair of goggles. Find a student who is not easily nauseated because the movement of the visual field induced by the goggles can produce dizziness and accompanying symptoms. Have the student initially wear the upside-down goggles and perform a variety of eye–hand coordination tasks. Shake hands with him or her, holding your hand in several different positions, making the student find your hand. Toss a foam ball back and forth, throwing it high and low. Have the student walk to a closed door, open it up, and walk through the threshold. Stand about 2 ft in front of the student, face to face, and have him or her look down at his or her feet. Because the field of view is upside down it will appear to the student that he or she is standing on your legs. If you now shake your legs or dance in place the student will feel as if he or she is moving. Ask the student to write his or her name on the blackboard, write an unfamiliar phrase, or trace the outline of a figure (a star or a square) you have drawn.

After letting the student do activities with the upside-down goggles, ask him or her to remove them and report the feelings with the goggles removed. Usually there is a feeling of relief and a sense of "strange familiarity" in returning to a familiar world. Now put the left–right reversing goggles on the student. Most people find these much more difficult to adjust to than the other goggles. Have the student repeat the exercises done with the upside-down goggles. He or she will probably experience much more difficulty and frustration than before. Start off with something simple. Have the student stand on one side of the room, walk about 10 ft away, stand slightly off to one side, and ask him or her to walk up to you and take an object from your hand. This task is usually difficult to do. After wearing the goggles for several minutes and doing a variety of tasks, have the student remove the goggles and report his or her impressions. Besides feeling relieved, the student is usually totally disoriented about where he or she is in the room. For other potential activities with prismatic goggles, refer to Benjamin and Lowman (1981).

DISCUSSION Adaptation to disoriented vision occurs slowly, so you can expect little improvement in performance during the demonstration. Students should be made aware that adaptation and adjustment do occur but usually only with prolonged continuous wearing of the goggles. When either pair of goggles is worn, the primary initial disorientation is to the apparent movement in the visual field. When the inverting goggles are initially worn and the head is moved up and down, the visual scene appears to be moving twice as fast in the same direction as the head movement. In most experiments this "swinging of the scene" has been reported to continue for several days. After a few days of continuously wearing the goggles, people are able to adjust their behavior to become accustomed to the distortion.

With the left–right reversing goggles there are two types of experiences that heighten the disorientation. First, when the head is moved right or left, the visual world appears to move twice as fast in the same direction as the head movement. Because people make many more left–right movements than up–down head movements, this swing of the scene is far more annoying and nauseating with left–right goggles than with upside-down goggles. Second, with upside-down goggles it is immediately apparent that there is a distortion because the many mono-oriented objects in the visual field make it obvious that the world is upside down. With the left–right reversing spectacles, the world looks normal, except when you move and try to coordinate your behavior. These goggles give an eerie, Alice-through-the-looking-glass quality to your perceptions. Everything looks normal (albeit reversed), but nothing behaves normally.

One common question asked is, Does the upside-down (or left–right reversed) world ever right itself? The answer I give usually compares perceptual distortion to language, as in the analogy made earlier. The distorted world is never righted. It makes no sense to ask which view is more correct or whether one view is mistaken for the other. They are both separate, distinct, yet correct views of the world. This experience is very analogous to that of experienced deep-sea divers who are easily able to adjust to the different depth cues necessary for underwater and out-of-water vision.

REFERENCES Benjamin, L. T., Jr., & Lowman, K. D. (1981). *Activities handbook for the teaching of psychology.* Washington, DC: American Psychological Association.

SUGGESTED READING Kohler, I. (1964). The formation and transformation of the perceptual world (H. Fiss, Trans.). *Psychological Issues, 3*(4), 1–173.

Rock, I. (1975). *An introduction to perception.* New York: MacMillan.

Snyder, F. W., & Pronko, N. H. (1952). *Vision with spatial inversion.* Wichita: University of Wichita Press.

15 CLASSROOM MEASUREMENT OF VISUAL ILLUSIONS

J. R. Corey and S. J. Tatz
C. W. Post College

This activity can be used with classes of small or medium size. No prior knowledge is required of the student unless the instructor wishes to incorporate some descriptive statistics. The instructor must prepare stimulus packets for each student from the masters included here and provide rulers, protractors, and so on for measuring.

CONCEPT

Students find visual illusions fascinating. Moreover, they serve instructional purposes, such as illustrating perceptual principles, (e.g., size contrast) and providing possible tests of theories of perception. They also can be used to illustrate psychophysical methods, that is, ways of providing a physical measure of a conscious experience.

However, most of the time, illusions are presented as mere demonstrations. Straight lines are seen to bend, or equal length lines are perceived as different. Rarely are students asked to quantify visual illusions because of measurement difficulties. We present three visual illusions that may be rapidly and accurately measured in the classroom or laboratory: the Müller–Lyer illusion, the induced tilt illusion and the horizontal–vertical/bisection illusion. These robust illusions rapidly provide data that may be then subjected to statistical analysis.

Müller-Lyer Illusion

Materials. The student is provided with photocopies of the stimuli shown in Figures 15-1 and 15-2 (the instructor will need access to a Xerox machine for the enlargement of figures; for best results, all dimensions must be doubled); if several stimuli are to be used they can be presented in a packet, stapled at the upper left-hand corner, and with successive stimuli separated by blank sheets to prevent see-through previews. Each packet could be assembled with the stimuli in a different random order (to control for order effects), and each stimulus could appear twice in each packet to provide more stable values for each condition and to allow measurement of reliability. Each student will need a 30-cm ruler and a pencil.

Instructions. Students are told the following: "For each figure, estimate the distance between the points of the two angles. Show your estimate by marking two dots on the straight line on the lower right with your pencil. Do not use a ruler or other aid."

Students are then told to exchange packets, to measure the distance between dots to the nearest millimeter for each stimulus, and to write the measurement on each page. The measurements can then be tabulated and an average obtained for each stimulus condition.

Induced-Tilt Illusion

Materials. Each stimulus (see Figure 15-3; for best results, all dimensions must be doubled) is presented flat on a table, with the student standing in front of it, looking down on it. A posterboard frame can be used, several inches in width, so that the opening just surrounds the stimulus circle; this will prevent the student from using edges or corners of the stimulus sheet as guides.

Students will need a pencil with which to respond and a protractor and straightedge to measure the responses.

Instructions. The student is told the following: "Stand in front of this stimulus looking down on it. Try to judge where the short line would hit the circle if it were extended and mark that point on the circle with your pencil. Do not trace the line out with your pencil or finger."

When all students have completed the task, they exchange stimuli and measure the response. The shorter line should be drawn out to the circle, and there should also be a line from the point of intersection to the student's response mark. With the protractor, the student will then measure the angle between the two lines to the nearest degree. This angle is called a *displacement error.* When the mark is on the side of the short line away from the long line (the most common direction), the displacement error is *positive;* when on the side toward the long line, the displacement error is *negative.* The measurements can then be tabulated and an average calculated for each stimulus condition.

The Horizontal–Vertical/Bisection Illusion

Materials. As usually pictured in the inverted *T* (see Figure 15-4) these illusions are confounded. Using the stimuli in Figures 15-4 to 15-7 (the instructor will need access to a Xerox machine; for best results, all dimensions must be doubled) a 2×2 factorial experiment may be carried out. Each of the stimuli is reproduced on separate sheets of paper. The thick standard lines are all 10 cm and the thin comparison lines are 18 cm. Each student requires a pencil and a 30-cm ruler after the task is completed.

Instructions. Each student receives all four stimuli in a counterbalanced or random order and is told, "Please mark the thin line at the point that it appears to be the same length as the thicker line." The students then record their age, sex, and social security number on the back.

The students exchange and measure the lengths of the marked comparison lines with a ruler. Double-checking may turn up errors and provide a discussion of reliability of measurement. Results are tabulated and means are calculated. The results of a $2 \times 2 \times$ subjects analysis of variance typically show a strong effect of the horizontal–vertical manipulation (see Figures 15-4 and 15-6 vs. 15-5 and 15-7) and the bisection effect (see Figures 15-4 and 15-5 vs. 15-6 and 15-7), but no interaction.

DISCUSSION   Many variations on these illusions can be constructed; the Müller–Lyer illusion may be studied with or without the central shaft or with the figure constructed solely of dots indicating the ends of each line. If the illusion persists in the dot form, for example, this shows that intersecting lines are not critical for the illusion. The fins may be drawn at different angles. With the induced-tilt illusion, the length of the inducing line, the length of the test line, and the angle between the two lines may be varied. The point of bisection may be varied in the horizontal–vertical/bisection illusion. These and other variations can provide many different individual projects for students who can easily construct their own stimuli. Other illusions can be found in the books cited in the Suggested Reading section.

SUGGESTED READING

Coren, S., & Girgus, J. S. (1978). *Seeing is deceiving: The psychology of visual illusions.* Hillsdale, NJ: Erlbaum.

Robinson, J. O. (1972). *The psychology of visual illusion.* London: Hutchinson University.

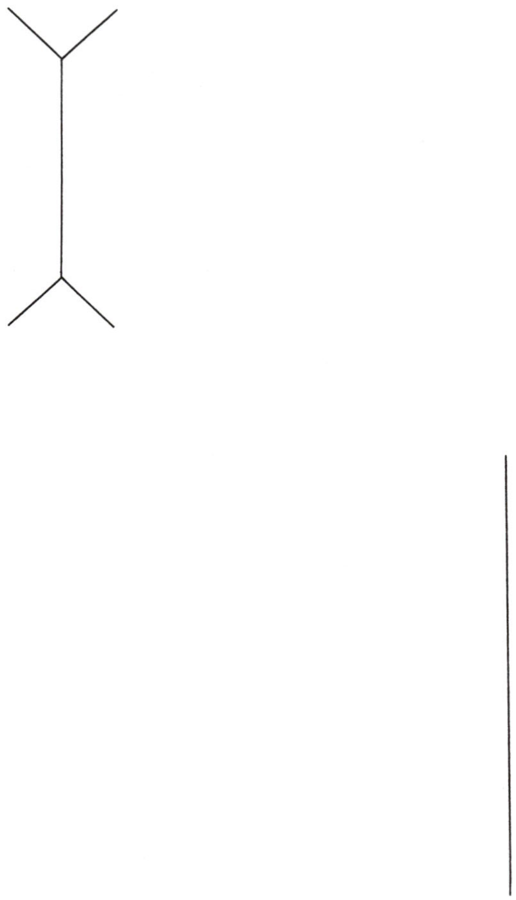

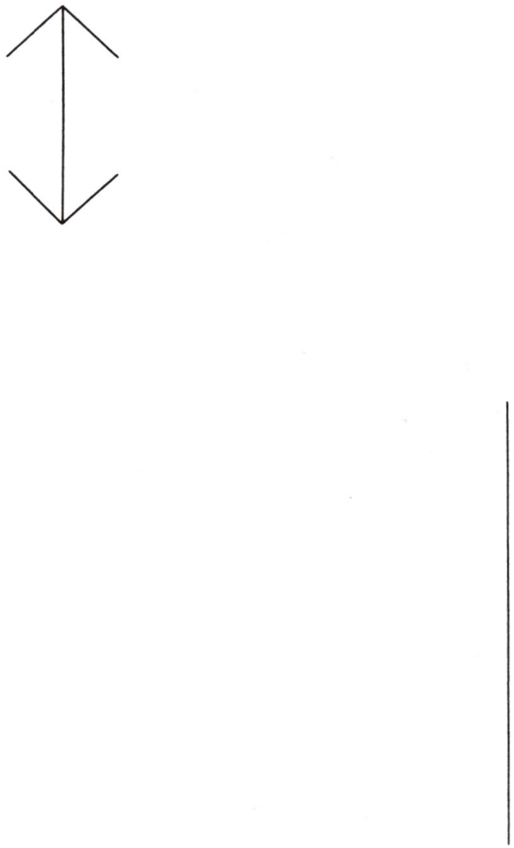

Figure 15-2. The "fins out" condition of the Müller–Lyer illusion. (For best results, all dimensions must be doubled.)

Figure 15-1. The "fins in" condition of the Müller–Lyer illusion. (For best results, all dimensions must be doubled.)

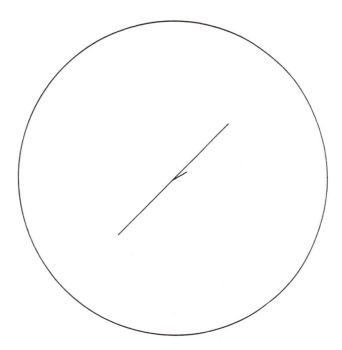

Figure 15-3. The induced-tilt illusion. (For best results, all dimensions must be doubled.)

Figure 15-4. The horizontal bisected standard for the horizontal–vertical/bisection illusion. (For best results, all dimensions must be doubled.)

Figure 15-5.   The vertical bisected standard. (For best results, all dimensions must be doubled.)

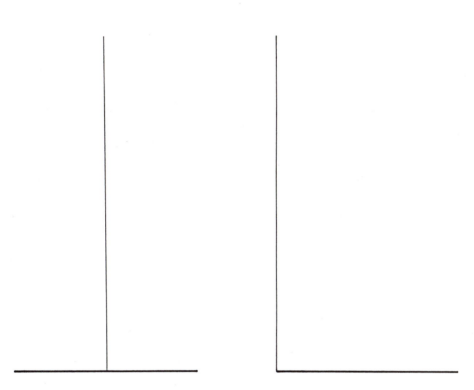

Figure 15-6. The horizontal nonbi-
sected standard. (For best results, all
dimensions must be doubled.)

Figure 15-7. The vertical nonbi-
sected standard. (For best results, all
dimensions must be doubled.)

16 AUDITORY SENSORY PROCESSES: THE TRAVELING WAVE ON THE BASILAR MEMBRANE

Kathy Barsz
Thomas More College

In this activity the only item you need is a 5- or 6-ft length of rope and a little practice to demonstrate to your class the traveling wave on the basilar membrane. This activity is best used as an introduction to a unit on the physical properties associated with the perception of sound.

CONCEPT

This activity is designed to show students a principle of auditory sensation, allowing them to observe the movement of the basilar membrane in response to a sound wave. The demonstration takes only a few minutes and is an excellent way to introduce the concept of pitch. Pitch is more interesting to students and more relevant to a psychology course but cannot be learned without first understanding how the auditory system responds to sound. Although the demonstration is technologically simple, it quickly and clearly communicates the notion of traveling waves, especially to students who have not studied physics. I have found that without the demonstration, the concept of the traveling wave is too complicated for many students to understand; they lose interest and further study of perception is stalled.

MATERIALS NEEDED

You will need a 5- or 6-foot length of clothesline.

INSTRUCTIONS

Tie one end of the rope to something that is 3–4 ft off the ground, such as a doorknob, and holding the other end, walk out so that the rope droops just a little in the middle. (You will have to practice getting the right amount of tension on the rope.)

Shake your end of the rope by flicking your wrist slowly; a traveling wave will be set up on the rope that travels from your hand and peaks at the end that is tied down; this is analogous to the traveling wave on the basilar membrane in response to a low-frequency tone. If you increase the speed at which you are shaking the rope, the traveling wave will now peak at a place closer to your hand. This shows that higher frequencies cause the traveling wave to peak closer to the vibrating oval window. When dealing with a complex sound, the membrane codes each overtone separately, with each one peaking at a different place on the membrane according to its frequency.

DISCUSSION

Because this activity is fairly simple and straightforward, it does not immediately lend itself to discussion and is best used as a way of demonstrating the physical process necessary to perception of sound. It is likely that this demonstration will lead to questions about the differences between frequency and pitch; the instructor should be clear in explaining these differences, as follows.

Frequency is the number of times a sound wave repeats itself. Thus, it is a physical entity. The traveling wave is a physical response of the basilar membrane. This demonstration shows the traveling wave as a physical movement, a concept that is sometimes hard to grasp until it is actually seen. *Pitch*, on the other hand, is the psychological perception of sound: how low or how high we perceive a sound to be (i.e., its tone). We use pitch to judge the identity of a sound, for example, to judge a person's gender by the height of his or her voice or to identify a melody by the sequence of its notes.

Frequency must be measured by a physical instrument (the oscilloscope or the frequency meter), whereas pitch must be measured using a psychological test such as a rating scale or discrimination task. The pitch of a sound is partly determined by its frequency.

In teaching sensation and perception to a psychology class, it is important that students have a basic understanding of the physical processes involved. This demonstration allows this to be done quickly and easily.

SUGGESTED READING

Bekesy, G. von. (1957). The ear. *Scientific American, 197,* 66–78.

Bekesy, G. von. (1960). Vibratory patterns of the basilar membrane. In E. G. Wever (Ed. and Trans.), *Experiments in hearing* (pp. 404–428). New York: McGraw-Hill.

17 USING DOMINOES TO HELP EXPLAIN THE ACTION POTENTIAL

Walter F. Wagor
Indiana University East

This activity is a graphic way to improve your students' understanding of the basic concepts of neural transmission. It is best to practice setting up dominoes before attempting this in class, and you may want to enlist some volunteers to help you to set up the demonstration. A stopwatch is not necessary, but it will enhance the impact. Your students need no preparation to benefit from this demonstration, and you can use it with any size class.

CONCEPT

Many students in introductory psychology classes find the chapter on the brain and biological bases of behavior to be difficult, especially the numerous concepts involved in the discussion of neural transmission (e.g., neural threshold, the all-or-none principle, and propagation of the action potential). To help students understand these concepts, Hamilton and Knox (1985) described an intriguing demonstration of a "live" neuron. Unfortunately, this demonstration needs 30 student volunteers, making the demonstration appropriate only for large classes (200 or more students). Those of us with much smaller class sizes need another visual way to help students understand the basic concepts of neural transmission.

The following activities are an elaboration of a mental exercise proposed by Schneider and Tarshis (1986) in their physiological psychology textbook. They suggested trying to visualize the "domino effect" of the action potential as it traveled along the axon. In the following activities, real dominoes are used to demonstrate the domino effect and several other concepts normally found in introductory explanations of neural transmission.

MATERIALS NEEDED

To perform these demonstrations you will need a smooth table-top surface (minimum of 5 ft long), two sets of dominoes (double 6s may work but double 9s are better), two stopwatches, and four 10–12-in. long sticks about $\frac{1}{2}$–$\frac{5}{8}$ in. square.

INSTRUCTIONS

Using these props, you can provide a visual aid for several important neural concepts. To illustrate how the action potential affects one area of the axon at a time and how it is sequentially passed on from one section of the axon to another, stand the dominoes on end, about 1 in. apart on the table, in a line about 3 ft long. To show students this sequential effect, knock down the first domino in the row, which will demonstrate how the "action potential" is then passed on along the entire length of the axon.

The concept of the neuron's refractory period and the fact that the axon is temporarily unable to convey a new action potential immediately is illustrated by the dominoes lying on the table. No matter how hard you push on the first domino, you will not be able to repeat the domino effect. It takes some time to set the dominoes back up (i.e., to produce another action potential). The time it takes to reset the dominoes is analogous to the refractory period. If you have some quick volunteers and a long enough line of dominoes, you may be able to have the first dominoes reset before the last ones are knocked down. You could then demonstrate the fact that more than one action potential could be traveling along the axon at the same time, although there has to be a certain amount of time between the potentials. If you cannot reset the dominoes fast enough, ask the students to imagine that someone could reset the dominoes fast enough so that several "waves" could be traveling along the axon simultaneously.

The all-or-none characteristic of the axon can be illustrated by pointing out that the push on the first domino has to be strong enough to knock it down. If it is, the action potential then perpetuates itself along the entire axon; if it is not, nothing happens beyond the first domino, the beginning of the axon. You can also demonstrate what happens in the axon collaterals (or branches) by forming a new line of dominoes that branches out to four or more collaterals. Students can easily see that the action potential affects all of the branches equally.

One additional concept that can be easily demonstrated with the dominoes is the advantage of a myelinated axon over an unmyelinated axon. You need to set up a row of dominoes as before, 4 ft long. Next to this row form a second row using the foot-long sticks. Place each stick on top of a pair of dominoes standing on end, one domino under each end of the stick. Place four of these stick–domino groups in a line, end to end, so that the falling dominoes of one group will hit the next group, causing it to also fall, and so on. You will probably need to practice setting up this line of stick–domino groups outside of class until you learn how to properly space them. By placing both of the above rows, the all-domino row and the stick–domino row, parallel to each other so that they begin and end along side of one another, you can demonstrate how much faster the action potential can travel if it can "jump" from "node" to "node" rather than having to be passed on sequentially, single domino by single domino. You could also use stopwatches to time this difference, thus reinforcing the point made visually.

DISCUSSION   When using these demonstrations in the classroom, you could choose to continue to describe the concepts you are about to demonstrate while you set up the demonstrations or it may be more convenient to use a number of pretrained volunteers to set up while you lecture. A potential problem with the latter approach is that students may be more interested in watching the other student volunteers instead of listening to the background explanation you are providing. Although that is still possible if you set up the demonstration yourself, at least students' attention will be focused on you, not on others. Use your own imagination and add to this list of concepts and activities that could be demonstrated fairly easily using dominoes.

REFERENCES   Hamilton, S. B., & Knox, T. A. (1985). The colossal neuron: Acting out physiological psychology. *Teaching of Psychology, 3*, 153–156.

Schneider, A. M., & Tarshis, B. (1986). *An introduction to physiological psychology* (3rd ed.). New York: Random House.

SUGGESTED   Kasschau, R. A. (1981). Conduction of a neuronal impulse. In L. T. Benjamin, Jr. &
READING   K. D. Lowman (Eds.), *Activities handbook for the teaching of psychology* (pp. 207–208). Washington, DC: American Psychological Association.

18 SENSORY INTERDEPENDENCIES

George M. Diekhoff

Midwestern State University

This activity involves students in a general discussion of sensory processing, although in large classes, only a sample of students can participate in each activity. Students do not need prior knowledge. The instructor will need to prepare a number of materials for the demonstrations and should do a few trial runs before presenting them to the class.

CONCEPT

With his doctrine of specific nerve energies (Goldstein, 1989; Muller, 1842), Johannas Muller formalized the observation that sensory experience depends less on the nature of the physical stimulus than on the projection areas in which the sensory nerve terminates. Thus, for example, stimulation of the optic nerve with light, pressure, or electricity results in a visual experience. The existence of separate, highly specialized sensory projection areas suggests that sensory experiences would be equally separate and independent. In fact, however, the senses are less independent than one might expect. The following activities are all aimed at demonstrating some of the interdependencies that exist between the sensory modalities.

INSTRUCTIONS

Exercise 1: The influence of smell on taste. Prepare bite-sized slices of apple and potato. Have volunteer subjects close their eyes and hold their noses while they are fed slices of apple and potato in a random sequence. The subjects' task is to identify what they are eating. The accuracy of their perceptions is given by the percentage of responses that are correct.

Next, repeat the procedure but have subjects breathe normally as they eat. Compare the accuracy of their taste perceptions with and without the contribution of the olfactory sense to show that the sense of smell is a major component of *taste*.

Exercise 2: The influence of temperature on taste. Prepare four small glasses (8 oz) of water, each with four pinches of sugar dissolved. The water in the glasses should be ice cold, cool, lukewarm, and hot, respectively. Have a volunteer subject taste each sugar solution with instructions to rank order their sweetness. (Obviously, the subject should not know in advance that the glasses contain equal amounts of sugar.) Reflecting the influence of temperature on taste, the cool and lukewarm solutions will be perceived as being sweeter than the ice cold or hot solutions.

Exercise 3: The influence of size on perceived weight. For this activity you will need two coffee cans, one 1-lb can and one 3-lb can, filled with sand until they weigh the same. Tell a volunteer subject that you are testing his or her difference threshold for weight. Have the subject lift each container and select the one that feels heavier. Despite their equal weight, subjects almost invariably identify the smaller container as weighing more.

The influence of visual size on perceived weight is well established. Smaller objects of a given weight are judged to be heavier than larger objects of the same weight. That is, what we call *weight* is, in part, the perception of density (i.e., weight/mass).

Exercise 4: Auditory–visual synesthesia. Read the list of vowel sounds shown below to your class with instructions to "Imagine that each sound has its own color. Your task is to match each sound to one of the following colors: red, yellow, white, black, blue."

Vowel sounds
ah, as in mama
eh, as in let
o, as in home
oo, as in boot

In a study of 400 nonsynesthetic subjects, Marks (1975) found evidence for a considerable degree of "cross-translation of the sensory modalities." Tabulate your students' most frequent responses to each of the vowel sounds and compare them with Marks's results:

Vowel sounds	Most frequent color response
ah	red or yellow
eh	white
o	red or black
oo	blue or black

DISCUSSION The sensory interdependencies demonstrated by the preceding activities illustrate two fundamental principles of perception. First, the gestalt Part–Whole Attitude (i.e., the whole is different from the sum of its parts) applies not just to stimulus elements *within* sensory modalities but *across* sensory modalities as well. Stimulus elements in one modality combine interactively with those in other modalities to determine the total sensory experience. Second, synesthetic experiences in particular suggest that incoming stimulation is translated into a data base that is not modality specific but to which all sensory modalities have access. Thus, an auditory experience can give rise to a visual impression because both visual and auditory systems access the same modality-nonspecific sensory data base. This notion also helps explain some other interesting facts of perception, including cross-modal transfer of perceptual learning, subjects' ability to match intensities across sensory modalities, and nonverbal infants' ability to recognize visually objects that have only been experienced previously through touch. Through the sensory-nonspecific data base, information presented in one sensory modality becomes available to the other modalities.

REFERENCES Goldstein, E. B. (1989). *Sensation and perception* (3rd ed.). Belmont, CA: Wadsworth.

Marks, L. (1975, January). Synesthesia: The lucky people with mixed up senses. *Psychology Today*, pp. 48–52.

Muller, J. (1842). *Elements of physiology* (W. Baly, Trans.). London: Taylor & Walton.

SUGGESTED READING Marks, L. (1975). On colored-hearing synesthesia: Cross-modal translation of sensory dimensions. *Psychological Bulletin, 82,* 303–330.

Matlin, M. W. (1988). *Sensation and perception.* (2nd ed.). Boston: Allyn & Bacon.

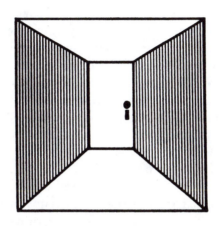

CHAPTER III
LEARNING AND MEMORY

Students are always curious about seeing how the concepts of cognitive psychology can be applied to their own learning abilities, and the activities in this chapter will help clarify their own learning and memory processes as well as give them some insight into your teaching methods. None of these exercises requires any prior knowledge of the subject, and some can enhance upper-level courses.

Activity 19 presents an innovative approach to multiple-choice testing, offering an alternative form of these tests that does not rely on rote memorization. Activity 23 tests students on their ability to use psychological sets in solving anagrams, and Activity 21 simultaneously gives students practice in strengthening memory and a good overview of the principles of memory and learning. Activity 22 is an excellent way to add perspective to discussions of creativity and problem-solving, showing as it does how mental "brute force" is the best, or only, option.

Operant conditioning is a primary concern in several of these activities; Activity 27 offers a classic operant chamber experiment with rats that will occupy at least seven class periods, while Activity 20 is a relaxed and enjoyable way to demonstrate learning techniques, particularly operant conditioning and observational learning. For an alternative or as a sideline to Activity 27, Activity 28 demonstrates operant conditioning with goldfish, a surprising but effective, low-cost, and esthetic choice. Activity 26 focuses on an important consideration in operant conditioning, namely the difference between punishment and negative reinforcement; this is a significant distinction, and one that is often difficult to explain clearly. Activity 24 is a thorough and straightforward explanation of how to discern and quantify improvements in learning ability that students can apply to their own work. For those who wish to see psychological principles applied more concretely to daily life, Activity 25 shows how marketing technology has benefited from an understanding of learning concepts in the selection of memorable (and therefore marketable) brand names.

Most of these activities can be done with classes of any size; preparation for the instructor varies but is generally not extensive.

19 A COGNITIVE TAXONOMY OF MULTIPLE-CHOICE QUESTIONS

Drew C. Appleby
Marian College

This activity can be used in any class in which students will be taking multiple-choice exams, although it fits most elegantly into a section on learning and memory. No prior knowledge is necessary for students. The only preparation required is copying the handout, but the author recommends making the extra effort to customize it.

CONCEPT

This activity describes a cognitive taxonomy (Bloom & Krathwohl, 1956) of multiple-choice questions that demonstrates how this type of question can be constructed to measure different levels of understanding of the same concept. The use of this taxonomy can increase comprehension, decrease student criticism of test questions, guide study techniques, lower test anxiety levels, and negate the old myth that multiple-choice questions can measure only rote-learned material.

MATERIALS NEEDED

The only materials needed are copies of the taxonomy to be distributed during a class period before the first test. Although the sample taxonomy that appears here can be reproduced verbatim, it is best used as a model for the construction of an original taxonomy. Constructing such a taxonomy will encourage teachers to take a hard look at the quality and type of multiple-choice questions (MCQs) that they write or chose from test banks. Some teachers may discover that most of their test items measure only surface understanding of the concepts they present to their students. Others may realize that their questions measure very complex relations that would be more appropriate for upper-level classes. Creating a taxonomy will also increase teachers' sensitivities to the educational objectives that they list in their class syllabi (e.g., to gain a thorough understanding of basic psychological terms, concepts, and methods). If a teacher decides to create an original taxonomy, it would be beneficial to choose a question topic (e.g., short-term memory) that fits the following criteria.

1. It will be covered on the first test.

2. It is complex enough so that a number of sample MCQs can be written about it on several levels of complexity.

3. It has been covered thoroughly in lecture or reading assignments so that students understand it on a number of different levels.

INSTRUCTIONS

After the taxonomy has been distributed, the class should be told that its purpose is to acquaint them with the different types of MCQs that they will encounter on their first test. The teacher should read each question aloud, wait for the class to answer it, read the explanation following it on the taxonomy, and then solicit questions regarding the nature of the thought processes required by the question. During this process, students begin to realize that they must truly understand, rather than merely memorize, the material that they are presented in class if they are to perform well on the tests. They should be urged to use or develop study techniques that will enable them to answer any type of MCQ on the taxonomy that is written about any of the material that is presented to them in the class. A teacher should be prepared to offer some helpful suggestions to students who suddenly realize that their lack of study techniques may limit their ability to perform up to their levels of expectation. A discussion of the "levels of processing" theory of memory (Craik & Lockhart, 1972) can be very beneficial at this point. Students seem to be particularly receptive to this theory when they realize how relevant it is to their academic performance.

There are several reasons why most teachers of the introductory class use MCQs to test their students. First, MCQs can be scored easily, quickly, and accurately. Second, MCQs can produce high levels of content validity in subject areas involving large quantities of widely divergent material. Third, MCQs are provided in abundance by the publishers of introductory psychology textbooks. Unfortunately, students do not always share their instructors' enthusiasm for these tests and often feel there is something inherently unfair or tricky about this type of test question, particularly those that they answer incorrectly. This results in one of the most unpleasant aspects of teaching the introductory class, the necessity of defending the validity of individual questions that are challenged by students when their tests are returned. These interchanges have the potential to provide very valuable feedback to both students and teachers, but this potentially beneficial effect is often overshadowed by the negative feelings produced when students believe that they are being tested unfairly and teachers feel that their authority is being questioned. Providing students with examples of the questions that they can expect on their tests decreases the frequency of their criticisms. It places the responsibility for missed questions on students who have failed to learn concepts on a variety of levels instead of on the teacher whose questions are labeled as tricky, ambiguous, or unfair by the students who miss them.

Perry (1970) described freshman-level students as dualistic in their thinking; that is, they believe that knowledge is either right or wrong in a very absolute and concrete way. They firmly believe that a teacher's primary purpose is to provide them with the facts and then to ask them to simply recognize or recall these facts, in the original form in which they were presented, on tests. Students operating in this stage feel most comfortable with, study for, and perform best on test items that are fact-oriented (i.e., items that test retention of terms and their definitions as they are presented in textbooks and lectures). Their level of discomfort rises dramatically as they are required to demonstrate increasingly deeper understanding of terms, principles, and theories with questions requiring practical application, organization, analysis, synthesis, or comparison.

Consider these comments: "You never told us you were going to ask this type of question!" "If I had known you were going to ask these types of question, I would have studied differently and gotten a better grade!" "I can't figure out what your questions mean, let alone answer them!" If a teacher has ever heard any of these comments after a first test, this taxonomy will be very beneficial. It can help students progress less painfully to a more flexible stage of cognitive development by introducing them to questions that require a deeper understanding of psychological concepts in a nonthreatening atmosphere (i.e., during a classroom demonstration instead of in a testing situation). Because many students have previously experienced only MCQs that measure straight facts, it is very disconcerting for them to suddenly encounter questions that require more complex understanding without any advance warning. Students appear to genuinely appreciate being exposed to the types of questions that they will encounter on their first test and report a correspondingly lower level of test anxiety. For many, it is the first time that a teacher has cared enough to take the time to show them exactly the types of questions that they will be expected to answer.

REFERENCES   Bloom, B. S., & Krathwohl, D. R. (1956). *Taxonomy of educational objectives: Handbook 1. The cognitive domain.* New York: McKay.

Craik, F. I. M., & Lockhart, R. S. (1972). Levels of processing: A framework for memory research. *Journal of Verbal Learning and Verbal Behavior, 11,* 671–684.

Perry, W. G., Jr. (1970). *Forms of intellectual and ethical development in college.* New York: Holt, Rinehart, & Winston.

1. Which of the following types of memory stores information for only about 30 seconds?
   a. short-term (STM)   b. long-term (LTM)   c. intermediate (IM)   d. sensory (SM)

This question tests a student's ability to recognize that a specific concept (e.g., STM) is associated with a single, important characteristic (e.g., it only lasts for about 30 seconds). This requires a student to merely *memorize a term and its definition.*

2. Which of the following is *true* about STM?
   a. Information stored in it is coded verbally.
   b. It can hold only about 5 to 9 bits of information.
   c. Information stored in it last only about 30 seconds unless it is rehearsed.
   d. all of the above

This type of question measures a student's ability to *learn a set of characteristics* that are common to a particular concept (e.g., that STM can hold only a certain type and amount of information for only a certain period of time). This requires a more thorough knowledge of a concept than does Question 1 but is still based primarily on memorization alone.

3. Joan just looked up a phone number, closed the phone book, and then repeated the number to herself as she was reaching for and dialing the phone. This is a good example of _____ .
   a. SM   B. STM   c. LTM   d. none of the above

This type of question measures a student's ability to *apply knowledge* to a real-life situation. This requires an understanding of the concept that goes beyond mere memorization of its definition or characteristics.

4. STM is to LTM as _____ is to _____ .
   a. verbal, semantic   c. 30 seconds, relatively permanent
   b. 5 to 9, unlimited   d. all of the above

This question measures a student's ability to *compare and contrast* two concepts (e.g., STM and LTM). This skill is based on, but goes beyond, the simpler abilities of memorizing a concept's definition (from Question 1) and its set of characteristics (from Question 2).

5. Which of the following is the correct sequence of memory stores through which information passes as it is processed by the human memory system?
   a. SM → STM → LTM   c. SM → LTM → STM
   b. STM → SM → LTM   d. STM → LTM → SM

A student must *learn a chronological relationship* among a series of variables (e.g., SM, STM, and LTM) to answer this question correctly.

6. Which of the following is the *best* explanation of why Tom has already forgotten the name of the person to whom he was introduced only 5 minutes ago?
   a. The name was never in Tom's STM.
   b. The name was lost from Tom's LTM.
   c. Tom did not successfully transfer the name from his STM to his LTM.
   d. Tom did not successfully transfer the name from his LTM to his STM.

The final question involves all the cognitive skills that were measured in the first five questions, plus it requires a student to *integrate knowledge* in order to produce a logical decision that is based on a thorough understanding of a concept (e.g., STM) that can be used to explain an example of complex human behavior (e.g., forgetting).

20 DEMONSTRATION OF LEARNING TECHNIQUES

Joan Young Smith
Grissom High School

■───■

This activity can either be presented to students with no prior knowledge about operant conditioning or after exposure to the concept. The primary purpose of the activity is for students to have a simple, concrete example to aid their learning of operant conditioning concepts. Other than obtaining the toy dispenser, very little preparation is required. You can use this demonstration with any size class, although each student will not be able to take a turn in larger classes.

■───■

CONCEPT   This activity illustrates the steps involved in various learning techniques, particularly operant conditioning.

MATERIALS NEEDED   You will need a toy peanut, candy, or bubblegum machine with a lever to pull in order to obtain the peanuts, candy, or bubblegum as well as an empty container similar to the candy machine in appearance.

INSTRUCTIONS   Assign appropriate reading materials to familiarize students with such terms as trial-and-error learning, operant conditioning, reinforcement, discrimination, generalization, observational learning, extinction, and motivation.

Place the filled peanut or candy machine on a table at the front of the room, making sure that all students will be able to see what is happening. Ask two volunteers to come inspect the machine and do whatever they wish to it (short of breaking it!). After several students have successfully pulled the lever for a reward of candy or peanuts, ask each remaining student to take a turn. Some students may refuse for various reasons. While this activity is in progress, ask the students to identify terms from the reading assignment that relate to the behaviors they are observing.

DISCUSSION   Many students will be able to relate the behaviors observed to trial-and-error learning, observational learning, and operant conditioning. Such questions as the following will help them to understand additional terms.

1. What would happen to your behavior if all peanuts and candy were gone? (extinction)

2. What would happen to your behavior if the machine were refilled? (spontaneous recovery)

3. What if you saw a candy machine and an empty instant coffee jar side by side? (discrimination)

4. What if you could not eat peanuts or candy because of health reasons? (effectiveness of a reinforcer, motivation)

5. What if you saw a second candy machine, filled, that was not exactly like but was similar to the first machine? (generalization)

If students have been introduced to variables, ask them to identify those variables and to speculate about possible variations. Each time I have used this activity, some unexpected teaching possibility has presented itself. I prefer to use it after introducing the terms so that students are able to recognize the behaviors representing the terms. However, it would be effective to demonstrate the behaviors before presenting concepts, to have students read or listen to lectures about the concepts, to demonstrate the behaviors again, and to then discuss what has been seen and heard.

SUGGESTED READING

Engle, T. L., & Snellgrove, L. (1969). *Psychology* (5th ed.). New York: Harcourt, Brace & World.

Kasschau, R. A. (1980). *Psychology: Exploring behavior.* Englewood Cliffs, NJ: Prentice-Hall.

Millenson, J. R. (1968). *Principles of behavioral analysis.* New York: MacMillan.

21 REMEMBERING LEARNING AND MEMORY

Barbara K. Sholley
University of Richmond

Both the teacher and the class will need to prepare for this activity—the students by reading background material and the instructor by typing up the lecture in individual sentences on separate pieces of colored paper. Classes of up to about 60 students can participate, and other than your "jigsaw" lecture, no materials are necessary. Because of the group process involved, the content of the lecture might be about half the amount ordinarily covered in an hour of lecture. The first time you try this, it might be a good idea to have the next class period flexible in case the activity runs over.

CONCEPT

Most introductory psychology texts, when describing human learning, provide mechanisms that could be useful for students to use when actually studying for exams, yet students don't seem to internalize this information for help with their own memories. One way to show them that learning about memory can aid their own memory and performance on examinations is by demonstrating specific concepts for them. One of these memory principles is that active rehearsal creates better retention, moving the material to long-term memory. By applying this principle, students are more likely to receive active reinforcements.

In my class, after teaching history, research design, and ethics, I teach learning so that students can apply psychological principles about human learning and memory to their own studying before the first examination.

MATERIALS NEEDED

Several strips of colored paper, for use as follows.

"Dismember" your lecture on memory by typing each sentence on a piece of colored paper. Each color represents a segment or chunk of the lecture: historical background, information processing, long-term memory, short-term memory, enhancing retention, memory aids, forgetting, and interference theory.

Each piece of colored paper contains several "bits" of critical information about verbal learning, remembering, or forgetting. For example, a bit of information from the interference theory chunk is the description of retroactive interference, while a separate bit is the actual paradigm. There is little depth provided in these bits, so the students will need to have done some background reading prior to the demonstration.

INSTRUCTIONS

Each student is given a strip of colored paper and must then locate and join ranks with other students who have the same color. The groups meet for approximately 10–15 minutes to determine how their bits fit together in order to form a coherent 5-minute lecture.

The group selects one member to deliver the minilecture to the rest of the class. After each minilecture, the class may question the group or the instructor so that all students have a complete understanding of the material.

This procedure works well, especially if the students have done the necessary reading. The students must develop examples (something often requested on exams), must be actively quizzed by peers, and must attempt to explain terms they have not previously encountered in lecture. The students learn how pieces of information fit together into logical blocks, how to organize a factual oral presentation, how rehearsal influences the quality of the presentation, and, of course, how teaching can be a learning experience. This also turns into a social experience because students provide support for their group representative, and sometimes the whole group delivers the lecture. It gives students a chance to participate fully in a lecture class. They are especially pleased (or relieved) to learn how to combat forgetting prior to the exam.

Although this technique can be somewhat chaotic, it is a good way to show students how memory operates for them. The demonstration uses a theoretical premise and makes it personally relevant. After all the students have delivered their lectures, discussion of how various principles were demonstrated is useful; discussions usually center on active learning, meaningfulness through examples, organization of memory into chunks, and use of memory enhancement devices when studying for exams. As a group, the students usually do well on exam questions about human learning and memory.

SUGGESTED READING

Houston, P. J. (1981). *Fundamentals of learning and memory* (2nd ed.). New York: Academic Press.

Jung, J. (1968). *Verbal learning.* New York: Holt, Rinehart & Winston.

Schwartz, S. (1986). *Classic studies in psychology* (pp. 57–66). Palo Alto, CA: Mayfield.

Wingfield, A. (1979). *Human learning and memory: An introduction.* New York: Harper & Row.

$^\square$22 BRUTE FORCE IN PROBLEM SOLVING

W. E. Scoville

University of Wisconsin—Oshkosh

This activity presents a problem to be solved by sheer effort rather than by creativity. The instructor might wish to try variations such as individual versus team efforts. No prior knowledge is necessary, and the instructor's advance preparation is minimal. This activity can be used with classes of any size. The recommended procedure is to distribute the problem during one class period and to discuss it the next.

CONCEPT
"Find the needle in the haystack" problems may be resistant to "creative thinking" solutions. Insight has its limitations with problems that are larger than they appear rather than simpler than they seem. Casually adding this puzzle to other materials on creative thinking and problem solving will bring this out very clearly.

MATERIALS NEEDED
Make as many copies of the unassembled puzzle pattern (Figure 22-1) as needed. A drawing of the completed puzzle (Figure 22-2) has been included just to prove it can be done. Alternate forms can be made by reverse engineering from a checkerboard pattern. Twelve or 13 pieces work well. Avoid unintended cues in the cutting and redrawing process.

INSTRUCTIONS
Challenge students to take the puzzle sheet home, to cut the pieces out, and to then form the 12 pieces into a regular checkerboard to be returned to class the next session.

DISCUSSION
Success should not be anticipated because the problem is much harder than it looks. Students will come to realize that there are thousands of ways to fit these parts together and no easy way to avoid repetition of previous errors. This is a task that is difficult because of the many possible combinations rather than because it requires creative insight. It makes a good foil for the creativity problems that are usually produced with such regularity. This activity also highlights the utility of the computer as a problem solver—patient, methodical, and very fast.

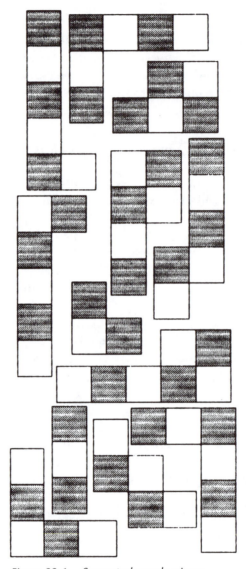

Figure 22-1. Separated puzzle pieces.

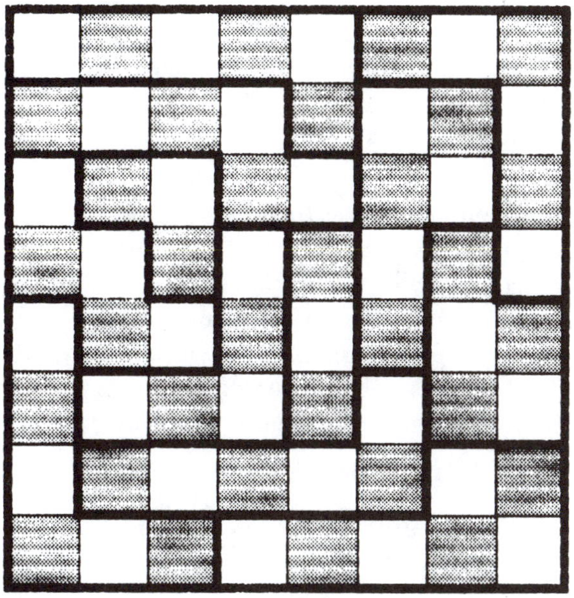

Figure 22-2. Puzzle pieces combined to form checkerboard.

23 PSYCHOLOGICAL SET AND THE SOLUTION OF ANAGRAMS

J. R. Corey
C. W. Post College

This is a paper-and-pencil activity that can be used with classes of any size, with students who have no prior knowledge of the topic. The instructor must provide the test page handout. This activity could be incorporated in discussions of perceptual set.

CONCEPT

The effects of psychological set (mental set or *einstellung*) have been demonstrated in areas ranging from problem solving to perception. A generalized tendency to respond in a certain way is first established and is then shown to carry over to a later task. In the present classroom experiment, two lists of six anagrams are presented. The first five may be unscrambled in only one way, establishing either an animal or vegetable set. The last target anagram on both lists is the same but could be solved as *ape* or *pea*. Statistical tests can then be performed to see if students tend to follow the set.

MATERIALS NEEDED

On one sheet of paper, provide the following instructions:

> This is a study of some factors that may affect the solution of anagrams, or scrambled words. On the next page is a list of letter combinations that can be unscrambled to yield common English words. No proper (capitalized) nouns, abbreviations, or foreign words appear.

> Please use this cover sheet to expose only one word at a time, and solve each anagram before going on to the next. Your instructor will provide you a hint if you find any anagram too difficult. Just raise your hand and your instructor will tell you the first letter of the solution. Please don't start on the next page until you are asked to do so.

> Example: DORW   Answer: _____

If part of this activity will include preparation of a written report in APA style, page 1 can also list the student's sex and age.

Page 2 will provide one of the following lists:
LULB, CALEM, NUKKS, SEUMO, BAZER, EAP (animal list),
NORC, NOONI, MATOOT, PREPPE, TEBE, EAP (vegetable list)

They should be printed in upper-case letters and spaced roughly equally down the page.

INSTRUCTIONS

Half the students should receive the animal list, and the other half should receive the vegetable list. Care should be taken to ensure that all students work independently and follow the instructions.

The instructor should also check careless answers (i.e., BULB for LULB) and should provide hints for students who need them. For students who are having real difficulty or distress, a second or third letter of the solution can be provided.

Table 1. *The Effect of Set on Anagram Solution*

	Psychological set	
Response	Animal	Vegetable
Ape	Follows set	Breaks set
Pea	Breaks set	Follows set

When all students have completed the task, answers should be collected and sorted into the 2×2 contingency table (Table 1). If a psychological set has been established, students receiving the vegetable list should be more likely to answer *pea* and the others to answer *ape*. These data may be analyzed by Fisher's exact probability test or by chi-square analysis.

Some students may write both answers for the target anagram. The instructor may choose to count only the first answer or to consider this a case of set-breaking when analyzing the data.

DISCUSSION

With most classes of introductory psychology students, between 80%–90% of students follow the established set. Some complain that they were misled into deducing that there was only one correct answer for each of the words. Careful rereading of the instructions dispels that notion.

Class discussion of further examples of psychological set (found in the Suggested Reading section) may lead to the role of set-breaking in creativity, scientific discovery, and art.

SUGGESTED READING

Luchins, A. S., & Luchins, E. H. (1959). *Rigidity of behavior.* Eugene: University of Oregon Press.

Saffren, M. A. (1962). Associations, set, and the solution of word problems. *Journal of Experimental Psychology, 64,* 40–45.

24 MEDIATION, DISCRIMINATION, AND QUALITATIVE SHIFTS IN PERFORMANCE

Salvador Macias III

University of South Carolina at Sumter

This activity provides a brief experiential introduction to problem solving and learning set. It can be used with students at any level and in any class in which all students can see the screen. Instructors must prepare 20 sets of three simple stimuli each for an overhead projector and must copy the answer sheet for students. There is no prior knowledge necessary for students.

CONCEPT

One of the more difficult ideas to explain to students is that of qualitative improvements in learning ability. That is, as children mature, they not only become better at various tasks but also do so because they have developed new methods of looking at problems and their internal relations, thereby devising more advanced solutions. Becoming more facile at an old strategy is indeed an improvement, but a quantitative one. Developing a new approach and style of perceiving problems is an even greater improvement, a qualitative one.

The problem for an instructor is to remind relatively advanced thinkers (college students) of the more primitive approaches they once used. A strategy that is obvious and easy to a college student may demand cognitive skills not present in young children. To unsophisticated thinkers, these "obvious" strategies are impossible, whereas the primitive strategies appear unnecessarily convoluted and complicated to advanced thinkers but are really more simple.

This activity uses a discrimination shift task to demonstrate problem-solving strategies: which strategies the students probably use, which others are possible, and how this information is available in a pattern of responses generated by this task. In solving a discrimination task, a variety of different strategies may be used. *Shifts* (changing the rule that correctly predicts the correct stimulus) allow one to see these different strategies by causing different patterns of responses according to what kind of shift is used and the cognitive skill of the subject.

MATERIALS NEEDED

An overhead projector and two transparencies are needed. Each transparency should be prepared as a series of 10 trials, each trial consisting of three stimuli that differ by color and shape. For example, Trial 1 might present a red triangle, a green square, and a blue circle. Trial 2 might present a red square, a green circle, and a blue triangle, and so forth. The positions of these should be completely random so that predictions according to position are not possible (see Figure 24-1). To limit stimulus presentations, a double-length sheet of paper with a wide horizontal slot cut in it can be used to expose one trial at a time. Also, I have found that using answer sheets

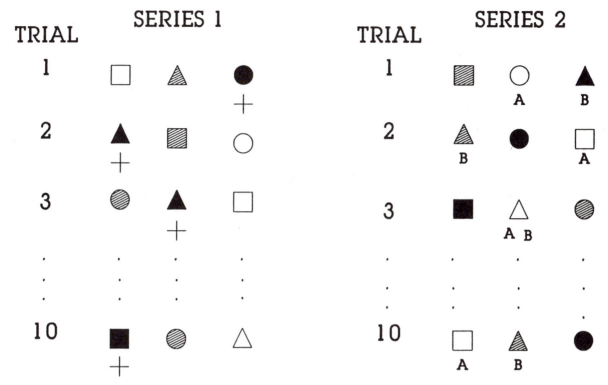

Figure 24-1. Random deviations of trial stimuli. (Correct answers are revealed after students have chosen an answer.)

with instructions and response blanks greatly facilitates the demonstration (see Answer Sheet).

This activity is taken from mediation, reversal–nonreversal learning experiments such as those performed by the Kendlers and colleagues (Esposito, 1975; H. H. Kendler, 1971; H. H. Kendler & Kendler, 1962; T. S. Kendler, Basden, & Bruckner, 1970; T. S. Kendler & Kendler, 1970; T. S. Kendler & Ward, 1972; Offenbach, 1983). Two series of 10 trials are presented. In Series 1 (the preshift trials), one dimension is relevant (e.g., color), with the correct choice always the same (e.g., blue). That is, selections of any blue stimulus, regardless of the shape, are correct. Students quickly discover this solution; my class averages are between 8 and 9 correct of the 10 trials.

Series 2 follows immediately. There are two separate discriminations presented in this series (the "shift" trials). One half of the class is assigned to Group A, in which the relevant dimension is still color but the correct value is changed, for example, to *green* (this is called a reversal shift). Group B has a harder task. Shape is the newly relevant dimension (a nonreversal shift). For example, *triangle* may now be correct.

One way to present two separate discriminations simultaneously is to label the correct choices by the letters *a* or *b* (see Figure 24-1) and to present the instructions as shown in the Answer Sheet. Students in Group A average around nine correct trials in Series 2; Group B students average approximately five to six. If calculating average numbers of correct responses is difficult (as in large classes), you may use a quick demonstration to compare the change in the number of correct choices over the two series. That is, by a show of hands, you can see that Group A students tend to improve from Series 1 to Series 2, whereas Group B students tend to perform more poorly on Series 2.

An important procedural reminder is to present only one trial at a time, covering both the previous and the later trials. The double-length sheet of paper with the slot cut in it greatly reduces the possibility that information will be presented at the wrong time. The instructor can present a trial, ask that the students respond, announce that the answer is forthcoming, show it, then go to the next trial, all while automatically covering all but the current information.

DISCUSSION   Group B students obviously have a more difficult task presented to them. This seems obvious because we assume the cognitive skill to recognize dimensional categories. Noticing that color is relevant in Series 1 causes both Group A and B to search for a relevant color in Series 2. This helps Group A and hinders Group B. But what if this cognitive ability is absent? What if a subject is unable to mediate by attending to categories? For example, 4–6-year-old children usually find that Task B is easier than Task A!

If categorical mediation is impossible, another strategy is necessary. It appears that younger children learn three separate discriminations—blue circle is correct, blue triangle is correct, and blue square is correct—and never notice the common feature of blueness that would allow a single rule to be learned. Thus, in a reversal shift, three new facts must be learned. For example, "pick the green triangle, the green circle, and the green square." In a nonreversal shift, with blue triangle, green triangle, and red triangle all correct, one of these is the same as Series 1 (blue triangle). In this series, only two new discriminations need to be learned, therefore, Group B is the easier task for these children.

The qualitative improvement of mediation, categorical attention abilities, and so forth, is usually obvious. After students have experienced the tasks themselves, it is a relatively simple matter to explain the less sophisticated strategies used by young children.

Incidentally, this task is also useful for discussions of cognition and perceptual learning as well as for methodological issues such as randomization, problem presentation, and so forth. I should also add that the typical data collected from these tasks are not the number correct in a series of 10 trials but rather are a trials-to-criterion measure. Usually, criterion is the number of trials necessary before there are nine correct responses in a string of 10 presentations. With group presentation and data collection, this is not possible, and the method described is adequate for this demonstration.

REFERENCES   Esposito, N. J. (1975). Review of discrimination shift learning in young children. *Psychological Bulletin, 82,* 432–455.

Kendler, H. H. (1971). Environmental and cognitive control of behavior. *American Psychologist, 26,* 962–973.

Kendler, H. H., & Kendler, T. S. (1962). Vertical and horizontal processes in problem solving. *Psychological Review, 69,* 1–16.

Kendler, T. S., Basden, B. H., & Bruckner, J. B. (1970). Dimensional dominance and continuity theory. *Journal of Experimental Psychology, 83,* 309–348.

Kendler, T. S., & Kendler, H. H. (1970). An ontogeny of optional shift behavior. *Child Development, 41,* 1–27.

Kendler, T. S., & Ward, J. W. (1972). Optional reverse probability is a linear function of the log of age. *Developmental Psychology, 7*, 337–348.

Offenbach, S. F. (1983). The concept of dimension in research in children's learning. *Monographs of the Society for Research in Child Development, 48* (6, Serial No. 204).

SUGGESTED READING

White, S. (1970). Learning theory function and child psychology. In P. H. Mussen (Ed.), *Carmichael's manual of child psychology* (Vol. 1). New York: Wiley.

Answer Sheet

For this demonstration, I will present two series of problems to you. In each series there are 10 trials. In each trial there are three stimuli. One of the stimuli has arbitrarily been identified as correct. Your task is to record in the spaces below which stimulus you think is the correct one for each trial. Place a mark in the position (left, middle, or right) occupied by the selected stimulus. After you respond the answer will be provided. If you are correct, circle that item.

For Series 2, the correct answers will depend on the group to which you have been assigned. Please note that you are either in Group A or in Group B (indicated below). The procedure is as with Series 1. The only exception is that correct choices will be indicated by the letters *A* or *B* placed beneath the appropriate stimulus.

	SERIES 1				SERIES 2: Group A or Group B		
Trial				Trial			
1.	____	____	____	1.	____	____	____
2.	____	____	____	2.	____	____	____
3.	____	____	____	3.	____	____	____
4.	____	____	____	4.	____	____	____
5.	____	____	____	5.	____	____	____
6.	____	____	____	6.	____	____	____
7.	____	____	____	7.	____	____	____
8.	____	____	____	8.	____	____	____
9.	____	____	____	9.	____	____	____
10.	____	____	____	10.	____	____	____
	Total correct ____				Total correct ____		

$\Box$ 25 MEMORY AND MARKETABLE PRODUCT NAMES

Walter A. Woods
Products and Concepts Research International

Although it may be true that a rose by any other name may smell as sweet, marketing specialists are aware that a product is more likely to sell if its name is one that is easily remembered. This activity demonstrates to students how learning concepts can be applied to marketing technology. No materials or prior knowledge is needed, and this activity can be used for students at levels ranging from high school to undergraduate courses. However, the activities (both in and out of class) extend over several class periods.

CONCEPT

A common problem encountered in marketing is that of selecting a name that will attract consumers. More often than not, the name will mean the difference between success and failure, because competitors can usually make physically comparable products.

Various theories have been proposed about what makes a good name. One of these theories is that short names are best and that shortness is a good criterion. But experience has shown that many short names are confused with other short names and cannot necessarily be recalled correctly. Another theory is that a name must be catchy. But no one has been able to say what catchiness is or how it can be identified.

It has been suggested (Woods, 1983) that the basic measure of a name that will attract consumers is its impact. *Impact* is said to be a function of (a) distinctiveness (prominence), (b) the capability to involve the perceiver, and (c) the ability to find a "memory address"—that is, its relevance to information already in memory. However, these attributes cannot be measured directly. The problem is, How can they be evaluated?

The principle behind Miller's (1956) concept of the "magical number seven, plus or minus two" provides an excellent tool for selecting impact names on the basis of memorability (Woods, 1981). Miller's concept is that, on average, about seven chunks of information can be retained in short-term (ST) memory (Gilmartin, Newell, & Simon, 1976) at one time. From ST memory, a chunk of information may find its way into long-term (LT) memory and may be retained. Information in ST memory that does not find its way into LT memory will be "bumped out" by new information. It is difficult to hold information in ST memory because people are constantly being bombarded with new information from many sources; if the average person has seven chunks of information in ST memory, one or more of these chunks will be lost quickly to new information.

If a respondent to a consumer name test is informed of seven names, some of these names may find their way into LT memory because of their relatedness to meaningful information already existing in LT memory (Simon & Chase, 1977). The worst names in the test will be bumped out immediately. Other names will be temporarily held in ST memory through rehearsal (i.e., by repeating them) until they find a LT memory "address" or are finally bumped out and lost.

Thus, if we ask test respondents to read a list of seven names, then disrupt the respondents for about 5 minutes by asking them irrelevant questions about their ages, birthdates, and so on, and then ask them to recall the names, some names will be recalled correctly, some will be partially recalled, and some will be entirely forgotten. It has been found that names that are accurately recalled by 75% or more of a test sample perform well in the market. If we find that none of the names are recalled by 75% or more of the sample, we conclude that we have no satisfactory names: Additional names must be created and tested.

If more than 7 names need to be tested, the names are split into separate lists of 7 each, and each list is tested separately. If the number of names available for testing is not divisible into groups of 7, additional names are created so that groups of 7 are available (e.g., if you have only 12 names, create 2 new ones). After the groups are independently tested, the 7 names with the highest scores from all of the groups are pooled into a new group for final testing.

MATERIALS NEEDED

No extra materials are needed for this activity.

INSTRUCTIONS

To demonstrate the seven plus or minus two principle, ask the class to prepare two lists of seven names each and to test these among friends and acquaintances using the process described previously. They should then calculate the recall percentages for each name. The seven highest scoring names are used for a final test.

Next, combine the names in both lists to produce a single list of 14 names. Test these names and again compute the recall scores. The results of the 7-names test can then be compared with the results of the 14-names test in order to test the validity of the seven plus or minus two concept.

DISCUSSION

It has sometimes been questioned whether a test of recall after a lapse of only 5 minutes is reliable. The reliability of the method has been demonstrated by comparing results after a lapse of 5 minutes with results after a lapse of 24 hours. It has been found that recall scores on individual names correlate quite highly. Furthermore, the proportions recalling the names under the two conditions do not vary more than about 5%.

As for validity, the real test for this is market performance. Names that have not performed well in recall tests have a poor record in the market. Names that have done well in the recall tests have a good record in the market.

Very few psychology students will ever be confronted with evaluating new product names, unless they choose to work in a field such as marketing. However, it is of value for students, as consumers, to understand the thinking and the processes that lie behind the identification of the products that are offered on the market. A name, in and of itself, does not make a product better than another that may have a less attractive name or a lower price. However, the principles that guide the choosing of the name reveal the psychology of memory and may make the difference between product success and failure.

REFERENCES

Gilmartin, E. J., Newell, A., & Simon, H. A. (1976). A program modeling short term memory under strategic control. In C. N. Cofer (Ed.), *The structure of human memory*. San Francisco: Freeman.

Miller, G. A. (1956). The magical number seven, plus or minus two: Some limits on the capacity for processing information. *Psychological Review, 63*, 81–97.

Simon, H. A., & Chase, W. G. (1977). Skill in chess. In I. L. Janis (Ed.), *Current trends in psychology*. Los Altos, CA: Kaufmann.

Woods, W. A. (1981). *Consumer behavior: Adapting and experiencing* (pp. 433–436). New York: Elsevier.

Woods, W. A. (1983, September 16). Gravy Train has it, Drive doesn't—How to measure "impact" of brand name candidates. *Marketing News*, Section 2, pp. 10–13.

26 TEACHING THE DISTINCTION BETWEEN NEGATIVE REINFORCEMENT AND PUNISHMENT

Robert T. Tauber
The Behrend College of Penn State

For those who have struggled to help students distinguish between punishment and negative reinforcement, this activity offers a simple solution. A transparency of the learning consequence matrix, an overhead projector, and copies of the quiz will be needed. Virtually any size class can participate in this discussion activity. Students need no prior knowledge of operant conditioning, and upper level students can often benefit from participating in this activity as well. The instructor may wish to go one step further and connect positive reinforcement with reward training, time-out with omission training, and negative reinforcement with escape and avoidance training.

CONCEPT

Negative reinforcement is often misinterpreted as punishment. Too much attention is paid to the word *negative* and not enough to *reinforcement*. The word *negative* is connotatively perceived as undesirable—negative attitudes, negative numbers, negative checkbook balances.

This activity demonstrates the important differences between negative reinforcement and punishment and provides students with an opportunity to experience firsthand the use of negative reinforcement in behavior modification.

MATERIALS NEEDED

You will need sufficient copies of the Negative Reinforcement Quiz (master supplied) as well as a transparency of the operant learning Consequence Matrix (copy supplied), with removable opaque tabs covering each of the four consequences.

INSTRUCTIONS

To introduce the concept of negative reinforcement, explain to the class that operant conditioning is one of the most researched and discussed topics in psychology, often spilling over into other disciplines such as education and management. When properly applied, operant conditioning can effectively modify the behavior of others. To apply such a "carrot and stick" approach successfully, users must understand which consequences are available as carrots to strengthen desired behaviors and as sticks to weaken undesired behaviors.

After this brief introduction, administer the Negative Reinforcement Quiz (nongraded) to the class so that students can commit themselves to their definition of negative reinforcement and to their understanding of when it should be used. When the students have completed the quiz, ask them how they answered Questions 1–5.

Those who take the quiz often incorrectly answer *punishment* or something similar for the first question. Following on this initial misunderstanding, they answer the other questions incorrectly and express vehement disagreement with the fifth question, which presents the idea of further use of negative reinforcement.

At this point, present the Consequence Matrix, with the opaque tabs covering each of the four consequences. The two column headings, "supply a consequence" and "remove a consequence," should be highlighted. Explain that one can only supply something or remove something: No other choices exist. Point out that the two row headings are "appetitive stimulus" (something desired) and "aversive stimulus" (something not desired).

Have students fill in the Consequence Matrix by combining each column heading with each row heading. It is soon obvious that only four combinations are possible. Without removing any of the opaque tabs covering the names of each consequence, ask students what it is called when someone supplies an appetitive stimulus. The answer, "positive reinforcement," is soon volunteered. Now remove the tab and reveal this as the correct answer. This consequence strengthens a behavior.

Now, ask students what it is called when someone removes an appetitive stimulus. Many students will offer the incorrect response, "punishment." You may have to offer hints or clues to elicit the correct answer, "time-out." Remove the second tab to show this answer. This is a consequence that weakens a behavior.

Consequence Matrix

Stimulus type	Supply a stimulus	Remove a stimulus
Appetitive stimulus (Something desired)	Positive reinforcement	Time-out
Aversive stimulus (Something not desired)	Punishment	Negative reinforcement

---

Continue by asking what it is called when someone applies an aversive stimulus. Again, the most likely answer will be "punishment." Remove the tab covering the term *punishment*. By now, you will have demonstrated one consequence to strengthen a behavior (positive reinforcement) and two to weaken a behavior (time-out and punishment).

Turn to the last quadrant of the Consequence Matrix and ask what it is called when someone removes an aversive stimulus. Almost reluctantly, most students will answer "negative reinforcement." Right they are. Given that the definition of negative reinforcement is "removing an aversive stimulus," ask students whether it is used to strengthen or weaken behaviors. Expect some hesitation in their response, for they will still be reluctant to admit the obvious—that negative reinforcement strengthens desired behaviors.

Using the matrix, one clearly sees that negative reinforcement removes an aversive stimulus, while punishment supplies an aversive stimulus. Negative reinforcement cannot be a synonym for punishment.

DISCUSSION   Refer students to the results of the quiz. Discuss the answer to the first question and remind them that "punishment" is not a synonym for "negative reinforcement." Point out that the correct answer to the second question should be "yes"; negative reinforcement strengthens a desired behavior. The correct answer to the third question should be "yes"; most people do look forward to having an aversive stimulus removed. Finally, because both positive reinforcement and negative reinforcement are used to start behavior, students answering "yes" for the fourth question and "no" for the fifth question might be asked to reconsider their answers.

As an example to illustrate the differences between negative reinforcement and punishment, offer the following statements: "If you clean your room, you will no longer have to stay inside," and, "Because you did not clean your room, you will have to stay inside today." These are examples of negative reinforcement and punishment, respectively. The first statement, in effect, says, If you do what I want you to do (clean your room), I will remove an aversive stimulus (you no longer have to stay inside). The second statement says, Because you did not do what I wanted you to do (again, clean your room), I will supply an aversive stimulus (you must stay inside).

Now have students create their own examples of contrasting statements. Test each example against the Consequence Matrix definition of "removing an aversive stimulus." Be on guard for student responses that are actually punishment, positive reinforcement, or time-out consequence statements. Have students rework incorrect examples until they are correctly worded negative reinforcement statements.

To understand operant conditioning, students need to understand each of the four available consequences. They need to realize that negative reinforcement and punishment are used for entirely different purposes: Negative reinforcement strengthens behaviors, whereas punishment weakens behaviors.

Point out to them that this misunderstanding is common. Even the professional literature is lacking in a thorough treatment of negative reinforcement; *Psychological Abstracts* from 1980 through 1985 lists 80 titles containing the term *negative reinforcement* and 362 containing the term *punishment*. Another example can be drawn from the popular media. In the movie "Ghostbusters," Bill Murray administers electric shocks to a male college student who gives incorrect answers in an ESP experiment. He defends his actions as negative reinforcement, when in fact supplying an electric shock (aversive stimulus) is clearly punishment.

SUGGESTED READING

Tauber, Robert T. (1982). Negative reinforcement: A positive strategy of classroom management. *The Clearing House, 56,* 64–67.

Tauber, Robert T. (1986). The positive side of negative reinforcement and the negative side of praise. *Durham and Newcastle Research Review, 10,* 299–302.

Tauber, Robert T. (1988). Overcoming misunderstanding about the concept of negative reinforcement. *Teaching of Psychology, 15,* 152–153.

27 A DEMONSTRATION OF CONTEXT-DEPENDENT LATENT INHIBITION IN OPERANT CONDITIONING

Melinda A. Sletten and Ernest D. Kemble
University of Minnesota: Morris

This activity requires preparation over at least 7 days and requires several rats and enough operant chambers to suit the number of rats and the number of students. If the instructor does the preliminary work, the last phase can be done in a single 2-hour lab session. Students need to be familiar with operant conditioning terms and procedures and with ethical principles for the treatment of animals (see Activity 80 in this volume).

CONCEPT

Latent inhibition refers to the retardation of Pavlovian or instrumental conditioning produced by the repeated presentation of a conditioned stimulus (CS) prior to its pairing with an excitatory or inhibitory unconditioned stimulus (US). This inhibitory effect is dependent on the context in which the initial CS presentations are introduced, however, and is not observed if the CS-only presentations occur in a setting differing substantially from that in which later conditioning is to be carried out. Unfortunately, most demonstrations of this important Pavlovian second-order conditioning phenomenon utilize electric shock as the US, which renders them inappropriate for most introductory laboratories. This exercise demonstrates context-dependent latent inhibition produced by the click of a feeding mechanism on the later acquisition of a bar-press response. Simple equipment, available or easily constructed in many laboratories, is utilized, and if the preliminary phases are completed prior to student participation, the activity can be completed within a single one to two hour laboratory period.

MATERIALS NEEDED

Sixteen or more albino rats serve as subjects. Testing is carried out in a small (approximately $29 \times 29 \times 11$ cm) operant chamber containing a relatively large (approximately 2×5 cm) removable lever and a source of water. The operant chamber should be equipped with a feeding mechanism that delivers 45-mg Noyes food tablets with a distinctly audible click. The combination of a small apparatus and a large lever assures a high operant rate of lever pressing and eliminates the need for shaping of the operant response. Half of the subjects are also exposed to a context control chamber. In our case, a $27 \times 13 \times 17$-cm black chamber was used, but any chamber differing markedly from the operant chamber should be satisfactory. If available, programming equipment should be used to time the testing intervals and record responses.

INSTRUCTIONS

Phase 1. The rats are placed on a limited food regimen (e.g., 30 minutes food access per day) for 24 hours prior to the beginning of the experiment and remain on this schedule throughout. At this time, half of the subjects are also randomly assigned to a latent inhibition group, and the remainder are assigned to a context control group. Twenty-four hours later, habituation to the apparatus and food tablets is begun. All subjects are placed in the apparatus, with the lever removed and with 20–30 food tablets present in the food cup for 10 minutes per day for at least 5 days or until the food tablets are readily consumed. In addition, context control rats are also placed in the context control chamber for 10 minutes per day for 2 days during this phase. It is important that the animals are thoroughly habituated to both the operant chamber and the food tablets and that no animal be exposed to the click of the feeding magazine during this phase.

Phase 2. During this phase, the rats are exposed to the click of the feeding magazine, which is unpaired with the delivery of food tablets. The rats are exposed to the clicks in pairs. A latent inhibition rat is placed in the operant chamber (with lever removed, no food tablets present, and the tube leading from feeding magazine to food cup disconnected), and a context control rat is placed in the context control chamber. Both chambers should be equidistant from the feeding magazine. Thirty clicks of the feeding magazine are delivered at random intervals during a single 10-minute period.

Phase 3. Twenty-four hours after the completion of Phase 2, all rats are placed in the operant chamber for a single 60-minute acquisition test. During this phase, the lever is inserted into the apparatus, the feeding magazine is connected to the food cup, and each lever press results in the delivery of a single 45-mg food tablet. The number of food-rewarded lever presses is recorded for four or more equal-time intervals during this single testing session to illustrate the increased rate of responding during the course of acquisition and the emergence of group differences in response rate. If time constraints do not permit student participation in the earlier phases of this experiment, Phase 3 can be completed within a single laboratory period.

DISCUSSION It has long been recognized that an association between the click of reward delivery mechanisms and positive reinforcers is important for the later shaping of an operant response. If this initial step is viewed as an instance of Pavlovian second-order conditioning, then the presentation of magazine clicks that are unpaired with reinforcer delivery should retard the acquisition of lever pressing among animals exposed to the clicks in the operant chamber (latent inhibition group) but not if the clicks are delivered in a markedly different environment (context control group). When this experiment was conducted in our Research Methods in Psychology course, the context control group showed significantly higher rates of response than did the latent inhibition group. This clear demonstration of context-dependent latent inhibition occurred despite the fact that our 24 rats were handled and tested by 24 inexperienced undergraduate students, and it nicely demonstrated the pervasive importance of latent inhibition. This was probably possible because the apparatus and procedures produced very rapid acquisition which, in turn, minimized the impact of repeated experimenter–subject interactions common to more extended testing procedures.

SUGGESTED
READING
Bitterman, M. E. (1975). The comparative analysis of learning: Are the laws of learning the same in all animals? *Science, 188,* 699–709.

Garcia, J., McGowan, B., & Green, K. (1972). Biological constraints on conditioning. In A. H. Black & W. F. Prokasy (Eds.), *Classical conditioning: II. Current research and theory.* New York: Appleton-Century-Crofts.

Holland, P. C., & Rescorla, R. A. (1975). Second-order conditioning with food unconditioned stimulus. *Journal of Comparative and Physiological Psychology, 88,* 459–467.

MacIntosh, N. J. (1974). *The psychology of animal learning.* New York: Academic Press.

Rescorla, R. A. (1976). Second-order conditioning of Pavlovian conditioned inhibition. *Learning and Motivation, 7,* 161–172.

Rescorla, R. A. (1980). *Pavlovian second-order conditioning: Studies in associative learning.* Hillsdale, NJ: Erlbaum.

Rescorla, R. A., & Wagner, A. R. (1972). A theory of Pavlovian conditioning: Variations in the effectiveness of reinforcement and nonreinforcement. In A. H. Black & W. F. Prokasy (Eds.), *Classical conditioning: II. Current research and theory.* New York: Appleton-Century-Crofts.

28 THE USE OF GOLDFISH IN OPERANT CONDITIONING

J. R. Corey
C. W. Post College

Most experiments involving animals are both complicated and costly; this one, however, is a clear and direct demonstration of operant conditioning that is easy and inexpensive to construct. No harm is done to the goldfish, and the entire class can take part in the training. Students do not need any prior knowledge of psychology, and a class of any size can participate. The instructor may wish to construct the conditioning chamber beforehand, or this can be done as part of the in-class demonstration.

CONCEPT

Operant conditioning demonstrations are powerful pedagogical devices that are out of the question in many high schools or colleges. Animal facilities for pigeons or small rodents are too expensive to maintain in a manner conforming to state, federal, and American Psychological Association (APA) regulations. Operant conditioning chambers (which should not be referred to as "Skinner boxes," in conformity with Skinner's wishes) are commercially available but are expensive (about $700). Home-made rat or pigeon chambers and associated electrical food dispensing and response counting circuits are almost impossible to construct out of components that are readily available. However, goldfish and other cyprinids are easy to maintain and can be trained to perform simple discriminated operants (Bitterman, 1965). Furthermore, the apparatus is easily constructed out of readily available materials. Expenses are reduced by the elimination of electromechanical food dispensers and counting devices and by the substitution of manual feeding and counting.[1]

MATERIALS NEEDED

Goldfish may be obtained from pet or department stores. Large (above 10 cm) fish are preferable because they are better able to perform the lever-pushing response. Keeping the fish healthy requires filtered or fresh water daily, and water out of the tap should stand for 1 day before use. Each fish should be housed in a 10-gallon or larger aquarium.

An operandum was constructed from a sensitive microswitch, a light-emitting diode (LED), and the barrel of a ballpoint pen. This was mounted on the outside of a water-tight plastic food container. A 3-VDC solid-state buzzer and two 1.5-V batteries were installed inside the container, and a switch and push button were mounted in the top (Figure 28-1). Figure 28-2 shows the wiring diagram of the circuit. The LED is lit only when the main switch is on. Then, either the operandum or the push button activates the buzzer. Food was delivered manually only after the buzzer was activated, either by the fish or the experimenter.

---

[1] A version of this activity was presented at the annual meeting of the Association for Behavior Analysis, May 1988.

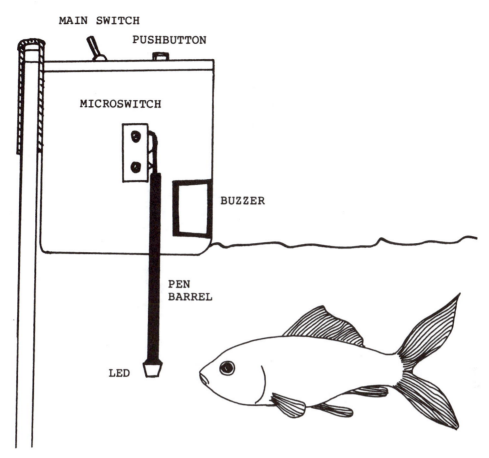

MAIN SWITCH

PUSHBUTTON

MICROSWITCH

BUZZER

PEN
BARREL

LED

Figure 28-1.   An illustration of the apparatus for training goldfish, showing the placement of the operandum, switches, and buzzer.

INSTRUCTIONS   Fish should be adapted to a feeding schedule in which food is presented for 5 min twice a day. Any food remaining uneaten after five minutes should be removed. The LED is always turned on during every training session and is left off when training is not proceeding. The buzzer should always be sounded immediately before food is delivered (a one-second delay is permissible). This magazine training is continued until the fish orients toward and eats the food immediately after each time the buzzer is sounded.

Short daily training sessions are terminated when the fish is satiated. Frequent deliveries of small amounts of food will accelerate training, but two sessions a day with a single pairing of the buzzer and food in each session should accomplish magazine training between 1 and 3 weeks.

Next, the buzzer and food are used to shape lever pushing. Approximations of lever pressing, such as swimming toward the lever, are reinforced initially by immediately sounding the buzzer and delivering food. Then closer and closer approximations are reinforced. Shaping proceeds until the fish reliably presses the operandum. Discrimination training involves alternating LED on and LED off periods. Lever pushing is reinforced only when the LED is on and extinguishes when the LED is off. Chaining may then be attempted by requiring a new response (swimming in a circle or jumping through a hoop) before the LED is turned on.

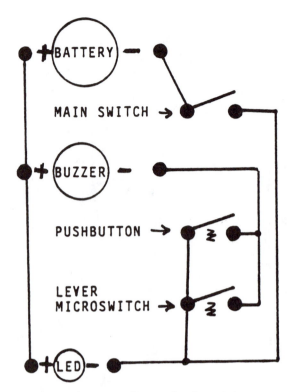

Figure 28-2.   The circuit diagram for the training apparatus.

DISCUSSION   Goldfish training can be done individually or by a group of students and can usually be accomplished in 1 or 2 months. Goldfish training takes much longer than pigeon or rat training, possibly because of more rapid satiation. The process could be accelerated by using frequent presentations of very small bits of food spread over several hours a day.

Once goldfish are trained, other demonstrations are feasible. For example, Anthouard (1987) found that fish (Serranidae) show social transmission of lever-pressing behavior. Is this also true of goldfish?

REFERENCES   Anthouard, M. (1987). A study of social transmission in juvenile *Dicentrarchus labrax* (Pisces, Serranidae) in an operant conditioning situation. *Behaviour, 103,* 266–275.

Bitterman, M. E. (1965). The evolution of intelligence. *Scientific American, 212,* 92–103.

CHAPTER IV
DEVELOPMENTAL
PSYCHOLOGY

These activities all differ both in approach and in level of complexity. Activity 29 offers a comprehensive survey of infant and child development. Activity 30 can be used with a class of any size and at any level and requires two class sessions. Activity 31 is a research and writing assignment that has students trace their own developmental history. Activity 33 is a historical outline of cultural and psychological developments in thinking about childhood, and Activity 32 demonstrates dietary effects on both physical and cognitive development. Activity 34 describes a "parent panel" for a study of adolescent development; it requires fairly detailed planning and works best with smaller classes. Activity 35 is a set of exercises that explore in some detail the "three tasks" of adolescent development—cognitive, social, and moral. Students should do some background reading beforehand; it works with any size class.

29 EARLY MOTOR AND VERBAL DEVELOPMENT

Peter S. Fernald
University of New Hampshire

L. Dodge Fernald
Harvard University

Before doing this activity, students will need some background in maturation processes before attempting to rank the developmental sequence that can be done in class on the chalkboard or separately on handouts. This activity is a good lead-in to a discussion about the developmental sequence, the distinction between abilities that are acquired through training and those that are acquired through maturation, and early intelligence testing.

CONCEPT

Several principles of human development, especially the cephalocaudal and proximodistal sequences and the role of maturation, are illustrated. Students should have some prior knowledge of the cephalocaudal and proximodistal sequences either through assigned reading or lecture.

MATERIALS NEEDED

Write the list of motor and verbal abilities on the chalkboard or mimeograph copies of the list and hand them out to the class.

Order of Development	Motor and Verbal Ability
_____	Walks alone; says several words
_____	Describes the difference between a bird and a dog
_____	Turns head to follow moving object
_____	Names penny, nickel, and dime
_____	Climbs stairs; says many words
_____	Laces shoes
_____	Sits alone for one minute; says "da-da"
_____	Tells how a baseball and an orange or an airplane and a kite are alike
_____	Puts on shoes
_____	Tells time to quarter-hour
_____	Runs; uses simple word combinations
_____	Walks while holding onto something

INSTRUCTIONS

Ask the students to rank the various abilities according to their developmental sequence beginning with 1, which indicates the first ability to develop, and ending with 12, the last ability to develop. After the students have completed this task, tell them the proper sequence, which is 4, 10, 1, 9, 5, 8, 2, 12, 7, 11, 6, 3. Then, to help students understand the sequence more clearly, put the list in its rearranged but correct order from first ability to develop (top) to last ability to develop. The list, with approximate ages, should appear as follows.

2 months	Turns head to follow moving object
9 months	Sits alone for 1 min; says "da-da"
1 year	Walks while holding onto something
1 year 3 months	Walks alone; says several words
1 year 6 months	Climbs stairs; says many words
2 years	Runs; uses simple word combinations
3 years	Puts on shoes
4 years	Laces shoes
5 years	Names penny, nickel, and dime
6 years	Describes the difference between a bird and a dog
7 years	Tells time to quarter-hour
8 years	Tells how a baseball and an orange or an airplane and a kite are alike

DISCUSSION

Ask the students the following question: In what ways are cephalocaudal and proximodistal development indicated in the sequence just described? Coax out of the students some examples illustrated in the sequence. An example of cephalocaudal development is that a baby turns his or her head to follow a moving object before he or she walks. The baby also puts on his or her shoes before he or she learns to lace them, a sequence that suggests proximodistal development.

Next, tell the students to put the letter *M* beside those abilities they believe are acquired chiefly through maturation and a *T* beside those that clearly involve training. Then ask them a second question: Is there any trend or pattern with regard to the abilities that develop primarily through maturation and those for which training is also required? Elicit through discussion the following points: The first 3 abilities develop chiefly through maturation with regard to the motor task, but training is involved with each of the verbal tasks; the last 6 abilities all involve some training. Thus, it would appear that training (learning) assumes greater importance for abilities occurring later in the developmental sequence.

Finally, invite students to construct an intelligence test for infants and young children, birth through 8 years, and ask them a third question: Would it be appropriate to use some of these items in such a test? Again, through discussion, elicit the following ideas. Intelligence, defined in general terms, is the ability to adjust to one's environment. Placed in the correct order, the items represent a progressive increase in capacity to adapt to and deal with the environment. In fact, several of the tasks are included in standard intelligence tests. Note also the changing nature of intelligence as one ascends the age scale, from a largely motor ability very early in life to greater verbal emphasis later on. Adult intelligence tests involve mostly verbal abilities.

30 IMPLICATIONS OF THE MILESTONES OF DEVELOPMENT

Eileen Astor-Stetson
Bloomsburg University of Pennsylvania

This activity is appropriate for classes of any size, from high school through a first course in developmental psychology. It extends over two class sessions, not necessarily consecutive. Students will develop their lists of milestones more easily if they have read the material on infancy. Obviously, the technique could be adapted for later stages of development as well.

CONCEPT

The milestones of development, such as walking, talking, or toilet training, are developmental tasks that indicate major physical, social, or emotional changes. Knowledge of the normal ranges of occurrence of the milestones is important for the identification of abnormality, for appropriate interactions with the child, and for reasonable expectations concerning behavior.

Most students readily agree it is important for people concerned with children to know the major milestones of development. However, many students, even when they have good insight into what the milestones of development are, are unable to explain their importance. This activity has two purposes: to allow students to discuss the implications of certain developmental achievements and to allow them to assess how knowledgeable they and their peers are in the area of infant development.

MATERIALS NEEDED

Make copies of the Suggested Data Sheet.

INSTRUCTIONS

Divide students into small groups and have each group develop a list a five milestones of infant development and their average age of occurrence. When students have completed their lists and shared them with the class, form a composite list.

Instruct the students to ask their friends when they think the average baby achieves each milestone. Friends' responses may be recorded on data sheets such as the one presented. A correct answer would score a 0, an answer one group too young or old a 1, an answer two groups too young or old a 2, and so forth.

DISCUSSION

When developing their milestones the students may discuss the physical, emotional, social, and cognitive implications of the event. For example, if a baby starts to walk at 12 months, this reflects more than just the normal development of bones and muscles. Rather, it also indicates that the physical world available to the baby has changed and that the nature of the baby's interactions with his or her caregivers is also changing. Students may also consider the implications of atypical development. A baby that is not walking at 2 years obviously deviates from the norm in physical development and may well have medical problems that need to be treated. But what other aspects of this baby's environment would be different from that of a more typical baby? How would adults and other children respond to this baby in a social context? Emotionally?

```
                        Suggested Data Sheet

Please indicate the age at which most babies have acquired each skill:
```

	Months						Score for each quest
	0–1	1–3	3–6	6–9	9–12	18–24	
1.							
2.							
3.							
4.							
5.							
				Total Score:			

Following data collection, students may discuss how knowledgeable their peers proved to be. The students may also discuss whether they expected differences in knowledge based on such factors as age or gender, why they held these expectations, and whether their expectations were met.

SUGGESTED READING

Bee, H., & Mitchell, S. (1984). *The developing person: A life-span approach* (2nd ed.). New York: Harper & Row.

Epstein, A. (1980). *Assessing the child development information needed by adolescent parents with very young children* (final report). Ypsilanti, MI: High/Scope Educational Research Foundation.

Stevens, J. H. (1984). Child development knowledge and parenting skills. *Family Relations, 33,* 237–244.

31 CHILDHOOD RESEARCH PAPER

Margaret S. Martin
Lander College

This activity demonstrates how to spark your students' interest in developmental psychology by having them apply the concepts of the course to their own developmental history. This paper can be adapted to any segment of the developmental life span, although the ages of traditional students place some limits on its use for adult development. Students are asked to research their history, illustrating specific references made in their text. Depending on the level of the class, you may wish to make the paper longer or limit the discussion to fewer aspects of development.

CONCEPT   The study of childhood in a developmental psychology course will give students unique insight into this content area when they are explicity asked to write a paper about themselves. Childhood, defined here as the period of growth and development up to adolescence, can be substituted by adolescence, or if you are teaching primarily older adult students, the period of young adulthood. In this assignment you are asking students to relate the concepts studied in their texts and in class to themselves.

INSTRUCTIONS   The following instructions to students may be used: Write a detailed paper of at least five pages describing your childhood growth and development. If possible, talk to relatives and others who knew you when you were young. Be sure to include subheadings and to cover the following areas of development: physical growth, motor development, language acquisition and first words used, particular habits or ways of expression, and anything else that may relate to this course about your environment, heredity, or behavior. Relate your behavior to specific references from your textbook. You are not required to include sensitive information about yourself.

If you decide to grade these papers, the following criteria may be used: inclusion of subheadings, grammar, relating behavior to specific references in the textbook, detail, and adequate coverage of different kinds of behavior.

SUGGESTED READING   Craig, G. (1983). *Human development* (3rd ed.). Englewood Cliffs, NJ: Prentice-Hall.

Gardner, H. (1982). *Developmental psychology* (2nd ed.). Boston: Little, Brown.

Reese, H. W., & Lipsitt, L. P. (1982). *Advances in child development and behavior.* New York: Academic Press.

$^{\Box}$32 GRITS AND DEVELOPMENT

Stephen F. Davis and Angela H. Becker
Emporia State University

This activity allows students to observe firsthand the physical and developmental effects of dietary deficiency. It extends over several weeks and will require the instructor to locate either a pregnant rat or a newborn litter of rats. Both the class and the instructor should be familiar with the American Psychological Association's code of ethics on the use of laboratory animals; the experiment should conclude with a return to a normal diet of the deprived rats.

CONCEPT

As a nation, the United States has become increasingly aware of, and concerned with, dietary influences on developmental processes, learned behaviors, and even personality factors. The amino acid *tryptophan* is a needed dietary component. One of its prescribed roles is to cause the release of growth hormone releasing hormone, which, in turn, causes the release of growth hormone. If tryptophan is lacking from the developing rat's diet, growth is retarded significantly. This phenomenon lends itself to an interesting and informative demonstration from which students can directly observe and learn several major psychological principles over a period of several weeks. For example, students can directly observe the effects of dietary differences on development. They then can determine if the dietary deficiency results in a learning deficit. Finally, an evaluation of the permanence of these developmental effects can be made.

INSTRUCTIONS

In order to conduct this project, you will need to acquire either a pregnant female rat or a litter of newly weaned rat pups. (The local pet store should be able to assist.) We recommend the first alternative because it will also provide students with the opportunity to observe the birthing process and the early development of the pups. At weaning (21 days of age) the students should randomly divide the litter into two groups. In order to make meaningful comparisons, there should be several males and females in each group. One group is then assigned to the "normal" feeding condition, whereas the second group is assigned to the "grits" condition. (Corn grits are used because they are deficient in tryptophan.) The remainder of the task is quite simple. The animals in the normal condition are simply fed standard rodent chow (e.g., Purina Laboratory Rodent Chow) on a free-feeding basis. The grits animals are fed instant grits (e.g., Quaker Instant Grits). For best results the grits should be mixed with warm water until the mixture is the consistency of thick soup. To approximate a free-feeding regimen, feed the grits animals in the morning and evening. (This will require only a few moments.)

Other than feeding the animals, your only other task will be to weigh the animals. Every other day, or even every third day, should be sufficient. You should notice that the normal animals quickly surpass the grits animals in terms of gross body weight. In our laboratory we have *consistently* found that after 8 weeks, normal animals always weigh between three and four times *more* than do the grits animals. Visually, this difference is most striking. When making such comparisons, be sure to compare males with males and females with females.

To determine whether learning ability has been imparied by the grits diet, you will need to construct a simple **T** maze. Nothing elaborate is needed, just something to force the animal to make a choice between two possible goals, one of which contains a reward. In order to ensure proper motivation, you should remove all food from your animals approximately 18–20 hours before the task begins. We have found that a piece of Fruit Loops cereal works quite well as the reward for a correct maze choice. Administer several trials (e.g., five or six) to each animal and record the number of errors each one makes before going to the correct goal. Use the mean number of errors per subject to determine if there are any differences between the groups. If you plan to test on more than one day, which is recommended, feed your animals a reduced amount *after* daily maze testing has been completed. Also, be sure to remove all food from their cages 18–20 hours before the next test session. A report by Remley, Armstrong, Gilman, and Mercer (1980) will provide helpful suggestions along these lines. Articles by Byrne and Smart (1980) and Fernstrom and Lytle (1976) also should be of interest.

To reverse the effects of the tryptophan deficiency, all you need to do is change the diet of the grits animals to the standard rodent diet you have been giving your normal rats. It will take some time, but the grits animals gradually will catch up with their normal littermates. Thus, the students also will see that the effects of a dietary deficiency are not irreversible in this case and therefore should be evaluated at all ages.

Obviously, the conduct of this project requires a rather substantial commitment of time and effort. Are the educational benefits in line with this expenditure of time and effort? The *very positive* reactions of our students would strongly suggest that they are. As already noted, the students observe firsthand the effects of a dietary deficiency on both growth and learning ability. They then are able to witness a reversal of the growth-related effects. Moreover, by directly involving your students in this project you also will have provided instruction in the conduct of an experiment, the procedures of careful data collection, and the ethics involved in animal research projects. The accomplishment of such educational objectives certainly appears to be in accord with the time and effort required to conduct this project.

REFERENCES

Byrne, E. A., & Smart, J. L. (1980). Delimitation of a sensitive period for the effects of early life undernutrition on social behavior of adult rats. *Physiology and Behavior, 23,* 131–133.

Fernstrom, J. D., & Lytle, L. D. (1976). Corn malnutrition, brain serotonin and behavior. *Nutrition Reviews, 34,* 257–262.

Remley, N. R., Armstrong, D. R., Gilman, D. P., & Mercer, L. F., Jr. (1980). Effects of early protein malnutrition on learning in the rat. *Bulletin of the Psychonomic Society, 16,* 377–379.

33 Teaching About the History of Childhood in Developmental Psychology Courses

Gregory F. Harper
State University of New York College at Fredonia

This discussion–activity can be used with any size class. No materials are needed, but an overhead projector could be used to show the historical outline. This would be a good introduction to a unit or course in child psychology, giving students a perspective that is likely to enhance the impact of subsequent material.

CONCEPT

Have you or your students ever asked the following questions: Why is child psychology a 20th-century phenomenon? What social factors have influenced the research agenda in the field? How has this research both reflected and influenced our conception of childhood as a cultural phenomenon?

This lecture–discussion provides a basis for answering those questions. It addresses (a) the historical origins of current child-rearing beliefs and practices (e.g., corporal punishment, or the notion of childhood innocence); (b) the extent to which factors that have traditionally influenced the treatment of children continue to do so; and (c) beliefs held by students about the proper treatment of children.

Because the discussion is intended to be illustrative, not exhaustive, I limit it to three representative periods of American history.

MATERIALS NEEDED

No materials are needed. I generally use the chalkboard to develop and organize the discussion, such that when the lecture is finished, the outline shown in Table 1 has been reproduced.

Obviously, you can use a transparency or slides to show this; however, I try to elicit student responses in developing the outline. The chalkboard lends itself to this type of spontaneity.

INSTRUCTIONS

Begin by listing and defining the major causal factors found on the left side of Table 1: infant mortality and life span, economic factors, sources of expert opinion on child development, and the major outcomes (i.e., stages of child development recognized, the value placed on children, general philosophy of child development, and representative practices).

Included here is a brief description of the historical eras represented, showing the interrelation of causal factors and outcomes. You may wish to research each of these areas more fully.

DISCUSSION

The theme of the culturally embedded context of conceptions about the child is basic to all other ideas in this discussion (Borstelmann, 1983). The prevailing historical view has been that the child is the servant of the society. Child nature, whether viewed as essentially evil or good, malleable or largely inherited, was viewed from

Table 1. *Factors Influencing Conceptualization of Childhood in Three Time Periods*

Factors	1700–1850	1850–1900	1900–present
Infant mortality	Very high	Lower	Very low
Birth rate	Very high	Lower	Very low
Economics	Agricultural	Industrial	Postindustrial
Stages recognized	Infant, adult	Infant, child, adult	Infant, child adolescent, adult
Value placed on children	Inheritor, laborer (economic)	Wage earner, old age security	Intrinsic
Expert	Religious leader	Physician	Many
Philosophy	Miniature adult	Sound mind, sound body	Natural needs

the perspective of adults. This view, in turn, was influenced by factors external to the child, whether religious, secular, social, or philosophical. The notion that the external environment should serve the child is a recent idea. The notion that children have unique needs and that they thrive best when these needs are met is an outcome both of child study and psychological theorizing (i.e., theories of Freud, Erikson, Piaget, etc.) and of a basic philosophical premise that the role of society in general, and parents in particular, is to nurture and develop whatever innate potential exists within the child.

Some possible questions for small group or class discussion are as follows:

1. What is the infant mortality rate now? Average family size? Average marriage (or reproductive) age? Do these factors continue to be related?

2. To what extent do economic factors influence our treatment of children? Do parents of different socioeconomic levels treat their children differently?

3. In the long view of history, are the current practices of placing children in daycare or childcare unusual?

4. What is the content of current expert advice on children? Who are the experts? What are parental goals for children today?

5. Why do people have children now that there are no economic incentives? How do their reasons for having children influence their day-to-day treatment of them?

6. Are we any less adult oriented in our conceptualization of childhood than in previous times?

7. To what extent do our views about the goodness of nature (i.e., the natural environment) influence our views about the "natural child"?

DESCRIPTION OF HISTORICAL ERAS

1700–1850

Infant mortality. Many writers (e.g., Aries, 1962) have argued that infant morality is the major factor influencing the conceptualization and treatment of children. High mortality rates are said to have prevented close emotional attachment or identification of parent with child. When most children died before 5 years of age, parents could not afford psychologically to become as emotionally invested in their children as is common today. Combined with a relatively short life expectancy, this created societal pressures for marriage at a young age and large numbers of children as a means of ensuring that some children would survive. Large families dictated early marriage to maximize childbearing potential; parents tended to be young and not necessarily more mature than young parents today.

Economics. American society at this time was largely agricultural. Large families meant more laborers, more efficient use of the land, and the assurance that wealth, which chiefly consisted of real estate, stayed within the family. More important, agricultural societies were not technological. This had two outcomes for children: (a) Children assumed adult occupational roles at an early age (i.e., the distinction between child jobs and adult jobs was largely one of size, speed, or judgment but not type of task; and (b) there was little value in formal education beyond learning the basics of reading, writing, and arithmetic. There was little need to see childhood as a distinct period of development or to see children as having unique characteristics apart from physical stature and mature judgment. Hence, children were generally regarded as small adults, held to the same standards of behavior, and they even dressed similarly. Failure to do so was perceived to be caused by weakness of character, breeding, temperament, or perhaps lax parenting. Evidence of this attitude can be seen in the treatment of children in, for example, Dickens's novels, family portraits, the absence of a literature on child care pertaining to children beyond infancy, and legal treatment that offered children no special considerations.

Sources of expert opinion. Clergy were the main source of expert opinion for this period. One cannot really characterize the treatment of American children at this time without acknowledging the strong religious influence on society in general. The treatment of many children was influenced by the prevailing Protestant religious philosophy emphasizing the sinful nature of humans (and children), the need to secure salvation for even the youngest child, and emphasis on outward manifestations of inward piety. The father was seen as the temporal authority and was generally justified in using any means, including physical punishment, to encourage such demeanor. Children were willful; breaking the will of the child was parental duty. However, parents were encouraged to teach by example; obedience through love was regarded as being superior to obedience through fear. In these Puritan-influenced societies, ignorance was seen as positively evil; salvation was impossible without knowledge (Borstelmann, 1983).

However, Greven (cited in Borstelmann, 1983) has suggested the coexistence of two parenting modes: the authoritative, as noted above, and the genteel. Genteel parents tended to assume the innocence of children and were more likely to be secular in their thinking. To them, parental love, reasoning, and even superior breeding or social status assured successful child rearing. Greven suggested that socioeconomic and geographic factors strongly influenced these views of children, a notion supported by Cable (1975). The writings of Newton and Locke are of this period, and the views they represent strongly influenced humans' views of themselves in the coming centuries. A shift can be seen in the latter part of this period toward what Wishy (1968) termed "the Child Redeemable." A large body of literature on child nurturing was suddenly available, offering advice on both practical matters and the moral training of children.

Outcomes. A summary of the outcomes of this period is as follows: There was a (a) blurring of the distinction between adults and children; (b) the father emerged as the authority figure; (c) corporal punishment was justified; (d) literacy was promoted; (e) the notion of parental responsibility for long-term outcomes of child rearing emerged; and (f) the family became the basic unit of socialization.

Infant mortality. There was a significant reduction in infant mortality attributable to improvements in medicine and in sanitation. Perhaps for the first time, parents could begin to measure their success not only in terms of the mere survival of their children but also in their continuing economic and social success.

Economics. The peak of the Industrial Revolution saw contradictory outcomes for children: A factory worker with a large family to feed naturally perceived this to be a disadvantage, and children became economic liabilities instead of assets. However, they were still viewed as necessary for "social security" in the absence of pensions and disability pay. Child-labor practices of the period reflected this contradiction: Children worked at adult jobs, but the horrendous working conditions threatened their very survival and contributed to the reforms that removed them from those settings. The demands of an industrial society included universal literacy and basic educational skills, contributing to the trend toward universal compulsory education. This need for education created the notion of childhood as preparation for adulthood, and the need to educate all children led to recognition of individual differences, age differences, and notions about aptitudes, skills, and abilities.

Sources of expert opinion. A reduction in infant mortality and an increased life span helped the physician to emerge as the expert not only on child health but also on child development. In the absence of a science of child development, physicians adopted a kind of analogy between mental and physical health. Many notions we have today about so-called "mental hygiene" derive from this time. Children were viewed as being mentally and physically delicate and therefore in need of protection from the corrupting influence of the outside world. Conversely, children needed to be toughened up by avoiding permissiveness or overindulgence.

Educational activities for children, in addition to being largely pre-occupational, included the idea that mental strength could be developed in a manner similar to physical strength; activities described as "exercises" were prescribed. The basic justification for much study was that it was difficult and required mental discipline to master.

The mother was viewed as the mentor of character development. Increasing attention was paid to the importance of early experience, proper environment, and the development of good habits. Children were seen as innocent, and their natural tendencies toward playfulness and affection as manifestations of goodness rather than evil.

Outcomes. The major outcomes are decidedly mixed: (a) One of the major reasons for having children (economic benefit) was removed; (b) as a result, children were abandoned and the founding of foundling homes and orphanages began on a large scale; (c) children worked in dangerous factories; (d) there was movement toward universal education; (e) individual differences were recognized; (f) childhood was identified as a separate period of development; and (g) there were improvements in the understanding of child health.

1900–Present

Infant mortality. Comparatively low infant mortality, combined with other factors, has resulted in a reduction in overall family size and a delay in the age at which individuals begin families. Improvements in birth control have made it possible for the first time for parents to consciously decide when or if they will have children.

Economics. American society is no longer industrially based. We are now in a postindustrial, technological or service-based economy, which requires increasing levels of education and psychological maturity in its workers. Thus, the total amount of time children spend in school has increased, and the age at which individuals enter the work force is delayed. Another outcome is the creation of a period during the life span—adolescence—when an individual is both physically and perhaps cognitively able to assume adult roles but is not permitted to do so. In contrast to most of human history, societies are increasingly age segregated, with few common areas of activity among children, adolescents, and adults. Economic benefit is no longer a reason for having children. Social security, pension plans, and disability insurance have all but freed children of any responsibility of the economic well-being of their parents. This has also freed parents to have children for only the best reasons. Parents can expect to measure their success as parents in the very long-term success of their children, a success measured not only in economic terms but also in terms of marital, occupational, and emotional happiness. Economic factors have also directly contributed to the decline of the extended family.

Sources of expert opinion. Physicians continue to occupy their now-traditional role as experts on child development, but they no longer hold a monopoly. As the definition of success in child rearing has expanded, so has the number of individuals prepared to give advice on various aspects of child development. These experts have, of course, been aided by advances in the scientific study of children. Most child rearing practices today are predicated on the notion, first championed by G. Stanley Hall (1891) and others, that children of various ages have needs that are distinct from one another and from adults. The overriding philosophy is to meet the needs of children and that, in turn, is the justification for studying child development.

Outcomes. In general, it can be argued that the last 70–80 years have been the best time in all of history to be a child, yet certain historical trends are still evident in the treatment of children: physical abuse, abandonment, unrealistic expectations regarding behavior, and so on.

REFERENCES

Aries, P. (1962). *Centuries of childhood: A social history of family life.* New York: Knopf.

Borstelmann, L. (1983). Children before psychology. In W. Kessen (Ed.), *Handbook of child psychology* (4th ed., pp. 1–40). New York: Wiley.

Cable, M. (1975). *The little darlings: A history of child rearing in America.* New York: Scribner's.

Hall, G. S. (1891). The contents of children's minds on entering school. *Paediatric Seminars, 1,* 139–173.

Wishy, B. (1968). *The child and the republic.* Philadelphia: University of Pennsylvania Press.

SUGGESTED READING

Greven, P., Jr. (1977). *The Protestant temperament: Patterns of child rearing, religious experience and the self in early America.* New York: Knopf.

deMause, L. (Ed.). (1974). *The history of childhood.* New York: Harper & Row.

34 Parent Panels: Bringing the Parent Into the Childhood and Adolescence Course

Janet Morahan-Martin
Bryant College

This activity is structured in a series of seven parent panels for a developmental psychology class and includes parent interviews and papers by students. However, the outline presented here could easily be adapted for one or two sessions in an introductory psychology class. This requires advance planning to arrange for the parents to visit class, and students need to have read the appropriate information ahead of time. If students do interviews or papers, that also should be done ahead of time. This would be best with classes of small to medium size if all students participate. It would be suitable for students at any level.

CONCEPT Parents play a critical role in the lives of children and adolescents. Frequently, however, in a course on childhood and adolescence, parents are relegated to a lesser role. Typically, in texts on childhood and adolescence, the study of parents focuses on genetics, modeling, and child-rearing patterns leading to adaptive traits or psychopathology in children. By implication, the emphasis is on how the parent molds or shapes the child. Although these approaches are valuable, I believe they do not adequately examine normal, healthy parenting or the interactive quality of parenting. The parent panels presented here provide a method of directly introducing parents to an undergraduate course. As the parents discuss their approaches to parenting, they bring to life the issues that parents face in raising their children. I have found using parent panels to be a particularly valuable method in teaching undergraduates who are not parents themselves.

Child rearing is an interactive process. The parent shapes the child and the child shapes the parent. Children continually change as they grow. As the child changes, so must the parent. The parent must adjust to the shifting needs of the child. Parenthood is thus a developmental process. Galinsky (1981) documented six stages of parenthood in her book *Between Generations.* Each stage of parenthood is characterized by themes and tasks that are largely determined by the child's developmental needs. These stages include expectant parents; parents of infants, toddlers, school-age children, and adolescents; and parents whose children are leaving home. Because these stages are the theoretical basis of the parent panels described here, I present a brief outline of the relevant issues for each stage.

During pregnancy, parents are in the first, or image-making, stage. The expectant parents accept the pregnancy, prepare for parenthood and for the birth. They build images of what the child will be like and what sort of parents they hope to be. Expectant parents also evaluate change in the relationships with their partners, parents, and friends. With the birth of the baby, parents enter the second, or nurturing, stage, which continues for about $1\frac{1}{2}$–2 years, when the child begins to say no. The key task of this stage for the parents is becoming attached to their baby. The parents face a changing sense of self because they must balance the needs of the baby with their own needs. They change in their relationship with each other and other significant people in their lives. During this stage, the parents compare the actual experience of parenting with their images of birth, their child, and themselves as parents. The third, or authority, stage of parenthood lasts from the time the child is about 2 until he or she is about 4 or 5 years old. As the child begins to become autonomous, the parents task shifts from nurturing to asserting responsible power and authority. The parents must determine acceptable limits for the child and how to enforce those limits and communicate with their child. In doing so, they must deal with their own often-shattered images of their not-so-perfect child and of themselves as the not-so-perfect parents. Also, they must deal with the child's sex role identity.

From the time that a child is about 4–5 until the approach of adolescence, the parent is in the fourth, or interpretive, stage. As the child's world expands beyond the safety of home and school, the parents' major task is to interpret the world to their child. This involves interpreting themselves to their child and interpreting and developing the child's self-concept as well as helping the child form values. The parents also must answer the child's questions about his or her expanding world and provide the child with access to the skills and information needed. The fifth, or interdependent, stage includes the child's teenage years. Parents must come to terms with the shock of their child becoming a teenager, and their images of themselves as parents must be reevaluated. Once again, the parent must renegotiate many of the issues of the authority stage: control, communication, understanding, and avoiding a battle of wills. They must deal with the child's sexuality and accept the teenager's identity and form new bonds with their almost-grown child. The sixth, or departure, stage happens when the child leaves home. This period is characterized by evaluations. As the parents prepare for the departure of the child, they review the child's years with them and reevaluate the entire parenting process. When the child actually leaves, the parents redefine their identities as parents of grown children, reexamine other important relationships, and measure their accomplishment and failures.

INSTRUCTIONS The parent panels are scheduled at the end of a unit of the appropriate developmental age of the child. Early in the semester, students choose the stage of parenthood they would like to present and form work groups on the basis of the stage they have chosen. These study groups are responsible for finding parents for the parent panel as well as conducting the session on the day of the parent panels.

Prior to the day of the panel presentation, all students are required to have read *Between Generations* on the appropriate parental issues for parents of children in the developmental age group being presented. Alternatively, other reading could be assigned. Additionally, each student in the study group for this parent panel is expected to conduct an interview with at least one parent of an appropriately aged child and write a paper summarizing the issues raised in this interview and whether the parent interview confirms the themes of parenthood raised by Galinsky (1981).

Students in the study group that is responsible for a given developmental age group are responsible for conducting the class on the day of the parent panel. However, it is recommended that the instructor introduce himself or herself to all of the parents who have volunteered to participate and briefly explain the purpose of their participation in the parent panel. On the day of the parent panel, the parents and members of the study group all sit facing the class. The parents, and their children if present, are introduced to the class by a member of the study group, who then briefly presents the issues of parenting that are relevant to the group and the findings from the interviews that the group conducted with other parents. The parents are encouraged to ask or comment on the presentation. Members of the study group then begin asking the parents about their experiences parenting a child of this developmental age. The study groups have previously been informed about open-ended questions and techniques for promoting discussion. Questions typically focus on the best and worst things about parenting a child of this developmental age; how the parents have changed; adjustments in their relationships with the child, their mate, other siblings, and their own parents; and in their life in general. Discussion among parents is encouraged, as are questions from the rest of the class. About 5–10 min at the end of the period is reserved for the parents to make comments and to again thank the parents for their participation.

DISCUSSION   Discussion is used to summarize the issues raised in the panel discussions. The focus is on developmental themes apparent from the parent panel and on contrasting the issues and themes of parents in this developmental age with parents in previous groups. Differences between styles of parenting are highlighted, as are the interactions between parent and child.

REFERENCES   Galinsky, E. (1981). *Between generations: The stages of parenthood.* New York: Berkeley Books.

35 THREE TASKS OF ADOLESCENCE: COGNITIVE, MORAL, SOCIAL

Mary Moore Vandendorpe
Lewis University

In this activity students should read the appropriate background materials before you engage them in this three-part discussion that is designed to bring the abstract theories they have read about to life. No materials are needed and any size class can participate.

CONCEPT   The cognitive theory of Piaget (1972), the moral theories of Kohlberg (1986) and Gilligan (1982), and the idea of social age-graded norms are key constructs for the study of adolescence. According to Erikson (1954), the formation of identity is aided by development in these areas.

Piaget postulated that formal operational thought requires an ability for hypothetical thinking and the generation of logical rules for abstract problems. Both Kohlberg (1986) and Gilligan (1982) proposed that adolescents become capable of moral reasoning and look beyond simple rewards and punishments. Kohlberg's theory is based on considerations of justice and equity, and seems applicable to most men. Gilligan's theory describes moral decisions as being based on relationships and responsibilities, and seems to be more relevant to women. In our society, age-graded norms are not highly visible because there is no single, universally recognized rite of passage. Nevertheless, adolescents are frequently caught between the norms for children and the norms for adults.

These developments make the adolescent's search for his or her own identity a difficult, although not impossible, struggle. They allow the teenager to generate several potential identities and to evaluate them in a reasonably logical manner. The adolescent can question beliefs and roles handed down by the family and society while still remaining sensitive to expectations about what his or her appropriate behavior should be. A successful resolution of identity depends on the ability to coordinate all of these elements.

INSTRUCTIONS   The activity is composed of three brief discussions:

1. After discussing the definition of the formal operations stage, introduce what I call the *"One Leg Scenario."* Ask the students, "Suppose that from this moment on, every human baby is born with only one leg. What would have to change?" Elaborate on the situation according to class questions; for example, state that the one-legged babies are normal in every other way. Then ask for ideas about what would have to change. The students quickly suggest changes in clothing, as well as in architecture. They often decide, for example, that stairs would disappear; the discussion will also include ideas of what cars and sports would be like. How would people travel—using crutches, riding on scooters, or just hopping on the one leg? Have the class consider how such an event might change our ideas of normality and might introduce new targets of discrimination. When the discussion seems to be finished, point out the

characteristics of formal operations that have become evident in the course of this exercise: hypothetico-deductive reasoning and consideration of every aspect of the problem.

This is a good example for the introductory class and can be a lead-in to discussions about divergent thinking and abnormal behavior as well as Piagetian stages.

2. Kohlberg's (1986) moral dilemma concerning Heinz and the druggist is cited in almost every text, but in my classes, two other moral dilemmas seem to be more realistic and interesting to undergraduates. They are exceeding the 55-mph speed limit and cheating in school.

Instruct the class to generate every reason that they can imagine for and against these two behaviors. Divide the class into small groups and have each group classify each reason according to its level of morality for both Kohlberg's (1986) and Gilligan's (1982) theories. They then decide what would be the appropriate rationale to use with an adolescent in order to encourage moral growth.

3. Students often fail to realize the impact of *norms* on our lives. Age-graded norms can be easily studied by asking the students how a freshman is supposed to act and how such expectations differ from those held for a senior. The major point, that norms are often age graded and that they have a strong, if usually unrecognized effect, on our lives, needs little elaboration.

DISCUSSION

The discussion should bring about an understanding of how these three abilities influence the development of identity. In order to emphasize themes of change and consistency, ask the students to write 10 answers to the item "I am . . ." in two sets—one for themselves currently and one for when they were 12 years old. Ask the students to describe the changes in their identity—such as viewpoint, sense of moral responsibility, and perception of self—that have occurred over time and also to note the similarities that have remained. Have them apply the theories discussed in this activity to their own development.

The second important area of discussion relates to the strong attraction many adolescents feel for ideologies. My classes have analyzed the ways in which the growing analytical ability, the stronger moral sense, and the need for controlling norms can make young people vulnerable to ideological groups: political extremists, religious cults, gangs, and so on.

REFERENCES

Erikson, E. (1954). *Childhood and society.* New York: Norton.

Gilligan, C. (1982). *In a different voice: Psychological theory and women's development.* Cambridge, MA: Harvard University Press.

Kohlberg, L. (1986). *The stages of ethical development from childhood through old age.* San Francisco: Harper & Row.

Piaget, J. (1972). Intellectual evolution from adolescence to adulthood. *Human Development, 15,* 1–12.

SUGGESTED READING

Thomas, R. (1985). *Comparing theories of child development.* Belmont, CA: Wadsworth.

CHAPTER V
SOCIAL PSYCHOLOGY

Each of the activities in this chapter is concerned with a different aspect of social psychology: As a whole, they offer a comprehensive overview of social psychological principles as they apply to the students' own experiences. Students who feel lost by dry theoretical explanations of social behavior will gain understanding through the active, participatory display of the theories provided in these exercises.

Activity 36 holds common human assumptions about behavior up to the light of empirical evidence, contrasting common sense judgment with testable hypotheses. Activity 38 tests the idea of "personal space" violation; this is a useful and intriguing experiment that should, however, be handled with care to ensure that students are not unduly upset or intimidated. Activity 40 uses an easy-to-learn game to show the different outcomes of competitive and cooperative behaviors within a group. It works best with small- to medium-size classes.

A very dramatic and engaging classroom experience should emerge from Activity 37, which is actually a problem-solving workshop requiring students to act out a conflict situation that makes almost daily newspaper headlines. This workshop spans three classes and, unlike the other activities in this chapter that require little or no preparation, requires extensive outside reading from the students as well as research on current events by the instructor. Activity 39 also deals with problem solving, but of a different nature: In this case, it focuses on the business world. The activity presents a complicated business problem and the psychological as well as the business ramifications of attempting a resolution. This is best suited to a more advanced class and fits in beautifully with a class on organizational psychology. Activity 41 replicates a famous study on obedience and aggression (although in a far more benign version) that should lead to some interesting classroom discussion.

36 HUMAN JUDGMENT VERSUS EMPIRICAL EVIDENCE

Jane A. Jegerski
Roosevelt University

This activity can be used with classes of any size. No prior knowledge is required, although you might wish to have students read the material on social norms and helping. No advance preparation is needed. This activity can be used in conjunction with a discussion of research methodology in field and lab settings or as an introduction to the value of research (as opposed to common sense) as a means of understanding behavior.

CONCEPT

This exercise demonstrates the need to test common social beliefs scientifically using a research study. This is accomplished using counterintuitive results from studies related to helping. The exercise also highlights the phenomenon of discrepant findings from laboratory study and field study and introduces a discussion of the norms that govern helping.

MATERIALS NEEDED

A copy of the Gruder, Romer, and Korth (1978) study on dependency and fault as determinants of helping behavior may be helpful.

INSTRUCTIONS

Present the design and procedure of the Gruder et al. (1978) study as follows:

> Randomly selected telephone subscribers received a "wrong number" phone call from a Mrs. Vernon, who was supposedly stranded on a nearby highway. She asked for Ralph's garage, and when she was told that she had the wrong number, she asked the subject to make the correct phone call for her in one of four randomly assigned ways:
>
> 1. Low dependency, fault. ". . . and I'm so upset. I was supposed to take the car into the shop last week to be repaired, but I forgot to do it. Now it's broken down."
> 2. Low dependency, no fault. ". . . and I'm so upset. The car was just repaired last week and it just broke down."
> 3. High dependency, fault. ". . . and I don't have any more change for the phone. Oh, I'm so upset. I was supposed to take the car into the shop last week to be repaired, but I forgot to do it. Now it's broken down."
> 4. High dependency, no fault. ". . . and I don't have any more change for the phone. Oh, I'm so upset. The car was just repaired last week and it just broke down."

The dependent measure was whether the subject helped by making the call.

After the class is familiar with the design of the study, have the students predict the results and tell why they made these judgments. My social psychology students invariably decide that the most help will be given to the target victim, Mrs. Vernon, in the high dependency, no fault condition and the least will be provided in the two fault conditions. Gruder et al. (1978) reported the following actual helping rates: high dependency, fault = 86%; low dependency, no fault = 69%; high dependency, no fault = 55%; and low dependency, fault = 52%.

DISCUSSION Discuss the results in relation to the hypothesized operation of two norms: the norm of social responsibility and the norm of self-sufficiency. Social responsibility suggests that we help others in need, especially when the victim's need is high (and being negligent about getting a car fixed can indicate greater dependency needs). The norm of self-sufficiency (that people take responsibility for their own welfare) would predict less helping when the victim's immediate dependency is low. It appears that these norms may be activated only in a realistic helping situation because the authors could not duplicate these results in a laboratory study in which subjects were asked to judge the likelihood of their helping in the four conditions.

Conclude the exercise with a discussion of possible reasons for the differences in helping responses in the lab and in the field settings (e.g., empathy as a mediator in the field, being asked the likelihood of helping rather than actually being asked to help). The discussion should emphasize the variable that might make the data run counter to one's intuitions about behavior.

REFERENCES Gruder, C. L., Romer, D., & Korth, B. (1978). Dependency and fault as determinants of helping. *Journal of Experimental and Social Psychology, 14,* 227–235.

SUGGESTED READING Agnew, N. M., & Pyke, S. W. (1987). This thing called science. In *The science game: An introduction to research in the social sciences* (4th ed., pp. 1–26). Englewood Cliffs, NJ: Prentice-Hall.

Christensen, L. B. (1988). What is science? In *Experimental methodology* (4th ed., 1–35). Boston: Allyn & Bacon.

Tedeschi, J. T., Lindskold, S., & Rosenfeld, P. (1985). An orientation to social psychology and its methods. In *Introduction to social psychology* (pp. 3–33). St. Paul, MN: West.

37 A PROBLEM-SOLVING WORKSHOP: THE MIDDLE EAST COMES TO PSYCHOLOGY CLASS

George Banziger
Marietta College

This simulation of conflict negotiation activity is appropriate for a social psychology course and spans three 50-minute class periods in which the instructor presents a background lecture during the first session and students are divided into groups for the simulation exercise in the last two sessions. In preparation for this activity, there is a fairly extensive outside reading assignment for the students. You may decide to adapt this activity to other issues, as well, such as the Vietnam war, abortion, Nicaragua, and so forth.

CONCEPT

International conflicts are played out on battlefields and at the negotiating table. These conflicts, and the attempts to resolve them, can be simulated at an interpersonal level to demonstrate the principles of conflict resolution (see Fisher, 1982; Myers, 1990) such as graduated reciprocation in tension reduction (GRIT), negotiation, and mediation. These simulations can also demonstrate the application of the principles of sensitivity groups, such as active listening (see Aronson, 1988), to the resolution of international conflicts.

MATERIALS NEEDED

Because some background preparation in the Middle East conflict is necessary, handouts or a presentation period on the history and culture of the area and on techniques of conflict resolution will be necessary.

Students will also need handouts describing the format of the simulation and listing suggested readings. Because good role playing is predicated on the performance of informed actors, some background reading is strongly recommended. This reading will include Fisher's (1982) chapter on international relations from a social psychology perspective, which should be familiar to all students. In addition, students assigned the role of Palestinians should read about the history and politics of Palestine (Friedman, 1989; Pipes, 1989); students assigned the role of Israelis should read about the history and politics of Israel (Spencer, 1988); and those assigned the role of U.S. negotiators should read about the history of United States–Israel relations (Quandt, 1977).

INSTRUCTIONS

Three 50-minute class periods are recommended, to be planned as follows:

1. The instructor lectures on the social psychology of international conflict, on problem-solving workshops, and on how they have been applied to international conflicts and gives an overview of the history, geography, and politics of the Pales-

---

Outlines of background material on history, culture, and conflict resolution, along with handouts describing the procedure for students, are available on request from the author at the Office of Continuing Education, Marietta College, Marietta, OH 45750.

tinian–Israeli conflict; at the end of the period, students are assigned randomly to one of three roles: Palestinians, Israelis, and U.S. negotiators.

2. The instructor briefly reviews the issue of Palestinian autonomy, which is the focus of the symposium (and the issue at which the 1979 Camp David accord left off), and divides the class into equal groups containing between 6–10 students. Each group will contain approximately the same number of Palestinians, Israelis, and negotiators. The students are encouraged to act out their assigned roles in a sincere, realistic, and informed fashion.

3. The second session of the workshop is continued during the last class. At the end of the workshop, students report on the status of their negotiations and present any solutions arrived at to the rest of the class. The instructor acts as a resource person, answering factual and policy questions to enhance in-role participation. Students are instructed to discuss the issue of Palestinian autonomy and the related problem of Israeli security by talking to each other as individuals and by listening to and reflecting others' feelings as is done in sensitivity groups. Arriving at a decision, however, is less important than their behavior in-role according to what they have read and heard.

DISCUSSION

To what extent were principles of conflict resolution utilized during the simulation? Was there any graduated reciprocation in tension reduction? Did the negotiations follow a pattern of increased concession-making, or did the participants harden in their positions?

From what was discussed in class about the parties to this conflict, do you think the acting Israelis and Palestinians behaved in role-appropriate ways? If they were truly role-appropriate, could a reconciliation ever be reached in sessions like these?

How is the conflict-resolution process affected by the introduction of violence (what if the participants had been armed)? Relate the latter question to the issue of competition versus cooperation, as it has been studied by social psychologists.

Did each side listen well to the other, or did it concentrate on expressing its own point of view? In real life could the two major parties involved in this conflict get together in this kind of situation?

The tendency in this simulation is to play the role of good student—in a kind of Pirandellian play within a play—and to move easily and swiftly toward conflict resolution. Students may need to be reminded that in the real world of international conflict, emotional positions are tenaciously held and players are more interested in promoting what they see as a God-given cause than in resolving a conflict with their ancient enemies.

Similar workshops led by professionals with real natives of these areas have shown, however, that some movement toward reconciliation can be made when individuals talk face to face, attempt to listen to the feelings of others, and utilize the principles of conflict resolution. As an additional requirement, students may be asked to write a short paper summarizing how their group performed, to what extent principles of conflict resolution were employed, and how the simulation could be improved.

REFERENCES

Aronson, E. (1988). *The social animal* (4th ed., pp. 325–364). New York: Freeman.

Fisher, R. J. (1982). *Social psychology: An applied approach* (pp. 473–515). New York: St. Martin's Press.

Friedman, T. L. (1989). *From Beirut to Jerusalem.* Farrar-Strauss.

Myers, D. G. (1990). *Social psychology* (3rd ed., pp. 483–514). New York: McGraw-Hill.

Pipes, D. (1989). *The long shadow: Culture and politics in the Middle East.* New Brunswick, NJ: Transaction.

Quandt, W. B. (1977). *Decade of decisions: American policy toward the Arab-Israeli conflict, 1967–1976.* Berkeley: University of California Press.

Spencer, W. (1988). *Global studies: The Middle East* (2nd ed.). Guilford, CT: Dushkin.

38 THE PERSONAL SPACE VIOLATION DEMONSTRATION

Peter R. Burzynski
University of Southern Indiana

Students will need to read background materials and will need to be exposed to the Ethical Principles in the Conduct of Research With Human Participants *before attempting this out-of-class field experiment. Except for copies of the handouts, no materials are needed. You can use this activity with any size class. The record sheet provided is for an unstructured observation, and the activity could be used in a methodology class as the first step in constructing structured observational forms.*

CONCEPT   Students can learn to evaluate the theoretical existence of "personal space," or the buffer zone we like to maintain around our bodies. This demonstration helps to reveal whether a penetrated or violated personal space can lead to discomfort or to a rise in aggressive feelings and behavior and can provoke discussions about stress-related illnesses or the sociopathology of criminal and aggressive behavior. The activity also requires that students evaluate the ethical considerations inherent in an exercise in which participants may be made to feel uncomfortable.

MATERIALS NEEDED   Each student will need to elicit the participation of two friends and two acquaintances. In addition, students will need instruction handouts, notebooks to record observations, and prediction and observation sheets like those shown at the end of this article.

INSTRUCTIONS   First, assign reading material that concerns the idea of personal body space (e.g., Cox, Paulus, & McCain, 1984; Rodin, Solomon, & Metcalf, 1976; Shiffenbaeur & Schiavo, 1976; Storms & Thomas, 1977). Emphasize those aspects of personal space violation that are especially sensitive to discomfort or may lead to aggressive behavior, namely, a feeling of constraint and a feeling of lack of control. Suggest also that other factors that may modify responses to personal space violation are sex-role behaviors (whether one feels more comfortable positioned closer to a same- or opposite-sex person) and degree of friendship (whether comfort is greater when friends or acquaintances are closer).

Next, offer students an opportunity to demonstrate the adequacy of the personal space theory in predicting emotional and behavioral responses. Give them a Prediction Sheet and an Observation Sheet and explain the situation you wish them to arrange.

Describe how the situation might vary with Participants 1–4 and have students complete the Prediction Sheet in class. Have the students hand in this sheet. After reading all the sheets, mark them and return them to the students. Then, indicate to the students that they have 2 days to arrange the four situations and to observe and record the results.

For each situation, students will select either a male friend, a female friend, a male acquaintance, or a female acquaintance to participate in the demonstration. A *friend* is defined herein as someone with whom the students share a regular, enjoyable relationship. An *acquaintance* is defined as someone known to the person but with whom a regular relationship is not established.

Before students conduct their demonstrations, it is very important that you discuss the ethical considerations involved in experiments in which people act as the subjects. Discuss the guidelines on ethical issues that are set forth in the American Psychological Association's *Ethical Principles in the Conduct of Research With Human Participants* (1982). The specific topics of informed consent, protection from mental harm, deception, and the right of subjects to withdraw from a study should be emphasized in the discussion.

After this, give each student a handout with instructions (see attached copy). Students will complete the demonstration on their own and will report on their findings to the instructor.

DISCUSSION   Students benefit from this activity in a number of ways:

1. They gain an appreciation of how difficult it is to organize and conduct a demonstration that is designed to study human behavior.

2. They formulate hypotheses and test them, thus experiencing the empirical method of data-gathering.

3. They learn about the complexities of describing emotional behavior or interpreting emotional responses from behavioral evidence.

4. They begin to inquire into the causes of undesirable behavior and to speculate on the predictability of human behavior in varying personal and social conditions.

5. Last but not less important, students will draw their own conclusions about the validity of the personal space theory.

The instructor of the class may help to focus thinking on these issues by reading aloud in class selected student explanations of predictions and outcomes. Students may then choose to debate or to defend these explanations.

REFERENCES   American Psychological Association. (1982). *Ethical principles in the conduct of research with human participants.* Washington, DC: Author.

Cox, V. C., Paulus, P. B., & McCain, G. (1984). Prison crowding research: The relevance for prison housing standards and a general approach regarding crowding phenomena. *American Psychologist, 39,* 1148–1160.

Rodin, J., Solomon, S. K., & Metcalf, J. (1976). Role of control in mediating perceptions of density. *Journal of Personality and Social Psychology, 36,* 988–999.

Shiffenbaeur, A., & Schiavo, R. S. (1976). Physical distance and attraction: An intensification effect. *Journal of Experimental Social Psychology, 12,* 274–282.

Storms, M. D., & Thomas, G. C. (1977). Reactions to physical closeness. *Journal of Personality and Social Psychology, 35,* 412–418.

Arrange to meet each friend or acquaintance separately in a room (in dorm, apartment, house, etc.) that has only one exit. By either removing chairs or placing objects on them, eliminate convenient places to sit down. Position yourself between the other person and the exit, beginning by standing 5 or 6 feet away. Maintain normal conversation while avoiding potentially emotion-charged topics. Some recommended topics are new music recordings, recent television shows or films, school activities, and so forth.

In the space of about 3–5 minutes, slowly shorten the distance between you and the other person. Avoid sudden or abrupt position changes but, rather, unobtrusively and continuously move closer. Try to maintain your position between the person and the exit, even if the person moves to get around you. At the end of 5 minutes, your position should be within 1 foot of the other person (if possible). *At no time should you attempt to physically restrain the other person from changing his or her position relative to yours.* At the conclusion of the time period, reveal to the person what you have been doing and why. Offer to answer any questions he or she might have. Be careful to do all that you can to ensure that the person is not unduly upset or confused.

During the 5-minute period, observe the following qualities of the person's response: (a) facial expressions (surprise, annoyance, enjoyment, suspicion, etc.); (b) amount of movement, toward or away from you or the exit; (c) the quality of his or her participation in the conversation, including level of volume or pitch, changing of topics, direct inquiry about what you are doing, and so on; and (d) any evidence of enjoyment, affection, anger, or aggression in his or her remarks or behavior.

Record your observations on the Observation Sheet. Compare these with the responses on the Prediction Sheet that you completed in class. On the back of the Observation Sheet, attempt to explain any differences between your predictions and the outcomes. Now hand in both of these sheets.

Prediction Sheet

Write a prediction for what the effect of your behavior will be (as described in detail on your instructions handout) on each of the following people:

1. A female friend:

2. A male friend:

3. A female acquaintance:

4. A male acquaintance:

Observation Sheet

Write your detailed observations of how your behavior (as described on your instructions handout) affected each of the following people:

1. A female friend:

2. A male friend:

3. A female acquaintance:

4. A male acquaintance:

---

39 FEDERATED SERVICES, INC.

Kenneth W. Olm
University of Texas at Austin

Alan L. Carsrud
University of Southern California

Do business and psychology make an agreeable marriage? This activity and exposure to a smattering of the recent publications about management style are evidence enough to convince most students that knowledge about psychological concepts is readily applied in the business setting.

At the minimum, students should be exposed to attitude theory and the research on the relation of attitude to behavior before engaging in this activity. However, if the activity is used near the end of the term when students have been exposed to a discussion of group norms, leadership, and principles of reinforcement, the discussion will be much richer. You will need to provide each student with a copy of the transcript. You can use this activity with any size class.

CONCEPT

This exercise is designed to encourage students to discuss the application of social psychology and personality theory within the context of everyday events in the business world.

MATERIALS NEEDED

You will need copies for each student of the case history materials on Federated Services, Inc., including Introduction, Current Situation, and Transcript.

INSTRUCTIONS

Students should be familiar with attitude theory and with research on the relation of attitude to behavior. Knowledge of cognitive consistency research and attitude change theory will improve students' responses to this exercise.

Have each student read all of the business materials from the perspective that he or she is the chairman of the board of this firm and has been handed the Transcript by an employee. Ask students to consider the employee's reactions and to gauge what they think the chairman would do.

DISCUSSION

Point out to the students that, despite the tone of the Transcript, the president was correct in expressing his concern about the attitudes and behavior of the employees. Focus the discussion around principles of social psychology. What effect will this meeting have on the employees' future attitudes and behavior? What are some alternative methods the president could have used, and how might these have been more (or less) effective in gaining the desired results? Will the president's way of dealing with the situation improve things, or should he be fired? Should any of the employees be fired? Will a lot of employees resign, and if so, why? What would make the others decide to stay? Students can also compare this management style with others that they have read about or experienced directly. Ask them to discuss their own working experiences and the ways in which work conflicts were handled.

Introduction

Federated Services, Inc., (FSI) is a relatively large wholesale and brokerage company dealing in building materials, hardware, and supplies. It serves 150 clients, 35 of whom own stock in FSI. The organization was founded over 22 years ago by a group of independent retailers who desired to lower their costs by controlling the intermediate supplier of their basic commodities. Sales revenues have increased every year, with a current sales volume of approximately $25,000,000.

In recent years, the company has faced increased competition in its geographic market area, which includes six states centered around Louisiana, from large national wholesale brokerage firms and chain operations. Because of the increase in competition and the fear of losing its clientele, the board of directors of FSI has been considering major changes in its strategic plan, including the relocation of its corporate headquarters. Possible strategic alternatives proposed in a recent study included buying out individual retailers to enter various markets directly. Although the board has talked with outside consultants, the majority of the board members and clients are from nonurban areas of the region and are reluctant to call upon outside help.

Currently, FSI is located in a small city that is not easily visited by the board. With the turnaround in the economy in recent months, there is a great deal of stress on FSI to supply its clients with goods and services in a very rapid and efficient manner. In fact, multiple distribution centers is a possibility under consideration.

All names are disguised in this material. No wording from the meeting transcript was altered or edited.

Current Situation

The president of FSI has held that position for more than 6 years. Originally trained as an accountant, he serves as the chief executive officer under the policy direction of a board of directors elected by approximately 35 stockholders, all of whom are active customers of FSI. The president owns no equity in the business.

Employment is fairly stable, with approximately 60 full- and part-time or temporary employees. There are four departments headed by four managers who report directly to the president. Although there is no exact designation of who is a "key" employee, there are 18 employees in key positions physically close to the president's office.

Pressures to expand markets and to offer greater assistance to clients, who in turn were subject to growing competition from chain operations, were causing increased tension at FSI headquarters. Reacting to these pressures, the president called a staff meeting early in June to relay his feelings about the current situation as he perceived it. Eighteen key employees, including all managers, attended the meeting.

The meeting was recorded by the president. A transcript was sent the next day to the chair of the board of directors. The chair in turn mailed a copy of the transcript to a former board chair, who was also a good friend. The chair followed up the mailing with several telephone calls to discuss the matter.

The former chair called a consultant to ask for her interpretation of the transcript and to solicit her advice prior to the next meeting of the board, about a month away. The current chair had not made a definite decision to place the matter of the staff meeting transcript on the agenda of the next board meeting.

Transcript of the President's Staff Meeting

Federated Services, Inc.
Recording of Staff Meeting in Office of President and Chief Executive Officer

June 12, 1984
Present: 18 key employees, including all managers

I am recording what I have to say today for the edification of those who can't be here today.

I am satisfied that many of you have seen the sign on the back end of a car that says, "I'm mad, Eddie"; well, I'm mad. I have spent a lot of time looking at FSI, FSI staff, and FSI attitude and I do not like what I see worth a damn. We have developed a bad attitude about our job, about our responsibilities, and about what we are doing here and I don't like it at all. Effective today Mr. and Mrs. Prima Donna do not work here anymore.

FSI, whether you like it or not, is a service organization. We are not a co-op, we are not a buying group, we are not anything other than a service to our dealers. We buy for their benefit, we work for their benefit, and

(Continued on next page)

(Federated Services, Inc.—*continued from previous page*)

contrary to popular belief, FSI does not exist to deliver you a paycheck with you putting forth just as little as you can do to earn it.

Ladies and gentlemen, I am here to tell you this morning you better start right now doing everything you can do. I don't care what your job description says. Your job is to do whatever you can to make things go better around here. About a year ago or less I had something to say about the manner of dress. That lasted about fifteen days. Nobody cares. I talked about being here at eight o'clock in the morning and leaving at five o'clock in the afternoon. That lasted about thirteen days. Don't care! Effective today every blessed one of you including myself are on probation. Your job will depend upon what you do around here effective immediately. Did you get that? You are going to prove that you have the need to work and want an opportunity to work and have a desire to work for FSI. That includes me, Bob, James, Charles, and every blessed one of us are on probation. If you can't work, if you won't work, the street is going to be awfully full of people. I don't believe that there is a soul sitting here that really has enough pride in his job to do the job the way it should be done. You screw it up, big deal! I have been advised of probably 10 or 12 situations this past week where we have cost a dealer anywhere from $20 to $200 just because of some stupid little mistake. That's bad, but that's not the worst part of it. The worst part of it was when the dealer told us about it, our attitude was "So what, I made a mistake, big deal!" That is not going to work any more. If you are not proud enough of your work to do every blessed bit of it, the best that you have the ability to do, I feel sorry for you but that's not the end of the story. How you do your job and how you present yourself represents you, represents your supervisor, represents FSI, and it represents me. And I don't like the way you all are representing me. I am satisfied your supervisor does not like the way you are representing him, and damn it, you should not like the way you are representing yourself.

If you do not have enough pride to do everything that you can do 8 hours a day the very best that you can, you're not good enough to work for me; and that's from the start of it to the end of it. Just because you wind up making a buy of $50,000 or $100,000 or negotiating a program that is going to put together 2, 3, or 4 million dollars' work of business for FSI, that's all fine and dandy, but if you do not pay attention to the last minute details that go along with supporting that, you haven't done your job and you're going to do your job or you will not be here. If you don't care how you work that's fine with me, but I care how you work. If you're not up to it we'll get somebody that is.

Sick time is provided for your benefit so that you are somewhat reimbursed when you happen to have an illness. It's not paid vacation, it's not a day off, it's not getting to leave early. It seems awfully strange to me when you start looking at about one-half to one dozen of you, you get sick an awful lot. I will be looking very carefully at sick time. Sickness is something that is going to occur. That's something that will occur especially if you are a mother. When you have a sick baby you have to take care of the sick baby and I understand that. The deal is the piddling little headaches and upset tummies and, probably more realistically, the desire to not have to work today or get off early on a weekend trip somewhere, et cetera, is not going to get it. You darn well better be sick. I have had an occasion, and not because I am backtracing and checking up on people, but occasionally I have had an opportunity to call somebody's home who was sick and guess what, there was nobody there. I don't know what you call it but I call that lying. Damn it, if you want the day off ask for the day off. Don't come up here telling me that you are sick. I expect every soul here at 8:00 a.m. in the morning and there are no excuses.

That railroad track out there has been out there for 100 years and it will be out there for 100 years more. You darn well better be cognizant of that train. When you figure it so darn close so that you can get here right at the stroke of 8:00, you're cutting it just a little bit too close. I said I didn't want to see any tennis shoes up here, and except for one occasion, I don't see them. I'm telling you right now I don't want to see any of the thong sandals up here, either. I do not want to see faded out blue jeans and I don't want to see sloppy tee shirts up here. This is a professional organization and you should come up here looking like a professional. When you come in here looking like a dump, you act like a dump, and you work like a dump. The way you dress demonstrates your attitude. I expect to see you up here looking presentable and ready to do a decent job. I am a little bit tired of walking around here and seeing some people just busting their butts trying to do a good job and walk around the corner and there's three or four of you huddled up and having a hen party or a bull session sitting on your butt not doing a thing. Buying Department, the next time Bob is out of town and I walk back to Sue's desk and I see five or six of you huddled up having a hen party every one of you are on the elevator. Process Department, next time I walk in there and see you all gathered around Jane's office you are going to be on the elevator going home. Lumber Department, I don't expect to walk back here and see everybody's feet propped up having a gay old time. If the dealers are not calling you with business you dang well better be calling

(*Continued on next page*)

them. I said a while ago and I am going to say it again, FSI does not exist just to deliver a paycheck to you. If business is not coming to you, you need to be thinking about why: "Maybe I haven't quite done the job that I ought to do, maybe the business is going somewhere else." I can tell you for a surety in some cases that is what the deal is. We feel as if an FSI dealer is obligated to us. Sweetheart, I am here to tell you it's just the other way around. We do not speak in terms of customer relations, because we feel like we have a captured audience out here. That's not true. They are your customer, they are your only customer. I am afraid that if we had to deal with the public on the basis that we are now dealing with our dealers there would be several of us getting very lean because we would be starving to death. Sure we have a lot of dealers out there that are going to give us their business in spite of everything we do. That may be unfortunate for them. When a problem develops that problem has not been adequately solved until you are happy, until the dealer is happy, the sawmill is happy, or the manufacturer is happy. If you finish up and you put to rest what you call a solution to the problem and everyone who has had to deal with that problem is not tickled to death, you have not adequately solved the problem.

Call backs. As usual, you consistently hear that "so and so is not calling me back." That may be and may not be. If you are smart, the next time I hear that "so and so did not call me back," I may come check it. If Sonny Smith calls you, if Lee Jones calls you, if Ben Brown calls you, if Bob Johnson calls you and you call them back and they are not there to take your telephone call, you best not depend on their people to get the message to those people that you called them back. If I can't look at your work papers and tell that you called them back, then I am going to assume that you didn't. That occurs a lot of times. It is probably the reason why in many, many cases people say "you didn't call me back." I know how difficult it is. You call somebody, they call you back, you call back and they are busy, they call you back and you're on the phone, and you play telephone tennis. That's fine and dandy. I have had a lot of telephone calls when I didn't get the message. I am sure the same thing occurs to them, so if you are smart and you want to make darn sure that you have your bases covered, you better have on your working papers a note that on a certain time you called back and that whomever you called was not available. If you cannot prove to me that you did call I am going to assume that you didn't. Every blessed part of your job down to the most minute detail is just as important as the first start on it. The expression, "Well, I'll fix that purchase order if it will make your job easier" stinks!! That purchase order is part of your job. If you don't want to do it, then, by God, we will get somebody that does. When a problem develops, it has really amazed me that we can screw up just about any way that we want to screw up, and you know it really doesn't get to be a big deal until we express the attitude, "So what, I screwed up. Big deal: That's your tough luck, buddy!" That's when the problem really starts. It seems to me in a lot of cases a lot of the stupid mistakes are just because we do not have our head where it ought to be. We are not concentrating on what we are doing. Reading the paper, reading the racing forms, placing bets with your bookie, that's all fine and dandy, if that's what you want to do, but 8:00 to 5:00 you are mine as long as you are working here, and I expect to see you attending to FSI business, and that is down to the most minute detail. I understand the problems, nobody has to tell me the difficulties that you have on a lot of occasions dealing with some of the FSI dealers in some situations. That is not an excuse. Effective right now the motto of FSI employees is YES, AND THEN YOU FIND A WAY. If you don't want to do it fine, we will get somebody that does. I have laying on my desk some information that was sent to me by a dealer where we screwed up. That dealer has informed the individual who screwed it up to fix it up and that individual's job depends on whether they get the thing straightened up or not. I am not going to say anything about it. About June 30, I will look into the situation and see if the problem has been settled. If it has, fine, if it hasn't one of the happy faces you see around here will not be here after that. That's only one of probably twenty or thirty that I have heard of in the last 2 weeks. And that's probably only one of another twenty or thirty that I will hear of in the next 2 weeks. But I tell you what I will hear: I will hear that that problem, wherever it occurred and however it occurred and whoever's fault it is, we have busted our butt to fix it. Our dealers are grown men, they can take bad news. You go do the best you can and if you can't change the situation and you tell them, "I have done all I can do and the result is still not good," they are grown men and they are just tickled to death that you cared enough to even try.

I do not really understand the attitude that is expressed when a dealer calls up here and wants something or has a problem, and we tell them on the phone before we have even wiggled our butt in our chair that we can't do anything about that, sorry, and hang up the phone. I do not understand where you get off on that. Lazy, I don't care, no job pride, I don't know where it comes from. But I will tell you where it is going, it is going out of this room from now on or it's going down the elevator with you for the last time. One or the other!! I am

(*Continued on next page*)

(Federated Services, Inc.—*continued from previous page*)

prepared right now to accept resignations from any or all of you, and I am prepared right now, if it necessitates it, to put every blessed one of you in the street. At that time and that time alone will we have an excuse for not doing our job. There is no excuse. You didn't try, you don't care, whatever, there is no excuse, none whatsoever. If you have attempted everything that you have the ability and the knowledge to do to solve a problem, until that has been exhausted, there is no excuse.

Does anybody have a problem with my drift going over your head? Has anybody misunderstood anything that I have talked about? I don't see any hands. I don't get mad very often, but I am mad now, and when I get mad I generally react. I am telling you here and now, folks, you better get serious about your job or you better get serious about finding another one. Any questions? If any of you care to resign, I will be in my office ready to accept them. They can be brief. You can just write "I quit" and sign your name. That's all I need to know. For those that stay and don't do your job, my note to you will be just as simple, "You're fired," and my name will be signed. Have you got it? Then go get it.

40 COMPETITIVE VERSUS COOPERATIVE BEHAVIOR

Frank Hollingsworth
Coatesville Area Senior High School

Small-to-medium classes will enjoy participating in these "circle toss" games in which a simple change of instructions will up the ante and provide a forum for discussing competitive and cooperative behavior. You will need one or more soft rubber balls. You may choose to have students either read the Psychology Today article cited or engage in the games without prior exposure to the concepts.

CONCEPT
Which activity would evoke a better performance level—competitive or cooperative? If this question were directed toward the average student, he or she would probably answer that competition is superior to cooperation. Although this assumption is widely held, is it valid? The following experiment was designed to allow students to compare performance levels resulting from both competitive and cooperative activity.

MATERIALS NEEDED
You will need a foam rubber soft ball.
   You may also choose to have students read the Kohn (1986) article, "How to Succeed Without Even Vying."

INSTRUCTIONS
The game is called *Circle Toss.* The object is to toss the ball to another member of the circle for 5 minutes, making as few errors as possible.
   The first game will be cooperative. Students should stand in a circle facing each other. Designate a student to begin the game by calling the name of another person in the circle and tossing the ball underhanded to that person. The receiver catches the ball and calls the name of another player and proceeds to toss the ball to that member.
   If a person makes a mistake, for example, drops the ball or throws it out of reach of the receiver, the scorekeeper will count it as one error. The activity should last about 5–7 minutes.
   After time is up, stop the game and tally the errors.
   The second game will be competitive. Start the game again, but this time tell the students that if they make an error they will be out of the game and the last person standing will be the winner. (A reward could also be promised to the winner.) Tell the players that they are not to call the person's name before they throw the ball. The object of the game is to keep the ball in play for 5 minutes with few errors. They should play until one player is left or 7 minutes have passed. Count the errors for this round.

DISCUSSION
Have students compare the results of both games. In which trial did their scores come out better? Why does competition have this effect? Is it only individual competition that has this effect? If the teams were cooperating within and competing

between, what effects might there have been? Does competition tend to enhance the motivation of those high in need for achievement? Does competition enhance the performance of a well-learned response and inhibit the performance of things less well-learned?

Have students consider why cooperation, rather than competition, produces greater benefits for the group as well as the individual, especially in light of the article from *Psychology Today*.

REFERENCES   Kohn, A. (1986, September). How to succeed without even vying. *Psychology Today*, pp. 22–28.

SUGGESTED READING   Axelrod, R. (1984). *The evolution of cooperation.* New York: Basic Books.
Orlick, T. (1978). *Every kid can win.* Chicago: Nelson-Hall.
Walker, S. (1980). *Winning: The psychology of competition.* New York: Norton.

41 THE AGGRESSION MACHINE: A SIMULATION

Stephen J. Dollinger
Southern Illinois University at Carbondale

You will need one deck of playing cards and two rubber bands for each participating group in this in-class simulation of an aggression experiment. Five students can participate in a demonstration, and a sixth student can act as the recording secretary. It is best if students know little about compliance, obedience, and aggression before engaging in this activity, which can serve as an excellent introduction to a unit on aggression.

CONCEPT

When the topic of aggression is introduced, this activity can be used to simulate (in a very general way) the classic aggression machine paradigm in which the "learner" of a task is given electric shock by a "teacher" for failing to deliver the correct answer to a question. In this paradigm, the subjects are led to believe that they are participating in a learning experiment; what is actually being observed is their capacity for aggression. The correctness of the learner's responses is not an objective quality but rather is subject to the discretion of the experimenter, who informs the teacher of any incorrect responses and explains the necessity of using electric shock in this type of "learning" experiment. The purpose of the simulation is to show how much shock the teacher is willing to administer.

Research with this paradigm has brought to light some troubling considerations regarding the issue of obedience (Geen, 1976; Feshbach & Weiner, 1986; Phares, 1984), especially with regard to the implicit pressure of authority figures (Milgram, 1974). One of the more interesting findings in the area is demonstrated in this activity: the matching escalation/de-escalation of aggression in the 2-person aggression–machine situation (Epstein & Taylor, 1967).

MATERIALS NEEDED

You will need a standard deck of playing cards and two rubber bands that are small enough to just fit around an adult's wrist. Six students can participate in each demonstration of this simulation, playing the following roles: 2 players, 2 partners (or "announcers"), 1 recorder (or "secretary"), and 1 experimenter. In a larger class, several demonstrations, with 5 players each, can be held simultaneously. You will need a deck of cards for each simulation.

INSTRUCTIONS

Explain to the class that this simulation is similar to an aggression experiment and that, in place of electric shock, aversive stimulation from a rubber band is used. (For ethical reasons, "shocks" are self-administered in this activity; judging from participants' comments, this did not undermine the effectiveness of the simulation.) Do not mention the escalation phenomenon.

Seat 2 volunteers facing opposite walls to prevent visual communication with one another. Provide them with numbered cards from 1 (ace) to 10, which will signify the intensity level of shock that they will apply to the other player when they win a trial of the game. Because participants cannot see each other, each player is assigned a partner who announces the opponent's chosen "shock intensity."

The basic procedure illustrates the randomness of the situation. Each trial consists of the experimenter drawing a card at random from those remaining in the deck. Each player is assigned a color, either red or black. The winner of each test is the player whose color is drawn from the deck by the experimenter. On each trial, the players are told who the winner is, and the winner selects a shock intensity level to be self-administered by the loser. For example, when a red card is drawn, the player whose assigned color is red is the winner; he or she will choose the shock intensity. The winner signals his choice by holding up a card with the appropriate number. The "shock" is effected by pulling the rubber band out to a distance roughly proportional to the specified shock intensity and then snapping the wrist (the greater the intensity required, the further out the band is pulled). The sequence and level of shock intensities is recorded by the secretary.

DISCUSSION

I have found that students initially select low-level intensities (1 or 2). During one demonstration that I conducted, a student decided, apparently on a whim, to administer a 5, and from that point on the aggression escalated. It is worth noting that at that point there was also an increase in class interest. As the players began to feel pain in their wrists, there was a de-escalation of the aggression as well as of class attention.

The debriefing can lead to a useful discussion about the kinds of messages each player thought the other was trying to communicate, the means of avoiding situations that involve this escalation of aggression, and the relevance of such phenomena when negotiating with aggressors or reducing international conflict.

Other issues that should be raised are the ethical considerations of this kind of experiment, particularly with regard to the Milgram (1974) study, in which subjects believed they were actually administering electric shock to other people, complete with simulated screaming. This can lead naturally into considerations of how aggression toward others can be made acceptable within certain contexts (as a scientific experiment, as a "necessary evil") or by the presence of an authority figure. This becomes especially interesting when it is applied to a discussion of current and historical events, which provide many examples of aggression toward a particular group being sanctioned for the cause of what is believed to be a greater good.

The discussion can conclude with a presentation of some of the newer findings about aggression.

REFERENCES

Epstein, S., & Taylor, S. P. (1967). Instigation to aggression as a function of degree of defeat and perceived aggressive intent of the opponent. *Journal of Personality, 35,* 265–289.

Feshbach, S., & Weiner, B. (1986). *Personality* (2nd ed.). Lexington, MA: Heath.

Geen, R. G. (1976). *Personality: The skein of behavior.* St. Louis, MO: Mosby.

Milgram, S. (1974). *Obedience to authority.* New York: Harper & Row.

Phares, E. J. (1984). *Introduction to personality.* Columbus, OH: Merrill.

CHAPTER VI
PERSONALITY, ABNORMAL,
AND CLINICAL
PSYCHOLOGY

To many students, personality and abnormal psychology are at the root of their fascination with psychology and represent what psychology is all about. These activities will allow them to use the concepts learned in class. Most of these activities require little or no prior knowledge of psychology on the part of the students, and most need minimal preparation on the part of the instructor. All are adaptable to any class size.

Activity 42 guides students through the completion of a psychosocial family tree and fits classes on clinical, counseling, or developmental psychology especially well. Activity 44 delineates the differences between state and trait in eliciting behavioral responses, and Activity 46 is a quick, easy demonstration of the illusion of control that lends itself to a discussion of gambling and other chance-based behaviors. Activity 49 looks at the role of paradigms in human behavior, giving students a case study to analyze.

Some of these activities attempt to give students a sense of actual clinical assessment and intervention. Activity 45 gives them a chance to use their knowledge in a mock assessment and intervention situation, and Activity 47 demonstrates verbal conditioning in the client–therapist relationship. Activity 48 has students role-play various kinds of abnormal behavior in a series of skits designed to accompany relevant lecture periods.

Activity 43 describes a two-sided, year-long assignment on personality theories. It relies on a solid understanding of the philosophy of science to be most effective.

42 THE PSYCHOSOCIAL FAMILY TREE

J. David Arnold

St. Lawrence University

The act of constructing a family tree can be adapted to suit courses in clinical, counseling, tests and measurements, social, developmental, and adjustment psychology as well as in abnormal and personality psychology. The instructor can demonstrate an example of the family tree on the board or can provide a handout when the assignment is made. Students need no prior knowledge and, except for the example of the family tree, no materials are needed. The activity itself is done outside class, and a week or more between the assignment and the due date is recommended. The family tree may be analyzed in small group discussions in class or in a written assignment.

CONCEPT

The psychosocial family tree is based on Bowen's (1978) multigenerational systems theory of family therapy. In short, Bowen's theory examines how transgenerational family psychosocial factors may contribute to the development of psychopathology. The following activity is a direct classroom adaptation of Bowen's family assessment diagram known in the family therapy field as the *genogram* or *familygram*. The genogram was originally designed for the clinical setting to schematically document psychosocial factors such as ethnic, religious, and occupational factors across at least three generations of a family. Subsequently, Bowen's genogram has been adopted as a means of studying the normal family life cycle (Carter & McGoldrick, 1980).

In the classroom, I refer to Bowen's (1978) genogram as a psychosocial family tree because it provides a more salient description of the activity, and the term *family tree* always seems to stimulate student enthusiasm for the project. This activity may be used as an example of family therapy assessment in clinical, counseling, or test and measures courses; the activity may also be used as a self-exploration exercise in any course that examines social influences or group processes, such as life-span development, adjustment, personality, social psychology, or relationship courses.

MATERIALS NEEDED

You will need large sheets of paper for drawing.

INSTRUCTIONS

The instructor may want to present a completed example of a psychosocial family tree on the board or on a handout before directing students on how to create their own psychosocial family tree (examples may be found in Carter & McGoldrick, 1980, or Papp, 1977). Students should use an oversized piece of paper when drawing their family trees in order to include all of the following information about three generations of their family.

Students can begin work either at the top of the paper, starting with their grandparents, or at the bottom of the paper, starting with their own generation (i.e., the student and his or her siblings and cousins). Female relations are represented by circles and male relations are represented by squares. Marriages are indicated by a horizontal line that connects the two spouses. The date of the marriage should be placed at the beginning of the marital line, and any subsequent separations or divorces should be noted by a slash on the marital line (one slash for a separation, two for a divorce). Multiple marriages may be diagrammed by branching off new marriage lines. Offspring are placed on descending vertical lines off of the marriage line in order of birth, from left to right. The spacing of offspring should be planned in such a way as to accommodate the offsprings' spouses and subsequent children. For example, if the first-born child has seven children, there should be sufficient space between the first- and second-born to include the seven children. For all family members, all of the following information (when relevant) should be written next to or within their circle or square: dates of birth and death; highest level of education; occupation; place of residence; chronic health problems, illnesses, or accidents; religious preference; cause of death; and the family's ethnic identity. Students will probably need time to consult with their parents or grandparents to gather some of this information.

DISCUSSION   After completing their family trees, most students will have learned something new about their family backgrounds. Many students report having interesting discussions with their parents and grandparents while working on their trees. Although this happens infrequently, some students may discover some aspect of their family background that is disturbing, and instructors should be prepared to refer these students for counseling.

To analyze their psychosocial family trees, students should begin by identifying certain patterns of continuity and discontinuity within and between generations of their family. For example, is going to college a typical or atypical pattern within and between generations of the student's family? Thus, for all of the demographic information listed for each family member, students should try to recognize as many trends as possible.

After patterns and trends have been listed, depending on the type of course, students should discuss the psychological significance of each pattern or trend. For example, if a couple is the first to get divorced in three generations of a family, will the couple's respective families accept the change in marital status, and how will the family reaction affect the couple's postdivorce adjustment?

The family's ethnic orientation is an important consideration when students examine their psychosocial family trees. I have students address their own family's ethnic orientation in terms of six factors: emotional expressiveness, the relative importance of extended family members, whether nonfamily members are ever treated as family, how problems (physical and psychological) are dealt with, attitudes toward work and money, and the extent to which religious and political ties are important. These factors are influenced by variables other than ethnic orientation alone. I have students use McGoldrick, Pearce, and Giordano (1982) as a reference guide to assess whether or not their families are representative of a particular ethnic orientation. Students learn about the ethnic origin of some of their family's values, how ethnic differences may contribute to interpersonal conflict, and how some families are less trusting of nonfamily members than are other families.

In summary, the psychosocial family tree may be used as a pedagogical tool to increase student understanding of the effects of family socialization on the individual, group, or clinical assessment of families. Although instructions for the construction of the psychosocial family tree will be consistent from course to course, instructors should design the student analysis of the family tree to illuminate their particular course content.

REFERENCES   Bowen, M. (1978). *Family therapy in clinical practice.* New York: Jason Aronson.

Carter, E. A., & McGoldrick, M. (Eds.). (1980). *The family life cycle: A framework for family therapy.* New York: Gardner.

McGoldrick, M., Pearce, J. K., & Giordano, J. (Eds.). (1982). *Ethnicity and family therapy.* New York: Guilford Press.

Papp, P. (Ed.). (1977). *Family therapy: full length case studies.* New York: Gardner.

43 AN EXERCISE FOR PERSONALITY COURSES ON METHODOLOGICAL ISSUES OF ASSESSMENT

George S. Howard and Paul G. Konstanty
University of Notre Dame

Although no materials are needed, the instructor must be familiar with the philosophy of science to skillfully pull off this two-fold activity, which spans the length of the personality course. Part of the activity entails small group projects in which class presentations and papers will be required. Another (seemingly unrelated) part is the assignment of a personal journal beginning with the first day of class. Students won't know until the end of the course, when they are asked to write an ungraded essay, how the two relate. Although students have an opportunity to delete parts of their journal entries, the instructor should be prepared to counsel or refer students who reveal problems with which they need help.

CONCEPT   At various points in the history of psychology, the study of persons has taken widely divergent conceptual and methodological twists. An important task for undergraduate psychology courses is to convey to students how the answers that psychologists arrive at are both a function of their approach to the questions and a function of the methods they use to secure data on those questions.

    This class project invites students in a personality class to reflect on how assumptions about human behavior and its possible causes are related to the methods of investigation deemed appropriate and how these methods, in turn, color the outcomes of empirical investigations. The exercise is intended to give students a glimpse of the fundamental problems that confront psychology in its continuing struggle to become a coherent intellectual enterprise.

MATERIALS   You will need a notebook (journal) for each student.
NEEDED

INSTRUCTIONS On the first class day, tell students that they will form small groups of four or five members each whose task will be to study various interesting individuals of their choice (suggestions garnered from Klos, 1976, and White, 1974, were helpful here). In our class, we included names from three categories: (a) well-known public figures (e.g., Richard Nixon, Phil Donahue, Howard Hughes), (b) acquaintances at school (e.g., several friends, an associate provost of the university, the personality course instructor), and (c) fictional characters (e.g., Garfield the cat, characters from novels). Fictional figures proved far less effective for demonstration purposes; therefore, we recommend that they not be used.

    In the second class, form the groups and have students decide who they will study. Instruct students "to use whatever methods of investigation possible, and any data sources available, to get to know this person." Assign each group one 15-minute block of class time during the first month or so to present their overall investigation strategy to the class and to receive constructive feedback (before investigation begins) from the rest of the class and from the instructor. We also gleaned research ideas from the course textbook (Mischel, 1981), class lectures, and consultation with other psychology faculty members.

Each group works together to plan and delegate tasks, and each student is responsible for a paper that will be graded. Projects should be completed early in the last month of the course.

On the first day of class, assign a concurrent project. Instruct each student to keep a personal journal for the next 3 months (see Hettich, 1976, for helpful suggestions on journals), requiring daily entries about events in their lives and their reactions to them. These should include any insights gained from their class work. The journals are graded on a pass/fail basis according to whether the student made an honest effort to perform the task. In our experience, there was enormous variability in the journals, which ranged in length from 19 to 175 pages. Offer students the option to remove information from the journal before submitting it to the instructor to discourage them from monitoring and censoring their thoughts.

One goal of the class projects was to highlight the implications that necessarily follow from making various ontological assumptions (in this case, about human nature) that lead to decided preferences for some types of theoretical explanations and methodological approaches to the exclusion of alternative theories and methods. In a critique of attribution theory research, Buss (1978) pointed out that attribution theorists prefer to view human behavior as being produced by efficient causes (those which bring about changes) but not by final causes (the end, or *telos*, for which change is produced). This forms the basis for the cause versus reason controversy current in psychology (see also Howard, 1984a; Rychlak, 1983; Secord, 1984). Whether one takes the perspective of the actor or the observer (which represents a methodological decision) will further cement whether investigations yield (efficient) causes as being responsible for human behavior or whether (final cause) reasons are seen as producing human action.

Direct students to consider both the group projects and their journals in light of Buss's (1978) observations. It immediately becomes obvious that reason explanations predominate in the journal, whereas both cause explanations and reason explanations occur in the group. In instances where the group secured data via interviews of their target person (or through autobiographies) and took the interviewee's word at face value, teleological (or final cause, or reason) explanations predominated. However, in instances where more traditional psychological research methods were used (e.g., experiments, surveys, standardized psychological tests), efficient cause explanations predominated.

Once students realize that the type of method chosen to investigate their subject largely determines the type of explanation they obtain, the crucial question in the exercise quickly becomes apparent. If human behavior is teleological in nature, or if it is due to efficient causal influences, or (the most likely possibility) it involves some combination of the two domains of influence, then why is traditional psychological research methodology incapable of considering final causal influences as Buss (1978) and others have suggested? An appropriate understanding of how this state of affairs has come about requires some background both in the history of science and the history of psychology. For our project, one class was devoted to a summary of this material, and students were urged to read from any of a number of works on this topic (e.g., Howard, 1984a, 1984b; Rychlak, 1977, 1983; Secord, 1984).

At the end of the course, give students a final, ungraded assignment. Because each student has used both an introspective technique (the journal) and an extraspective one (the group project) to understand another person, each student might have some opinion regarding the validity of these two types of accounts. Ask students to write a brief essay in answer to the following questions: "Suppose someone were to read your journal and your paper on the group project. Which account would give them a better understanding of the person they were reading about? Give specific examples and reasons for your preference (if you have one) for one style of explanation over another."

In my class, the essays were read by both the instructor and a student who was not in the class to judge which type of account each student seemed to prefer. They concluded unanimously that the first person account was greatly preferred, the third person account least preferred, and a combination of the two received about-average preference.

DISCUSSION

This project directly involves students in activities that approximate some of the tasks engaged in by personality researchers, clinicians, theoretical and philosophical psychologists, theologians, novelists, and other professionals who strive to understand human beings. It gives them first-hand contact with the problems and procedures of this kind of research as well as a closer understanding of why the failure to achieve totally satisfactory explanations in particular domains often sets in motion the processes of fundamental change (cf. Howard, 1982).

Students also become aware that this conceptual (or theoretical) and methodological symbiosis is not unique to psychology but is a fundamental activity for all sciences. The problem presented in this activity is similar to that faced by quantum physicists several decades ago (Capra, 1982; Prigozine & Stengers, 1984).

Another point to bring up in discussion is the attitude held by many researchers that the subject is a passive respondent to external influences or a simple possessor of certain traits and states that are held to be responsible for his or her actions. Rarely do researchers consider behavior as meaningful action directed toward the goals and purposes of the active agents involved in the performance. If our research asks only extraspective, efficient cause questions, our empirical answers will be of this sort. It is only when we entertain research questions aimed at elucidating individuals' teleological powers that we can obtain evidence of purposeful human action by active agents.

These activities integrate personality theory and personality research more fully into a set of common problems and goals shared by psychological investigators. The process is more satisfying for students, who may integrate this newfound awareness with their work in other courses.

REFERENCES

Buss, A. R. (1978). Causes and reasons in attribution theory: A conceptual critique. *Journal of Personality and Social Psychology, 36,* 1311–1321.

Capra, F. (1982). *The turning point.* New York: Simon & Schuster.

Hettich, P. (1976). The journal: An autobiographical approach to learning. *Teaching of Psychology, 3,* 60–63.

Howard, G. S. (1982). Improving methodology via research on research methods. *Journal of Counseling Psychology, 29,* 318–326.

Howard, G. S. (1984a). A modest proposal for a revision of strategies in counseling research. *Journal of Counseling Psychology, 31,* 430–442.

Howard, G. S. (1984b). On studying humans. *The Counseling Psychologist, 12,* 101–109.

Klos, D. S. (1976). Students as case writers. *Teaching of Psychology, 3,* 63–66.

Mischel, W. (1981). *Introduction to personality* (3rd ed.). New York: Holt, Rinehart, & Winston.

Prigozine, I., & Stengers, I. (1984). *Order out of chaos: Man's new dialogue with nature.* Boulder: New Science Library.

Rychlak, J. R. (1977). *The psychology of rigorous humanism.* New York: Wiley-Interscience.

Rychlak, J. R. (1983). Sorting out theory from method and vice versa. *New Ideas in Psychology, 1,* 255–261.

Secord, P. F. (1984). Determinism, free will, and self-intervention: A psychological perspective. *New Ideas in Psychology, 2,* 25–33.

White, R. W. (1974). Teaching personality through life histories. *Teaching of Psychology, 1,* 69–73.

SUGGESTED READING

Wittgenstein, L. (1953). *Philosophical Investigations.* Oxford: Basil Blackwell.

$^{\square}$44 TRAIT VERSUS SITUATION AS A PREDICTOR OF BEHAVIOR: A STUDY MODELED AFTER THE THEORIES OF BEM

Darlene Kennedy and Bernard Mausner
Beaver College

■————————————————————————————————————■

This activity must be planned several weeks in advance. You will need access to videocassette recorder for students who are assigned the role of experimenters in this out-of-class interviewing activity. Additionally, you will need to send away for copies of the Gottschalt Hidden Figures Test and the State–Trait Anxiety Inventory. Instruction sheets to be given to students are supplied at the end of the article. After the outside interviews are completed, a class discussion and debriefing session is recommended. Students should have prior knowledge of the ethics of research with human participants, and the instructor should discuss issues of confidentiality and deception.

■————————————————————————————————————■

CONCEPT

This activity centers on one of the most lively issues in contemporary personality theory. Appropriate for classes in social psychology, personality, or research methodology in psychology, the activity also offers several side benefits: Students learn about the technique of role playing, how to administer an individual test of perceptual skill, and how to operate videotaping equipment.

In the study of personality theory, psychologists are divided in their views of how individual behaviors are formed. Those who believe that the source of behavior is internal maintain that people are quite consistent within their personality traits and generally act the same way in all situations. Those who believe that behavior is externally controlled find that people act differently, according to the situation they are in (Pervin, 1984). A compromise position suggests that people vary in their degree of consistency in any trait and, furthermore, that certain situations elicit certain behavioral traits (Bem, 1983; Bem & Allen, 1974).

Another area of personality relevant to this activity is anxiety, although here again there is a division of opinions about the definition of anxiety. Spielberger (1972) noted that the difficulty arises from the different ways in which the term is used. One definition describes anxiety as an unpleasant emotional state characterized by feelings of tension and worry and by the arousal of the autonomic nervous system—an anxiety state that is evoked when a person feels that a situation is potentially dangerous or threatening. A second definition describes it as a relatively stable individual difference in anxiety-proneness between people—trait anxiety that is not manifested in behavior. This experiment will use Spielberger's State–Trait Anxiety Inventory (Spielberger, Gorsuch, & Lushene, 1970).

MATERIALS NEEDED

In addition to a videocassette recorder and video camera, you will need the Gottschalt Hidden Figures Test (Educational Testing Service, 1962) and the State–Trait

Table 1. *Pearson Correlations for Trait and State Anxiety Measures of Female Undergraduates Consistent in Anxiety: Results of Two Experiments*

Variable	STAI Hidden Figures State scale	STAI Interview State scale
STAI Trait scale		
1985	.709*	.843*
1986	.685*	.620*
STAI Hidden Figures State scale		
1985		.867*
1986		.707*

Note. STAI = State–Trait Anxiety Inventory.
* $p < .05$.

Anxiety Inventory (Spielberger et al., 1970). Instruction handouts for experimenters and interviewers should also be distributed to those who need them.

INSTRUCTIONS   Several weeks ahead of the actual demonstration date, ask the students to say whether they think they are consistent or inconsistent in their anxiety level. They can rate this on a scale of 1 (*very consistent*) to 5 (*very inconsistent*). Those with 1 or 5 rankings will be the subjects.

Divide the rest of the class into pairs; these will be the experimenters, who will work in teams. Each pair must arrange to test 2 subjects during outside class time (procedure takes about 45–60 minutes). Give the experimenters copies of the instruction handouts.

After the testing is completed, conclude with a debriefing of the subjects and a discussion.

Table 1 shows the results from this experiment as it was conducted in 1985 and again in 1986 with female undergraduates at a small northeastern liberal arts college. Correlations were performed on the results of the consistent subjects between the STAI Trait measure and STAI State measure given after an interview, between the STAI Trait measure and the STAI State measure given after a hidden figures task, and between the two state measures. All comparisons revealed significant correlations, indicating that subjects who reported consistency in their anxiety actually exhibited this consistency.

Table 2 shows that none of the correlations for the inconsistent subjects were significant in either year. This shows that these students had inconsistent anxiety levels, depending on the nature of the task.

Table 2. *Pearson Correlations for Trait and State Anxiety Measures of Female Undergraduates Inconsistent in Anxiety: Results of Two Experiments*

Variable	STAI Hidden Figures State scale	STAI Interview State scale
STAI Trait scale		
1985	.376	.141
1986	.333	.361
STAI Hidden Figures State scale		
1985		.014
1986		.417

Note. STAI = State–Trait Anxiety Inventory.

Students who are involved in this experiment will gain an understanding of ways of testing predictions from personality theory. They will learn about the theories suggesting that behavior is internally controlled versus externally controlled and will also learn the compromise position offered by Bem (1983).

Several questions will occur from the results of this experiment. What do the results of the study disclose about a person's perceived consistency in behavior and his or her actual results according to the State–Trait Anxiety Inventory? Which task had anxiety levels that varied more? Did either task seem to provoke more anxiety than the other? What mechanisms did the subjects appear to be using in order to combat anxiety? When the trait versus state anxiety results were compared, should the scores have been consistent or inconsistent across the measurements for the two types of subjects?

This theoretical conflict offers plenty of room for discussion. What is the nature of anxiety, and how does it fit into the distinction between state and trait anxiety?

REFERENCES

Bem, D. J. (1983). Toward a response style theory of persons in situations. In R. A. Dienstbier & M. M. Page (Eds.), *Nebraska Symposium On Motivation 1982: Personality—Current theory and research* (Vol. 30). Lincoln: University of Nebraska Press.

Bem, D. J., & Allen, A. (1974). On predicting some of the people some of the time: The search for cross-situational consistencies in behavior. *Psychological Review, 81*, 506–520.

Educational Testing Service. (1962). *Hidden Figures Test—Cf-1* (Developed under NIMH Contract M-4186). Princeton, NJ: Author.

Pervin, L. A. (1984). *Current controversies and issues in personality* (2nd ed). New York: Wiley.

Spielberger, C. D. (1972). Conceptual and methodological issues in anxiety research. In C. D. Spielberger (Ed.), *Anxiety: Current trends in theory and research* (Vol. 2). New York: Academic Press.

Spielberger, C. D., Gorsuch, R. L., & Lushene, R. E. (1970). *Manual for the State–Trait Anxiety Inventory*. Palo Alto, CA: Consulting Psychologists Press.

1. Do not tell the subjects that anxiety is being measured. Refer to the State-Trait Anxiety Inventory as the "self-evaluation quenstionnaire." Tell the subject that you are gathering information on characteristics of students at this college (or school) and ask if he or she has plans to go to college or graduate school after graduating. If the subject says yes, administer the college/graduate school interview; if not, administer the job interview.

2. Have the subject fill out the trait section of the self-evaluation questionnaire. Then, test each subject on both tasks, having one subject perform Task 1 first and the other perform Task 2 first. Ask the subjects to fill out a STAI State measure after each of the two tasks.

Task 1: Have the subject role-play an interview and videotape it with you. Tell the subject that this will be good practice and that you will play the videotape back so that he or she can see how he or she did. One of the experimenters will have to role-play the interview while the other operates the camera. Immediately after seeing the tape, the subject should fill out the state section of the questionnaire. Mark the form with a *1* without letting the subject see you mark it.

Task 2: Tell the subject that another characteristic you are looking at is the IQ scores of students at this school, and have the subject complete the following task taken from an intelligence test (the Hidden Figures Test). The subject will have 10 minutes for each section (20 minutes total). Immediately after finishing the test, the subject should fill out a second state questionnaire. Again, mark the form *2* without letting the subject see.

3. After the experiment, subjects must be debriefed, and you should explain to them what the experiment was actually about. It is also very important not to pressure or intimidate the subjects in any way during the experiment and to offer any subjects who are uncomfortable the option of removing themselves from the experiment.

4. The state and trait anxiety measures may be correlated to determine the consistency or inconsistency of anxiety in the subjects. Significant correlations should be obtained from consistent subjects, showing consistent anxiety levels across the three scales. The analysis of inconsistent subjects should show low correlations to indicate that anxiety levels varied depending on the situation.

Ask whether the subject intends to go to college or graduate school after graduating or look for a job.

College or Graduate School

1. Have you thought about the kind of program you want to follow? What is it?

2. How could you convince the school that they should accept you into their program?

3. Imagine that you are being interviewed by a member of the college faculty. How would you explain your interest in going to his or her department?

4. Since (college) graduate school is very expensive, how could you explain your need for a fellowship, scholarship, or job?

Job Interview

1. What kind of work do you hope to be doing 10 years from now?

2. How could you convince a company that they ought to hire you?

3. Imagine that you are being interviewed for a job. How would you explain to the person interviewing you that you would be a good bet for the job?

Play back the tape while the subject watches.

45 BRINGING THE CLINIC INTO THE UNDERGRADUATE CLASSROOM

David M. Young

Indiana University—Purdue University at Fort Wayne

Students develop hands-on skills in problem formulation, classification of disorders, developing treatment plans, and assessing the prognoses of actual or simulated clients in this exercise. Although a film or video presentation of a clinical interview works best, you can do this activity with an audiotaped interview or even a written history. The simulation procedure generally should be introduced 4 to 5 weeks into the course, after students have been prepared in the background they will need to engage in this miniclinic assessment exercise. A full class session for the actual presentation of the interview, the assessment, and ensuing discussion is recommended. The student worksheets for completing the assessment are provided.

CONCEPT

Many notable teachers of psychology, textbook authors, and practicing psychologists (Benjamin & Lowman, 1981; McKeachie, 1978; Radford & Rose, 1980) have implored professors to give undergraduate students the experience of actually working at the tasks that psychologists perform. In many undergraduate lecture courses, students become oriented to what clinicians do and may even observe audiotaped or videotaped examples of clinical activities. Yet, because of ethical concerns (e.g., confidentiality problems, using untrained students to make interventions or important decisions regarding a client) or the sheer numbers of students involved, psychology students are rarely directed to attempt the hands-on exercise of clinical skills. When students are tested in abnormal psychology courses, they are often expected to make diagnostic decisions, provide a prognosis, and define the relevance of particular forms of therapy for different disorders—all based on fragments of hypothetical cases, often presented in the form of multiple-choice items. This article describes a method that involves students in the relevant simulation of a variety of clinical experiences. We have employed these techniques or "miniclinics" in several courses that contain units related to clinical assessment and intervention (e.g. abnormal, child development, and introductory psychology courses).

MATERIALS NEEDED

Besides the three student worksheets that are replicated here, the most important element of the miniclinic exercise is the case material presented by the instructor—ideally, written background information and films or videotapes. Satisfactory but less revealing and stimulating for discussion are written case histories.

Recently, there has been an increase in both the quality and the selection of clinical vignettes (both actual and simulated productions). These are often available from book publishers for a small fee or at no charge to instructors who have adopted the publisher's text book in abnormal psychology.

The film catalogues of colleges and universities are another excellent source of such material. The film "Otto—A Case Study in Abnormal Behavior" (Film No. EC1404, 16; available from the Audio-Visual Center, Indiana University, Bloomington, IN 47405-5901) features a case enactment designed to be studied from the basic models of psychopathology and treatment. This fine film may be ordered separately or in a series of films displaying various representative scholars discussing the hypothetical Otto from their own model of therapy.

The paper-and-pencil materials include three worksheets: (a) Intake and Problem Formulation, (b) DSM-III Classification, and (c) Treatment Plan and Prognosis. These forms should be reproduced for each student.

INSTRUCTIONS Undergraduate students are assigned at random to one of several "clinic" groups representing a model or school of psychopathology (e.g., psychoanalytic, behavioral, client-centered, existential, biological). We have found that groups of 6–10 students function effectively for these exercises. During the course of the semester, as clinics are convened, students are rotated to other models. This procedure ensures that each student is exposed to the full complement of therapeutic approaches and helps each student develop ease of communication with other members of the class.

The clinic simulation procedure is generally introduced approximately 4 or 5 weeks into the semester. This timing permits the instructor to cover, in standard sequence, introductory chapters on abnormal psychology, the various models or approaches to psychopathology, the chapters on classification and assessment procedures, and at least one content chapter focusing on the disorders themselves. These chapters are usually followed by material covering the remaining diagnostic categories. The experienced instructor will frequently find that most textbooks follow this fairly standard sequence.

Critical to the success of the exercise is the effective introduction of the material in chapters about models of psychopathology and the *Diagnostic and Statistical Manual of Mental Disorders, Third Edition (DSM-III*; American Psychiatric Association, 1980). When these chapters are taught (and they should be introduced early in the course), it is important to prepare the students for the eventual clinic exercise by demonstrating how a case can be viewed by the various models, regardless of the diagnosis agreed upon from the *DSM-III*. For example, depression can be viewed as resulting from a chemical imbalance, from a reduction in reinforcement, or from a symbolic loss accentuated by a fixation in the oral stage of development. Thus, before students are actually given the clinic assignment, it is important that they have understood to some degree the ideas behind the various models, the nature of the classification system, and at least one area of disorders outlined in the *DSM-III*.

Time requirements for the exercise vary with the depth of each instructor's involvement with the procedure. For example, some instructors may not wish to have the clinic groups complete each form for each case presented. However, after the stimulus case has been presented, at least 30 minutes of discussion and processing should be made available for the groups. Additional time for a general review of each group's findings, a discussion of agreement within and among groups, and a presentation of new material by the instructor is needed. For thorough processing of the exercise, a full hour should be allotted. Group discussion and the processing of information can be carried over from one class session to the next. However, we have found the process to be smoother when the entire exercise is completed within one class session. Problems of absenteeism, retention of the case material, and so forth are minimized when closure is achieved within one class period.

Students in each of the miniclinics are presented with an overview of the nature of the learning task. Prior to the actual presentation of case material, students in each clinic are reminded of the particular concerns and variables relevant to their discipline. The psychoanalytical group is, for example, cued to look for important features of early childhood, for current defense mechanisms employed, and for the possible forms that an eventual transference might take. Similar coaching is directed toward members of other miniclinics. These instructions are provided to students in a general session so students can become further aware of the differentiation in task and approach of the various therapeutic schools.

When clinic assignments and the general review have been completed, the full case presentation is made, starting with background information provided by the instructor. Each group also receives a copy of the written case history. It is helpful to select cases with a good deal of background information so that students from each clinic have enough potential information to make a case for the relevance or efficacy of their mode. After the background information is presented, the recording of the case is played. Next, students divide into clinic groups to discuss the case and to complete the paper-and-pencil assignments. While the students are working in their groups, it is helpful for the instructor to interact with each group in progress.

The paper-and-pencil assignments consist of three worksheets: Intake and Problem Formulation, DSM-III Classification, and Treatment Plan and Prognosis. Students are instructed to tailor their observations to their assigned perspective on the Intake and Problem Formulation Worksheet. For example, under the Historical Antecedent section, behaviorists are encouraged to note possible early learning histories, psychoanalysts are told to report possible developmental trauma, and students in the physiological clinic are directed to focus on possible early signs of neurological disorder, brain injury, congenital problem, and so forth. Each student is required to complete this form, although group discussion may take place before each student has completed the assignment.

The DSM-III worksheet requires students in each of the clinics to review all five axes of the *DSM-III*. Of course, students are informed that they will rarely utilize all axes in classifying a case. As with the Intake and Problem Formulation Worksheet, each student is required to complete a form after group discussion. Students are encouraged to stick to their guns even if others in the clinic disagree. Because of this practice, reliability estimates may be made for each clinic.

The classification exercise is followed by the completion of the Treatment Plan and Prognosis Worksheet. It is here that students are able to exercise the most creativity and to display familiarity with their assigned model of practice. Interventions should be justified on the basis of problem documentation and relevance to the student's particular mode. The prognosis section is also to be completed with reference to the assigned model and with consideration of the available resources and circumstances relevant to the model (e.g., How well would an older adult with an IQ of 75 do in traditional psychoanalysis?).

With the worksheets completed, the full class reassembles to process the results of the exercise. The instructor leads a discussion of each worksheet activity, highlighting the points of view for each model represented. In addition, a discussion of agreement or disagreement on diagnosis, etiology, and treatment both within and among groups may be held. Rough estimates of percent agreement within groups may be calculated by simply dividing the number of agreements (with the correct diagnostic category) by the combined number of agreements and disagreements within each group. It should be made clear to students, however, that this number is only a rough estimate that is probably inflated because it does not account for the number of agreements that would be expected by chance. It is probably not worth the time it would take to labor through a complete explanation of the probabilities of chance agreement for each diagnostic category.

DISCUSSION The miniclinic method presents several advantages to the instructor as well as a few potential stumbling blocks. Advantages include teaching students the rigors of keeping within theoretical models, teaching the logical connection between an etiological conception of problems and interventions associated with particular models, and exploring the problem of how models relate (or do not relate) to the current classification system. Finally, students are able to learn clinical material without rote. They learn that the *DSM-III* is a real tool and enjoy exercising their diagnostic skill through safe risk taking in the miniclinic.

The problems associated with this process include the always-present possibility that passive students will remain passive and let others complete the exercise. The medical students' disease syndrome and the phenomena of the "instant expert" can also be stimulated by this activity, yet early warnings and effective feedback in class can do much to prevent these problems.

One final and nontechnical note summarizing the process is in order: Both students and instructors who use this process find it a lot of fun!

REFERENCES American Psychiatric Association. (1980). *Diagnostic and statistical manual of mental disorders* (3rd ed.). Washington, DC: Author.

Benjamin, L. T., & Lowman, K. D. (Eds.). (1981). *Activities handbook for the teaching of psychology.* Washington, DC: American Psychological Association.

McKeachie, W. J. (1978). *Teaching tips: A guidebook for the beginning college teacher* (7th ed.). Lexington, MA: Health.

Radford, J., & Rose, D. (Eds.). (1980). *The teaching of psychology: Method, content and context.* New York: Wiley.

SUGGESTED READING Spitzer, R. L., Skodoe, A. E., Gibbon, M., & Williams, J. B. W. (1981). *DSM III casebook: A learning companion to the diagnostic and statistical manual of mental disorders (third edition).* Washington, DC: American Psychiatric Association.

DSM-III Classification Worksheet

Name: _____

Date: _____

Section: _____

Case: _____

Clinic Assigned: _____

AXIS I: Disorders Usually First Evident in Infancy, Childhood or Adolescence
Assessment data:

DSM-III
classification: _____
AXIS II: Personality Disorders
Assessment Data:

DSM-III
classification: _____
AXIS III: Physical Disorders and Conditions
Assessment Data:

DSM-III
classification: _____
AXIS IV: Severity of Psychosocial Stressors (1-7)
Assessment Data:

DSM-III
classification
(1-7): _____
AXIS V: Highest Level of Adaptive Functioning in Past Year (1-7)
Assessment Data:

DSM-III classification
(1-7): _____

Notes, Ideas, and Questions for Discussion

```
┌─────────────────────────────────────────────────────────────────────┐
│                    Treatment Plan and Prognosis Worksheet             │
│                                                                       │
│                                          Name: _____   │
│                                          Date: _____   │
│                                       Section: _____   │
│                                          Case: _____   │
│  Clinic Assigned: _____ │
│                                                                       │
│  Summary of needs (conditions):                                       │
│                                                                       │
│                                                                       │
│  Unanswered questions and further assessment needed:                  │
│                                                                       │
│                                                                       │
│  Recommended interventions (with rationale):                          │
│                                                                       │
│                                                                       │
│  Prognosis (related to specific problems):                            │
│                                                                       │
│  _____  │
│                                                                       │
│                  Notes, Ideas, and Questions for Discussion           │
│                                                                       │
│                                                                       │
│                                                                       │
└─────────────────────────────────────────────────────────────────────┘
```

46 THE ILLUSION OF CONTROL

Stephen J. Dollinger
Southern Illinois University at Carbondale

All you will need is a deck of standard playing cards and a dollar bill to conduct this quick, easy activity. Students need no prior knowledge, and the demonstration can be done in a single class session. The activity is appropriate for classes of any size and leads to a lively discussion of superstitious behavior and gambling.

CONCEPT

This activity involves a simulation that illustrates research methodology in experimental personality psychology and serves as a preliminary introduction to lecture material on the topic of illusion of control.

Langer (1975) showed that people often believe that they can exert control in totally chance situations. Examples of this are apparent in lotteries, horse races, or ESP tasks. This illusion is most likely to be evident when a chance situation incorporates cues from similar skill situations, cues that suggest that skill factors might be effective in determining the outcome of the chance. For example, one's odds of winning the lottery do not change by virtue of one's choosing or being assigned a ticket; nevertheless, many people feel more confident when they feel that they are in a position of active, rather than passive, participation. The concept of illusory control becomes especially interesting in light of such phenomena as compulsive gambling, superstitions, and mania (Ayeroff & Abelson, 1976; Benassi, Sweeney, & Drevno, 1979; Burger & Schnerring, 1982; Golin, Terrell, & Johnson, 1977; Stern & Berrenberg, 1979).

MATERIALS NEEDED

You will need a standard deck of 52 playing cards and a $1 prize. At least four participants (preferably about 20 participants) are needed to conduct the simulation.

INSTRUCTIONS

As you enter the classroom, take the dollar bill from your wallet and, holding it high, announce that the class will begin with a brief card game. State that the person drawing the highest-valued card will win the dollar.

Hand a card to the first person, direct the second to draw his or her own card, and alternate in this way until everyone has a card. Now ask the students, before looking at their cards, to write down what their level of confidence is that they will win. After all participants have received a card and written down their subjective probability of winning, have the students look at their cards and determine who the winner is.

Now have a class member calculate a composite result of the two groups' (choice and no choice) responses.

In keeping with the illusion of control phenomenon, subjects choosing their own cards were more confident (choice group mean = 55%) than those whose card was assigned (no choice group mean = 45%). Both groups were markedly overconfident when the base rate odds were considered (11% probability with the nine participants in the class providing these data).

DISCUSSION   I use this simulation, as well as a discussion about the Illinois State Lottery and its workings, as a lead-in to lecture material on the illusion of control. The simulation has been effective in eliciting intently focused attention and enthusiastic participation in the lecture material and its implications. For example, it elicited a number of self-disclosures about the students' own gambling activities and other comments about the personal relevance of the phenomenon. You can also bring up factors that contribute to the illusion of control, such as superstitions. What kinds of superstitions do students use when taking final exams or playing in a big game? Have these superstitions ever been connected to the actual outcome, or has the belief in them actually helped to assuage some of the anxiety inherent in such situations? Ask students to consider the contradictions between the illusion of control held by gamblers and racetrack bettors and the loss of control from which compulsive gamblers suffer. The argument is often made that success in racetrack betting does require a certain knowledge of the situation (what the horses are like, how they run in certain conditions, how the jockeys have been doing lately, and so on). How true is this, and can other types of gambling make a similar claim?

REFERENCES   Ayeroff, F., & Abelson, R. P. (1976). ESP and ESB: Belief in personal success at mental telepathy. *Journal of Personality and Social Psychology, 34,* 240–247.

Benassi, V. A., Sweeney, P. D., & Drevno, G. E. (1979). Mind over matter: Perceived success at psychokinesis. *Journal of Personality and Social Psychology, 37,* 1377–1386.

Burger, J. M., & Schnerring, D. A. (1982). The effects of desire for control and extrinsic rewards on the illusion of control and gambling. *Motivation and Emotion, 6,* 329–335.

Golin, S., Terrell, F., & Johnson, B. (1977). Depression and the illusion of control. *Journal of Abnormal Psychology, 86,* 440–442.

Langer, E. J. (1975). The illusion of control. *Journal of Personality and Social Psychology, 32,* 311–328.

Stern, G. S., & Berrenberg, J. L. (1979). Skill-set, success outcome, and mania as determinants of the illusion of control. *Journal of Research in Personality, 13,* 206–220.

47 SIMULATION FOR TEACHING PERSONALITY PSYCHOLOGY: VERBAL CONDITIONING, NEED FOR APPROVAL, AND LOCUS OF CONTROL

Stephen J. Dollinger
Southern Illinois University at Carbondale

This activity demonstrates the paradigm of verbal conditioning, showing students how this conditioning can be influenced by factors such as the client's need for approval and whether the client possesses a stronger external or internal locus of control. It requires little preparation beyond writing up a list of verbs and can be used with any class size.

CONCEPT

Verbal conditioning is a research paradigm that was used frequently in the 1960s to study personality. The method (from Taffel, 1955) is particularly interesting because it was thought to reflect what happened in psychoanalysis—that the verbal commentary of the analyst might serve to reinforce the patient's verbal behavior. Performance in this task is related to several personality variables, especially the need for social approval and locus of control constructs. Persons with an internal locus of control, who believe that life's rewards and punishment are under their own control, are more likely to resist outside influence. Persons with a high need for social approval are likely to be especially susceptible to verbal conditioning, as are those with an external rather than an internal locus of control.

MATERIALS NEEDED

You will need a list of 30 verbs (any, chosen by the experimenter) and a list of six pronouns used by the subject (I, You, He, She, We, They).

INSTRUCTIONS

Select two students, one as the experimenter and one as the subject. Have the subject wait outside the classroom while you explain the procedure to the rest of the class. After it is clear to them, have the subject re-enter and begin the demonstration.

The experimenter asks the subject to make a sentence using one of the six pronouns on his or her sheet with a verb given by the experimenter. The experimenter states the verb slowly and then systematically reinforces (with verbal comments such as "um hmmm" or "good") any sentence beginning with "I" or "We." Over a series of trials, it becomes evident whether conditioning is taking place if the subject produces more first-person (i.e., self-disclosive) sentences. The experimenter keeps track of the pronouns used for each sentence, and the data are examined when the task is completed.

DISCUSSION

In my class, the experiment yielded a weak conditioning effect on intermediate trials, which disappeared on later trials. Discussion after the simulation revealed that the subject was herself actively experimenting "to try to figure out the rules of the game." This response was particularly interesting in light of the locus of control construct in which research has shown that "externals" perform better as subjects, whereas "internals" are resistant to influence.

Discussion of the task opens up a discussion of the topics of need for approval and locus of control. Have students consider the differences in external and internal locus of control: How do they see themselves? Why do they believe in the idea of external (or internal) locus? What evidence exists to support or to weaken either argument? How important is social approval to them? (For research on verbal conditioning and these personality variables, see Crowne & Strickland, 1961; Doctor, 1971; Getter, 1966; Marlowe, Beecher, Cook, & Doob, 1964; Strickland, 1970. For lecture ideas, see Millham & Jacobson, 1978; Phares, 1978.)

This simulation is valuable in motivating student interest in the material, especially because it requires active participation that is less threatening than might be the case with other kinds of exercises in personality psychology. The simulation is more similar to a role-playing activity than an exercise in self-disclosure that might provoke feelings of vulnerability. And yet, there is considerable room for spontaneity and a wide latitude of possible responses in the simulations. Ask students to discuss any experiences in their own lives that parallel the findings shown in this demonstration. Without allowing students to disclose highly sensitive information about themselves, encourage them to speak of situations in which they have influenced others, or have been influenced themselves, by this kind of conditioning. The discussion could lead to the application of this principle in various settings, including therapist–client relations, work settings, and so on.

REFERENCES

Crowne, D. P., & Strickland, B. R. (1961). The conditioning of verbal behavior as a function of the need for social approval. *Journal of Abnormal and Social Psychology, 63,* 395–401.

Doctor, R. M. (1971). Locus of control of reinforcement and responsiveness to social influence. *Journal of Personality, 39,* 542–551.

Getter, H. (1966). A personality determinant of verbal conditioning. *Journal of Personality, 34,* 397–405.

Marlowe, D., Beecher, R. S., Cook, J. B., & Doob, A. N. (1964). The approval motive, vicarious reinforcement and verbal conditioning. *Perceptual and Motor Skills, 19,* 523–530.

Millham, J., & Jacobson, L. I. (1978). The need for approval. In H. London & J. E. Exner (Eds.), *Dimensions of personality* (pp. 365–390). New York: Wiley.

Phares, E. J. (1978). Locus of control. In H. London & J. E. Exner (Eds.), *Dimensions of personality* (pp. 263–304). New York: Wiley.

Strickland, B. R. (1970). Individual differences in verbal conditioning, extinction and awareness. *Journal of Personality, 38,* 364–378.

Taffel, C. (1955). Anxiety and the conditioning of verbal behavior. *Journal of Abnormal and Social Psychology, 51,* 496–501.

48 UNDERSTANDING ABNORMAL BEHAVIOR: WEARING THE OTHER SHOE

Antonio E. Puente
University of North Carolina at Wilmington

This activity is suited for an abnormal or psychopathology course. No materials are needed. The instructor must devote time out of class coaching student volunteers and must be willing to set up appointments with other professionals whom the volunteers will interview. Volunteers will present skits on the day that the disorder they have researched is being introduced by the instructor.

CONCEPT

Students tend to form stereotypes about mental illness and to distance themselves from it rather than attempt to confront and understand this complex, abstract set of behaviors. One way to sensitize students to abnormal behavior is to have them view it from the perspective of the person who is mentally ill. This exercise is best applied in courses, such as psychopathology or abnormal psychology, where a series of lectures on abnormal behavior is presented.

MATERIALS NEEDED

Students should have access to texts and other outside resources that objectively describe abnormal behavior. Wherever possible, arrange interviews for students with professionals who are willing to discuss the challenge of viewing behavior from the standpoint of the client or the patient.

INSTRUCTIONS

This activity should precede the lectures on specific forms of abnormal behavior.

Announce to the students that they may volunteer to participate in a research project that will culminate in a skit that uses role-playing to demonstrate abnormal behavior. Provide the volunteers with readings, appointments with mental health professionals, or both. Before students begin researching their topics, instruct the student volunteers as well as the class to write a brief paragraph describing their preconceived notions of the disorder to be studied. This serves as the pretest.

The instructor should meet with the student volunteers to develop a game plan because, once confronted with the complexities of the task and the time between assignment and presentation, the volunteers may stray from their intended goals. Informal and intermittent contacts with students during the planning period provide the student with direction and support.

On the day of the lecture on a specific form of mental disorder, the student who has researched that disorder presents a 5–10 minute skit. A skit can be performed by a single student volunteer or by several volunteers who act out the roles of psychologist, parent, and friend as well as patient. The skit should depict typical behaviors seen in persons with that disorder. There should be at least one skit for each of the major disorders. Students from the audience may ask questions of the "patient."

It is important to point out that the instructor must be prepared to deal with inappropriate self-disclosure on the part of both the student actors and the rest of the class. This problem is best avoided by structuring a pre-skit discussion in which the importance of objectivity and the inappropriateness of a class as a setting for self-disclosure are addressed.

Once the skit has been completed, ask the class and the student volunteers to write a posttest paragraph describing their views of the disorder.

DISCUSSION

The paragraphs written in the pretest and posttest serve as the basis for the class discussion. The "patient" should discuss with the class how his or her views of the disorder changed as well as what was unusual about being a "patient." Encourage the students to compare how their original perception of the abnormal behavior changed as a function of the activity. Direct the class discussion to focus on a more accurate appreciation of disordered behavior while taking care to keep students from losing sight of their objectivity and from bringing up their own problems for discussion. While emphasizing that students should not act out personal problems they are experiencing, the instructor should also screen students who may identify closely with some disorder. An example is an anorexic student who volunteers to act out anorexia for the class. It is helpful to emphasize the distinction between acting and self-disclosing.

Participants and classmates alike should be encouraged to avoid stereotyping as a means to understand the complexities of abnormal behavior. Applicable ethical principles should be discussed at this point. Of special relevance are the issues of responsibility, objectivity, integrity, confidentiality, and, above all, the welfare of the patient.

SUGGESTED READING

Fadiman, J., & Kewman, D. (1979). *Exploring madness.* Monterey, CA: Brooks/Cole.

Gardner, N. (1974). *The shattered mind.* New York: Vintage.

Sechehaye, M. (1951). *Autobiography of a schizophrenic girl.* New York: Signet.

Sheehan, S. (1982). *Is there no place on earth for me?* Boston: Houghton Mifflin.

Spitzer, R. L., Skodol, A. E., Gibbon, M., & Williams, J. B. (1983). *Psychopathology: A case book.* New York: McGraw-Hill.

49 PARADIGMS ON THE ETIOLOGY AND TREATMENT OF ABNORMAL BEHAVIOR

Janet Morahan-Martin
Bryant College

This activity can be used with any size class and requires little preparation beyond photocopying the handout. It offers instructors a good opportunity to illustrate what may appear to be an esoteric concept to students and is best suited to classes that have had some exposure to abnormal psychology.

CONCEPT

Paradigms play a powerful role in how we view human behavior, affecting the questions we ask, the causes we attribute to certain behaviors, and the way we treat them. Paradigms also reflect assumptions that we hold about behavior. As psychologists, we have been trained to understand how paradigms affect our judgments and assumptions about behavior; however, this concept can be confusing and difficult to understand for students. To the introductory students especially, this idea may reinforce a belief that psychologists never agree and therefore, are incompetent and don't know what they are talking about. To upper-level students, the role paradigms play may be more obvious. However, students may still find it hard to understand their own implicit assumptions about the causes of behavior as well as what constitutes normal and abnormal behavior.

This activity illustrates the role of paradigms in human behavior and can furthermore be used to reveal to the students their own assumptions about normal and abnormal behavior and to introduce a discussion on the history of abnormal psychology.

MATERIALS NEEDED

You will need a copy of the case handout for each student.

INSTRUCTIONS

Have the class read the case and answer the questions. This may be done with the entire class participating, or the class may be broken into smaller groups that first discuss the case and then present their answers to the entire class.

DISCUSSION

After eliciting answers from the class, ask the students to attempt to classify their answers according to the psychological paradigms being used in the course. It is useful to focus on the causes of behavior that are not attributed and to ask why. For example, students frequently do not question whether the cause of Ellen's behavior may be physical. This can be an opportunity to stress that problems in behavior may be physical in origin. A discussion of how treatment follows cause can be elicited by asking the class if the treatments they recommended followed from causes that they attributed to Ellen's behavior. The discussion can then focus on what assumptions about normal and abnormal behavior the students have made in their answers. Finally, this discussion can be used to introduce a survey of the history of abnormal psychology by questioning why no one suggested that Ellen is possessed by the devil or that she is suffering from masturbatory insanity or an imbalance of bodily fluids.

SUGGESTED READING Davison, G., & Neale, J. (1990). *Abnormal psychology* (5th ed.). New York: Wiley.

The Case of Ellen

Ellen S. was referred to the clinic shortly after her "miscarriage." She was a 32-year-old woman who was employed as an administrative assistant for Mr. Johnson. She and Mr. Johnson had recently terminated their 2-year-old love affair because Mr. Johnson was unwilling to divorce his wife because of his children.

Although medical tests indicated that she was not actually pregnant, Ellen had shown classic symptoms of early pregnancy during the 3 months that she believed she was pregnant. She ceased menstruation, was chronically fatigued and nauseated, and had gained weight.

Ellen was raised by fundamentalist religious parents with whom she still lived. She had been told repeatedly about the sins of sex and alcohol. Her affair with Mr. Johnson was her first relationship.

Assume you are Ellen's therapist:

1. What issues do you think are important to the development of Ellen's problems?

2. How would you treat Ellen?

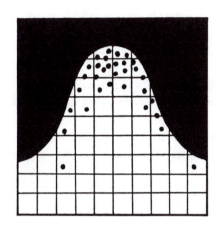

CHAPTER VII
STATISTICS

Statistics may be the hardest part of a psychology course to teach in a way that captures the students' interest and attention. These nine activities address this concern by presenting creative approaches to teaching statistical concepts. Most of them require no prior knowledge of statistics, and several use a game-of-chance format to illustrate probability and variability.

Activity 50 demonstrates the normal probability curve. Activity 52 does require some prior study of measures of central tendency. Activity 53 is an especially good way to introduce general statistical principles in a nonthreatening way; Activities 51 and 54 use games, and Activity 55 lets students analyze their own exam scores. Activity 56 explains the standard error of the mean, and Activity 57 applies statistical analysis to a real-life situation, in this case that of personnel assessment.

For basic information about statistics, the reader is referred to Appendix B in this volume or to any solid introductory statistics text.

50 NORMAL PROBABILITY CURVE

Peter S. Fernald
University of New Hampshire

L. Dodge Fernald
Harvard University

This activity can be used with any size class. You will need 10 cups, each containing 15 pennies. Students need no prior knowledge, and this provides them with an excellent introduction to the concept of normal distribution and the bell-shaped curve.

CONCEPT

This activity helps students understand the bell shape of the normal probability curve. Aside from clarifying an important statistical concept, it also demonstrates the fact that various human characteristics, such as height, time estimation, and midterm grades, are typically distributed according to this curve.

MATERIALS

You will need 10 paper cups, each containing 15 pennies.

INSTRUCTIONS

Begin by making the following statement to the class:

> I wish to demonstrate some principles of probability. The demonstration requires that 10 students each toss a set of 15 pennies, but before we do this I want each of you to guess the outcome by answering these questions: Which distribution—5 heads, 7 heads, or 13 heads—will occur most frequently? Which least frequently?

Ask the students to write their answers on a sheet of paper.

Give one box of pennies to each of 10 students in the class. Ask them to shake the boxes and throw the pennies out carefully onto their desks or writing tablets for 10 trials. For each trial, the student or a student sitting nearby should record the number of heads. While the students are tossing coins, draw Figure 50-1 on the chalkboard.

DISCUSSION

After the students have completed and recorded their 10 tosses, describe to the class the bell shape of the normal probability curve:

> The normal probability curve is bell-shaped. Scores at the middle of the scale occur more frequently than those at the extreme ends. Hence, 7 heads should occur more frequently than 5 heads, which in turn should occur more frequently than 13 heads. Let's check our results to see if such is the case.

Ask the 10 students to indicate the number of times they obtained 7 heads. Sometimes it is satisfactory to have the students call out their findings. Otherwise, they

---

Adapted from the *Introduction to Psychology Student Guidebook* (5th ed.), by L. Dodge Fernald and Peter S. Fernald. Copyright (c) 1985, Wm. C. Brown Company. Used by permission.

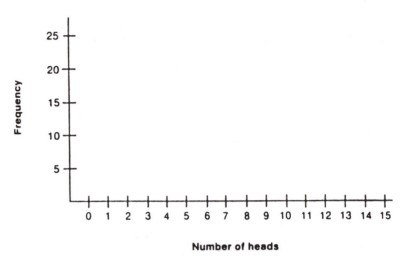

Figure 50-1. Frequency distribution for tossing 15 pennies.

can indicate the number of trials on which a particular number of heads occurred by simply raising their hands with the appropriate number of fingers extended. Tally the number of times that 5 heads and 13 heads were obtained in the same manner. Then ask the class, Did 7 heads occur more frequently than 5 heads? Did 5 heads occur more frequently than 13 heads? Typically, the data are exactly as predicted. Plot the obtained frequencies for 5, 7, and 13 heads on the graph on the chalkboard (see Figure 50-1).

Indicate to the class that in order to be sure the curve is really bell-shaped you wish to obtain the frequency for every point on the horizontal axis of the polygon. In the same manner as described previously, ask the students to indicate the number of times that other combinations of heads occurred (0, 1, 2, and so forth). Plot all points for 0–15 heads on the graph. After connecting all the points, ask the class, Is the curve bell-shaped? Again, the results typically are as predicted, and the mean will lie between 7 and 8, approximately at 7.5.

Students usually attribute greater significance to these points if they are informed that many human characteristics show a distribution similar to the normal probability curve. These characteristics include height, time estimation, academic ability, introversion/extroversion, and perhaps grades on an examination, to mention only a few. To illustrate this point, plot a frequency distribution for one such characteristic on the chalkboard. Time estimation data, for example, is very quickly obtained by asking students to estimate a 30-second time interval. This part of the demonstration/discussion should not be attempted unless at least 50 scores can be obtained. Fewer than this number may not produce a normal curve.

SUGGESTED READING

Downie, N. M., & Heath, R. W. (1983). *Basic statistical methods* (5th ed., Chap. 7). New York: Harper & Row.

Witte, R. S. (1985). *Statistics* (2nd ed., Chap. 6). New York: Holt, Rinehart, & Winston.

51 PROBABILITY AND CHANCE VARIATION

Jane A. Jegerski
University of Illinois

You will need a set of dice for every three students, copies of the illustration of all possible outcomes, and several calculators for this activity in which you teach students the game of craps, divide them into groups of three, and use the game as an entertaining way to teach the statistical concepts of probability and chance error.

CONCEPT

Two characteristics of the dice game craps—portability and high interest to participants—make it ideal for use in teaching some of the basic concepts of probability and chance variation. This exercise uses student-generated data from craps games to apply basic notions of probability and to introduce three concepts: the law of averages, expected versus observed values, and standard error.

MATERIALS NEEDED

You will need one set of dice for each student triad and a copy of the illustration displaying all possible dice outcomes for students unfamiliar with dice games. Students will also need calculators to compute statistical outcomes.

INSTRUCTIONS

Present the basic rules for craps, as follows:

> Roll two dice. If a 7 or 11 shows up, you win. If a 2, 3, or 12 show up, you lose. If any number from 4 through 10 (except 7) shows up, you earn a *point throw:* To make the point or win, you must roll the same number again before throwing a 7; no other number matters. If you throw a 7 after a point throw, you lose and must pass the dice. For any other outcome (win or lose on the first throw or win after a point throw), you can roll the dice again (another "come out" throw).

Group the shooters into triads, with one student as the recorder and two as shooters. The recorder role can be rotated within the triad to give everyone a chance to shoot. The recorder lists the sum of each roll (2–12) in a separate column for each player, leaving a blank row space between numbers when the dice are rolled for each new come out throw. The recorder also keeps track of wins and losses. The shooters roll against each other, preferably by throwing dice against a wall as a backboard to help defeat controlled throws. Students roll 100 times and then stop recording.

DISCUSSION

When the shooting is over, direct each triad of students to answer the following questions.

1. What is the probability of rolling each number (2–12) on one roll? (Use the possible outcomes illustration.) Find the proportion of each outcome in your 100 rolls. How close were these actual proportions to the expected values?

2. What are the probabilities of winning, losing, or continuing on the first roll? Can you figure out the probability of winning on the second roll if you have thrown a

point on the first roll? Why or why not? (Answer: No, you need to know which point number was rolled because of differing probabilities). Can you figure out the probability of losing on the second roll? Why or why not? (Answer: Yes, because there is only one way to lose on the second roll, by throwing a 7, for which $p = .17$, after throwing a point on the first roll for which $p = .67$; to gauge losing on the second roll, $p = .67 \times .17$, or $p = .11$.)

3. What is the expected value of one roll? (Answer: 7) What is the expected value of the sum of 50 rolls? (Answer: 350) What is the observed value for the sum of your first 50 rolls? (Note: Fifty rolls, instead of all 100 rolls, are used in these calculations to accommodate time constraints and to minimize computational error.)

4. How many wins and losses occurred during the first 100 rolls? If you had been betting, would you have come out ahead, broken even, or fallen behind if you had kept the size of your bets the same?

After all the student triads have completed the exercise, enter their observed frequencies in a table on the blackboard with the possible rolls of dice (and their expected values) down the side and the student group number across the top. Sum the row frequencies for the rolls of dice and list the expected values for these totals. Next, ask students to gauge which observed frequencies are closest to the expected frequencies—an individual group's frequencies ($n = 50$ rolls) or the class's total frequencies ($N = 500$ rolls)? The total frequencies will be closer to the expected frequencies than any of the small group results (usually). However, both observed frequencies will deviate from the expected values by some amount. This is called *chance error*. As the number of tosses goes up, chance error (expressed here as a percentage of the sum of the tosses) goes down. The likely size of this chance error can be computed and is referred to as the *standard error* (SE) of the sum (of the rolls of dice). The standard error for the sum can be calculated by multiplying the square root of the number of rolls times the standard deviation of the chance model (Freedman, Pisani, & Purves, 1978a).

Thus, for 50 rolls, $SE = \sqrt{50} \times 2.45 = 17.32$, and for 500 rolls, $SE = \sqrt{500} \times 2.45 = 54.78$.

Note: Some teachers may prefer to go directly to the standard error of the mean, the standard deviation of the chance model divided by the square root of the sample size, rather than first presenting the standard error for the sum and next presenting the standard error for the average as the standard error for the sum divided by the number (of rolls of dice), as I do.

If this exercise were repeated every day, about 68% of those repetitions would have total sums of rolls between 3,445 and 3,555. About 68% of the time, the triad groups of students would get between 333 and 367. Conclude the discussion by emphasizing the difference between the standard deviation (which applies to a list of numbers) and the standard error (which applies to chance variability around an expected value).

REFERENCES   Freedman, D., Pisani, R., & Purves, R. (1978a). *Statistics*. New York: Norton.

SUGGESTED   Diagram Group. (1975). *The way to play*. New York: Bantam Books.
READING   Freedman, D., Pisani, R., & Purves, R. (1978b). *Instructor's manual for statistics*. New York: Norton.

$\square$52 ON THE AVERAGE . . .

Kurt Salzinger

Polytechnic University and New York State Psychiatric Institute

This activity can be used with classes of virtually any size, although the instructor may not be able to use all the students' answers in larger classes. The instructor will need to provide copies of the printed material to be analyzed. The students' tabulations can be done in or out of class. Students will need to have studied measures of central tendency.

CONCEPT

Benjamin Disraeli long ago divided lies into "lies, damned lies, and statistics." The point of this exercise is to show that we can find truth in average statistics if we understand what kind of average is used. Measures of central tendency are good sources for study because they do differ from one another, particularly for skewed distributions. In addition, samples of such distributions are often readily available to the student. What is more, it is constructive to have students see how we operationalize our concepts, that is, how we quantify them so that we can measure them, which in turn allows us to arrive at precise conclusions about our hypotheses.

The basic problem to be examined is whether different definitions of *average* result in the same conclusion. We will study verbal behavior. Suppose you wish to examine the hypothesis that one text is more difficult than another. You decide to measure difficulty by how many letters each word contains. This brings up the following problems: How can we select a representative sample? How large should the sample be? How can we summarize the average difficulty of each text using an adequate index of central tendency?

MATERIALS NEEDED

The basic materials are any English texts that differ from one another in manifest difficulty. Contrasting sources of word length can be found in novels versus textbooks or in such magazines as the *Reader's Digest* versus the *New York Review of Books.*

INSTRUCTIONS

Students should obtain their data from the same source so they can see how measures change as a function of the size and type of the sample. In this way, the class can divide the work of counting the length of words. The count can be performed by hand. Starting with a text sample of 200 words, each student can prepare a table listing word length (ranging from 1 letter to the length of the longest word) along the left hand side of a sheet of paper. Next to each word-length, students will enter a tally mark for each same-size word that appears in text. The computer buffs in the class can enter the text into a computer and write a program to provide the three measures of central tendency and the frequency distributions that we will examine.

Next, students can chart frequency distributions, with the number of letters displayed along the abscissa and the number of words corresponding to each word length displayed along the ordinate. The points should be connected so that students can clearly see that the distribution is skewed, that is, that the shorter words (three to four letters long) are the most frequent. This will show that the distributions are indeed skewed. Students should then compute the arithmetic *mean*, that is, the total number of letters divided by the total number of words. Next, students should compute the *median*, that is, the middlemost score, and finally, they should calculate the *mode*, the most frequently occurring word length.

Depending on how much time the teacher wishes to devote to this project, he or she can determine how many 200-word samples are to be collected by each student. In any case, the samples from each student can then be combined to produce a larger sample of word length, and each sample can be compared with every other sample to see how similar they are when they are of the same set and how different they are when they are from different sets. The distributions of each set can then be combined into one large distribution, and the two distributions can be compared. For example, the combined distribution of all samples from the *Reader's Digest* could be compared with the combined distribution of all samples from the *New York Review of Books*.

DISCUSSION   Have the students compare the frequency distributions, means, medians, and modes first for the samples of the same text and then for the samples of the different texts. This should give students an intuitive idea of inferential statistics, which one uses to determine whether two sets of data differ from one another. Thus, students will be able to see (a) how one must establish that the difference between two sets of data exceeds the differences one finds among samples within a given set of data; (b) that some measures of central tendency differentiate the various samples better than others; and (c) that for word-length distributions the mean is the largest, the median is next in size, and the mode is the smallest. Finally, the student should be able to conclude whether the two sets of data differ in difficulty.

The word length measure was explored many years ago for cases of disputed authorship. Mendenhall (1887, 1901) examined the frequency distributions of the writings of Shakespeare and compared them with those of Bacon. He found, interestingly enough, that Shakespeare had a mode of four letters, whereas Bacon had a mode of three letters. Students might find a renewed interest in Shakespeare knowing that he prefers four-letter words. More recently, and in a more sophisticated way, Mosteller and Wallace (1964) returned to the problem of applying statistics to disputed authorship in a book. Finally, students might find of interest Huff's (1954) *How to Lie With Statistics*, in which the author describes how one can use different measures of central tendency to make different points.

REFERENCES   Huff, D. (1954). *How to lie with statistics*. New York: Norton.

Mendenhall, T. C. (1887). The characteristic curves of composition. *Science, 9* (Suppl.), 237–246.

Mendenhall, T. C. (1901). A mechanical solution of a literary problem. *Popular Science Monthly, 60,* 97–105.

Mosteller, F., & Wallace, D. L. (1964). *Inference and disputed authorship: The Federalist*. Reading, MA: Addison-Wesley.

53 MEASURES OF CENTRAL TENDENCY IN DAILY LIFE

Lita Linzer Schwartz

Pennsylvania State University: Ogontz Campus

This is a simple, nonthreatening way to introduce your students to a unit on statistics. All you need are some examples of scores or measurements, such as scores on the last test or heights of the students in your class. Students need no prior knowledge, and you may use this with any size class.

CONCEPT Exactly what is meant by the word *average?* This activity clarifies the meaning of this word in statistical terms.

MATERIALS NEEDED You will need several groups of scores or measurements. Test scores, heights, ages, and so on, are possible examples (see Example Worksheet).

INSTRUCTIONS After defining the terms *mean, median,* and *mode* for students, direct them to find these measures for each group of figures selected.

DISCUSSION Are all three measures of central tendency equal? Are there situations for which one measure of central tendency is more appropriate than another? Why? Which measure of central tendency is most often used in newspaper reports (e.g., of number of pizzas eaten per person annually in the United States, of male and female incomes, of books read)?

Students can explore central tendency measures through many related activities. Have students ask a variety of people what *average* means to them. Students should also ask these people how they would find the average.

Some students might be interested in learning about what is average for infants and toddlers. They can obtain a grid from a pediatrician or family physician that shows range, mean, and average deviations for children's heights and weights at different ages. (This will also be available in standard child development texts.)

Have students keep records of their spending in different categories (e.g., food, movies, sports activities, books) for 4 weeks. At the end of this period, have them compute weekly and total means, medians, and modes. (They may be shocked!)

Given the following group of test scores, find the range, mean, median, and mode of the scores:

<pre>
88 39 83 65
72 67 93 75
60 74 47 74
74 82 97 81
89 86 73 77
</pre>

Range _____   Median _____

Mean _____   Mode _____

Question: If the three 74s were changed to 64s, in what way would this change the figures computed?

54 TEACHING THE CONCEPT OF STATISTICAL VARIABILITY

Ashton D. Trice and O. Ashton Trice
Mary Baldwin College

Epp P. Ogden
Salem College

This is actually three activities that, when used together, can be used effectively to teach the concept of probability. The dart game was designed for small lab classes of about 12. You may want to use volunteers to demonstrate the exercise for larger classes. The penny toss game can be used as a large group activity. The study diaries are done individually out of class.

CONCEPT

In teaching statistical concepts to beginning psychology students, we have found that variability is the first major stumbling block. Routinely, 40–50% of our students are unable to compute or interpret measures of variability by the end of the semester when we teach by didactic methods alone. Students who have difficulty with variability are somewhat more math anxious, have had fewer advanced math courses, and fail to solve formal operational tasks at a higher rate than those students who show little difficulty with the concept (Trice & Ogden, 1985). Because variability underlies the concepts of normal distribution, correlation, and significant differences, we developed a series of highly concrete exercises to give students a feel for the concept before moving on.

These exercises were developed in the context of an hour-long weekly lab adjunct to an introductory psychology lecture course, with out-of-class weekly exercises aimed at developing study skills (Trice & Trice, 1986). In a pilot program, we found that students exposed to this series of exercises scored an average of 83% on a test of concepts and calculations about variability, whereas those exposed to an equal amount of didactic teaching scored an average of 59%.

MATERIALS NEEDED

You will need darts and a dart board, a cup and pennies, and study diary notebooks.

INSTRUCTIONS

Dart board. In this exercise, students throw seven darts at a target 15 feet away. The target is the size of a legal pad page, which is marked by a straight line down the center. Students are instructed to aim as close to the center line as possible. Students place a legal page over the target for their first attempt (darts that miss the target are rethrown) and then practice throwing for 15 minutes in groups of 4 students. (By working in groups of 4, 12 students can complete the exercise during a 60-minute lab period). A second page is placed over the target at the end of the practice period, and a second set of throws is collected.

The holes in the paper represent data points. Each student measures the deviation from the target and constructs a line graph with the seven points and the target point on the line for each set of throws. Students then calculate and place the mean throw on the graph. Typically, students improve (decrease variability) considerably with practice, but the mean throws for the two sets are rarely much different, and the second mean throw is frequently farther away from the target point on the line graph than the mean of the first set of throws, underscoring the point that a data set must be represented by both a measure of central tendency and a measure of variability.

Students can measure the mean deviation from both the target and the mean point on the line graph with a ruler, first without consideration of directionality and then by considering directionality using positive and negative signs for the vectors. This exercise allows students to grasp why the mean deviation from the mean is undefined, since it will always be $0/N$.

Give students the following instructions:

1. Place an $8'' \times 14''$ piece of paper over the target. Throw your darts. If you totally miss the target, rethrow those darts. Remove the paper, and practice with your group for 15 minutes. Now put a second piece of paper over the target and throw as before.

2. Use a ruler to measure how far each throw for both tries was from the target line. Did you improve? (What was your average miss for the first try, and what was your average miss for your second try?)

3. Now compute where your average hit was by using a plus sign for those hits that were to the right of the target and a minus sign for those to the left of the target. Compute the average by using the usual formula for the mean ($\Sigma x/N$). Did your average hit improve? If not, why?

4. Now compute the deviations from the mean, first without using the plus and minus signs and then using the signs. What do you notice about the mean deviation when you use the signs?

Penny toss. The penny toss is an extension of the dart game and is typically used as a larger group activity. A piece of wrapping paper is placed on the floor. A cup is used as a target. Seven pennies are thrown at the cup. They are removed and marked. Cartesian coordinates are drawn, and the exercises described for the dart board are followed for both axes. We have found it useful to collect only two data sets, one thrown at close range and one at a considerable distance. Although the means are typically very close, the deviations are usually quite different.

Students then can find the center of the distribution by plotting the intersection of the means on the two axes.

Study diaries. The study diary exercise follows the mathematics of the preceding two exercises and, as a secondary benefit, points out to students how poorly they "guesstimate" the amount of time they study. Students provide a guesstimate of their average study time per week. This figure is divided by 7 to provide a target for daily study time. Students then keep careful study diaries for a week. These diaries are kept to an accuracy of 1 minute. For example, if a student begins studying at 8:09 and is interrupted by a phone call at 8:17, she or he is expected to clock out for the duration of the call. The study diaries for this exercise consist of single lines that are divided into four columns: (a) clock in, (b) clock out, (c) course studied, and (d) activity (reading, writing, completing worksheets, etc.).

Tell students not to total their study times until the meeting of the laboratory section. There, students compute the number of minutes for each day (we have found waking-to-bed days more useful than midnight-to-midnight days). Students then compute deviations from target study times, mean study times, and daily deviations from the means. It is at this point that the computation of the standard deviation is introduced.

DISCUSSION With as many as half of today's college students unable to perform satisfactorily on abstract reasoning tasks, it seems expedient to us to introduce new concepts in a concrete form (Schwebel, 1975). Although these three exercises seem to have a positive impact on students' later ability to compute and interpret variability, they are clearly only exemplars that instructors can take as starting points. Introduced in these materials are statistical concepts that come into play later in the teaching sequence (e.g., working with Cartesian coordinates and comparing two data sets in terms of both means and variability). It has been our experience that use of these exercises reinforces content (effects of practice on performance, specific measurement vs. subjective ratings).

It is important to include group activities, such as the coin toss activity, because students seem to learn a great deal from the verbal interactions with peers (Seashore, 1910), and such interaction may improve students' attitudes toward math content.

REFERENCES Schwebel, M. (1975). Formal operations in first-year college students. *College Psychology, 91,* 133–141.

Seashore, C. E. (1910). The class experiment. *Journal of Educational Psychology, 1,* 25–30.

Trice, A. D., & Ogden, E. P. (1985). Correlates of math anxiety in college students. *Math Matters Journal, 4,* 56–63.

Trice, A. D., & Trice, O. A. (1986, August). *Evaluation of the study skills laboratories for introductory psychology.* Paper presented at the 94th Annual Convention of the American Psychological Association, Washington, DC.

55 Don't Change! First Impressions Are Always Best, or Are They?

Stephen F. Davis, Cathy A. Grover, and Jeffrey S. Kixmiller
Emporia State University

This activity can be done with any size class and poses a question that will capture students' interest and illustrate statistical principles and reasons of central tendency at the same time. No materials are needed except the students' exam papers. (Obviously, this activity cannot be used early in the term unless it is modified, perhaps by using exam papers from a previous class.)

CONCEPT

Many of us can recall taking an examination with the teacher's admonition, "Don't change your answers, trust your first impulse," ringing in our ears. As teachers, we have no doubt perpetuated this myth ourselves.

Recent reports indicate that this is not necessarily the best idea. Although the numbers of answers that are changed are not astoundingly high, it seems clear that, if you feel confident of your change, you may increase your grade (Best, 1979). More specifically, Benjamin, Cavell, and Shallenberger (1984) surveyed the published research data on answer changing and reported that (a) the median number of changed answers was 3.3% and (b) an improvement in scores was consistently reported.

Clearly, this topic has the potential for stimulating a lively, interesting, and informative class discussion. Although this discussion will be applicable at any point during the psychology course, the fact that it can be supplemented with some easily gathered data makes its inclusion in the section on statistics and methodology a natural.

INSTRUCTIONS

Present this activity the next time your class has a test or exam.

After collecting and grading the tests, check the number of erasures and strike-overs and determine (a) the percentage of answers that have been changed and (b) the number of students whose test scores increase, decrease, or remain the same as a result of answer changing.

Although most investigators (e.g., Sitton, Adams, & Anderson, 1980) have failed to find a gender effect, Skinner (1983) did report that women changed significantly more answers than did men. If you have a large group of students, you may also want to evaluate this factor.

Students will want to know which items are changed most often, those that are easy or those that are more difficult. To differentiate between the two, group items into easy or hard categories based on the number or percentage of students passing each item (you may wish to modify your definitions several times to see if it has any effect on the number of changes that are observed for each type).

Be sure to work through all the calculations of means, medians, and percentages with your students.

DISCUSSION	This is a straightforward demonstration whose main purpose is to illustrate statistical principles. The background articles, however, can provide an excellent lead-in to discussions about this kind of test-taking behavior. You can ask students why this idea (about not changing your first answer) has persisted and to what extent they believe it themselves. Ask them why they change certain answers and leave others alone, how they handle questions whose answers they really don't know, and if they think that answer-changing is a sign of careful thinking or of indecision.

REFERENCES	Benjamin, L. T., Jr., Cavell, T. A., & Shallenberger, W. R. (1984). Staying with initial answers on objective tests: Is it a myth? *Teaching of Psychology, 11,* 133–141.

Best, J. B. (1979). Item difficulty and answer changing. *Teaching of Psychology, 6,* 228–230.

Sitton, L. R., Adams, I. G., & Anderson, H. N. (1980). Personality correlates of students' patterns of changing answers on multiple-choice tests. *Psychological Reports, 47,* 655–660.

Skinner, N. F. (1983). Switching answers on multiple-choice questions: Shrewdness or shibboleth? *Teaching of Psychology, 10,* 220–222.

$^\square$56 SAMPLING SAMPLING DISTRIBUTIONS

William J. Hunter
University of Calgary

This activity is designed to be flexible, applicable to any readily available data, and adaptable to any level of instruction. It teaches students to calculate and understand the concept of the standard error of the mean. The only preparation required is the copying of the tabulation sheet. Twelve students participate; for large classes, groups of twelve can be used.

CONCEPT   Specifically, the concept examined herein is the standard error of the mean. More generally, this activity will provide a basis for discussing the interrelations of sampling, statistical testing, and research design. The level of the discussion can be toned up or down to fit the instructor's purpose.

MATERIALS NEEDED   You will need a measurement device (tape measure, short quiz, survey, etc.) and copies of the Sampling Distribution Tabulation Sheet.

INSTRUCTIONS   Select 12 students or organize the class into groups of 12.

Gather data on any convenient variable (e.g., length of left forearm in finger widths, shoe size, favorite number) so that each student has a "score" on the variable.

Have students compute the means (the sum of scores divided by the number of students) and standard deviations (which measure the spread of scores) for the set of 12 observations, entering their calculations under Round 1 on the tabulation sheet. These are the *population* mean and standard deviation. (The population, of course, is 12).

Pair the students (group them in samples of two). Ask them to find the mean and standard deviation of their two observations and to record the results for the six pairs on the tabulation sheet (under Round 2). Repeat this step for samples of 3, 4, and 6 students (entering results under Rounds 3–5).

Calculate—or have students calculate—the means and standard deviations of the sample means and record them in the summary section of the tabulation sheet.

DISCUSSION   It will quickly be apparent that the mean of the sample means (Rounds 2, 3, 4, and 5) is equal to the population mean (from Round 1). It will also be clear that the larger the size of the sample, the smaller the standard deviation of sample means (SD_M) will be. At this point, it will be fairly easy for students to grasp the idea of plotting the sample means in a frequency chart (e.g., the six means from Round 1), and most students will see that as sample size increases, the shape of this sampling distribution of means will approach normal. It is useful to point out that the sampling distribution of means is a hypothetical distribution of the means of all possible samples of a given size. (Note that this is not what the demonstration did, since doing so would require sampling with replacement, but the demonstration could be extended to include all possible samples as an out-of-class activity.) Because the differences between the means in the sampling distribution are due to random sampling (or sampling error), the standard deviation of the sampling distribution of means is called the standard error of the mean (SE_M). Because we know the relation between standard deviations and areas under the normal curve, it becomes possible to discuss the likelihood that a given sample mean belongs to a given population. Specifically, we can use the following test: $Z = x - M/\sigma_x$, where $\sigma/x = SD/\sqrt{N - 1}$.

This, then, becomes a model for all inferential statistics: any inferential statistic = an observed difference/variation due to sampling. Encourage students to see that this step (statistical testing) plays a very specific role in experimentation: given a well-designed study, all but two causes of group differences have been eliminated (sampling error and treatment effect). Statistical testing eliminates the former so that the experimenter may conclude that the treatment is the cause of the observed difference. It is not necessary to present the full discussion to derive benefit from this activity—even discovering that the mean of the sample means equals the population mean can be sufficiently beneficial in some classes.

Sampling Distribution Tabulation Sheet

A. Tabulation of Scores and Means

	Round 1			Round 2		Round 3		Round 4		Round 5	
	Student and score			Group	Mean score	Group	Mean score	Group	Mean score	Group	Mean score
1	___	7	___	A	___	A	___	A	___	A	___
2	___	8	___	B	___	B	___	B	___	B	___
3	___	9	___	C	___	C	___	C	___		
4	___	10	___	D	___	D	___				
5	___	11	___	E	___						
6	___	12	___	F	___						

B. Tabulation of Group Means and Standard Deviations

Group	n	M	SD
Round 1	12	___	___
Round 2	2	___	___
Round 3	3	___	___
Round 4	4	___	___
Round 5	6	___	___

[□]57 STATISTICS FOR PERSONNEL ASSESSMENT

Alan L. Carsrud
University of Southern California

■──■

This is a detailed exercise that applies statistical procedures to business management. Students, serving as "consultants," will use statistical methods to find the most qualified applicant for a hypothetical administrative assistant position. The instructor should review the pertinent material in the students' statistics text with the class prior to beginning the assignment. Students will also need calculators. This activity can be used with classes of any size.

■──■

CONCEPT

This exercise attempts to accomplish two key goals. One is to teach students to apply statistical concepts and procedures to real-life data. The second and more important goal is to teach students to use statistical data in decision making, in this case, personnel decisions.

MATERIALS NEEDED

Students should have calculators and their statistics texts to help them complete the exercise. They will also need copies of the tables and the Descriptive Statistics Worksheet.

INSTRUCTIONS

Begin by providing students with the following background information:

> Ms. Karen Hammer, President of Trans Oceanic Shipping Company, must hire an administrative assistant. Ms. Hammer would like to hire the best possible person for the job. Trans Oceanic Shipping Company has received resumes from 10 applicants. After reviewing these resumes, Ms. Hammer has noticed that all 10 people meet the minimum criteria for the position. However, she must select only 1 person, and she has no idea who is the best candidate.
>
> Not knowing what to do, Ms. Hammer asks Professor Carsrud for help. Professor Carsrud suggests that she hire one of his students to aid her in selecting the right candidate. Ms. Hammer agrees and, because you are an enterprising young business student who sees the chance to apply some of the concepts you've learned in class (and also to earn a big consulting fee), you volunteer.
>
> You go to Trans Oceanic Shipping Company armed with two standardized personnel tests, Test A (the Minnesota Clerical Test) and Test B (the Clerical Aptitude Test). Both measures are believed to be good predictors of management success. Test A consists of 50 true/false items. It is scored on a 50-point basis, with 1 point given for each correct item (50 = *perfect score*, 0 = *none correct*; $M = 25$, $SD = 5$). Test B is made up of 30 multiple-choice questions. One point is given for each correct answer on Test B (30 = *perfect score*, 0 = *none correct*; $M = 15$, $SD = 5$). Test scores for each applicant are provided in Table 1.

1. Students should first consolidate the data into one handy table so that it is possible to see all the scores at a glance. Although Table 1 does this to some extent, a

Table 1. *Applicant Test Scores*

Applicant	Test A	Test B
1	30	25
2	18	14
3	35	15
4	27	10
5	25	27
6	42	25
7	21	21
8	35	18
9	47	20
10	35	25

frequency distribution will allow the user to easily determine such things as the range of scores and how often each score appears. Instruct students to put the data for Test A and Test B into frequency distributions, listing data for each candidate under the following row heads:

Score Test A   Frequency   Score Test B   Frequency

2. Tell students that one important aspect of any performance measure is the type of data (nominal, ordinal, interval, ratio) it uses. This will determine what purpose the data will be used for as well as which mathematical operations, if any, are appropriate to use. Ask students to decide which type of data the test scores represent. Why?

3. Descriptive statistics, such as mean, median, and mode, can also be helpful in giving us a better overall picture of the data. In addition, these statistics are useful as base data in more complex formulas. Give students the Descriptive Statistics Worksheet and instruct them to provide data for Test A and Test B.

4. We have already discussed the importance of frequency distributions. When there are only 10 scores, it is not difficult to construct a frequency distribution, but it would be difficult if there were 1,000 applicants and the scores ranged from 1 to 500. In a situation like this, it is often wise to group data into intervals. In our consulting scenario, let us suppose that Ms. Hammer has decided she would like the applicants placed in one of five groups, depending on their scores on Test B. Ask students to use the test score data from Table 1 to determine the most appropriate class interval size. What would be the midpoint of each interval? Tell students that, to impress Ms. Hammer, they might wish to construct a frequency histogram for the scores of Test B.

5. Recall that the scores of Test A are from a standardized personnel test with a mean of 25 and a standard deviation of 5. If we were to chart the scores of everyone who had ever taken the test, they would form a normal distribution. If graphed, the data would look like the bell-shaped curve. Ask students to determine how our sample (the 10 applicants) compares with the overall population (refer them to their Descriptive Statistics Worksheet) by plotting a graph of the test scores on a separate piece of paper.

Direct students to answer the following questions by examining the graphed scores: Is the curve skewed positively or negatively? What does this tell them about our sample? How would they explain this to Ms. Hammer? If they assume that the

```
┌─────────────────────────────────────────────────────────────────────────────┐
│                        Descriptive Statistics Worksheet                       │
│                                                                               │
│ Fill in the proper data for each test.                                        │
│ ─────────────────────────────────────────────────────────────────────────── │
│ Statistic                              Test A                          Test B │
│                                                                               │
│ 1. Σ X                                                                        │
│                                                                               │
│ 2. Σ X²                                                                       │
│                                                                               │
│ 3. (Σ X)²                                                                     │
│                                                                               │
│ 4. Mean                                                                       │
│                                                                               │
│ 5. Median                                                                     │
│                                                                               │
│ 6. Mode                                                                       │
│                                                                               │
│ 7. Range                                                                      │
│                                                                               │
│ 8. Standard deviation                                                         │
│       N                                                                       │
│       N − 1                                                                   │
└─────────────────────────────────────────────────────────────────────────────┘
```

Statistic	Test A	Test B
1. ΣX		
2. ΣX^2		
3. $(\Sigma X)^2$		
4. Mean		
5. Median		
6. Mode		
7. Range		
8. Standard deviation N $N-1$		

scores on Test A are normally distributed, what percent of the scores would fall between 20 and 30? Why? What percentile does the score 32.5 correspond to? Why?

6. Ms. Hammer does not understand what the test scores of the 10 applicants represent. To better illustrate the test scores and each applicant's standing in the population, direct students to turn the scores into standard scores, or Z scores. The Z score shows an individual's standing relative to the mean of the group. The higher the Z score, the more an individual's score deviates from the mean of the group. Students can compute the Z score for Test A using the following formula:

$$Z = \frac{X - M}{SD}. \tag{1}$$

Table 2. *Test A Scores and Performance Ratings*

Applicant	Score	Rating
1	15	5
2	33	7
3	20	5
4	24	6
5	18	4
6	41	8
7	10	3
8	30	6
9	45	9
10	26	5
11	40	7
12	47	9
13	43	7
14	16	3
15	36	6

7. We assumed that both personnel tests were good predictors of management performance. However, by looking over the results, the test scores seem inconsistent; for example, the highest score on Test A (47) is only a medium score on Test B (20). This makes it hard to decide on whom to hire. Direct students to decide which test to use for selection by determining the validity of each test. One way to determine the validity of the tests is to see if there is a correlation between personnel test scores and actual job performance. If the test scores predict actual job performance, the test can be used to determine who is most likely to succeed.

Tell students that Ms. Hammer has asked them to compute a correlation coefficient for each of the personnel tests. They are given access to the personnel files of all the current assistants (15 in all). Here they find the assistants' performance ratings given by their supervisors. The performance ratings are on a 1–9 scale (1 = *very poor*, 9 = *excellent*). The performance ratings will be used as a measure of job success. The 15 assistants are then given both personnel tests. Test scores on each test are correlated with corresponding performance ratings to see which test yields the highest correlation and, therefore, is better at predicting future job success.

Tell students to correlate Test A scores and performance ratings (see Table 2) using the following formula:

$$r_{xy} = \frac{\Sigma \, xy}{(N)(SD_x)(SD_y)}, \tag{2}$$

where Σxy is the sum of the corresponding deviations of x and y from their corresponding means. Ask students how they would interpret this correlation. Is there a high or low correlation?

Now direct students to correlate Test B scores with their corresponding performance rating (see Table 3). Again, ask students to interpret this correlation and to identify high or low correlations.

8. Direct students to choose the test that Ms. Hammer should use to make her decision. Which candidate should be hired as the new administrative assistant?

Table 3. *Test B Scores and Performance Ratings*

Applicant	Score	Rating
1	11	5
2	14	7
3	20	5
4	12	6
5	18	4
6	20	8
7	14	3
8	12	6
9	25	9
10	14	5
11	22	7
12	29	9
13	12	7
14	10	3
15	15	6

DISCUSSION Following the exercise, tell students to discuss their decisions and the process of using statistical information to assist in making personnel decisions. Focus some of the discussion on Type I and Type II errors.

SUGGESTED READING

Anastasi, A. (1982). *Psychological testing.* New York: MacMillan.

Goldstein, G. & Hersen, M. (1984). *Handbook of psychological assessment.* Elmsford, NY: Pergamon Press.

American Psychological Association, Division 14. (1980). *Principles for the validation and use of personnel selection procedures* (2nd ed.). College Park, MD: Author.

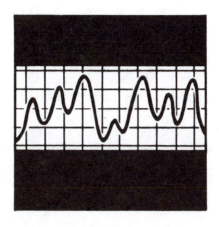

CHAPTER VIII
SPECIAL TOPICS

These activities all address special concerns that do not fit neatly into any specific chapter. All can be used to enhance a traditional psychology curriculum, and they vary in degrees of difficulty and the type of preparation needed for each. Activity 58 is an amusing ice-breaker with a dual purpose: While teaching students the fundamentals of research methodology, it breaks down their resistance to class participation. Activity 59 lets students experience, temporarily, the challenges faced by persons with disabilities, and Activity 67 gives students a firsthand look at the psychological services in their own community.

There are two activities that can be used to teach the history of psychology: Activity 65, in which students debate differing psychological theories within a historical framework, and Activity 60, a longer and more involved activity for creating cognitive maps of the history of psychology, itself an interesting skill for students to learn. In a similar vein, in Activity 61 a formal debate of research findings is set up that requires students to adopt a critical approach to research as well as develop their own research skills.

Other activities are concerned with physiology: Activity 68 focuses on altered states of consciousness, specifically meditation, whereas Activities 69 and 71 look scientifically at concepts such as biofeedback, stress, and relaxation. In Activity 64, students become the instructors, designing and creating their own poster session as a group; in that case the poster session was open to the entire school as well as other psychology sections.

Students can gain a better understanding of their own and others' behavior through four of the activities in this chapter: Students are guided through the process of self-directed behavior change in Activity 62. In Activity 66, the reactions to external pressures of passive, aggressive, and assertive personalities are contrasted. A tongue-in-cheek analysis of self-fulfilling prophecies is provided in Activity 70. In Activity 63, students are kept in touch with their own thoughts and actions by keeping a journal in which they apply psychological principles to daily events. In Activity 72, the effects of role models on personal aspirations are explored.

$^{\square}58$ WILL CLASS PARTICIPATION "KILL" YOU? REFUTING A COMMON IRRATIONAL BELIEF BY TEACHING RESEARCH METHODS

Bernardo J. Carducci
Indiana University Southeast

■——■

This activity is an icebreaker that can be used with classes of any size at any level. It is a good activity to use on the first day of class. No prior knowledge is required of students and no advance preparation by the instructor is needed. The activity familiarizes students with several terms relevant throughout the course. This activity can also be used to introduce methodology.

■——■

CONCEPT

One of the biggest frustrations faced by those teaching large sections of psychology courses (e.g., introductory psychology) is getting students to overcome their apprehension about speaking up in class. The purpose of this activity is to present a demonstration designed to establish a norm of class participation during the first class meeting while introducing some basic principles of research methodology. On the basis of the irrational belief held by many students that speaking up in class will "kill" them, this demonstration uses a very simple pretest–posttest design to test in a rational manner this irrational belief right before the students' eyes. I recommend that this activity be conducted during the first class meeting, before the students settle into a mode of nonparticipation.

MATERIALS NEEDED

The only thing needed is a balled-up piece of paper.

INSTRUCTIONS

The following steps each correspond to a basic methodological principle:

Step 1. Statement of rival hypotheses: I'll bet your life I'm right! Start the activity by giving a simple definition of a hypothesis. Then give the following two hypotheses:

Student: Speaking up in class will kill you.

Instructor: Speaking up in class will not kill you.

Tell students that you have such faith in your own hypothesis that you are willing to bet their lives on it.

Step 2. Selection of subjects: Follow the bouncing ball. If the class size is sufficiently small or if you have enough time for all students to participate, proceed to Step 3.

For large classes, demonstrate the process of randomly selecting subjects. Wad up a piece of paper and throw it out into the classroom or lecture hall. The person who catches it is your first subject. Standing at his or her seat, this person then throws the ball out in any direction, and the next person to catch it is the second subject. (Subjects should remain standing.) Continue this procedure until you feel you have a sample of adequate size. Now ask the students to come to the front of the classroom.

Step 3. Pretest measure: Are all of the subjects alive? At this point, the operational definition of "alive" must be clarified because it is imperative that all of the subjects be alive at the start of the demonstration to provide a fair test of the hypotheses. To do this, make the distinction between being "alive" (i.e., thinking and feeling) and being alive but "brain dead." For the purpose of the demonstration, you will want to assume that everyone is both alive and thinking. You can point out that because the subjects were able to follow your directions up to this point, it is safe to assume that all of them fit the operational definition of being alive prior to the introduction of the treatment.

Step 4. Introducing the treatment: Speaking up in front of the class. Ask the students to describe what they feel would be a fair test of which of the two hypotheses is correct. An obvious treatment is to ask the subjects to speak directly to the class, giving their name, proposed major, and something they like to do in their spare time.

Step 5. The posttest measure: Are you still alive? Because nobody actually died after speaking, the students can conclude that, at least in this course, speaking up in class will not kill you.

You might point out to them that this is an extremely powerful test of the hypothesis. If standing up in front of the entire class will not kill them, surely they are clearly out of danger when speaking from the safety of their desks, surrounded by their friends.

Step 6. A lesson in the formulation of alternative explanations: Suppose somebody did die? To get the students participating immediately in a class discussion, ask them to speculate about what alternative explanations might be used to explain the highly unlikely possibility of someone's actually dying during the demonstration (e.g., selecting a sickly or intoxicated subject). In addition, how would the demonstration have to be modified to control for such explanations, thus providing a more valid test of the hypothesis?

Step 7. A note on ecological validity: See, talking during the discussion did not kill you. Before terminating this activity, you might point out that because those students who participated in the postdemonstration discussion in Step 6 are still alive, you now have further evidence to support the ecological validity of your hypothesis. In addition, to test the generalizability of this conclusion, encourage the students to participate in their other classes as well and report the results back at the next class meeting.

DISCUSSION
This teaching activity is designed to help establish a norm of class participation by stimulating some discussion during the first class meeting while introducing some basic principles of research methodology. The demonstration allows for discussion at each step, and it gives students a firm enough understanding of these basic principles to begin to discuss in more detail the experimental method and such concepts as independent and dependent variables and the notion of experimental control. To maintain the norm of class participation throughout the semester, instructors are encouraged to use other teaching activities presented in this handbook designed to stimulate student discussion.

Suggested Reading

Buss, A. H. (1980). *Self-consciousness and social anxiety.* San Francisco: W. H. Freeman.

Cozby, P. C. (1985). *Methods in behavioral research* (3rd ed.). Palo Alto, CA: Mayfield.

Eisenberg, A. M. (1975). *Living communication.* Englewood Cliffs, NJ: Prentice-Hall.

Friedman, P. G. (1980). *Shyness and reticence in students.* Washington, DC: National Education Association.

59 Experiential Activities for Generating Interpersonal Empathy for People With Developmental Disabilities

Charles Denton Fernald
University of North Carolina at Charlotte

Sue Sampen Fernald
University of North Carolina at Chapel Hill

This activity contains five simple demonstrations, which can be done in class and require readily available materials, that are designed to sensitize students to the experience of persons with disabilities. Students need no prior knowledge and there is no preparation except for gathering the materials. The discussion could be expanded to include the long-term effects of physical disabilities on social or cognitive development.

CONCEPT

What does it feel like to have a developmental disability such as mental retardation, autism, or cerebral palsy? People with these disabilities experience the world around them very differently from the ways others do. The activities described here are designed to give students some personal experiences that might simulate the experiences of people with developmental disabilities. These experiences may help students to understand, appreciate, and empathize with persons with disabilities.

EXERCISE 1

UNDERSTANDING LANGUAGE

Some people with disabilities have problems with understanding speech and following instructions. The following are some tasks that can help the students understand how this might feel.

For the foreign language task, select a paragraph written in a foreign language that you can read smoothly. Give instructions for an activity in another language. You should use gestures and be emphatic about trying to get the students to understand.

For the missing words task, write out a set of instructions for an activity, then erase one or two key words in each sentence. Read the instructions, being careful not to put in the missing words.

For the complicated task, use one set of simple materials, (e.g., origami paper, rope for knots, neckties) for each student. Write out a set of instructions for a complicated task (e.g., origami paper folding, macramé or other type of knot, tying a necktie). Then read the instructions aloud and have the students try to follow them without any demonstration.

Questions for discussion include the following: How did it feel when you did not understand what you were supposed to be doing? How might you act if you were constantly in similar situations?

EXERCISE 2   TROUBLE CONTROLLING MUSCLES

Some persons with disabilities have difficulty controlling their muscles and so cannot move their limbs the way they want to move them.

For this task you will need a small paper bag for each student. Each student places a paper bag over his or her hand, holds a pencil with the bag, and then writes a short paragraph or copies a simple design from one drawn on the blackboard.

Questions for discussion include the following: How did it feel when you could not do what you wanted to do with your own muscles? How would you react if the teacher were constantly telling you to write more neatly?

EXERCISE 3   DIFFERENCES IN PERSONAL SPACE

Some persons with disabilities feel uncomfortable when others get too close (or too far away). What is normal distance for you may seem too close (or too far) for them. Also, some persons with disabilities do not like to be touched. There are others who like to be touched more than usual.

No extra materials are needed for this task. Have the students stand face to face close together in pairs. Their faces should be very close together (nose to nose). Then have them carry on a conversation (e.g., about the latest movie they saw, etc.).

Now have them pair off again, but this time have them stand with about 6 feet of open space between them, and converse this way.

Pairing off a third time, the students should decide which member of each pair will do the talking. Have them stand very close together. The talker will tell the other student to do several tasks, but while doing so, will touch the other student a lot (e.g., feel hair, stroke face, roll up sleeve, etc.). The task can be fairly complicated (e.g., "Please take this book into the hall, but before you do that, get out five pieces of paper and bring them to me along with three pencils"). Students may also reverse roles.

Questions for discussion include the following: What does it feel like to have someone too close (or too far away) when you are having a conversation? What does it feel like to have someone touching you too much while he or she is talking to you? Were you able to follow the instructions?

DISCUSSION   People often assume that personal experiences, such as understanding language, moving muscles, and interacting with others, are identical for everyone. The activities of this section suggest that the experiences of people with disabilities may be very different from those who have no disabilities.

Some final questions you may want to ask students are as follows: How have these activities changed your understanding of what it must be like to have a disability? How might the different experiences of persons with disabilities affect the way they act? How would you react if you had these experiences every day? Do you think that these activities will have any impact on how you will treat and react to persons with disabilities?

Suggested Reading

Telford, C. W., & Sawrey, J. M. (1981). *The exceptional individual.* Englewood Cliffs, NJ: Prentice-Hall.

Thompson, R. J., Jr., & O'Quinn, A. N. (1979). *Developmental disabilities: Etiologies, manifestations, diagnoses, and treatments.* New York: Oxford University Press.

60 COGNITIVE MAPS OF THE HISTORY OF PSYCHOLOGY

George S. Howard
University of Notre Dame

This activity requires an hour or so of the instructor's time and the time of one colleague to produce the map and to copy the comparison maps for presentation to the class. Although students could do this at the end of an introductory course, more advanced students are likely to be more suitable. The maps are constructed outside of class, and at least one class session should be devoted to the discussion. Small to medium classes would work best. This activity highlights the role of values in education and methodology, and the organization required contributes to study skills.

CONCEPT

There is simply no way of giving a completely objective account of any series of historical events. The conscientious historian can only strive to offer an account that is as faithful to the facts as is humanly possible. However, the ways in which events, people, and actions are related to one another represent a hermeneutic (or interpretive) act. All historical analyses involve some degree of storytelling, and whenever one tells a tale, the author paints the account (accentuating some persons and events while downplaying others) and draws out themes and implications in a somewhat idiosyncratic fashion.

Like all history telling, books and courses in the history of psychology involve storytelling of a (presumably) nonvicious sort. Of course, texts and courses will strive for, and attempt to convey the impression of, objectivity and accuracy in their account of psychology's path into the present. However, history of psychology courses can also be used as vehicles for making points typically associated with courses in methodology in history. Namely, instructors might demonstrate to students how an account of the history of psychology is slanted by the narrator's background, interests, and purpose in recounting that history.

Most maps are designed to give a pictorial representation of some geographical area, such as the United States. Such a map is called realistic or accurate if its *scale* is correct, that is, if the ratio of actual geographic distances throughout the country to distances between points on the map is constant throughout. However, even if a map's scale is correct, it might still be virtually worthless as a road map for example. One can appreciate this by thinking of a map where lines that depict highways are so thick that the lines become indistinguishable around metropolitan areas. One would be hard-pressed to know from the map whether it were easy to get from one highway to another. Such a map might be described as potentially misleading or even useless.

When the map analogy above is applied to courses in the history of psychology, issues of scale might correspond to questions of seeing that the various approaches and schools (e.g., cognitive, humanistic, psychoanalytic, etc.) and context domains (e.g., clinical, experimental, developmental, etc.) are represented appropriately in the text, the course, or both. Conversely, questions of utility might be thought of as relating to the author's and instructor's purposes in characterizing psychology's history in the way he or she does (e.g., I want students to see the importance of good experimental method to generating knowledge of human action; I want students to see how psychology has prospered the more it comes out of the lab and deals with real human problems; I want students to see that great ideas spring directly from the personalities and childhood experiences of theorists, etc).

Have you ever seen those pictures that are supposed to represent the cognitive map of the United States in the minds of New Yorkers? They are gross distortions of the scale of the country: the East Coast (New York, Boston, Philadelphia, Washington, DC, and Miami) comprises about 75% of the map area. The Middle Atlantic, Midwest, Plains, Southeast, Southwest, and Rocky Mountain states occupy about 5% of the area of the cognitive map (represented by dots referring to Chicago and Texas). Finally, the West Coast (meaning Los Angeles and San Francisco only) occupies the remaining 25% of the map.

The notion of proper scale on this map is stood on its head, and it is this purposeful distortion that creates the utility of the map. It represents a sarcastic commentary on the perceived egocentrism and hubris of New Yorkers. (Having spent well over half of my life in the New York metropolitan area, I find such a view of Gothamites hard to believe. However, sayings such as, "Whenever you're west of the Hudson River, you're camping out" do convey a certain attitude.)

The point of this exercise is to trace the cognitive map of a few observers of the history of psychology in order to better appreciate (a) the complexity of the discipline's past and development; (b) the issues of objectivity and perspective inevitably encountered in the writing of any historical explanation; and (c) to gain a richer appreciation of how a writer's experiences and interests influence that author's writing of history.

MATERIALS NEEDED

You will need large pieces of paper, as well as pencils, rulers, and (if desired) colored pencils, felt-tip pens, crayons, and so on for creating the maps.

INSTRUCTIONS

It may be helpful for the instructor to draw his or her own cognitive map of the history of psychology (call this Map A) before studying Figure 60-1, which represents my attempt to draw my own cognitive map (Map B). Invite a faculty colleague (typically in an area different from your subspecialty) to do the same exercise and refer to this map as Map C. Have a small group of students construct a similar map using the course text as a guide; this will be Map D. (Incidentally, my students found this exercise to be a wonderful way to "organize the facts" in preparation for the final examination). Finally, have a few students (about three) trace their understanding of the history of psychology (Maps E–G).

A few days before the class on cognitive maps, each person who will be producing one of the maps should be instructed to trace his or her view of the history of psychology on one piece of paper. Each "historian" should feel free to organize the scheme in any way she or he feels most comfortable. Last, I suggest that each historian try to extend the history into the present, perhaps even mentioning specific faculty that the students in the class might know personally. I never put a time limit on the construction of the map, but anything over an hour tends to be overkill. The students who are reviewing the course text are the only historians allowed access to any reference materials.

For the class discussion, copies of Maps A–G are given to all students and the class is urged to make comments on any of the maps; point out comparisons between

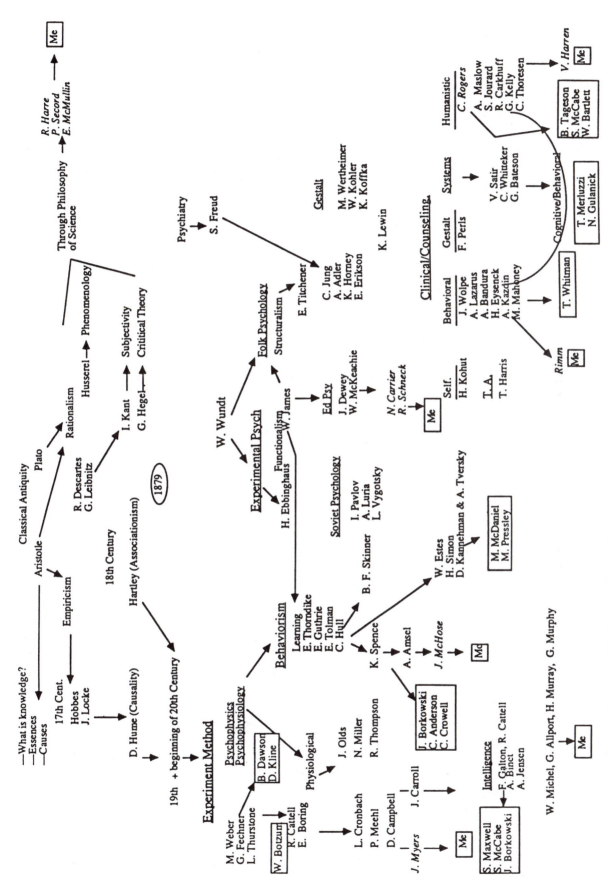

Figure 60-1. Howard's cognitive map of the history of psychology.

or among the maps; note organizing characteristics implicit in any of the maps; comment on noteworthy omissions; and so forth.

It generally takes several minutes of silence for students to absorb the material in the various cognitive maps, but once comments begin they can flood out. The determination of which cognitive maps are "most accurate," "best organized," "most understandable," and so forth is itself an interpretation based on the cognitive map of the history of psychology that the student himself or herself has developed. Thus, students often actively disagree with one another regarding which exhibit is, for example, most accurate.

Several issues almost always arise in these discussions. For example, how does the historian organize the account? Is time the central organizing concept? Do schools of thought (e.g., psychoanalytic, humanistic, behavioral) figure heavily in the presentation of people, events, and so forth? Are there any content domains (e.g., counseling, learning, industrial) seriously overdeveloped or underdeveloped? Do the maps represent all of psychology or only American psychology? When does the history of psychology begin in each map? Were there any patterns in the maps that might have been predicted before actually seeing the data (e.g., faculty histories more elaborate than student histories; the exhibit based on the course text being more logical or better organized than other maps; the map writer's known interest [and lack of interest] in specific subspecialties leading to great detail in predictable and perhaps unpredictable areas and to lack of attention to others).

For purposes of discussion, consider my map (see Figure 60-1). Individuals enclosed in boxes are members of the Notre Dame faculty. Students are often surprised at where their teachers show up in these histories. The few names in italics represent the individuals with whom I had personal contact, who introduced me to that particular area. There are seven identifiable influences on my thinking, but none of my colleagues show as being influenced by more than two sources. Does this speak to how well people know themselves—and what factors influenced their thinking—versus how well they know others and their thinking?

I did not edit (read or correct for embarrassing errors and omissions) my history of psychology. Did you notice that only two women (Karen Horney and Virginia Satir) appear? Where are Anna Freud, Ann Anastasi, Charlotte Buhler, Leona Tyler, Sandra Scarr, Anne Roe, Janet Spence, Jane Loevinger, Eleanor Gibson, Eleanor Maccoby, and others? Oops! Sorry. An almost equally embarrassing oversight involves the fact that there is almost no representation of developmental and social psychology in my cognitive map. Surely Jerome Bruner, Leon Festinger, J. McVicker Hunt, Stanley Milgram, Robert Sears, Stanley Schachter, and many others should have been named. I also seem to have devoted more time and attention to psychology's roots in philosophy than do most psychologists. Finally, some of the connections that I made reflect somewhat idiosyncratic knowledge that I have garnered over the years. For example, few would think of William James as influencing behaviorism, or Clark Hull leading to B. F. Skinner, to name two instances. Finally, the influence of individual thinkers on other individuals seems to dominate the overall structure of my cognitive map rather than content domains or theoretical systems.

There is enormous variability in the ways in which different people organize their maps. There is also surprisingly little overlap among the individuals who show up on the various maps, once one gets past the obvious choices such as Freud, Wundt, James, Skinner, Piaget, and Rogers. Both of these tendencies point out clearly to students how much of the map-making activity of history writing represents a (somewhat) subjective construction of the author.

Finally, I always make a related point that the path of biological evolution represents the story of those who have temporarily won the battle for survival only to lose at a later date (e.g., dinosaurs), or those who won and also then evolved into a different species (e.g., lizards to apes to humans). However, most of the variability attributed to genetic mutations was immediately nonviable and thus never shows up in the historical record of the evolution of life. What remains is only a partial record. The history of psychology is of the ideas that proved to be good; the bad ones quickly drop out of sight. This, however, is true of almost all history telling. History tends to become the history of the winners. Few people have an interest in telling and retelling the tales of the losers. Yet, it is still an open debate as to whether consumers of history would be better served if we were to dwell on the lessons to be learned from the losers rather than on what we believe is to be gained from a study of the winners.

SUGGESTED READING

Boring, E. G., & Lindzey, G. (Eds.). (1967). *A history of psychology in autobiography* (Volume I-V). New York: Appleton-Century-Crofts.

Collingwood, R. G. (1946). *The idea of history.* Oxford, England: Clarendon Press.

Hexter, J. H. (1971). *The history primer.* New York: Basic Books.

Kendler, H. H. (1987). *Historical foundations of modern psychology.* Chicago: Dorsey.

Leakey, T. H. (1987). *A history of psychology.* Englewood Cliffs, NJ: Prentice-Hall.

Mandelbaum, M. (1977). *The anatomy of historical knowledge.* Baltimore, MD: Johns Hopkins University Press.

Martin, R. (1977). *Historical explanation.* Ithaca, NY: Cornell University Press.

61 USE OF DEBATES IN INTRODUCTORY PSYCHOLOGY

Janet Morahan-Martin
Bryant College

This activity is best suited for small to medium classes and would be especially suitable for an honors class. Although it is intended for the introductory course, it could be adapted to other courses. The instructor must plan ahead of time how the debates will fit into the course schedule and set up the debate team assignments in the first few weeks of the term. The instructor will need to place materials relevant to the debates on reserve in the library. A rating scale for group debates is provided. You may choose to have the student observers evaluate the debates as well.

CONCEPT

Psychology is a field of controversy. Psychological issues are debated in the media and in courts. Legal proceedings sometimes find psychologists offering conflicting interpretations of the same facts. Psychologists of different paradigms perceive and interpret information differently and frequently argue over these differences. All of this is hardly new to the psychologist. Psychologists debate among themselves; unfortunately, students often interpret this as yet another sign of psychology's inability to understand behavior rather than it being indicative of scientific inquiry and ongoing research. Introductory psychology courses typically survey an enormous amount of material. The challenge in teaching an introductory course is to help the students understand that this material is subject to various interpretations and to involve them in the debate process.

One approach to involve students in the controversies in psychology is to use a structured debate format in the classroom. This activity is a discussion of how debates can be used in an introductory psychology course. This technique can also be used in other psychology courses.

MATERIALS NEEDED

Each debate topic requires one position paper supporting and one position paper opposing the issue. The instructor can choose topics and articles and make them available to the class.

Rubenstein and Slife's (1988) *Taking Sides: Clashing Views on Controversial Psychological Issues* is a good sourcebook, and it offers 19 ready-made debates. Each issue is posed as a question (e.g., "Can suicide be rational?") An article supporting and one opposing are presented for each issue, as well as a summary, points and counterpoints, and concluding challenge questions.

INSTRUCTIONS

Before the beginning of the semester, choose the debate topics to be used. These should be incorporated in the syllabus so that a debate will end a unit on a relevant issue. For example, the issue "Can intelligence be increased?" could close a unit on psychological testing. As much as possible, the upcoming issue should be referred to in the context of reviewing the material of that unit. This helps to integrate the issue into the unit material, maximizing the relevancy of both.

Introduce students to the debate topics and debate format on the first day of the course and have them form debate teams of three to four students within 1–2 weeks. Each team is required to submit a list of the issues they would like to debate in rank order, so that student preferences can be considered in making debate assignments. Letting students choose their team members and topics can help promote a greater feeling of group cohesiveness and commitment. Each issue should have two teams assigned to it: one pro and one con. Again, student preferences can be taken into consideration in assigning pro or con teams, although arbitrary arrangements will sometimes be necessary. Assignment to the pro or con side of a debate can be made either when debates are initially assigned or 1–2 weeks before the debate. The latter allows students to investigate the overall debate issue and may help minimize a narrow focusing of research on one side of a given debate.

Research requirements for the team presentation can vary according to the instructor's intents. This project can be the basis of a focused research project. It is helpful to place some introductory material on reserve in the library as well as require research into professional journals. Encourage students to interview professionals who specialize in their chosen area and to conduct surveys. Students may be required to hand in an annotated bibliography or a summary of their research either prior to or on the day of the debate. It is important to inform students of the relative importance of research when assignments are made.

It is helpful if all students not on the debate team are required to prepare for the issue to be debated as well. If possible, have students read articles on the pro and con sides of the debate. This will force students to be prepared for the debate and encourage them to think actively about the debate issue prior to class.

On the day of the debate, introduce the topic and summarize the debate at the end of the period. It may be helpful to take a vote of the class's position before and after the debate. During the debate, it is important that the instructor not let the debater focus on him or her. The instructor may wish to sit on the side of the class and avoid eye contact with the debate teams.

Debate formats can vary. One possibility is a formal debate with constructive and rebuttal speeches (Dick, 1972). An alternative is to have team members assume roles for the debate (Gallagher, 1987). In this format, each team would have three roles: *stater*, *prover*, and *attacker*. Team members should determine in advance which roles each of them is to take. The stater presents the position taken by the group, outlining the basic arguments of the team, and also concluding the debate with a summary of the team's position. The prover is responsible for citing relevant research to support the arguments. The prover should thoroughly understand the research supporting the team's side of the issue. The attacker will probe the opposite team for weaknesses in their arguments and should be familiar with the articles and materials being used by both teams. This role may be assumed by one student or the entire team. All team members should be responsible for defending the team's position against the attacker and class questions. Each team should be expected to plan its presentation and attack format in advance. Direct reading of prepared statements should be discouraged. Debates can be evaluated by the teacher and class members using the Rating Scales for Group Debates provided at the end of the article.

Students not on the debate team should participate actively in the debate. They may ask for clarification as well as question any team member. However, it is important that the team make their initial presentation before the class takes over. Active class participation before the teams have finished their presentation can disrupt the team's ability to make their presentations. The student audience can also be involved by taking a vote at the end of the debate. Students also may take part in the evaluation process.

Time management is essential. Both sides must have time to present their entire debate, attack, and defense. Allot a certain amount of time for each team member and also for class questions. Sometimes the instructor will have to terminate a line of questioning if it becomes repetitive. Finally, time should be left for class discussion afterward.

DISCUSSION

Discussion should center around the issues raised in the debate. Take a final vote on the debate and ask students why they have or have not changed their position. They can cite the strong and weak points in the debate.

Use this opportunity to clarify any questions and misinformation as well as to cite the relevancy of the topic to related subjects in the course.

REFERENCES

Dick, R. (1972). *Argumentation and rational debating.* Dubuque, IA: William C. Brown.

Gallagher, D. (1987). *Using "taking sides" in the classroom.* Guilford, CT: Dushkin.

Rubenstein, J., & Slife, B. (1988). *Taking sides: Clashing views on controversial psychological issues* (5th ed.). Guilford, CT: Dushkin.

SUGGESTED READING

Slife, B., & Rubenstein, J. (1988). *An instructor's manual for Taking sides: Clashing views on controversial psychological issues* (5th ed.). Guilford, CT: Dushkin.

Rating Scale for Group Debates

Group _____ Title   Pro or Con _____

Group Members: <u>Class Time</u> (Circle)

Stater _____

Prover 1 _____

Prover 2 _____

Prover 3 _____

Attacker _____

<u>Team</u> Grade Equivalent –	Failure		Poor			Excellent		
	F 0	D 1	CD 2	C 3	BC 4	B 5	AB 6	A 7
1. Did the team appear to have done its homework?								
2. Was the team presentation well organized and effective?								
3. Did the team make its presentation interesting to the class?								
4. Was the team empirical as it presented and defended its points?								
5. Did the team go beyond the issue as presented in the text?								
6. How effective overall was the team's presentation?								
<u>Offensive</u> 7. Was the team perceptive to the weak points on the opposite side and able to put the other team on the defensive?								
<u>Defensive</u> 8. Was the team able to defend itself against the attacks of the class and the other team?								
9. Team Grade								
Grade Equivalent –	F 0	D 1	CD 2	C 3	BC 4	B 5	AB 6	A 7

(Continued on next page)

(Rating Scale—*continued from previous page*)

Grade Equivalent –	Failure		Poor		Excellent		

A. Stater: Name _____

	F | 0	D | 1	CD | 2	C | 3	BC | 4	B | 5	AB | 6	A | 7
1. Use of and knowledge of research								
2. Effective presentation								
3. Effective in defense								
4. Effective in offense								
5. Overall Grade								

B. Prover 1: Name _____

	F | 0	D | 1	CD | 2	C | 3	BC | 4	B | 5	AB | 6	A | 7
1. Use of and knowledge of research								
2. Effective presentation								
3. Effective in defense								
4. Effective in offense								
5. Overall Grade								

C. Prover 2: Name _____

	F | 0	D | 1	CD | 2	C | 3	BC | 4	B | 5	AB | 6	A | 7
1. Use of and knowledge of research								
2. Effective presentation								
3. Effective in defense								
4. Effective in offense								
5. Overall Grade								

D. Prover 3: Name _____

	F | 0	D | 1	CD | 2	C | 3	BC | 4	B | 5	AB | 6	A | 7
1. Use of and knowledge of research								
2. Effective presentation								
3. Effective in defense								
4. Effective in offense								
5. Overall Grade								

E. Prover 4: Name _____

	F | 0	D | 1	CD | 2	C | 3	BC | 4	B | 5	AB | 6	A | 7
1. Use of and knowledge of research								
2. Effective presentation								
3. Effective in defense								
4. Effective in offense								
5. Overall Grade								

Comments on team or individuals _____

_____

_____

_____

_____

62 A MODULE FOR A SELF-DIRECTED BEHAVIOR CHANGE PROJECT

Janet Morahan-Martin
Bryant College

This activity can be used with classes of virtually any size, although the written progress reports should be considered because the project extends over several weeks and includes small group meetings outside of class. The instructor should be thoroughly familiar with some of the sources cited, but there are no materials or equipment needed. Some discussion of the treatment of privileged information that emerges in group meetings is appropriate, and teachers should consider the ethics of requiring an intervention such as this and possible alternative assignments.

CONCEPT

An activity requiring students to change their behavior is an excellent method of the direct application of the principles of psychology. Such programs, often called self-modification or self-change projects, have been used in a variety of courses, including behavior modification techniques, adjustment, and counseling. Most self-modification projects are behavioral or cognitive or both, although some have involved the application of other paradigms as well. Both instructors and students are enthusiastic about using them.

The format for self-modification projects described here involves (a) frequent reporting of the steps involved in the project and weighing these steps into the final project grade; (b) bringing in outside advisers on the major group of projects to lecture on that topic; and (c) forming support and discussion groups of students involved in similar projects.

MATERIALS NEEDED

Watson and Tharp's (1989) *Self-Directed Behavior: Self-Modification for Personal Adjustment* may be useful. The authors detail behavioral and cognitive techniques for self-change, guiding the reader through the entire process step by step. The chapters are general to any type of behavioral self-change, but are supplemented by frequent examples as well as a section at the end of many chapters that provides specific ideas for common projects, involving topics such as anxiety, assertiveness, smoking, alcohol and substance abuse, depression, social skills and relations, study skills, and time management. Included at the end of each chapter is a series of specific graduated steps in planning and implementing a self-change program.

INSTRUCTIONS

Have the students form groups according to their goal choices, with each group working on a different area. Groups should meet weekly throughout the semester.

Divide the activity into three phases. In the first phase, have students specify a goal for change and conduct a 2–3-week baseline observation period. While still in this period, have them start the second phase: planning the initial contract. Allot a span of about 5 weeks for the implementation of their contract. In the third phase, students plan and implement termination.

At each phase, specific steps adapted from Watson and Tharp (1989) are incorporated into the syllabus and required as written assignments of the students. These help shape the final paper by gradually taking the students through the required approximations and skills necessary for each aspect of the project.

Prompt feedback from the instructor and from other students should be provided at each step to students in the self-modification groups. Completion of each step is weighted in the project grade along with the final paper. Student feedback indicates that requiring weekly or biweekly steps is worth the extra time and work involved because it builds commitment; keeps the students up to date; provides outside comments on their progress, which in turn helps them to modify their program; and provides the basis for the final written paper.

The following is a description of the process in its three phases.

I. Specify goal and conduct observation
   A. Goal setting
      1. List five personal goals you would like to achieve.
      2. Choose a specific goal and subgoals and write an initial contract.
         a) Plan ahead for obstacles by evaluating the pros and cons of change and evaluating self-efficacy beliefs.
         b) Build commitment by anticipating tempting situations and making public commitments.
   B. Baseline observation period
      1. Plan and implement the specific methods that will be used during this time. Behaviors must be recorded daily and include antecedents, behaviors, and consequences. A structured diary, frequency count, or rating scale must be used. This will last about 2 or 3 weeks.
II. Formal contracts
   A. Planning
      1. On the basis of your observations, identify and evaluate the antecedents of your behavior and the consequences of your behavior.
      2. Identify antecedents of your desired and undesired behavior and devise a specific plan to increase or decrease stimulus control using at least two of the following: self-instructions, narrowing antecedent controls, reperceiving antecedents, changes in the chain of events, thought stopping, and precommitment.
      3. Develop specific plans to reach your behavioral goals and subgoals using each of the following techniques at least once: substituting new thoughts and behaviors, shaping, overt and covert modeling, and rehearsal.
      4. Plan at least four ways that you will provide appropriate consequences for desired behavior throughout the project. At least three consequences must involve rewards. (Steps 1–4 are completed during the baseline observation period.)
      5. The initial contract is due. It should include a summary of your observation period, your specific goals and subgoals, specific methods and rules for obtaining each goal, recording methods, feedback, and escape clauses. The techniques used in Steps 1–4 may be incorporated into the contract, which should be signed and witnessed. The self-modification project begins immediately.
   B. Implementation and self-modification
      1. At the end of the first week and for each remaining week of the self-modification project, students are required to complete a graph of their behavior.
      2. At the end of the second week and throughout the rest of the activity, students evaluate their progress weekly, rewriting their

contracts as necessary. They must also prepare a specific program in advance for dealing with high-risk situations and lapses.

III. Termination

1. One to 2 weeks before the end of the contract period, students build a program for termination. They must make use of the following: thinning of reinforcement, finding social or natural reinforcement, program for transfer, and plans for reinstatement.

Bringing in advisers to discuss the major topics has been a very popular idea. Select presentations based on the students' own interests and have students incorporate material from them into their contracts. Typical presentation topics can include stress management, assertiveness training, relaxation techniques, nutrition, time management, and study skills. I have invited health educators and members of the college's Center for Student Development to make these presentations. Some of the guest lecturers may also be available to consult with individual students and groups. Students have often reported that these presentations were helpful in integrating two or more topics into one goal (e.g., including stress and time management into a nutrition program).

DISCUSSION

The groups formed at the beginning of the term will be meeting for regular discussions to provide emotional support. They talk about the steps they have completed, their progress and difficulties, alternative behaviors, and future plans. Previous research has indicated that students work better and learn more in cooperative settings (Johnson, Maruyama, Johnson, Nelson, & Skon, 1981) and that groups encourage cooperation among students (Bouton & Garth, 1983). Feedback from students confirms that groups have had a similar positive effect on the quality of their self-modification projects as well as their commitment to and enjoyment of the project.

REFERENCES

Bouton, C., & Garth, R. (Eds.). (1983). *Learning in groups.* San Francisco: Jossey-Bass.

Johnson, D. W., Maruyama, G., Johnson, R., Nelson, D., & Skon, L. (1981). Effects of cooperative, competitive, and individualistic goal structure on achievement: A meta-analysis. *Psychological Bulletin, 89,* 47–62.

Watson, L., & Tharp, R. G. (1989). *Self-directed behavior: Self-modification for personal adjustment* (5th ed.). Monterey, CA: Brooks/Cole.

SUGGESTED READING

Barton, E. J. (1982). Facilitating student veracity: Instructor application of behavioral technology to self-modification projects. *Teaching of Psychology, 9,* 99–101.

Berrera, M., Jr., & Glasgow, R. E. (1976). Design and evaluation of a personalized instruction course in behavioral self-control. *Teaching of Psychology, 3,* 81–84.

Hamilton, S. B. (1980). Instructionally based training in self-control: Behavior-specific and generalized outcomes resulting from student-implemented self-modification projects. *Teaching of Psychology, 7,* 140–145.

63 Journal Writing Across the Psychology Curriculum: A Tool for Increasing Understanding of Course Material and Enhancing Personal Growth

Connie Schick
Bloomsburg University of Pennsylvania

J. David Arnold
Saint Lawrence University

In this activity, the volume of writing required makes it most suitable for small- or medium-sized classes. The journals promote active involvement with the course content as well as self-awareness. The use of journals requires significant advance planning, as well as a consideration of the ethical issues raised by the potentially personal nature of the entries.

CONCEPT This technique is designed to encourage student self-awareness and interaction with course material through the use of informal written entries, which become a semester-long record of student progress and change. The journal can be "graded" periodically and used as source material for a part of the final exam.

Writing has become an increasingly emphasized skill in college curricula. However, students often dislike writing because they associate it with preparation of formal papers; emphasis on grammar and spelling; and investigation of dry, personally irrelevant topics. One method for overcoming the reluctance of students to write—and to facilitate their carrying the skill into later life—is to introduce them to journal writing, which is designed to promote students' understanding of their thoughts and feelings regarding course materials (Walvoord, 1986). Britton and associates (Britton, 1970) classify journals as "expressive writing," intimate in tone and close to the writer's train of thought. Journals are both a dialectical tool to increase students' self-consciousness about their thinking (Berthoff, 1981) and a "seedbed" for more formal or public writing (Macrorie, 1976).

Fulwiler (1982) placed journals midway between diaries and class notebooks. As interdisciplinary writing tools, journals are useful in numerous settings, with students of varied writing experience (Fulwiler, 1980; Macrorie, 1970).

Journals serve two major purposes: (a) an aid to self-exploration and self-growth and (b) a method of organizing, assimilating, and objectifying thoughts and reactions that occur during reading of topical materials in preparation for classroom discussion. Academically, writing about one's thoughts is similar to the "recite" stage of the SQ3R method because it encourages more complete and logical statement of opinions and insights. Added advantages of journalizing include the following: (a) physical health may be improved either by providing an outlet for suppressed traumatic events or a new coping strategy (Pennebaker & Beall, 1986); (b) presenting oneself openly and nondefensively, even on paper, may teach one that self-disclosure brings "real" feeling and acceptance from others (Rogers, 1969); and (c) learning how and when to self-disclose increases one's personal courage, interpersonal skills, and ability to accept and use feedback from others (Jourard, 1963, 1971).

Suzuki said that every human being is "so constituted by nature that he can become an artist of life" (cited in Shapiro, 1978, p. 163). Journal writing gives students a new method for putting brush to canvas, so to speak.

MATERIALS NEEDED   Journal notebooks are all that is required.

INSTRUCTIONS   Do not request—or expect—polished or edited papers. If students are to become aware of thoughts and perception patterns, the stream-of-consciousness writing style works best. You must be invited to the students' thought processes as an observer, encourager, devil's advocate, and sounding board, never as a critic, editor, or judge.

Students often reveal more than in class or face-to-face meetings. Alert students to the limits of their journal disclosures. If journalizing is to encourage soul-searching and fledgling self-disclosure, facilitate the process by stressing confidentiality and your intention to respond as "another human being," suggesting where they might find more information or get expert advice. You do not need to be a clinician or counselor to use journals, but you do need to know how to refer if one of your students seems to need referral, and some will!

Provide a clear statement of purpose for the journal, indicating whether students will receive further instructions or specific assignments during the semester. Inform them initially of the ultimate use and disposition of the journal. If it will eventually be submitted intact and used as a basis for a paper or final, keep it in a folder, possibly with a table of contents. They should be assured of its return if you want personal self-disclosure.

Grading should be done on the basis of whether students are journalizing as you direct—correctly and on time—and applying themselves to the task of self-exploration, or of interaction with the reading or applied situations with which the journal entries are concerned.

Give students a course outline including (a) number and length of entries; (b) what to journalize and how (e.g., style, person, application, or potential use); (c) due dates (i.e., stressing the importance of frequent writing for personal growth and of writing while they read for understanding of course materials); and (d) grading procedure (e.g., unsatisfactory/redo and satisfactory).

Finally, stress that you realize that they can invent information and situations, but remind them that it does not hurt you or help them. The method is designed to further their own learning process, gain a skill they might find useful in the future, and—by the way—get feedback from you that might facilitate their progress. Journalizing is their task and like most learning techniques, works only as well as it is applied. You are there to see they complete the journal, but the content is theirs.

There are various types of journal entries. Among these are (a) thoughts concerning readings, classroom activities, or life experiences, which are used as "advanced organizers," passports to class, checks to be sure understanding or synthesis, or both, has occurred; (b) logs for practicum or clinical experience or to trace development of skills or dealing with an ongoing situation; (c) real or imaginary dialogues or letters and reports of critical incidents and how they did (or could) affect the student; (d) rough drafts of papers, potential research ideas; (e) descriptions of situations or portraits of others or self; (f) future dreams, wishes, goals, entries that are especially useful in clarifying values, delineating knowledge of situations and one's personal strengths and weaknesses, and doing "reality checks"; (g) list making, especially as it aids time management, planning skills, and insight into oneself and one's personal environment; (h) seeing through another's eyes, real or imaginary; and (i) reactions to having read entries in class or to a classmate to develop self-disclosure, feedback, and active listening skills.

By using two adjacent loose-leaf pages, a four-column journal format can accommodate an ongoing dialogue. For example, Column 1 can be used to summarize readings, class notes, or self-explorations; Column 2, for raising questions, making comments, or synthesizing; Column 3, for instructor feedback; and Column 4, for student reflections later in the semester.

You may write to us for sample course outlines and finals. Schick will provide samples in the areas of the psychology of adjustment as well as senior seminars on ethics and applications for psychology in the future and environmental psychology. Arnold has samples on relating, liking, and loving as well as psychology history and systems.

DISCUSSION

Most of your discussion will be in your responses to students' journal entries. Walvoord (1986) has listed several response methods: (a) appreciation; (b) clarification or restatement or both; (c) challenge; (d) personal reflection; (e) encouragement to pursue topics further in the journal, classroom, library, or outside of the academic setting; and (f) request for revision of the entry into a more polished piece of writing.

You should react more to content than to mechanics, mirror student comments when useful, never deny the validity of student opinion, and offer general advice when appropriate (Browning, 1986). Students quickly learn your shorthand, which is necessary considering the volume of journal entries you will be receiving. For instance, marks and words suffice when longer statements are unnecessary, such as for insights or statements you especially like or feel the student should reread, reconsider, or notice (e.g., !!, yea!, boo!!, really?, Irrational Belief #_____).

REFERENCES

Berthoff, A. E. (1981). *The making of meaning.* Upper Montclair, NJ: Boynton/Cook.

Britton, J. (1970). *Language and learning.* Harmondsworth, England: Penguin Books.

Browning, N. F. (1986). Journal writing: One assignment does more than improve reading, writing, and thinking. *Journal of Reading, 30,* 39–44.

Fulwiler, T. (1980). Journals across the discipline. *English Journal, 69,* 14–19.

Fulwiler, T. (1982). The personal connection: Journal writing across the curriculum. In T. Fulwiler & A. Young (Eds.), *Language connections: Writing and reading across the curriculum* (pp. 15–32). Urbana, IL: National Council on the Teaching of English.

Jourard, S. M. (1963). Healthy personality and self-disclosure. *Mental Hygiene, 43*, 499–507.

Jourard, S. M. (1971). *The transparent self* (rev. ed.). New York: Van Nostrand Reinhold.

Macrorie, K. (1970). *Telling writing*. Rochelle Park, NJ: Hayden.

Macrorie, K. (1976). *Writing to be read* (2nd ed.). Rochelle Park, NJ: Hayden.

Pennebaker, J. W., & Beall, S. K. (1986). Confronting a traumatic event: Toward an understanding of inhibition and disease. *Journal of Abnormal Psychology, 95*, 274–281.

Rogers, C. (1969). *Freedom to learn*. Columbus, OH: Charles E. Merrill.

Shapiro, D. H., Jr. (1978). *Precision nirvana*. Englewood Cliffs, NJ: Prentice-Hall.

Walvoord, B. E. F. (1986). *Helping students write well: A guide for teachers in all disciplines* (2nd ed.). New York: Modern Language Association of America.

SUGGESTED READING

Baldwin, C. (1977). *One to one: Self-understanding through journal writing*. New York: M. Evans.

Fox, R. (1982). The personal log: Enriching clinical practice. *Clinical Social Work Journal, 10*, 92–102.

Fromm, E. (1971). *Escape from freedom*. New York: Avon Books.

Hoffman, S. (1983). Using student journals to teach study skills. *Journal of Reading, 26*, 344–347.

Krishnamurti, J. (1953). *Education and the significance of life*. New York: Harper & Row.

Progoff, I. (1975). *At a journal workshop*. New York: Dialogue House Library.

Rainer, T. (1978). *The new diary*. Los Angeles: J. P. Tarcher.

Swenson, C. R. (1987, September). Using journal writing with students. In K. F. Hays (Chair), *Keeping personal journals: Our students, our clients, ourselves*. Symposium conducted at the 95th Annual Convention of the American Psychological Association, New York.

64 PRESENTING DATA-BASED PROJECTS BY MEANS OF A POSTER SESSION: GUIDELINES AND CAUTIONS

Ashton D. Trice
Mary Baldwin College

This activity is an alternative to the traditional written research report and is suitable for any class in which a research project would ordinarily be required. There is no advance preparation for the teacher, but some class time should be spent introducing the concept of a poster session early in the term.

CONCEPT

Empirical research is often a requirement in undergraduate and graduate psychology courses. Most often research is reported by written papers or by oral presentations, and it is often difficult to see the research through the prose or the oratory. Although teaching students to write standard scientific prose and to make oral presentations are objectives in most psychology curricula, often the primary objective in assigning a data collection and interpretation project is to familiarize students with issues in the design and procedures of research. As evaluators, though, we may focus our feedback on the presentation vehicle, as it is often easier to copy edit than it is to make fundamental critiques of methodology.

I first used a poster session in class by accident: Several sessions of an extension graduate course in educational psychology had been cancelled, so I offered my students the choice between writing a research paper or doing a poster session. The decision was nearly unanimously in favor of the poster, and in the course evaluations, the poster session was indicated consistently as the most useful part of the course. In fact, several students went on to take their posters to state conventions.

Posters have a number of advantages:

1. Posters focus attention on the data rather than on the writing or oral communications skills of the students and are an efficient means of sharing results among students. Students can view about 20 posters in an hour and ask questions of the presenters.

2. Posters can be posted publicly for students' review outside of class time. I often use a combination of these two techniques when posters are developed. In several classes: I schedule an in-class presentation hour during which presenters stay with their posters for half of the class period and then become the "audience" for the other half of the presentation.

3. Poster displays share departmental activities with other students who might become interested in the courses and with colleagues who can get an idea of what is taking place in the psychology course both within and outside of the psychology discipline.

4. Posters focus on graphics, an underpracticed skill.

5. Posters encourage students to practice clear, concise writing. Because the conventions of professional organizations are increasingly using posters as a means

of data dissemination, using them in classes practices a useful professional skill that is usually taught either incidentally or not at all. Many state psychological associations have student poster sessions, and students are ready to go.

6. Students like posters. Consistently, the poster process is rated highly in my course evaluations.

Old posters that are either particularly effective or particularly ineffective are useful, as are guidelines published by various conventions.

I require my students to compose their posters on my personal computer (PC). This greatly assists the revision process and allows for high-quality posters that students can take to professional meetings. Because posters emphasize graphics, using a PC minimizes teaching particular skills in the area of graphics (e.g., Leroy lettering) and minimizes costs, which can be high if rub-on or friction lettering is used. The principal complaints students have voiced are that (a) posters took too long to produce, (b) some students already had considerable skill in graphic layout, and (c) the grade might be influenced by the graphic quality of posters.

My machine is particularly user-friendly and easy to learn, and its graphic capabilities are astonishing. Less friendly and capable systems may not have these advantages, but limiting the poster production to the capabilities of a single system seems to diminish competition among students to produce the "slickest" poster and again focuses attention on data rather than on skill with the communication medium.

The poster project seems to work best when it is done in small groups rather than individually. Students, however, are nervous about receiving a grade on such an unorthodox requirement and being graded on the work of several individuals. Each year I have students who quietly slip me a typical "term paper" treatment of the project as insurance against the possibility that the group project will not be up to their expectations.

Set clear guidelines. The text of a poster will typically be between 250 and 500 words (1–2 typewritten pages). I have given students the following outline, suggesting that each subtopic be given only one sentence:

A. Introduction
 1. Statement of the general problem
 2. Statement of the scope of the problem
 3. Summary of the most relevant study from the literature review
 4. Statement of the hypothesis to be tested
B. Method
 1. Description of the subjects, which may take two sentences
 2. Description of the setting
 3. One sentence description of each instrument used
 4. Statement of the experimental design
 5. Description of the procedures
C. Results and Discussion
 1. A statement of the results in the same syntax as the hypothesis
 2. One-sentence amplifications of each figure caption
 3. A statement of the significance levels
 4. A brief conclusion

5. A statement of the limitations of the study
6. A statement of the implications of the study for future research or practice

No one ever follows the outline exactly, but this suggestion seems to shape competent texts.

There are certain cautions: If everyone started using poster sessions, the novelty would wear thin and their motivational appeal would diminish. Likewise, the skills practiced do not cover the wide range of professional skills we would like our students to have. Certainly I would not recommend the use of the poster session for all project reports for an entire curriculum. I have found this activity of best use in introductory psychology, behavior modification, and research methodology courses in which a pilot study is required. In fact, the poster session seems most appropriate for classes in which a data-based research project is required that composes only a small portion of the total class grade (although we now require a poster defense of senior theses at my present institution, which supplements the written research paper).

Grading posters can be difficult. I have used a modified Guttman technique in which posters are graded on seven dimensions: clarity of text, clarity of graphics, clarity of figure captions, adequacy of experimental design, appropriateness of data analysis techniques, a clear relation between statement of the problem and data collection process, and overall quality of presentation. Each dimension is rated 0 (unacceptable), 1 (acceptable), or 1.5 (outstanding). The usual standards of 90% = *A*, 80% = *B*, and so on can then be applied. Because the texts are short (and if on a PC easy to modify), there is ample time for students to receive at least one round of feedback before the session.

65 ROLE-PLAYING ACTIVITY: THE 1924 AMERICAN PSYCHOLOGICAL ASSOCIATION PRESIDENTIAL ELECTION

Ronda J. Carpenter
Roanoke College

This role play of an actual American Psychological Association (APA) presidential election will require the construction of a sign, a lectern for the nominees, voting ballots for the class, and announcements describing the activity. It is designed for a history of psychology course and can be used with any size class. As written, the activity includes seven male roles. The instructor may wish to use this format but choose a different historical period or take other steps to ensure the participation of women in the role playing as well as the questioning.

CONCEPT
In the early 1920s functionalism was still the dominant school of psychology, although behaviorism was gradually gaining acceptance. This activity familiarizes students with the ideas and work of six functionalists and with the challenge of behaviorism. Role playing involves students more directly than a lecture often does; it also provides an opportunity for students to give oral presentations informally.

MATERIALS NEEDED
The following items are needed: a sign posted on the classroom door indicating that the APA is meeting therein; a lectern with appropriate identification (e.g., "APA Presidential Election"); name tags for the six candidates and instructor; ballots for all students, with a place for the voter's signature; and announcements describing the activity.

INSTRUCTIONS
At least one class meeting prior to the activity, distribute an announcement of the forthcoming election, such as the following one.

ANNOUNCEMENT
From the office of Louis Terman
President of the American Psychological Association

1923

Six candidates for President of the APA for 1924 will meet at (college/university) on (date) at (time) in (classroom) . Each candidate will speak for __ minutes. He will present his views about psychology and summarize his contributions to the science and profession. The six candidates are James R. Angell, Harvey A. Carr, James McKeen Cattell, John Dewey, G. Stanley Hall, and Robert S. Woodworth.

Six volunteers are obtained to play the roles of the candidates. The instructor plays the role of Louis Terman, and the remaining students constitute the electorate.

Instruct candidates to prepare a campaign speech that (a) summarizes the candidate's contributions to psychology and (b) presents his views about the proper object of study and methodology of the discipline. Information about the candidates' lives and views may be obtained from any standard history and systems textbook.

Instruct the other students to be prepared to (a) challenge the candidates' views from a behaviorist standpoint and to (b) "elect" the man who actually was selected as APA president in 1924.

On election day, post the sign on the classroom door and provide a lectern and name tags for the candidates.

Playing the role of President Louis Terman, introduce each candidate and moderate the questioning after the speeches. Encourage candidates to challenge each other and call on other students to question the candidates' views.

Distribute ballots to the electorate and candidates. Collect and tally the signed ballots, and announce that G. Stanley Hall has been elected, again, to the presidency of APA.

DISCUSSION

In the next class meeting, the ascent of behaviorism and the decline of functionalism can be discussed, with references to points brought up in the campaign speeches and audience response.

In a large class, additional roles may be included. For example, E. B. Titchener, John B. Watson, Mary Cover Jones, and Albert P. Weiss could challenge the candidates' views about the nature of psychology from the floor. The exercise could also be adapted to other periods in the history of psychology.

The success of the activity depends on the quality of the students' preparation and their willingness to act in the roles. I used this activity with a small class in history and systems. Afterward, the students admitted an initial reluctance, but all reported that they enjoyed the role playing as a different way to learn and as a "break from just lecture and discussion."

SUGGESTED READING

Angell, J. R. (1988). The province of functional psychology. In L. T. Benjamin, Jr. (Ed.), *A history of psychology: Original sources and contemporary research* (pp. 324–332). New York: McGraw-Hill.

Schultz, D. P., & Schultz, S. E. (1987). *A history of modern psychology* (4th ed.). San Diego, CA: Harcourt Brace Jovanovich.

Watson, J. B. (1988). Psychology as the behaviorist views it. In L. T. Benjamin, Jr. (Ed.), *A history of psychology: Original sources and contemporary research* (pp. 401–406). New York: McGraw-Hill.

66 SATURDAY NIGHT AT THE MOVIES: DEMONSTRATING THE DIFFERENCES BETWEEN ASSERTIVE, AGGRESSIVE, AND PASSIVE BEHAVIOR

Bruce G. Klonsky
State University of New York at Fredonia

In this activity the instructor will need to present a background lecture describing assertive, aggressive, and passive behavior before asking four volunteers to role play these behaviors before the class. The situation depicted in the skit is one with which everyone will be able to identify. No materials or other preparation is needed for this activity, which should go a long way toward bringing the class to an understanding of assertive behavior.

CONCEPT

This activity illustrates the basic differences between assertive, aggressive, and passive behavior, and the probable consequences of using such behaviors. A role-play skit featuring a noisy couple at a movie theater provides an experiential activity in which students can demonstrate assertive and nonassertive behaviors. This teaching activity is best suited for introductory-level undergraduate courses in personality, adjustment, and applied psychology.

MATERIALS NEEDED

This role-playing demonstration can be carried out in an ordinary classroom. All that is needed is a row layout similar to the kind encountered at a movie theater such as the one depicted below:

$$X \quad X \quad X \quad X$$
$$O \quad O \quad O \quad O$$

INSTRUCTIONS

Before engaging in this activity, I have found that it is best to provide the class with definitions and descriptions of assertive, aggressive, and passive behavior (e.g., Alberti, 1977; Gambrill & Richey, 1985). *Assertive behavior* can be defined as the honest, relatively straightforward expression of both positive and negative thoughts and feelings. Assertive behavior is socially appropriate behavior that takes the feelings and welfare of others into consideration. Assertive people believe that they have the same rights, responsibilities, and personal worth as other people. Assertive people convey a confident demeanor with their facial expressions, eye contact, gestures, and verbal messages. Their verbal behaviors include the use of "I" statements and words that express feelings and describe rather than evaluate.

Aggressive behavior lacks the "finesse" of assertive behavior. In this role-playing situation, aggressive behavior can be described as hostile or coercive words or actions that communicate disrespect toward others. Aggressive nonverbal behaviors include threatening hand gestures, a rigid posture, glaring or unbroken eye contact, scowling, and a short speaking distance between the person and recipient of the behavior. Aggressive verbal behaviors include statements of blame, name-calling, loud or sarcastic vocal qualities, "loaded" or evaluative words, interrupting, and monopolizing. People who behave aggressively typically believe that they have more rights and fewer responsibilities than others and that they have more personal worth than others.

Passive behavior fails to express ideas, opinions, or feelings well. There are two major categories of passive behavior: (a) "doormat" (dependent) and (b) indirect (passive–aggressive). Passive-dependent people typically withdraw, flee, or give in when they encounter a difficult situation. The indirect, or passive–aggressive, person can be likened to a "mad dog in a lamb's suit" and deals with difficult situations with a concealed attack. Passive people typically exhibit behaviors such as low voice volume, lack of eye contact, hesitant speech, and smiling when communicating a serious point. Passive people (the doormat variety in particular) often are self-critical and do not express personal preferences. Passive-dependent people also feel that other people have more rights than they do and that they have more responsibilities but less personal worth than others. Passive–aggressive people's beliefs about their rights and responsibilities are more similar to the directly aggressive than to the passive-dependent people.

The class is then given a series of situations to analyze. They are given four possible responses to each situation and asked to label the assertive, aggressive, doormat (passive–dependent), and indirect (passive–aggressive) behaviors. The following item, based on material in Chapter 15 of Alberti's (1977) book, is an example of such a situation of the four alternatives provided for the students:

You invite a friend who lives out of state to spend his or her 2-week vacation with you at your home. It is now 1 month later and your friend shows no intention of leaving or reimbursing you for food and telephone bills. You would like your friend to leave. Provide the appropriate labels for the following four ways of handling this situation: (a) You do not mention anything about your expenses or feelings because you do not want to damage the friendship (doormat behavior). (b) You leave a note saying that you are terribly sorry, but your mother (or father) has decided to live with you and you will need the room (indirect behavior). (c) You tell your friend that you really value his or her friendship but his or her extended visit is putting a strain on it and you have to ask him or her to leave (assertive behavior). (d) You put all of your friend's belongings out on the doorstep with a note saying "Don't call me; I'll call you" (aggressive behavior).

Finally, the greater payoff of assertive behavior as compared with the aggressive and passive alternatives is emphasized. Assertive behavior is explained to be more likely to yield social rewards and greater life satisfaction.

INSTRUCTIONS   After preparing the class, ask for 4–7 student volunteers for a demonstration/skit that uses role playing. Indicate that the demonstration/skit includes the following roles: (a) the noisy couple; (b) the manager of the movie theater; (c) the person who has undergone assertiveness training (i.e., an assertive moviegoer); (d) the passive–dependent (doormat) moviegoer; (e) the passive–aggressive (indirect) moviegoer; and (f) the aggressive moviegoer. If you only get four volunteers, you can use the roles of the noisy couple, the manager, and the assertive person (i.e., playing the passive–dependent role "before therapy" and the assertive role "after therapy").

The contents of the roles are discussed with the volunteers. The noisy couple is instructed to continue talking until the manager is asked to intervene. The manager is asked to respond to the assertive person's request for action in dealing with the noisy couple. The passive–dependent moviegoer's role involves shifting to another seat in the theater or leaving the theater without asking the chatty couple to refrain from talking. The passive–aggressive moviegoer's role involves placing some object near the chatty couple's seats (e.g., banana peel or full cup of soda) so that they might trip as they leave their seats. The aggressive moviegoer's role involves the use of inflammatory name-calling (e.g., "Look, you dimwits, why don't you shut up so I can hear the movie! I paid good money for this!") and threatening gestures (e.g., raised fist) in dealing with the noisy couple in front of them. This aggressive approach does not get the couple to stop talking and creates a heated confrontation.

The assertive moviegoer is the "star" of the skit. The assertive moviegoer is asked to first use a *minimal effective response*. The minimal effective response is behavior that would ordinarily accomplish one's goal with a minimum of effort and negative emotion, and a very small likelihood of negative consequences. In the theater role play, a minimal effective response might be in the form of a "friendly request" such as "I wonder if you would please be a little more quiet. I'm having a problem hearing the movie." The assertive moviegoer then has to demonstrate that he or she has the confidence to "escalate" when his or her minimal effective response fails. When the couple resume chatting, then the assertive moviegoer engages in the following first-order escalation in a more businesslike voice: "Look, would you please be a little more quiet? I simply can't hear the movie." A second-order escalation is made necessary when the chatty culprits respond to the first-order escalation by continuing to talk and making remarks such as "What's this guy (lady) so uptight about? The creeps they let into these movies. . . ." The assertive moviegoer's second-order escalation might be something along the following lines: "Look, if you people don't quiet down, I'm simply going to call the manager." When the chatty couple see the assertive moviegoer begin to call the manager over, they are asked to respond along the following lines: "Okay, buddy (lady), okay" and become silent. Another possible counterresponse might be "This guy (lady) is buggin' me. He (she) is really gettin' on my nerves. Let's sit somewhere else (or leave)."

DISCUSSION   It is useful to follow the role playing with a review of techniques that therapists use during assertiveness training (e.g., behavior rehearsal, role modeling, shaping, reinforcement, etc.) and an indication of how such techniques might be applied to develop the social skills necessary to handle situations requiring assertiveness (e.g., the movie situation, asking someone out for a date, returning merchandise to a store). An excellent review of such training techniques is found in behavior therapy textbooks (e.g., Rimm & Masters, 1979).

Additionally, it is useful to discuss how important one's interpretation of his or her own behavior is. For example, a person might be acting in assertive fashion but mislabeling his or her behavior as overly aggressive or as not assertive enough.

Also focus the discussion on age, sex, and cultural differences in assertive behavior. Applications of assertiveness training to job-hunting situations and to anger management also make interesting discussion topics. I have found that students enjoy taking and scoring assertion measures such as the Gambrill and Richey Assertion Inventory (Gambrill & Richey, 1985) and the Rathus Assertiveness Schedule

(Rathus & Nevid, 1980). Such scores take on more meaning for the students after the role playing and accompanying class material on assertive behavior.

REFERENCES   Alberti, R. E. (Ed.). (1977). *Assertiveness: Innovations, applications, and issues.* San Luis Obispo, CA: Impact.

Gambrill, E., & Richey, C. (1985). *Taking charge of your social life.* Belmont, CA: Wadsworth.

Rathus, S. A., & Nevid, J. S. (1980). *Adjustment and growth: The challenges of life.* New York: Holt, Rinehart & Winston.

Rimm, D. C., & Masters, J. C. (1979). *Behavior therapy: Techniques and empirical findings* (2nd ed.). New York: Academic Press.

SUGGESTED   Alberti, R. E., & Emmons, M. L. (1974). *Your perfect right: A guide to assertive* **READING** *behavior.* San Luis Obispo, CA: Impact.

67 USING STUDENT COMMUNITY SERVICE AS PART OF A HIGH SCHOOL PSYCHOLOGY COURSE

Thomas Lestina
Naperville Central High School

Students are eager to gain experience in the real world, and instructors are not likely to suffer for volunteers when they offer students the option to do community service for a term project. Instructors must be willing to volunteer time outside of the classroom to organize and supervise student volunteers in various settings such as hospitals and mental health facilities. Once you establish community contacts for your students, you will have put the program in place for coming semesters. It is recommended that you combine the project with relevant reading and writing assignments.

CONCEPT

It has been said many times that actions speak louder than words. In teaching a behavioral science, this theory becomes more of a reality. When students have the chance to observe behavior in real life, outside of a lecture or a classroom activity, they become more personally aware of the concepts being taught.

Because of my belief in expanding psychology outside of the classroom, I suggest that students, when possible, should become involved in a community service project or practicum.

MATERIALS NEEDED

No extra materials or equipment are needed.

INSTRUCTIONS

The organization of a community service project is the most difficult step. Determine how many students are willing to volunteer their time and how often. Offering volunteer work as an option for a semester project will usually generate ample student interest. Teachers must also be willing to volunteer extra time to organize and oversee the activity being planned.

After sufficient interest has been shown, identify several organizations in need of volunteers. One can usually find willing recipients by contacting local or state inpatient mental health facilities, community living facilities for retarded adults, or even nursing homes. The psychology students at Naperville Central High School visit a state mental health facility two evenings of every month. There are currently 180 students visiting eight different wards.

When pursuing a program such as this, teachers must stress the importance of fellowship and planned activities; otherwise, students may want to participate more out of curiosity than for humanitarian reasons. It is best to assign several more reliable students to be leaders; they can contact the facility supervisors and coordinate activities with them. Most of the residents enjoy seeing young people who are willing to play bingo, shoot pool, help write letters, sing, dance, plan holiday parties, or just sit and talk.

It is important to discuss each evening's activities and observations on the following school day. I also suggest the use of related activities for the student participants.

One excellent additional activity is to assign the reading of one or two books (see the Suggested Reading section) and to have the students write a paper comparing the residents, setting, treatment, and staff of the institution portrayed in the book with those of the institution at which they volunteer. Students should present their papers to the class so that (a) all students can get an idea of the books' differing perspectives and (b) students who read the same book can compare their observations. By using this as a project, you can combine volunteer experience with reading and writing. An activity such as this not only increases students' knowledge of certain aspects of human behavior but also increases interest in a school's psychology program. In Naperville we have used this activity for 11 years, and the psychology enrollment has increased from 10 sections in 1975 to 21 sections in the 1986–1987 school year.

SUGGESTED READING

Donaldson, K. (1976). *Insanity inside out.* New York: Crown.

Gordon, B. (1986). *I'm dancing as fast as I can.* New York: Bantam Books.

Greenberg, J. (1977). *I never promised you a rose garden.* New York: Signet.

Kesey, K. (1977). *One flew over the cuckoo's nest.* New York: Penguin Books.

Rebeta-Burditt, J. (1986). *The cracker factory.* New York: Bantam Books.

68 CONCENTRATIVE MEDITATION

Linda Leal

Eastern Illinois University

In this activity the class will need to practice for several successive class sessions and practice out of class as well before meditative states can be achieved. No materials are needed unless you choose to measure physiological changes before and after the meditation exercise. Any size class can participate, although a large class will present more of a challenge.

CONCEPT

Over the years psychologists have investigated various altered states of consciousness. An altered state of consciousness exists whenever there is a significant change in the quality of ordinary perceptual functioning. Concentrative meditation is one method used to alter consciousness that is easy to learn and to demonstrate in the classroom.

The primary goal of meditation is to achieve a state of deep relaxation by restricting the flow of incoming sensory information, accomplished by concentrating exclusively on one repetitive stimulus in order to block out all other sensations and thoughts. Concentrative meditation is, therefore, a systematic narrowing of attention that seems to slow the metabolism and help produce feelings of well-being. Today many psychologists view meditation as a viable method for dealing with stress. The purpose of this exercise is to introduce students to the concept of conscious alteration by allowing them practice in concentrative meditation.

MATERIALS NEEDED

No materials are needed unless you want to measure physiological changes before and after meditating. If you have the necessary equipment (i.e., sphygmomanometer) students can measure such physiological responses as heart rate, blood pressure, and so forth both before and after meditating. A cautionary note: Often the biological effects of meditation are not evident until individuals are well practiced in achieving a meditative state. If physiological responses are measured, discussion should then include the possibility that students' expectations about changes in their physiological functioning may be influencing the measures obtained.

INSTRUCTIONS

After introducing the class to the concept of concentrative meditation, instruct students to sit quietly and breathe in and out as usual for approximately 30 seconds.

Next, ask them to concentrate on each breath by lowering their eyes and focusing their attention on breathing in and out. Direct them to concentrate on the rise and fall of the abdominal area and at the same time say to themselves "in" and "out." They are to think of nothing except the rise and fall of the abdomen and the corresponding thoughts of in and out. This is practiced for several minutes. Initially, many students have trouble concentrating their full attention on their breathing; reassure them that this problem will diminish with practice.

On the second practice day, instruct the students to close their eyes as they concentrate on their breathing. Remind them to focus all of their attention on breathing in and out from the abdomen.

SPECIAL TOPICS

Practice meditation for several additional class dates (as often as time permits). In order to promote class discussion, meditation is best practiced at the beginning of the class period. Additionally, encourage students to practice meditation outside of class and report on their experiences. Inform them that the usual procedure is to meditate for approximately 20 minutes daily.

DISCUSSION

The following questions may be used to guide discussion:

1. Why should meditation promote feelings of well-being and relaxation? Researchers have reported that the physiological effects of meditation are related to lowered activity of the sympathetic nervous system, the branch of the autonomic nervous system that functions as the arousal center during emergency or stressful situations. The most common bodily change reported is *hypometabolism*, which is characterized by decreases in the body's metabolic rate as reflected by lowered oxygen consumption, in heart and respiration rates, and in carbon dioxide production.

Recently several researchers have suggested that just sitting quietly results in similar physiological effects. The fact that other activities achieve the same results, however, does not negate the value of meditation as one way to control stress.

Another possible explanation as to why meditation promotes relaxation is cognitive in nature. When people concentrate all of their attention on one stimulus (breathing), they cannot simultaneously be paying attention to other stressful thoughts. Meditation may be helpful, therefore, in distracting attention away from whatever is bothering people.

2. Why is it difficult to keep distracting thoughts from entering consciousness while meditating? Repeated presentation of any one stimulus often results in *habituation*, or a decrease in sensory responding. This may occur during meditation as people continue concentrating on one stimulus. Another possibility that has been suggested is that the mind is undisciplined. Only through repeated practice can people "train" themselves in the art of deep concentration.

3. Does meditation lead to heightened state of consciousness, alertness, or creativity? Although long-term meditators have made these claims, most reports are based on personal accounts or poorly controlled studies. An important point to keep in mind is that although the physiological correlates of meditation can be readily measured, there is no scientific evidence that meditation produces a heightened state of conscious awareness.

SUGGESTED READING

Carrington, P. (1977). *Freedom in meditation.* New York: Anchor Books.

LeShan, L. (1974). *How to meditate.* Boston: Little, Brown.

Naranjo, C., & Ornstein, R. E. (1977). *On the psychology of meditation.* New York: Penguin Books.

Pagano, R. R., & Warrenburg, S. (1983). Meditation. In R. J. Davidson, G. E. Schwartz, & D. Shapiro (Eds.), *Consciousness and self-regulation* (pp. 152–210). New York: Plenum Press.

Wallace, R. K., & Benson, H. (1972). The physiology of meditation. *Scientific American, 226,* 84–90.

69 PHYSIOLOGICAL EFFECTS OF TRYING TO RELAX

James P. Motiff
Hope College

A thermister or any biofeedback or temperature-recording device that measures to tenths of a degree is needed for this demonstration. This is a simple, easy way to illustrate the mind–body effect and a good introduction to related activities in this chapter (e.g., Concentrative Meditation, Biofeedback on a Budget). Students need no prior knowledge, and this activity is suitable for any size class.

CONCEPT

It is well accepted that actively *trying* to relax seldom works because the physiological mechanisms of any effort involve stress and a corresponding sympathetic autonomic (fight or flight) response. Several points can be learned from this demonstration: (a) autonomic nervous system (ANS) activity (sympathetic arousal) causes peripheral vasoconstriction, which can be measured as finger temperature; (b) vasoconstriction and a decrease in finger temperature indicate stress, and vasodilation and an increase in finger temperature indicate relaxation (a shutting down of the stress effect on the sympathetic ANS); and (c) actively trying to do anything results in a decrease in finger temperature even when one makes a deliberate attempt to raise finger temperature.

MATERIALS NEEDED

You will need a thermister to register finger temperature. However, any biofeedback or temperature recording device that measures to tenths of a degree will work.

INSTRUCTIONS

Ask for a volunteer who thinks he or she will be able to produce an increase in finger temperature. Have this student come up to the front of the room and attach the thermister to the second pad of a noncalloused finger.

Measure the student's baseline temperature and then instruct the student to begin raising the skin temperature. Tell the student to try as hard as possible to warm the finger, indicating that the greater the increase in temperature, the greater the student's skill. Under the stress of this attempt, the finger temperature will actually fall.

DISCUSSION

This activity will enhance a discussion of the mind–body relation because it shows clearly that meeting the challenge of trying to raise finger temperature produces just the opposite response. The mental activity of trying increases sympathetic arousal and the correlated decrease in blood flow and temperature that results from peripheral vasoconstriction.

As an adjunct to this demonstration, instruct the class and the student volunteer in *passive relaxation*, in letting go, in changing the mental focus to thoughts of relaxing in the warm sunshine at a favorite beach. This passive relaxation produces an increase in finger temperature.

SUGGESTED
READING

Danskin, D. G., & Crow, M. A. (1981). *Biofeedback: An introduction and guide.* Palo Alto, CA: Mayfield.

70 BIOLOGICAL BASES OF BEHAVIOR AND THE SELF-FULFILLING PROPHECY

Fred L. Nesbit
Sauk Valley Community College

In this activity, the instructor is likely to get a lot of discussion from this simple, straightforward exercise in which students survey their friends and relatives for incidence of a recessive trait and are asked to correlate the trait with other traits and characteristics. No materials are needed, students do not need prior knowledge, and it can be used with any size class.

CONCEPT
This is a simple demonstration that is very effective in illustrating basic patterns in biological heredity as well as the self-fulfilling prophecy. Students perform a project on the basis of their own ideas or "prophecies," which are suggested to them by the instructor. It serves as a good introduction to these topics and others such as stereotyping and discrimination.

INSTRUCTIONS
At some point during the study of heredity and behavior, instruct the students to look at the back of their hands, particularly their fingers. Explain that the hair on the first finger section connected to the knuckle is the result of a dominant gene and thus is likely to be found; hair on the second (midsection) is the result of a recessive gene and is therefore not likely to be found. Announce that you are seeking the identity of those rare individuals with "middigital hair."

Spirited chatter will quickly break out as several students stare at their hands in disbelief. They have just discovered that they possess this mysterious, rare condition you have described. The existence of only a minority of individuals with this condition permits a review of the expected ratio of occurrence in the phenotype for biogenic traits.

Ask the students to check among family members for evidence of middigital hair and to make a list of significant characteristics that their hairy relatives may share.

DISCUSSION
When the students return to class with their lists of hairy relatives and the traits they may share (but without any prior comment on the significance of these traits), the timing is right for a discussion.

Have the students consider the meaning and consequences of hairy middigits and introduce the concept of the self-fulfilling prophecy. This concept relates to the idea that an expectation about the occurrence of an event or behavior may act to increase the likelihood that the event or behavior will indeed occur. If people think that individuals with certain characteristics are lazy, for example, they may treat them in a way that actually brings about laziness on the part of the stereotyped group. To make them think about possible implications for behavior that arises biologically from middigital hair (when, of course, there are none), propose a series of what ifs: What if it has something to do with untrustworthiness? it is related to irresponsibility? On exposure to moonlight, does it lead to werewolfism?

General laughter always erupts at this last suggestion, breaking the tension and permitting you to drive home the point about the self-fulfilling prophecy. If this group were an isolated subculture, it would be easy to imagine that a peculiar biological trait such as this might become falsely associated with certain expected behaviors. Over time, it could lead to discrimination and subsequent psychological and socioeconomic impairments. Campaigns might be run with such slogans as "Beware of those with middigital hair." This concept, quickly grasped, provides perfect timing for a discussion of racism and sexism, and for identification of the causes of most racial and sexual differences as being cultural rather than biological. Implications for research can also be explored by introducing the distortions arising from experimenter effects in behavioral research and by discussing Rosenthal's Pygmalion effect.

This demonstration moves swiftly, and it always seems to get quickly and clearly to the major applications.

SUGGESTED READING

Archibald, W. P. (1974). Alternative explanations for the self-fulfilling prophecy. *Psychological Bulletin, 81*, 74–84.

Craig, C. J. (1980). *Human development.* Englewood Cliffs, NJ: Prentice-Hall.

Rosenthal, R. (1976). *Experimenter effects in behavioral research.* New York: Halstead Press.

Rosenthal, R., & Jacobson, L. (1968). *Pygmalion in the classroom: Teacher expectation and pupils' intellectual development.* New York: Holt, Rinehart & Winston.

Skrypnek, B. J., & Snyder, M. (1982). On the self-perpetuating nature of stereotypes about women and men. *Journal of Experimental Social Psychology, 18,* 277–291.

Williams, H. K. (1977). *Psychology of women: Behavior in a biosocial context.* New York: Norton.

$\square$'71 BIOFEEDBACK ON A BUDGET

Margaret S. Martin
Medical University of South Carolina

In this activity the instructor will need to order biodots before asking the class to keep a 3-day journal recording emotional states. No other materials are needed and any size class can participate. As always in journal-writing assignments, students should be cautioned about inappropriate personal disclosures.

CONCEPT

Biodots are temperature-sensitive, small, round pieces of plastic that can be affixed to the "webbing" between the left thumb and forefinger. They have an adhesive backing and will stay in place for a few hours. As the temperature of the skin goes up the Biodot changes color. Biodots can be used to demonstrate biofeedback (on a limited budget), perform a variety of experiments, and show the relation between emotion and color. It is assumed that the temperature of the skin on the extremities changes in response to the emotional state. A journal may be kept noting color and thoughts at random times during the day.

MATERIALS NEEDED

You will need Biodots, which can be ordered from the ACCTion Consortium, 303 17th Ave, N.E., Hampton, IA 50441.

INSTRUCTIONS

The following instructions to students may be used: "Keep a 3-day journal of your observations while wearing a Biodot. At 10 random times during the day note the color of your Biodot, your activities, and your thoughts. Bring your journals to class at the end of this period."

Because some students may include personal, sensitive information about themselves, I suggest that the instructor not read student journals or caution students about including inappropriate or very personal data.

DISCUSSION

A general class discussion might follow small group discussions of no more than three or four students in each small group. It is preferable to allow students to select the groups they want to be in for this activity.

The following questions may be used to stimulate student thinking: Did your Biodot show any consistency between color and activity? Between color and thoughts? What color did your Biodot turn prior to a test, speech, or some other anxiety-producing activity? In what situations did your biodot show the "relaxed state"?

SUGGESTED READING

ACCTion Consortium. (1978). *Biofeedback, biodots, and stress: Teacher's guide.* Hampton, IA: Author.

Davis, M., McKay, M., & Eshelman, E. (1980). *The relaxation and stress reduction workbook.* Richmond, CA: New Harbinger.

Restak, R. (1984). *The brain.* New York: Bantam Books.

Spielberger, C. D., & Sarason, I. G. (1985). *Stress and anxiety* (Vol. 9). Washington, DC: Hemisphere.

Wortman, C. B., & Loftus, E. F. (1988). *Psychology.* New York: Knopf.

72 THE INFLUENCE OF ROLE MODELS AND MENTORS ON CAREER DEVELOPMENT

Michele A. Paludi
Hunter College of the City University of New York

Charles Epstein
Burke Marketing Research

This activity can be done with any size class, although you may want to divide the class according to college major or career aspirations if it is very large. The activity is recommended as a separate unit on achievement motivation, work, or career development but may also be integrated into discussions of developmental tasks or adolescence–young adulthood and career counseling.

CONCEPT
This activity will acquaint students with the role played by certain individuals in developing their career identities.

Career development continues to be an active area of research and theory (Betz & Fitzgerald, 1987). Among the many topics related to this inquiry are individuals' aspirations, motivation, attributions, as well as barriers to success (e.g., fear of failure, sexual harassment). Relative to these topics has been a decade-long focus on *mentoring* and *role-model choice* and their benefits to career development.

Individuals differentiate the terms *role model* and *mentor* along the dimensions of input on career advancement (e.g., political contacts, job-specific skills) and duration of the relationship (e.g., class instructor for one course vs. a 3–4-year relationship that included the functions of advisor, instructor, and sponsor of research). Mentors are seen as being more likely than role models to have a long relationship with their protégés as well as to actively promote their careers.

The personality characteristics most often listed by college and graduate students as ones that they emulate in a role model are the following: achievement oriented, scholarly, supportive, loving, ambitious, self-confident, sincere, genuine, caring for others, interested in other things besides career, and socially adept. These characteristics are also listed among those that students emulate in a mentor; however, the ordering is as follows: supportive, caring for others, genuine, sincere, achievement oriented, loving, socially adept, and interested in other things besides career (Paludi, Waite, Hoewing-Roberson, & Jones, 1988).

Arguments in favor of having mentors generally stress the importance of an individual's identification with the mentor, the importance of the information provided by the mentor's behavior, and the positive incentive through illustrative success (e.g., Gilbert, Gallessich, & Evans, 1983; Wallston, Cheronis, Czirr, Edwards, & Russo, 1978). Furthermore, the sex of the role model and mentor relates to men's and women's self-assessment of competency, aspirations, and self-worth (Farylo & Paludi, 1985). For example, women students paired with women mentors reported higher satisfaction with their student role than men or women students paired with male mentors (Gilbert et al., 1983).

MATERIALS NEEDED Materials were developed by the Hunter College Women's Career Development Research Collective in 1988 on the basis of experiences with role models and mentors.

INSTRUCTIONS Administer the following questions to students individually or in groups according to potential college major, interests, career aspirations, part-time employment, and so forth.

Many people have described a role model as an individual who has one or more personality characteristics that are admirable. A role model is someone whom we may want to emulate: We may want to be as kind, as smart, or as funny as he or she is. We may think of our teacher in high school or junior high school as a role model. We may want to be like him or her in some way when we are older.

For the next few minutes, think of the characteristics you admire in people—in your family members, teachers, friends, sisters, brothers, and yourself. In addition, think of some individuals who have the characteristics you admire, such as humor, compassion, kindness, independence, ability to talk on a variety of topics, competence, athletic ability, and so forth.

Think of the first person that comes into your mind when you consider a role model. Answer the following questions about this person:
1. Is this person female or male?
2. What is the relationship of this person to you (e.g., parent, teacher, friend)?
3. List five characteristics of this person that make you think of him or her as your role model.
4. Now look at the five characteristics you listed in Question 3. Please put them in order from the most important (to you) to the least important.

Now that you have described your experiences with a role model, do a similar thing for your mentor. A mentor has been described as an individual with whom one works closely on a specific project. A mentor is someone who actively promotes your skills and assists you with your career goals. For example, a mentor is someone who talks positively about your work, helps you to get jobs or information about college, and invests time in your future. A mentor is an advisor, friend, and guide into a new experience. He or she is someone with whom you have interactions, perhaps even on a day-to-day basis.

Think about an individual who fits these descriptions of a mentor and answer the following questions:
5. Is the person female or male?
6. List five reasons why you refer to this person as your mentor.
7. Please list five characteristics of this person that you like.
8. Do you believe your performance in school has been helped by the advice and encouragement given by this person?
9. Do you believe this person considers herself or himself as important to your career development as you think she or he is?
10. Will you ask this individual for help in making decisions about your future plans? Why or why not?
11. Do you believe this person's gender was an important characteristic for you? Why or why not?

Ask students to share their responses with their group or the entire class.

Look for ethnic, racial, and sex similarities and differences in students' responses and discuss some of the benefits and the disadvantages of sharing gender or background in a mentor–protégé relationship. Discuss career development and the impact of role models and mentors on adolescents' and adults' vocational choice.

DISCUSSION

This exercise has been effective in discussing sociopsychological and structural influences on academic success and career choice. As has been pointed out in the literature on adolescents and career development (see Betz & Fitzgerald, 1987), there is a fundamental problem concerning career choice during adolescence. Career decision making is important during this stage of the life span, yet many adolescents make this decision by prematurely closing on a career choice as a result of aimless diffusion. Furthermore, their competencies, abilities, and values are not fixed at adolescence. Consequently, adolescents may not know what information to seek about careers, how to go about it, where to look, or with whom to discuss their vocational development.

Students who have discussed their responses to these survey questions have reported contacting the individuals they listed and establishing a collaborative relationship with them. Discussing ideas and plans with someone whom they admire can help adolescents make more accurate, realistic choices about college majors and career goals. Topics that get raised in these discussions include individuals' perceptions of the time commitment involved in careers, individuals' ability to juggle career and family lives, difficulty in selecting a mentor, attributions mentors make for the successes of their protégés, male–female verbal and nonverbal communication patterns, drawbacks to having a mentor (e.g., harrassment, social organization of collegial ties, retention of women and ethnic minorities in college or graduate school, and reentry students' mentor–protégé relationships).

REFERENCES

Betz, N., & Fitzgerald, L. (1987). *The career psychology of women.* New York: Academic Press.

Gilbert, L. A., Gallessich, J. M., & Evans, S. L. (1983). Sex of faculty role model and students' self-perceptions of competency. *Sex Roles, 9,* 597–607.

Farylo, B., & Paludi, M. A. (1985). Developmental discontinuities in mentor choice by male students. *Journal of Social Psychology, 125,* 521–522.

Paludi, M. A., Waite, B., Hoewing-Roberson, R., & Jones, L. (1988). Mentors vs. role models: A clarification of terms. *International Journal of Mentoring, 2,* 20–25.

Wallston, B. S., Cheronis, J., Czirr, R., Edwards, S., & Russo, A. (1978, March). *Role models for professional women.* Paper presented at the meeting of the Association for Women in Psychology, Pittsburgh, PA.

SUGGESTED READING

Collins, E. G., & Scott, P. (1978). Everyone who makes it has a mentor. *Harvard Business Review, 54,* 89–101.

Hetherington, C., & Barcelo, R. (1985). Womentoring: A cross-cultural perspective. *Journal of the National Association of Women Deans, Administrators, and Counselors, 48,* 12–15.

CHAPTER IX
ETHICS

The study of ethics should be an integral part of any psychology course, and these activities provide several vehicles for presenting ethical issues both in research and in practice. Activity 80 is not an actual classroom demonstration but a thoughtful and important consideration of the issues involved in animal research. Activity 74 provides an exercise designed to be completed while watching television, and Activity 76 describes one that uses print media; both will bring issues of animal research directly into the student's work. Both will also require some familiarity with ethical principles in laboratory research with animals. Activity 75, which also deals with the ethics of using animals in research, is suitable for a class that has had no prior exposure to the topic.

Activity 77 considers the problems and questions that arise from using human participants in a research study and gives students a familiarity with the basic tenets of ethics in research; Activity 73 is set up as a role-playing exercise that replicates a well-known, ethically controversial experiment. Activity 79 uses a set of skits to illustrate obedience and the ethical questions tied to it.

Activity 78 gives students a firsthand look at deception in an experiment. It is a potentially disturbing exercise, but is also a very instructive one; the instructor must debrief the class thoroughly on its completion. Activity 81 explores the relation between ethics, values, and behavior.

For a bibliography of texts on various ethical questions, please refer to Appendix E in this volume.

73 ETHICS OF RESEARCH WITH HUMAN PARTICIPANTS

Robert T. Brown
University of North Carolina at Wilmington

■──■

This activity can be used in small to medium classes of high school or college students. Students must read the American Psychological Association's (1982) Ethical Principles in the Conduct of Research With Human Participants *and a research proposal outside of class. If your school has an institutional review board, you may wish to rewrite the proposal following that format and to assign roles to reflect the actual composition of the committee. The activity takes at least two class sessions. Although this activity could be modified to be a written assignment for larger classes, the role playing produces more understanding of the difficulties and ambiguities in applying the* Ethical Principles.

■──■

CONCEPT   Increasing interest in teaching ethics to undergraduates in psychology is reflected in recent presentations and papers (e.g., Haemmerlie & Matthews, 1988; Mathews, 1989) as well as in expanded coverage of ethics of research in undergraduate psychology textbooks. Didactic presentation of ethical conflicts or case histories of violation of ethical principles, however, rarely interests students. In this exercise, students become actively involved with ethical issues by role playing being members of an ethics committee. They evaluate a proposal for research using human participants in terms of the APA *Ethical Principles.* The proposal involves considerable deception.

The proposal, in the general format used by institutional review boards (see accompanying handout), matches as closely as possible an ethically controversial study by Zimbardo, Anderson, and Kabat (1981). To disguise the fact that the proposal came from an actual experiment, the investigator was listed as Philip G. Odrabmiz (Zimbardo spelled backward). Hunt (1982) dealt with ethical issues of this and other experiments, provided additional information on the Zimbardo et al. (1981) procedures, and described the reactions of one of their subjects.

Zimbardo et al. (1981) told subjects that they would be participating with two other subjects (actually confederates) in a study of the effects of hypnotic training on group creative problem solving. In fact, the purpose was to test a hypothesis that hypnotically induced deafness would evoke paranoid reactions. The hypothesis was derived from a theory by Maher (1974) that paranoid reactions common to elderly people may result from deafness of which they are unaware; the elderly interpret an inability to hear others as resulting from others whispering and trying to keep things from them. Paranoia thus results from an incorrect attribution: "People must be talking about me because I cannot hear them." Zimbardo also told subjects that they would be able to work with him on subsequent research, which was not true (Hunt, 1982). An ethical dilemma exists: The experiment has important theoretical and practical implications but is deceptive both in procedures used and incentives offered subjects.

In the experiment itself, all subjects were hypnotized. Experimental subjects were given the posthypnotic suggestion that at the outset of the subsequent problem-solving exercise they would become deaf. Thus they did not hear the other two "subjects" in the group exercise.

The actual results were that subjects with hypnotically induced deafness showed high levels of paranoid reactions and stress relative to control subjects, confirming the hypothesis.

MATERIALS
NEEDED

Students will need copies of the APA *Ethical Principles* and copies of Request for Permission to Conduct Research With Human Subjects (included at the end of this exercise).

Instructors will need a copy of the *Ethical Principles*; articles by Zimbardo et al. (1981) and Hunt (1982), which should be available in most libraries, to be used in preparing the request; and a discussion of research using deception, available in most experimental psychology textbooks.

INSTRUCTIONS

Assign the *Ethical Principles* to be read outside of class.

Explain and discuss basic aspects of principles using a few examples from *Ethical Principles* in Session 1 and assign students to read, outside of class, the proposal for research using human subjects.

In Session 2, divide the class into several "ethics committees," each of which should have about six members. Instruct each committee to (a) evaluate the proposal relative to the *Ethical Principles* and recommend that it be accepted, rejected, or revised for further consideration; (b) justify their recommendations; and (c) if their recommendation is to reject or revise, to justify objections in terms of specific *Ethical Principles*. A time limit to reach a decision can be set; 30–40 minutes is generally sufficient.

During this part of the exercise, the instructor role plays the investigator, providing details about any parts of the proposal that appear unclear, answering questions, and attempting to justify the proposed procedures. Instructors need to be very familiar with the Zimbardo et al. (1981) and Hunt (1982) research, as well as with general arguments regarding the use of deception. Some basic knowledge of hypnosis is also helpful. (This role has occasionally been quite challenging!)

After the committees have reached decisions, ask each to report its recommendation and justification. Keep a record on the blackboard. Encourage dissenting members to make minority reports.

Announce that the proposal was derived from an actual published experiment that was controversial enough to be the focus of an article on deception and hold up copies of the articles. Lead a discussion on the implications for knowledge of the ethics committees' actions. Consider (a) the benefits of knowledge to society versus cost to individual subjects and (b) ways to reduce deception. You may wish to address the issue of what knowledge would have been lost if the student ethics committees had turned down the Zimbardo et al. (1981) research or, for example, Milgram's (1974) studies on obedience.

DISCUSSION

Reports of student ethics committees have shown that virtually all committees rejected the proposal outright or requested revision. Of the 16 committees for which reports were available, only 1 approved the proposal, 7 rejected it outright, and 8 requested major revisions. Recommendations differed, however, and lively discussions among committees were common. The most frequently requested revision was to eliminate the statement that subjects would be able to work with the experimenter on future research. Some committees also requested that the subjects be fully informed about the actual purpose of the experiment with that knowledge then removed from the subjects while they were hypnotized.

The exercise has been conducted in a variety of ways. Student ethics committees have been constituted in two ways. Particularly when time has been a factor or the students have limited background, students have simply been instructed to play the role of members of an ethics committee. When more time was available with upper level college students, they were asked to play the role of specific professionals who might serve on a university institutional review board, such as a physiologist, a philosopher with expertise in ethics, a social psychologist who conducts research with human subjects, a social worker, a physician, and a minister. Specific assignment of roles tends to sharpen and increase discussion within committees and lead to some interesting positions. In one case, the student role playing a minister rejected the proposal outright because hypnotism was supposedly a satanic state in which the person could become inhabited by the devil!

The exercise was originally designed for use in undergraduate courses in experimental psychology. Evaluating the overall effectiveness of the exercise on a scale from 0 (*exercise was not at all valuable*) to 7 (*exercise was very valuable*), 96 students in six classes taught by three different instructors gave a mean rating of 5.9.

The exercise has also been used successfully with high school juniors and seniors in Summer Ventures, a summer program in North Carolina for mathematically and scientifically gifted high school juniors and seniors.

REFERENCES

American Psychological Association. (1982). *Ethical principles in the conduct of research with human participants*. Washington, DC: Author.

Haemmerlie, F. M., & Matthews, J. R. (1988). Preparing undergraduates for paraprofessional positions: What, when, where, and how are ethical issues taught? *Teaching of Psychology, 15,* 192–194.

Hunt, M. (1982). Research through deception. *New York Times Magazine,* 12 September. (Reprinted in *Annual Editions: Psychology.*)

Maher, B. (1974). Delusional thinking and cognitive disorder. In H. London & R. E. Nisbett (Eds.), *Thought and feeling: Cognitive alteration of feeling states* (pp. 85–103). Chicago: Aldine.

Matthews, J. R. (1989, August). *Teaching of ethics and ethics of teaching.* Paper presented at the 97th Annual Convention of the American Psychological Association, New Orleans.

Milgram, S. (1974). *Obedience to authority.* New York: Harper & Row.

Zimbardo, P. G., Anderson, S. M., & Kabat, L. G. (1981). Induced hearing deficit generates experimental paranoia. *Science, 212,* 1529–1531.

Note. You may not run any subjects, for pilot work or for the main study, until you are informed that the proposed research project has been approved. Significant changes in procedure must also be cleared through the Ethics Committee.

Investigators: <u>Philip G. Odrabmiz and students</u>   Department: <u>Psychology</u>

Status: <u>XXX (PGO)</u>   Faculty   <u>XXX</u>   Student

Title of Project: <u>Effect of Hypnotically Induced Hearing Loss on Perception</u>

<u>of Paranoia</u>

Source of Subjects <u>General psychology subject pool</u>

1. Attach a brief description of the project in sufficient detail to permit full evaluation concerning protection of human subjects. Include purpose of the experiment, manipulation performed and responses to be recorded, activities in which subjects engage, special incentives or rewards, and tests and questionnaires.

2. Will subjects be at physical, social, or psychological risk? If yes, describe:
   Yes, subjects in the ``deafness without awareness'' condition (see Description of the Experiment) may experience severe stress and paranoid reactions, frustration, and hostility during testing.

3. Describe steps taken to minimize risk:
   The duration of stressful situation is only 30 minutes. Extensive debriefing will be done to remove any stress or other adverse reactions. (See Description of the Experiment.)

4. Are any illegal activities involved? If so, describe in detail separately:
   No

5. Is prior written fully informed consent to be obtained from subjects or others?
   No
   Describe procedure for obtaining consent:
   Subjects will sign up for an experiment on the effects of hypnosis on problem solving.
   If no, reason:
   Fully informed consent would inform subject of the true purpose of experiment and render the results meaningless.

6. Is any deception involved? If yes, describe:
   Yes. Subjects are told that they are participating in an experiment on the effects of hypnosis on problem solving, but in fact experimental subjects will have hypnotically induced hearing loss. The purpose is to examine the effects of that loss on paranoid reactions.
   Describe debriefing:
   See the section on debriefing in the Description of the Experiment.

7. Describe security procedures for assuring confidentiality of subjects' identification:
   No names will be recorded on any data sheets. All information will be coded.

Investigator's assurance:
   I have read the institutional guidelines on the use of human subjects in research and agree to abide by them. I also agree to report any significant changes in procedures or instruments to the committee for additional review.

Signatures *Philip A. Odramiz*

Faculty advisor if any _____

Background

Paranoid reactions are often observed in people who suffer gradual hearing loss later in life. These reactions include delusions of persecution. Maher (1974) has suggested that the relation may stem from the person's not being aware of the hearing loss and therefore interpreting his or her inability to hear others as resulting from their whispering and trying to keep things from him or her. Thus, paranoid reactions result from an incorrect attribution: "Those people must be whispering about me because I cannot hear what they are saying."

Purpose

The proposed research is an experimental test of a hypothesis drawn from Maher's explanation. In particular, the experiment is designed to determine whether normal young humans who have a temporary induced hearing loss will show greater paranoid reactions than control subjects who have normal hearing. The temporary hearing loss will be induced through hypnotic suggestion.

Subjects

Subjects will be undergraduate students in introductory psychology who will receive credit toward the research requirement of the course. They will also be told that they may be able to collaborate with the experimenter in subsequent research. (They will probably not be able to collaborate; the suggestion is made to interest subjects in participating in the project.) Only subjects who are determined to be highly hypnotizable on standard tests of hypnotic susceptibility will be used.

Manipulation to Be Used and Measures to Be Taken

Training. Subjects will be informed that they will be participating in a study testing a hypothesis that training in hypnosis improves creative problem solving by groups of people. As an initial step in the experiment, all subjects will be taught self-hypnosis skills and how to use hypnosis to increase concentration and control pain and other physical states. In addition, all subjects will fill out several standard personality inventories including sections of the Minnesota Multiphasic Personality Inventory (MMPI) and our paranoia scale (see the Rating Scales section).

Testing. In the test session, subjects will be randomly divided into three groups that differ in the suggestion made under hypnosis. All subjects will be hypnotized and will listen to deep relaxation music. Posthypnotic suggestions will then be made for subjects to respond in a particular way to the word *focus* on a projection screen in the problem-solving setting. "Deaf without awareness" subjects will be told that when they see the word they will be unable to hear until they are tapped by the experimenter. They will further be told that they will not remember these instructions. "Deaf with awareness" subjects will be given the same instructions about responding to the word but will be told to remember the instructions. "Hypnosis control" subjects will be told that they will scratch an itchy ear when they see the word and that they will not remember the instructions. Each subject will be hypnotized individually but will be led to believe that he or she is participating with two other subjects in a study of group problem solving. (The other subjects will actually be confederates of the experimenter.) After being released from hypnosis, each subject and the two confederates will work on a set of problems presented on slides on a projection screen. The confederates will act out a well-rehearsed, animated conversation prior to projection of the first slide to establish that they happen to know each other and that they should work together. They will invite the subject to work with them, and slides that contain the problems will then be shown. The first slide will be *focus*, which induces the posthypnotic suggestion. From this point on, subjects with hypnotically induced deafness will not hear the other two and should perceive themselves as being left out of the group. Subjects without awareness will not know that they have been made functionally deaf. During the test session, subjects will be scored for paranoid behavior by trained observers who will not be aware of what condition each subject is in. During the session, some "problems" will be Thematic Apperception Test cards. After the session, all subjects will again complete the MMPI and paranoia scales. The experimental session will last 30 minutes.

(*Continued on next page*)

(Experiment Description—*continued from previous page*)

Debriefing

Because deafness without awareness subjects are expected to experience high levels of paranoia and other negative reactions, extensive debriefing will be provided. Subjects will be told the actual purpose of the experiment, its value, and why it was necessary to use deception. Each subject will be rehypnotized and told to recall all events experienced during the session. Confusion and tension will be removed. Subjects will be reevaluated 1 month later as a follow-up.

Rating Scales

Observers rate the subjects, from 0 to 100, on the following scales: confused, relaxed, agitated, irritated, friendly, and hostile.

Subjects rate themselves, from 0 to 100, on each of the following subscales of the paranoia scale: relaxed, agitated, happy, irritated, friendly, hostile, intellectually sharp, confused, vision, hearing, creative, and suspicious.

74 CONSIDERING ANIMAL RESEARCH AND ETHICS WHILE WATCHING TELEVISION

Ellen P. Reese
Mount Holyoke College

This activity can be used with high school or college classes of any size. Students need to be familiar with the Guidelines for Ethical Conduct in the Care and Use of Animals (American Psychological Association, 1986) and Principle 10 (Care and Use of Animals) of the Ethical Principles of Psychologists (American Psychological Association, 1989). This activity can be done in or out of class, but class discussion is beneficial. If there is no class section on ethics, the activity can be incorporated into a discussion of methodology. The instructor needs to copy the handout.

CONCEPT

This exercise, which can be used in class or as a homework assignment, has several goals: (a) increase students' awareness of the special abilities of other animals and their role in the ecosystem; (b) alert students to potential misrepresentations of scientific information as presented in the media; (c) focus students' attention on a variety of ethical issues that may arise from our interactions with other animals, both inside and outside of the laboratory, and point them toward possible solutions to problems that arise; and (d) help students adopt a scientist's perspective when they witness or participate in events that take place outside of the classroom and (e) to help them think in terms of questions for research and ways of answering those questions.

INSTRUCTIONS

Preferably, the instructor will preview a film that will be shown in class and will review the form with the students. This will allow the instructor to provide background information on the species to be observed and to alert the students to sections of the form that are especially relevant. All students can then view, analyze, and discuss the same situation and receive informed feedback from the instructor. Subsequently, or alternatively, students may watch one (or more) television programs or read one (or more) articles on their own. Public television airs several suitable programs: "Wild America"; "Wild, Wild World of Animals"; "Nature"; "New Wilderness"; "World of Survival"; and "Nova." Some episodes of the National Geographic specials and other science programs are also appropriate. The form is designed for use by students who will watch one or more television programs on their own, but it can also be used for tapes or films shown in class. The evaluation section (D1) can be attached to all assignments and the feedback used to revise the activities of the course.

DISCUSSION

In regard to the general questions on the form, most species that are featured in television programs have some sensory and motor abilities that are superior to our own. For example, many hawks can spot a moving mouse from a mile high, cheetahs

---

can sprint 70 miles an hour, and the sense of smell of many animals is far more acute than ours, which is one reason dogs are used to locate drugs and missing persons. Bats and porpoises can hear much higher sounds (ultrasound) than we can, while elephants and some species of whales can hear much lower sounds (infrasound) and can communicate over distances of miles. The social behavior of other species is particularly interesting to students. The males of several birds, including pigeons and doves, share the incubation of eggs and the brooding of the young, and in most familiar species, both parents feed the young. In the case of the rhea (a cousin of the ostrich), it is the male that incubates the eggs and later leads the chicks to food. Coots and moorhens have two clutches of young each year, and the older ones help feed their younger siblings. In a pride of lions, it is the females that do most of the hunting, but elephants are probably the most matriarchal of societies. Wolves are often held up as a model of social behavior, perhaps because all members of the pack care for the young.

In regard to the questions about ethical issues, the attitude of the narrator is noted because of its probable and often subtle effects upon the viewer. On "Wild America," Marty Stouffer always seems respectful and admiring, no matter what the species. However, on "Wild, Wild World of Animals," William Conrad (or his script writer) is frequently condescending and tends to make frivolous remarks at the animals' expense. Other ethical questions relate to the treatment of the animals whose behavior the scientist is studying. Even observations in the natural environment can raise problems. Jane Goodall is among those who have reported how difficult it is to refrain from intervening when a wounded animal is repeatedly attacked by members of its group or is starving to death because it cannot keep up with its mother. But intervention would interfere with the natural ecology and would reduce the validity of the observations.

The final section asks the student to frame a question for research and to then design a study that might answer that question. This is a difficult task, even for a sophisticated scientist, but with the help of the instructor and contributions from other students, the exercise can provide an introduction to the methodology of science.

It is essential that student reports form the base for classroom discussion: Many students will be sensitive to issues not raised in preliminary discussion, and these should be considered. In addition, some student reactions may be based on erroneous interpretations or the application of inappropriate criteria; these issues should be clarified.

REFERENCES   American Psychological Association. (1986). *Guidelines for ethical conduct in the care and use of animals.* Washington, DC: Author.

American Psychological Association. (1989). *Ethical principles of psychologists.* Washington, DC: Author.

Title of episode: _____

Species _____ Location _____

Program (or other source) _____Channel _____ Date _____ Times _____

A. General
   1. Briefly describe or summarize the program including its main purpose or message.

   2. What are some of the special abilities of the species described (e.g., its sensory capacities, motor abilities, social behavior) and how do they compare with our abilities?

   3. What did you learn that changed or challenged your views or opinions?

   4. What additional information would you need to draw the conclusions suggested by the program?

B. Ethical Issues
   1. What was the attitude of the narrator (author, experimenter) toward the animals (e.g., admiration, respect, concern, indifference, condescension, ridicule, other)? Please provide an example.

   2. Did the program convey an awareness of ethical concerns regarding preservation of national habitats, treatment of laboratory animals, and so forth?

   3. If ethical problems arose, what was their impact on or cost to the individuals or species?

   4. Were these costs justified in terms of potential benefits to other animals, to people, or to science?

   5. If, after considering all of the issues involved, you feel that you have identified any ethical problems with the material you have watched, specify what these are and what is being done or might be done to alleviate the situation.

   6. If you do believe that there is an ethical problem with the material you have watched, is there something you as an individual might do to contribute to its solution?

   7. Has this program modified your views or ethical issues? In what way?

C. Questions for Research
   1. Are there any scientific questions that arise from what you have seen (e.g., what do we not know about the species' biological needs, sensory capacities, social behavior, learning capacities, other)?

   2. How might you find an answer to one of the above questions:
      a. What behavior would you observe and how would you measure it?

      b. Under what conditions?

      c. What results might you predict?

(*Continued on next page*)

(Television Analysis—*continued from previous page*)

D. Value of this Exercise
  1. How much did you learn (educational value) from this exercise? Use a 7-point scale on which 1 = *you learned nothing* and 7 = *it was maximally educational.*

      Educational value ————————————

  2. How interesting was this exercise? Use a 7-point scale on which 1 = *it bored you to tears* and 7 = *it was extremely interesting.*

      Interest value ————————————

  3. Would this be a good program to show in class (if it is available)?

      ————————————————————

  4. For what topics would it be most appropriate?

Other Comments or Suggestions

75 ETHICS IN ANIMAL RESEARCH

Margaret S. Martin
Lander College

This activity involves small group discussion and can be used with high school or entry-level college students. No advance preparation of materials is required, but both the teacher and the students need to have read materials on the ethics of animal research. The brevity and lack of detail in the "case" and the generality of the discussion questions means that the class discussion is likely to be wide-ranging and to tap students' feelings about the subject as much as their knowledge.

CONCEPT

The consideration of ethical principles in research is a vital issue today in psychology. Ethical principles are extended to animal studies as well as to studies done with human subjects. The American Psychological Association has published articles and guidelines on issues involving both groups of subjects. The following class activity will stimulate discussion that may be directly related to these guidelines.

INSTRUCTIONS

Have students form small groups of three or four and read the following comments: "As a college ethics committee, outline a report to be presented to the president of your college. Identify the ethical problems and steps you would take to remedy these problems. Also, indicate procedures that should be taken to prevent other occurrences."

Have a spokesperson from each group briefly present his or her report to the class for discussion. When the students understand their task, read aloud the following situation or hand out copies to each group:

> Professor Onetrack has abruptly had his research budget cut by 25%. On the verge of a breakthrough in his medical experiments, he is determined to keep his research program operating. Dean Determined argues that the college needs to put more funds into the remedial program to better prepare students for degree programs and to increase graduation rates. Recently, Professor Onetrack bought some experimental animals from John Cutrate to help reduce some of the effects of his budget cut. During a demonstration of one of his experimental procedures to a community hospital group, Nancy Nurse recognized her missing pet poodle, which had been implanted with an electrode. She is suing the professor and the college for $500,000.

DISCUSSION

The discussion can focus only on the ethical pros and cons of animal research or can be expanded to research on humans. If so, be sure to include comments on Milgram's (1963) obedience studies. This discussion can be guided by some of the following questions: Should animals be used in research? If animals are to be used in research, what should be some guidelines for researchers to follow? How do ethical practices differ for animals and humans?

Consider the principle of "harm avoidance" in the American Psychological Association's (1981, 1982) ethical practices statement and relate it to animal research. Also consider how you can provide "debriefing" in an animal study.

REFERENCES American Psychological Association. (1981). Ethical principles of psychologists. *American Psychologist, 36*, 633–638.

American Psychological Association. (1982). *Ethical principles in the conduct of research with human participants* (2nd ed.). Washington, DC: Author.

Milgram, S. (1963). Behavioral study of obedience. *Journal of Abnormal and Social Psychology, 67*, 371–378.

SUGGESTED READING Evans, J. D. (1985). *Invitation to psychological research.* Holt, Rinehart & Winston.

Rollin, E. B. (1985). The moral status of research animals in psychology. *American Psychologist, 40*, 930–936.

76 ANALYZING THE VALUE AND ETHICS OF ANIMAL RESEARCH THAT IS REPORTED IN THE POPULAR PRESS

Ellen P. Reese
Mount Holyoke College

This activity is appropriate with classes of virtually any size. Students need to be familiar with the American Psychological Association's (1986) Guidelines for Ethical Conduct in the Care and Use of Animals. The students are asked to analyze an article from the popular press. This could be done in writing by individuals or as a small group activity during class. In any event, the instructor may wish to use the questions from the form provided in this activity in a handout to guide the review of the article.

CONCEPT

This activity is designed to help students relate behavioral research with nonhuman animals to events in their own world. The general form provided here requires students to (a) analyze an animal study that has been reported in the popular press, (b) assess the implications of the study for human behavior, and (c) judge the extent to which the study complies with ethical guidelines for research with animals.

The example is a study of the long-term effects of exposing prenatal rat pups to caffeine. The study was reported in the monthly newspaper of the American Psychological Association, the *APA Monitor*, and the form has been completed with answers that would be appropriate for an analysis of this article.

Instructors can adapt the form for a study reported in the text, or they or their students can bring in articles from popular magazines. The questions on ethical issues (see the section on Ethical Issues) can be incorporated in discussions of any area of animal research.

DISCUSSION

The several hundred college freshmen who have completed this exercise have generally done well with the questions that require them to analyze the study. This requires careful reading and takes approximately 1 hour; however, given the relevance of the study to human prenatal development, most students find the exercise worthwhile. The most common omission has been a failure to note the importance of following the rat pups to maturity, which provides the information that the learning deficits increase with age. This study illustrates one of the major arguments for research with nonhuman animals: The short life of some animals, including rats, permits scientists to study the life-span development of behavior as well as the cross-generational effects of various events that may occur during pregnancy.

The section on the interpretation of the study that follows seems more difficult for students to answer. If the exercise is introduced with references to fetal alcohol syndrome and other known effects of substance abuse during pregnancy, most students see implications for human mothers. They have more trouble with the questions about generalizing from animal studies to human behavior and designing additional studies. These questions will benefit from a class discussion in which the students can present and discuss their responses.

As would be expected, the section on ethical issues produces responses that reflect a range of positions on animal rights: animal welfare issues. Other responses are more directly related to the procedures used in the study. Several students have said that the high dosage was unreasonable for a rat. As I read the study (Paragraphs 1 and 5), the rat mothers were given the *equivalent* of what would be 12 cups for a human, and many women do drink 12 or more cups a day. Other students have objected to the study on the grounds that there were too many groups and that the middle dose of 8 cups could have been eliminated. In my view, the middle dosage provided very important information. Without these subjects, one might assume a linear increase in effects from the lowest to the highest dose. In fact, the effects of the 4-cup dose were minimal and those of the 8-cup dose seem to have been similar to those of the 12-cup dose. Prenatal caffeine intake appears to become particularly dangerous for rats somewhere between the equivalent of 4 and 8 cups per day, something we would not know if the middle dose had been eliminated. A few students have said they would not approve the study because the number of subjects was not stated. I applaud that response but point out that the information would have been included in a technical report of the research. A detailed, and readable, discussion of alternatives to the use of nonhuman animals in research and education is presented in the 1985 report of the Office of Technology Assessment.

REFERENCES American Psychological Association. (1986). *Guidelines for ethical conduct in the care and use of animals.* Washington, DC: Author.

Caffeine Slows Pup Learning
Carol Turkington

Giving pregnant rats the equivalent of several cups of coffee daily during a critical period of pup development causes a number of behavioral and neurochemical changes in the offspring, according to researchers at the Hebrew University and the Wiezman Institute of Science in Israel.

Rat dams who got low doses of prenatal caffeine (four cups daily) during the last week of pregnancy gave birth to hyperactive pups. High doses (12 cups) caused significant learning disabilities in the pups that lasted throughout the animals' lives, Brina Frieder said at the annual Society for Neuroscience meeting in Washington this fall.

Recent research has indicated that women who use psychotropic drugs during pregnancy bear children who show lasting behavioral changes, including some types of learning disabilities and attention-deficit disorders. These drugs apparently interfere with normal brain development that occurs during midpregnancy.

Frieder and her colleagues in Israel determined that interfering with a rat's rapid brain development during the final week of pregnancy is the most likely to produce deficiencies in the ability of the animal to perform in situations that require sustained attention or complex learning ability.

The researchers gave caffeine to pregnant rats in drinking water during the last seven days of pregnancy. Three groups of pregnant rats were treated with varying doses of caffeine equivalent to four, eight, and 12 cups a day. The study followed the pups into adulthood, and compared their physical and behavioral development to that of rat pups born to animals that didn't get caffeine.

Four cups of caffeine daily caused hyperactivity in the offspring but no serious learning problems. But those with mothers given the two higher doses showed learning deficits on learning tasks that required sustained attention, such as complex visual or auditory discrimination. And researchers found that the higher the dose, the more marked the disability. The rats had no problems in simple motor learning or spatial orientation tasks.

In addition to the learning deficits, the animals that were prenatally exposed to the higher doses of caffeine were much more obese in adulthood than those in the low-dose or control groups. Both the obesity and the learning disability became more severe with increasing age.

Neurochemical studies of the rat mothers revealed an increase in protein concentration in the cortex and hippocampus of those that had received the highest doses, and an increase in choline uptake in those that had received lower doses.

Note. From the APA Monitor, *February 1987, 18(2), p. 27.*

Analysis of an Article Describing Biobehavioral Research (Form Completed for Study on Effects of Prenatal Caffeine)

A. The Study
 1. Purpose
  To discover the long-term effects of exposing prenatal rats to caffeine.
 2. Procedure
  a. Independent variable (what was studied to observe its effects on behavior; how was this variable manipulated?):
   The equivalent (for humans) or 4, 8, and 12 cups of coffee was given in mothers' drinking water during last week of pregnancy.
  b. Dependent variables (what effects did experimenter look for and how were they measured?):
   Behavior: activity level, ability to learn simple motor tasks and complex visual and auditory discriminations.[1]
   Physical development: weight.
   Neurochemical changes in brains of mothers: protein concentration and choline uptake.
  c. Controls (what was done to minimize the possibility that the results might be due to the passage of time or some other condition unrelated to the study?):
   The same measures were taken for rats whose mothers did not receive caffeine.
 3. Results (summarize the main results of the study)

Dosage	Behavioral effects	Physiological effects
Low	*Hyperactive, but no learning disabilities.*	*Mothers: increased choline uptake.* *Pups: ? (neurochemical studies not reported)*
Medium, high	*Hyperactive; impaired learning for complex visual and auditory discriminations (deficits increased with age).*	*Mothers: increased protein concentrations in cortex, hippocampus.* *Pups: increasing obesity with increasing age (neurochemical studies not reported).*

 4. Interpretation
  a. If one assumes some similarities in the prenatal development of different species of mammals, what are the implications of the study for human behavior?
   Substances consumed during pregnancy may have long-term harmful effects on children. If caffeine does all of this, what about nicotine, alcohol, marijuana, cocaine, and other drugs? (The article mentions long-term damage to children of women who take psychotropic drugs during pregnancy.)
  b. What are some potential problems in generalizing from a single study on rats to human behavior?
   Rats are not people (the physiology of pigs is closer to ours). The rats' gestation period is 3 weeks, and caffeine was given during the last week, the period of most rapid development of the brain. The study of psychotropic drugs with humans refers to brain damage during midpregnancy. Researchers need to know the effects of various drugs throughout pregnancy; these effects may be different for different species.
  c. What other studies might be run?
   Other laboratory studies might include replications of this experiment with other species as well as studies of other drugs. Clinical studies would include testing for learning deficits in children of mothers known to have taken caffeine or other drugs during pregnancy. Such studies should include long-term follow-up assessment.

---

[1] The article does not give details, but typical discrimination tasks might require the rat to press one lever in the presence of one tone (or a particular visual pattern) and another lever in the presence of a different tone (or different visual pattern). Responding on the appropriate lever would be rewarded with food.

(continued on next page)

(Article Analysis—*continued from previous page*)

B. Ethical Issues
1. In answering these questions, assume you are on a review board and must approve, suggest modifications, or reject this study before it is conducted.
    a. Justification (before approving or rejecting a study, review boards try to decide whether the probable results of the study justify any costs to the subjects):
    What are the probable costs to the animals in this study?
    Presumably the rats were killed at the end of the study. There was no impairment of spatial orientation or simple motor learning, so the animals could function in a laboratory environment even though they might not have survived in the wild. Their obesity may have been uncomfortable.
    What are the potential benefits to people, other animals, science (see Part A, Number 4)?
    b. As far as you can tell, is the study well designed so as to produce clear and important results?
    Yes: appropriate controls and follow-up.
    c. How do the experimenters maximize what can be learned from the study?
    Different dosages; several behavioral and physiological measures; study continued until rat pups were adults.
    d. Are there any alternatives to the use of live animals in conducting the study? (Are there any reasons why people, tissue cultures, or computer simulations could not have produced intelligible results?)
    People: *a review board would deny on ethical grounds.*
    Tissue cultures: *would not allow for effects on learning. Need live animals to study behavior.*
    Computer: *do not know enough to program relevant information into the computer.*
2. Procedures. If the experiment is justified, can you think of any ways to reduce stress to the subjects or reduce the number of subjects and still answer the questions the study is designed to answer?
    (*This question should always be included. I see nothing to question in the caffeine study, but students may.*)
3. Would you approve the study as described? State reasons why or why not.

Note. Answers are in italics.

□ 77 THREE EXERCISES ON THE ETHICS OF RESEARCH ON HUMANS

Joan E. Sieber

California State University, Hayward

In this activity there are three exercises that can be done individually, in small groups, or in general class discussion. These exercises are appropriate for students at any level, in virtually any size class. No prior knowledge is required, and the only advance preparation for the teacher is copying material. The first exercise familiarizes students with the ethical principles that they will need to apply to proposed research plans in the other exercises. Exercise 1 can be a stand-alone discussion or used with Exercises 2, 3, or both.

CONCEPT

At every stage in the planning and conduct of research, there are important decisions to be made. These decisions involve ethical as well as scientific elements. Unless the decisions are ethically sound, they will not be scientifically sound. Many students think *ethics* simply means being nice or honest. As these exercises show, ethics means far more. Students are often surprised to realize that unethical research typically occurs because the scientist has been thoughtless and acted in a hurry, not because the scientist is a bad person. This activity and the exercises within it are designed to help the student overcome some of the kinds of thoughtlessness that naturally arise when one is intent on doing a research project.

MATERIALS NEEDED

You will need to make copies of the three ethical principles, the sample letter, and the research project description.

INSTRUCTIONS

Exercise 1. Have students study the handouts listing the three main ethical principles for research on humans and the six scientific norms based on those principles. Ask them to explain how each norm relates to the principles designated. You may wish to divide the class into small groups, with each group then presenting its conclusions to the rest of the class.

The Three Basic Ethical Principles

The following three ethical principles should guide research on humans:
   A. *Beneficence*—maximizing good outcomes and avoiding unnecessary risk.
   B. *Respect*—concern for autonomy of persons and courtesy.
   C. *Justice*—fair procedures and fair distribution of costs and benefits.
   These three basic principles translate into six norms of scientific behavior:
   1. *Valid research design.* Only valid research yields correct results. Valid design takes into account relevant theory, methods, and prior findings (Principles A and B).

2. *Competence of researcher.* Even well-designed research may yield invalid results or cause harm if the researcher is inadequately supervised or insufficiently qualified (Principles A and B).
3. *Identification of consequences.* Possible risks and benefits should be identified and considered before the research is conducted (Principles A–C).
4. *Selection of subjects.* The population sampled should (a) be appropriate to the purposes of the study, (b) be the one that benefits from the research, and (c) not include persons having very limited power and autonomy (Principles A–C).
5. *Voluntary informed consent.* Voluntary informed consent of subjects should be obtained beforehand. *Voluntary* means freely, without threat or undue inducement. *Informed* means that subjects know what reasonable persons in that situation would want to know before giving consent. *Consent* means explicit agreement to participate. Informed consent requires clear communication that subjects comprehend, not complex technical explanations or legal jargon (Principles A–C).
6. *Compensation for injury.* The researcher is responsible for what happens to subjects and should compensate them for injury (Principles A–C).

Exercise 2. This exercise is designed to test students' abilities to apply the above norms and principles. Describe to them each of the following research plans and have them discuss the ethical considerations of each. Compare their responses with the answers given here.

A. You plan to study the effects of competition on ability to solve math problems. Half of the subjects will be told that you want to see what approach they take in solving math problems. The other half will be told that you want to see which person chooses the best approach.

   Answer: This study requires withholding some information. Include in the informed consent statement that you cannot give subjects full information about the study ahead of time but that you will explain it all to them afterward. Those who do not like having information withheld may decline to participate.

B. You plan to compare the intellectual skills of retired people to those of sophomores. To recruit sophomores, you plan to arrange for volunteers to receive an *A* in their psychology course and for nonvolunteers to have their grade lowered. To recruit retired people, you plan to go to a retirement community each evening next week, knock at people's doors, and ask them to work some puzzles without explaining all of the details of the study because most would not understand.

   Answer: For retired people to be meaningfully compared with sophomores, they must have equally good education, vision, test-taking skills, and so on, assumptions that are sure to be false. The recruitment of sophomores involves undue inducement and coercion. Elderly people are likely to be frightened and unwilling to let strangers in at night. It is unacceptable to assume that one should not give an adequate explanation just because the subjects would not understand a technical explanation.

C. You plan to compare marijuana use in freshmen and seniors. Because you may want to reinterview some subjects later, you plan to write their names and phone numbers on their data sheets. You plan to promise confidentiality so that subjects will trust you and to keep the data in your room in a locked file.

Answer: This is a study of criminal behavior. You should not promise confidentiality because you cannot assure it. Your data could be subpoenaed and you might have to choose between going to jail and handing over the data. If you hand over the data, subjects can sue you for breaking your promise of confidentiality. Research on criminal behavior is risky and should be left to professional scientists who are knowledgeable about the risks and about how to minimize them.

D. You plan to study the effects of an educational (cable) TV curriculum on learning to read. You give access to the cable TV program to 100 homes with 5-year-olds whose parents want their child to watch the TV curriculum daily. You get permission to test those 100 children in 2 months, along with 100 matched control children who will not have access to the cable TV.

Answer: Because you do not know whether the curriculum will be effective, it is fair to "deprive" the control group for a while. Inform both sets of families and even things up later by giving the control families access to the cable TV after the study is over. (See Conner, 1982, for a description of the evaluation of "Sesame Street" and a discussion of the ethics of random assignment of subjects to conditions.

E. To study self-esteem in children, you plan to have 8-year-olds draw pictures of themselves and their friends and to answer some questions. You plan to ask a teacher friend of yours to let you test some of her students.

Answer: This study involves special problems of consent having to do with children, coercion, and institutional responsibility. Children are easily coerced and cannot legally consent. Parents and persons in charge at institutions (e.g., schools, jails, hospitals, places of employment) may exert subtle pressures for conformity to their wishes; hence, autonomy and freedom from coercion may be difficult to ensure. Most schools probably would require that you get consent from the school board or the parents. You should also give each child an independent opportunity to decline to participate.

Exercise 3. Students should be led through a discussion of the elements of informed consent before beginning this exercise.

The Elements of Informed Consent

Federal law governing human research requires that informed consent statements include the following:

1. Explain the purpose of the research, the expected duration of subjects' participation, and a description of the procedures. Describe the procedure in terms sub-

jects understand. Avoid jargon or explanations that are irrelevant to deciding whether to participate.

2. Describe any foreseeable risks or discomforts to subjects.
3. Describe any benefits reasonably to be expected from participation.
4. Describe alternatives to participation when appropriate.
5. Describe how confidentiality will be maintained.
6. For risky research, say whether compensation for harm is available.
7. Indicate whom to contact for answers to questions about the research and subjects' rights or in case of research-related injury.
8. Indicate that participation is voluntary, refusal to participate will involve no penalty or loss of benefits to which subjects are otherwise entitled, and subjects may discontinue participation at any time.

Ask students to write a clear, friendly letter soliciting participation in the research project described in the research project description (see the sample letter and description below). With the students, compare their letters with the sample letter.

Suggested Letter for Exercise 3

(Veterans Administration hospital letterhead)

Dear Patient,

We need your help in a new study on taste sensitivity and preference. The results of this study may help doctors and dietitians plant diets to improve health and may add to the understanding of taste perception.

In this study, we will find out how readily a person detects and identifies sweet, sour, salty, and bitter tastes, and what tastes they prefer. This information will be analyzed in relation to some information from patients' medical records. Persons participating in this study can expect to spend about 20 minutes on each of 5 different days. Participants will be asked to taste plain water and samples of water mixed with small amounts of some safe substances that normally are used to season food; they will be asked to answer some questions about how the samples taste and which ones they prefer. There is no foreseeable risk or discomfort. Participants' identity and personal information will remain confidential.

Your participation is strictly voluntary. You may withdraw your participation at any time. Your decision as to whether to participate will have no effect on any benefits you receive or wish to receive from any agency. For answers to questions pertaining to the research, research participants' rights, or in the event of a research-related injury, contact me at _____ (name, address, telephone number).

Eating disorders (e.g., cravings and aversions) have been observed among psychiatric patients receiving lithium treatment. You are a research psychologist at a Veterans Administration hospital and you propose that acuity for detecting and recognizing the four basic tastes (sweet, sour, salt, and bitter) be measured and preferences be determined among patients undergoing lithium therapy and matched controls. You wish to test the hypothesis that lithium-medicated subjects have altered taste perception thresholds and taste preferences. The substances will consist of pure water and small concentrations of the following substances diluted in water: sucrose (sweet), salt, citric acid (sour), and quinine sulfate (bitter). These substances normally are used as food additives at higher levels of concentration. Three small samples will be presented simultaneously, two identical and one different, with the position varied so that odd and identical samples are tried equally. Paired comparisons and a hedonic rating scale will be used to measure taste preference. Data acquired through taste testing will be analyzed in relation to age, sex, smoking history, duration of lithium administration, and current lithium concentration. Five 10–15 minute sessions per subject are required. Three threshold tests for each of the four test substances will be conducted on separate days. On the 5th day, preference testing will be conducted.

78 ETHICAL PRINCIPLES AND DILEMMAS IN THE PRACTICE OF PSYCHOLOGY

Peter S. Fernald
University of New Hampshire

L. Dodge Fernald
Harvard University

This activity can be used with students at any level and with classes of any size. However, with larger classes, the preparation of "individual personality profiles" could become time consuming. The activity involves getting and writing samples during one class and giving feedback and having class discussion during a subsequent class. It is best used in conjunction with a discussion of personality, or possibly parapsychology. Deception is used on students during the exercise as a starting point for discussing the ethics of deception as well as other ethics issues.

CONCEPT

Using high-probability statements taken from an astrological source, this classroom demonstration illustrates the willingness of students (and presumably other laypeople) to believe bogus personality assessments. This activity addresses concerns about the American Psychological Association's (1981) *Ethical Principles of Psychologists* and the dilemmas psychologists face in their efforts to protect the welfare of clients, students, and subjects.

MATERIALS NEEDED

Each student will receive a presumably individual "personality analysis." The analyses are actually identical, a set of 12 high-probability statements taken from an astrological source (Forer, 1949). The analysis is the following:

> You have a strong need for other people to like you and for them to admire you. You have a tendency to be critical of yourself. You have a great deal of unused capacity which you have not turned to your advantage. While you have some personality weaknesses, you are generally able to compensate for them. Your sexual adjustment has presented some problems for you. Disciplined and controlled on the outside, you tend to be worrisome and insecure inside. At times you have serious doubts as to whether you have made the right decision or done the right thing. You prefer a certain amount of change and variety and become dissatisfied when hemmed in by restrictions and limitations. You pride yourself on being an independent thinker and do not accept others' opinions without satisfactory proof. You have found it unwise to be too frank in revealing yourself to others. At times you are extroverted, affable, sociable, while at other times you are introverted, wary, and reserved. Some of your aspirations tend to be pretty unrealistic.

Adapted from the *Instructor's Manual* of *Introduction to Psychology* (5th ed.), by L. Dodge Fernald and Peter S. Fernald. Copyright 1985, Wm. C. Brown. Used by permission.

To enhance the credibility of the personality analyses, the instructor can handwrite them. However, because this procedure is time consuming, it is appropriate only for small classes. For large classes, use of a word processor will be most efficient. However, students in large classes often sit close to one another, which makes it likely that some will read each other's analysis, thus letting the "cat out of the bag" prematurely. Two procedures minimize this possibility: First, program the word processor to generate different sequences of high-probability statements so that on quick glance the identical reports do not appear to be identical. Second, tell students that the analyses are quite personal and for this reason they should keep their respective analyses to themselves.

INSTRUCTIONS   Tell students you would like to demonstrate a fascinating phenomenon called graphology, which is the analysis of human character through handwriting. Give them the following instructions, which will add substantially to your credibility:

> As you know, in addition to my interest in graphology, I am an experimental psychologist. Hence our purpose here is to demonstrate, using experimental procedures, the cues a graphologist uses. We will design a situation in which all cues, other than those involved in handwriting, are controlled or held constant. To do this, all subjects must follow these directions:
>
> 1. You are to write "The quick brown fox jumps over the lazy dog," a sentence that contains all 26 letters of the alphabet. If each of you were to write a different sentence, the contents of the sentences would include cues to your personalities. For example, one student might write, "Two dollars says you can't analyze me," and another might say, "This course is fun," and I would know that the former student liked to wager, and the latter enjoyed psychology. As you can see, having each of you write the same sentence not only gives me a chance to see how you form all the letters of the alphabet, but it also eliminates any cues present in the content of your sentences.
>
> 2. I want you to write on the sheets of paper I give you, since the type of paper you use can tell me something about you. For example, using inexpensive paper might indicate frugality. For similar reasons, I want you all to use the same pen as there are obvious differences between one who purchases an expensive pen and one who uses red or green ballpoint pen and still another who uses a dull pencil.
>
> 3. I could probably tell something about you from your name, as names often give clues to racial or national stereotypes, which, as we will see later in the course, have some validity. For these reasons, I want you to use a number, perhaps your social security number, instead of your name. Be sure to remember your number so you will know which personality report is yours at the next class meeting.

At the following class meeting, return to every student his or her personality analysis. Then, ask each student to read the analysis and, without showing it to or discussing it with anyone else, to rate it on the following five-point scale: 5 = excellent appraisal, 4 = good appraisal (more right than wrong), 3 = average appraisal (about half right), 2 = poor appraisal (more wrong than right), and 1 = very poor appraisal.

Collect the ratings and then indicate on the chalkboard the frequency of the various rating. Typically, most students give "excellent" or "good" ratings to their personality descriptions, a finding that is consistent with published studies using similar procedures (Forer, 1949).

Now ask a student to read aloud his or her personality appraisal. Repeat this step until it is clear that all of the appraisals are identical. Students are usually amazed and amused to discover that everyone has the same description. Inform the class that most of the statements were taken from an astrological source.

Some students may feel angry, embarrassed, or both about the deception. It is important, therefore, to explain the reasons (indicated below in the Discussion) why deception was used and why they were so easily duped. Help them understand, accept, and feel comfortable with any embarrassment and anger resulting from their being tricked. One way to do this is to point out that even personnel managers, who are supposed to be experts in appraising human behavior, are readily taken in by these same personality descriptions (Stagner, 1958).

DISCUSSION Ask the students if the demonstration indicates anything about the dangers of deception in the use of psychological assessment techniques and, from a more general standpoint, in the rendering of any and all psychological services. Typically, students will readily realize that the dangers are very great and that many people are easily duped by self-proclaimed experts having little or no training in psychology. Palmists, crystal-ball gazers, and others who take on various professional-sounding titles (e.g., psychotherapist, counselor, healer) often have large followings of people who are impressed by their seemingly accurate but fraudulent descriptions of personality.

This should elicit a discussion of the control of psychological practice and the problems of licensing and certification. It is important to address the question of why the demonstration succeeded (i.e., why so many students were easily duped). There are a number of possible explanations, but three seem especially relevant: First, many students do not realize the statements are intentionally general and vague. Second, because students share a number of common concerns, traits, conflicts, interests, and motives, many of the astrological statements are in fact accurate. Third, by virtue of training, role, and title, the instructor is considered an authority, and the proper role of the student is to believe the teachings of the instructor or the authority figure.

The latter explanation raises an important ethical issue relevant to the present demonstration. Is the instructor who intentionally dupes students, possibly causing them unnecessary embarrassment and anger, acting in an ethical and professional manner? To facilitate discussion of this question, read to the class the following statement, which is the first three sentences of the preamble to the *Ethical Principles of Psychologists* (American Psychological Association, 1981)

> Psychologists respect the dignity and worth of the individual and strive for the preservation and protection of fundamental human rights. They are committed to increasing knowledge of human behavior and of people's understanding of themselves and others and to the utilization of such knowledge for the promotion of human welfare. While pursuing these objectives, they make every effort to protect the welfare of those who seek their services and of the research participants that may be the objects of study. (p. 633)

Intentionally deceiving students is clearly inconsistent with psychologists' ethical principles, which emphasize both respect for the worth and dignity of the individual and protection of the welfare of those (students, in this instance) seeking psychological services. On the other hand, psychologists are also committed to "increasing knowledge of human behavior and of people's understanding of themselves and others and to the utilization of such knowledge for the promotion of human welfare" (American Psychological Association, 1981). It may be that lecturing about the dangers of self-proclaimed experts who take advantage of an uninformed public is, from an educational standpoint, far less effective than having students experience the deception firsthand. Stated more simply, in this case *experiential learning* may be more effective than learning through instruction (lecture). If this is so, are the possible negative effects of deception more than compensated for by the students' enhanced critical and mental faculties, their realizations that "even I can be duped," and that "I must do my best to evaluate critically the claims of individuals claiming expertise"?

The ethical dilemma described here is not unusual. Two well-known examples are Milgram's obedience to authority experiments (Milgram, 1974) and Zimbardo's prison study (Zimbardo, Haney, & Banks, 1973). In both cases the dignity and welfare of both students and subjects were at risk, and at the same time, the surprising findings of those studies posed here, as in all instances, concerns trading one form of human welfare for another.

REFERENCES

American Psychological Association. (1981). *Ethical principles of psychologists.* Washington, DC: Author.

Forer, B. R. (1949). The fallacy of personal validation: A classroom demonstration of gullibility. *Journal of Abnormal and Social Psychology, 44,* 118–123.

Milgram, S. (1974). *Obedience to authority.* New York: Harper & Row.

Stanger, R. (1958). The gullibility of personnel managers. *Personnel Psychology, 11,* 247–352.

Zimbardo, P. G., Haney, C., & Banks, W. C. (1973). A Pirandellian prison. *The New York Times Magazine,* pp. 38–60.

SUGGESTED READING

Fernald, P. S., & Makarewixj, J. F. (1967). Use of personal validation. *Journal of Counseling Psychology, 14,* 568–569.

$\square$79 OBEDIENCE AND ETHICS

Cynthia A. Erickson, Cathy A. Grover, and Stephen F. Davis
Emporia State University

This activity requires much advance preparation, and the effectiveness of the presentation depends almost entirely on the quality of the skits. It can be used with virtually any size class. If there is no section specifically dealing with ethics, the discussion can be included in the social psychology unit.

CONCEPT

For several reasons Milgram's (1974) work on obedience to authority is considered to be one of the most important psychological studies to have been conducted. Ethical difficulties and the implications for the appropriate treatment of subjects (human or animal) are highlighted by this work. This project also is important because of the implications it made about how people interact with and respond to authority figures. Milgram demonstrated that normal people are capable of doing atrocious things to others, such as administering electric shock. The Milgram study and its underlying significance can be difficult to explain to beginning psychology students in the context of a lecture presentation.

MATERIALS NEEDED

You will need copies of the scripts for three skits, which are described in the next section and are available on request. Be sure to give your drama department sufficient time to prepare for the presentation. We have found that 3–4 weeks of advance warning is appreciated.

INSTRUCTIONS

One way to make this and similar studies clear and meaningful is to arrange for the school drama club or members of the community theater to act out three skits. For maximum effectiveness, these skits should be presented during a single class period. Prior to the start of the skits, write the word *ethics* on the chalkboard and say nothing about it until the skits have been completed.

The first skit is an accurate and serious dramatization of one of Milgram's (1974) studies. It will help to have the drama club view the film produced by Milgram and his colleagues (Johnson, 1965). Also included in this skit are scenes of 2 subjects after completion of the experiment. The first scene depicts a subject who is pleased with his or her performance. The second shows a subject who is deeply disturbed by the thought that another human being may have been harmed or killed.

Skit 2 is set in a prison camp in Nazi Germany. A paper-pushing administrator, with back to the camp, is ordering the removal of 125 more inmates. The guards are following orders, obeying authority figures. Unlike the subjects in Milgram's (1974) study, the guards have something to lose if they do not comply.

The third skit is a more recent example of group conformity and obedience to authority. The setting is Jonestown, the scene of the infamous group suicide. Several hundred people obeyed Jim Jones and took their own lives. Showing the film *The People of People's Temple* (Gottleib & Ruxin, 1979) to the actors as part of their preparation for this skit will assist them.

You should plan to allow approximately 30 minutes for the presentation of the skits. Each of the skits we have prepared lasts no longer than 7 or 8 minutes. However, it takes a couple of minutes to arrange even the most elementary props for the next skit and for the actors to take their places. We have also found that these skits are far more effective when the actors are clothed in black. This seems to heighten the tension in the room.

DISCUSSION The final portion of the class period is devoted to a discussion of the skits. Some of the more effective questions for these sessions include the following:

1. Have you been in a situation in which you had to obey authority? What was your reaction to this situation?

2. How many of you feel that you would respond in a manner similar to Milgram's (1974) subjects? Why or why not?

3. How does the Milgram experiment relate to the other skits?

4. If this study was repeated today, would similar results be obtained? Why or why not?

5. Should the Milgram study be repeated? Why or why not? Would you like to serve as a subject?

6. Ask the actors to describe how they felt about the various parts they played in the skits.

7. Yale University subsequently paid for psychological treatment for several of Milgram's subjects. What ethical responsibilities do researchers have when they are using human subjects?

8. What changes have occurred in the ethical treatment of subjects since the Milgram study was conducted? Do you feel that these changes may have been a direct result of this widely publicized experiment?

9. Do such ethical considerations extend to the use of animal subjects as well? Why or why not?

10. Should subjects be informed about the purpose and the results of psychological research they have participated in?

One might question whether the educational gain of this project is worth the efforts that have been expended. Our experiences have led us to answer with a resounding yes! Student reactions have been extremely favorable. Students are appreciative of the change of pace provided by the skits. Class discussions, as well as examination scores, indicate that their understanding of this area of research and the ethical responsibilities of psychologists is superior to that of previous classes taught via the lecture-only method. In one class period you will have presented a seminal piece of psychological research, exposed the students to other real-life forms of obedience to authority, and discussed the ethical treatment of human and animal subjects—all without even delivering a lecture!

REFERENCES Gottleib, D., & Ruxin, J. (Producers). (1979). *The People of people's temple* [Film]. Wilmette, IL: Film, Inc.

Johnson, C. (Ed.). (1965). *Obedience* [Film]. New York: New York University.

Milgram, S. (1974). *Obedience to authority.* New York: Harper & Row.

80 ETHICAL ISSUES IN THE USE OF ANIMALS IN EDUCATION

Ellen P. Reese

Mount Holyoke College

■──■

This is not an activity per se but a discussion of the selection and use of animals for educational and research purposes. Alternatives are presented for various conditioning paradigms. This article is a rich source of ideas for teachers planning to use or discuss animals in the classroom. Students who will work with animals would also benefit from reading this article.

■──■

DISCUSSION   Any use of animals—whether for food, entertainment, education, or research—involves ethical questions about which people have strong and divergent convictions. In this regard, the American Psychological Association (APA) has been a leader in enunciating ethical principles and guidelines for research with nonhuman subjects (see the *Guidelines for Ethical Conduct in the Care and Use of Animals* [American Psychological Association, 1986] at the end of this activity). One provision of the *Guidelines* encourages teachers to include instruction and discussion of the ethics and values of animal research in any course that involves or even discusses the use of animals. The purpose of this section, therefore, is to present some background information about the use of animals by psychologists and to provide some activities that will involve students in the kinds of ethical decisions that anyone working with animals is forced to make.

Use of Animals in Psychological Research

Nearly all psychologists conduct their research with human subjects. Of the 8% of psychologists who do work with animals, most study rodents. Furthermore, a survey conducted by the APA (1985) showed that of the 252,000 animals used in university psychology laboratories, 51 were dogs and 1,502 were cats; rodents composed more than 95% of the total. To put these figures into perspective, it should be noted that more than 4 billion animals are slaughtered for food each year and that more than 10 million animals are euthanized by animal shelters. There are no precise figures on the use of animals in all areas of research, but the U.S. Office of Technology Assessment estimates between 17–22 million vertebrates were used in 1983, of which 12–15 million were rats and mice (Office of Technology Assessment, 1985, p. 10). Most of these animals were not used in studies of behavior but in medical research or in testing the safety of drugs, pesticides, food additives, building materials, and other products.

Justification of Animal Research

The APA *Guidelines* (Section VI) require that any research with animals be justified. It must not be trivial. Instead, it must meet at least one of the following criteria: (a) increase knowledge of the processes underlying the evolution, development, mainte-nance, alteration, control, or biological significance of behavior; (b) increase under-standing of the species under study; or (c) provide results that benefit the health or welfare of humans or other animals.

The potential scientific importance of a study must also outweigh any harm or distress to the animals, and, in arriving at this judgment, the psychologist should assume that any procedures that cause pain in humans will also cause pain in other animals.

Before selecting a species for a particular study, psychologists must consider such possibilities as tissue cultures or computer simulations and, if an intact animal is needed, the species must be well-suited to answer the questions posed.

Because people do not always agree on the potential importance of a study or the potential for distress to the animals, no research may be conducted until it has been reviewed by an animal care and use committee whose members include a veterinar-ian and a member from the local community.

Alternatives to Animals in Behavioral Research

For now and for the forseeable future, there are few alternatives to the use of live animals when one is studying behavior. The main alternatives to behavioral research with nonhuman animals is research with humans, and human volunteers are by far the most frequent subjects in psychological research. When animals are used, their number must be kept to the minimum compatible with scientific validity, and every-thing feasible must be done to ensure their humane treatment.

Use of Animals in Education

It is the view of APA that alternatives to the classroom use of animals should be found whenever possible. Such alternatives could include the use of films or tapes, or the observation of animals in settings other than the classroom. When animals are used, their treatment must be in adherence with APA's (1986) *Guidelines for Ethical Conduct in the Care and Use of Animals* (provided at the end of this activity) and in accordance with all applicable federal, state, and local laws and regulations.

The APA *Guidelines* state that live animals may be used for educational pur-poses only after review by a local committee charged with that responsibility. The purpose and justification should be clear, and alternatives such as films and other demonstrations should have been considered and found inadequate. A sample fac-ulty proposal that has been used for this purpose can be found at the end of this activity.

Guidelines for Classroom Activities Involving Live Animals

1. Integrate the activity into the course. All too often, students view labs, dem-onstrations, and films as "enrichment" activities that have little relation to the "real" content of a course. Students view the text and lectures as being important because they constitute the basis for examinations; other activities may merely pro-vide a welcome diversion. Students are most likely to take an activity seriously if they see its relation to other course content including applications to human behavior, if they write (and get credit for) some sort of report on the activity, and if relevant questions appear on an examination.

2. *Before introducing animals into the curriculum, provide information about the species.* Television programs, films, and articles from nature magazines are excellent sources of information. If students are to appreciate the complexities of behavior, if they are to be able to interpret any data they will collect, and if they are to have informed opinions about generalizing from animal studies to the solution of human problems, then they should know as much as possible about the animal they will be studying.

3. *Whenever appropriate, consider settings other than the classroom.* Field trips to zoos, aquaria, and animal parks, as well as to local farms and riding stables, can provide an opportunity for students to record several classes of behavior in any of several species. Birds, squirrels, and other small mammals can be observed in parks and at home feeding stations.

Even though it is usually not possible to manipulate specific variables at, say, a zoo, students can define and record social behavior and can identify the variables that may affect it. These might include the composition of the social group, the complexity of the enclosure, the time of day, the season of the year and, of course, the intrusiveness of the observers. These kinds of observational recordings can provide a basis for discussing the potential importance of several variables and the problems that arise if one wants to design an experimental study with appropriate controls.

4. *In the laboratory or classroom, observe the animal in as "free" an environment as possible before introducing any constraints.* A large and "enriched" area allows animals to exhibit a range of species-specific behavior. For rats, mice, or gerbils, provide a running wheel, tunnels (avoid anything with sharp edges), a ladder to a platform, objects and paper to manipulate and chew, and shavings. For the small Japanese quail (Reese & Reese, 1962), provide shrubs and branches to perch on and hide under, water and flat rocks in a container large enough for bathing, and sand or Fuller's earth for dust bathing (also good for gerbils). Food and water should always be available. Providing levers, foot pedals, pecking keys, and so on allows baseline measures of these activities in an enriched environment for possible comparison with baselines later obtained in standard apparatus. Students can observe and record an animal's behavior and plot an *ethogram* or behavior profile. (see Activity 2, "Observational Recording of Rodent Behavior: Behavior Profile or Ethogram"). They can graph and compare the profiles of related species (e.g., two rodents), the behavior of an animal with and without a familiar conspecific (use social pairs because the introduction of an unfamiliar animal usually produces aggression), or the behavior of parents and young.

Selecting and defining the behavior to measure and deciding upon an appropriate recording procedure are educational goals in themselves. When several classes of behavior are to be recorded, interval recording provides the most information. Sulzer-Azaroff and Reese (1982, chap. 4) describe several procedures and include a field activity on recording the behavior of fish in a community tank.

5. *Learn as much as you can from any animal studied.* Preliminary readings and films prepare students to see and appreciate nuances of behavior that they might otherwise miss. Similarly, observations in an enriched environment provide invaluable preparation for subsequent work with the animal. For example, if operant

conditioning or discrimination training is to be attempted, it is as important for the student to know what behavior *not* to reinforce as it is to know what to look for when shaping some activity. It is also informative to note the differences in behavior that occur in enriched and restricted environments.

Even when one activity is of primary interest, data on other classes of behavior are important. In conditioning experiments, for instance, students should learn that changing the frequency of one class of behavior is likely to affect the frequency of many other classes of behavior. So, while one student in the group is recording pecking by a pigeon or lever pressing by a rat, another student can record everything else the animal is doing. The resulting graph will show a high rate of "other" behavior during baseline or operant level, a decrease as pecking or lever pressing is conditioned, and a recovery of other activities when pecking or lever pressing is extinguished. The curves of the conditioned behavior and other behavior are essentially mirror images. These graphs can then be related to the preferred method of decreasing behavior, namely the reinforcement of some other behavior. In training a color discrimination in birds, for example, the goal is to keep the bird pecking one color key (a lighted disk) and stop pecking when the key is another color. To accomplish this, the students reinforce pecking when the key is red and turning a circle when the key is green. It takes only about 5 minutes to have a bird responding appropriately, and there is no need to use aversive procedures (including extinction) to find out if it has color vision. This is also the favored reductive procedure in behavior modification: You might reduce hyperactive or disruptive classroom behavior by reinforcing academic work, reduce aggressive or asocial behavior by reinforcing cooperative behavior, or break a dog from jumping on visitors by training it to sit by your side when someone comes to the door.

Ethical Issues

The APA (1986) *Guidelines* oppose the use of aversive stimulation and invasive procedures when animals are used for the teaching of psychology; the occasional exceptions for advanced courses require convincing justification, even when the instructional goals cannot be achieved in any other way. Guidelines universally recommend using as few animals as possible in order to accomplish the purpose of education or research.

In research, various experimental designs can reduce the number of animals needed. In education, a few animals can sometimes illustrate several basic principles of psychology. It is also possible to conserve animals by having students work together in small groups and by teaching the animal different things in successive labs.

Species Appropriate for the Classroom

A great deal can be learned from studying the behavior of any species, but some adapt more readily to laboratory housing than do others. Orlans (1977) is an excellent source of noninvasive studies of animal behavior in species ranging from protozoa to small mammals. Abramson (1986) emphasized learning studies in a variety of invertebrates and included drug effects (ant, earthworm), genetic analyses (fruitfly), and lesions (ant, earthworm), as well as several projects on classical and operant conditioning and discrimination. Studies of avoidance conditioning are included; however, even with invertebrates, there is no reason to expose an animal in the classroom to electric shock or a strong concentration of acid when light avoidance illustrates the same points more humanely. Abramson classified in his short article more than 50 studies of learning in invertebrates and listed commercial suppliers, descriptions of apparatus, and review papers for work with seven species.

The animals most often used in classroom studies of learning are small rodents (rats, mice, gerbils) and domesticated birds (pigeons, doves). These animals adapt readily to laboratory housing, and all exhibit interesting social and parental behavior in addition to providing "typical" data on learning. They can therefore be used to provide instruction in a variety of areas such as observational recording, social behavior, and developmental changes, as well as for studies of learning. Doves are excellent animals for ethological studies (Gurley-Fellars, 1981), as are some species of fish. The blue gourami is widely available and exhibits fascinating courtship, breeding, and parental behavior (Thompson & Pollak, 1981). These and other fish are used in research on learning, but conditioning takes more time than is usually available for undergraduate instruction. Excellent species for both learning and ethological studies are rats and mice (Christiano, 1983), gerbils (Hunt & Shields, 1978; Plant, 1980), chicks (Rowland, Jordan, & Orson, 1984), and the Japanese quail (Reese & Reese, 1962).

Disposition of Animals

The ultimate disposition of an animal is a major concern when selecting a species for study. Serious problems arise—for students, for instructors, and for our profession —when animals are used to illustrate a few principles of psychology and then are killed for lack of an appropriate alternative. The local review board (APA *Guidelines*, Section XC) must not only approve any use of animals for educational purposes but must also determine appropriate options for disposing of any animals used. Rats and mice are especially likely to be killed at the end of a semester because they have short life spans (2–4 years) and may become difficult to work with if they are not handled frequently. Pigeons and ring neck doves, on the other hand, can live 20 years or more, and they can be used repeatedly to illustrate the acquisition of many different discriminations. Ring doves are much smaller than pigeons and easier to house and maintain.

CONCLUSION   The study of psychology is always closely tied to ethical considerations, whether the subjects in an experiment are human or nonhuman animals. The use of animals in the psychology laboratory can be very instructive, but it should be considered carefully and undertaken only when no reasonable alternative is available; in such cases, the instructor should supervise the students to ensure that the animals are being treated humanely.

REFERENCES
Abramson, C. I. (1986). Invertebrates in the classroom. *Teaching of Psychology, 13,* 24–29.

American Psychological Association. (1986). *Guidelines for ethical conduct in the care and use of animals.* Washington, DC: Author.

Christiano, J. M. (1983). *Experiments in operant conditioning* (2nd ed.). Bayport, NY: Life Science Associates.

Gurley-Fellars, L. (1981). Non-destructive animal study: Ring doves, a model case. *American Biology Teacher, 43,* 420–425.

Hunt, D., & Shields, R. (1978). Using gerbils in the undergraduate laboratory. *Teaching of Psychology, 5,* 210–211.

Office of Technology Assessment. (1985). *Alternatives to animal use in research, testing, and education.* Washington, DC: Congress of the United States.

Orlans, F. B. (1977). *Animal care from protozoa to small mammals.* Menlo Park, CA: Addison-Wesley.

Plant, L. (1980). The gerbil jar: A basic home experience in operant conditioning. *Teaching of Psychology, 7,* 109.

Reese, E. P., & Reese, T. W. (1962). The quail, *Coturnix coturnix,* as a laboratory animal. *Journal of the Experimental Analysis of Behavior, 5,* 265–270.

Rowland, D. L., Jordan, E. K., & Orson, M. (1984). On the use of chicks as experimental laboratory subjects. *Teaching of Psychology, 11,* 45–46.

Sulzer-Azaroff, B., & Reese, E. P. (1982). *Applying behavioral analysis: A program for developing professional competence.* New York: Holt, Rinehart & Winston.

Thompson, T., & Pollak, E. I. (1981). Using the blue gourami in ethological and embryological studies. *American Biology Teacher, 43,* 98–100.

Suggested Reading

Alper, J. (1986, May). Depression at an early age. *Science 86,* pp. 44–50.

Public Affairs Office. (1987, November). *The use of animals in psychological research.* Washington, DC: American Psychological Association.

Keehn, J. D. (1977). In defense of experiments with animals. *Bulletin of the British Psychological Society, 30,* 404–405.

Keehn, J. D. (1986). *Animal models for psychiatry.* Boston: Routledge & Kegan Paul.

Kellert, S. R., & Westervelt, M. O. (1984). Children's attitudes, knowledge and behaviors toward animals. *Children's Environments Quarterly, 1*(3), 8–11.

Miller, N. E. (1985). The value of behavioral research on animals. *American Psychologist, 40,* 423–440.

Rumbaugh, D. M. (1985). Comparative psychology: Patterns in adaptation. In A. M. Rogers & C. J. Scheirer (Eds.), *The G. Stanley Hall Lecture Series* (Vol. 5, 7–53). Washington, DC: American Psychological Association.

Snowdon, C. T. (1983). Ethology, comparative psychology, and animal behavior. *Annual Review of Psychology, 34,* 63–94.

Educational Use of Animals: Faculty Proposal
© Ellen P. Reese, 1986, Mount Holyoke College

Note that numbers and letters in parentheses refer to sections of the APA *Guidelines for Ethical Conduct in the Care and Use of Animals.*

Instructor: _____ Semester, Year _____ Est. No. Students _____
Course No. _____ Title _____

A. Teaching Format. (check all that apply)
_____ Classroom demonstration (X,B)
_____ Supervised laboratory (X,A,E)
_____ Student projects (X,A,E,F) All students conducting independent projects must complete the form, *Ethical Issues in Animal Research: Proposal for Student Projects* (copies available from department secretary); the proposal must be approved before the student may start with animals.

(Continued on next page)

(Faculty Proposal—*continued from previous page*)

B. Animals
    1. Species (VII-1) _____
    2. Number of animals needed (VII-2) _____
    3. Where will the animals come from? (IV) _____
    4. What will be the disposition of these animals? (XI) _____
    _____

C. Supervision (II)
    1. Who will conduct the demonstration(s) or supervise the laboratory section(s)? _____
    _____

    2. Who will have day to day responsibility for the welfare of the animals throughout their stay in the laboratory? _____
    _____

D. Justification of Proposed Use of Animals (VI, X)
    1. What is the purpose of the demonstration(s)? _____
    _____

    2. Have you considered alternatives such as films, videotapes, computer simulations, or other models? _____
    _____

    3. What will the students learn from live animals or animal preparations that they could not learn from such alternatives?
    n.b. If you know of any data showing that the use of animals is more effective than alternatives in achieving these or similar goals; please forward information and references to Ellen P. Reese who is documenting and coordinating such data.
    _____

    4. Will you include instruction and discussion of the ethics and values of animal research in this course? (X,D) _____
    5. Will students have the option of substituting other work if they do not wish to participate in the activity(ies) you have planned? _____

E. Procedure(s) (VIII)
    1. Briefly describe the procedures to be employed, noting any that might produce pain or distress for the animal. (See student proposal form for procedures that may induce distress and suggestions for ways to reduce such distress.)

    If the animals are to be deprived of any basic necessity, state what will be withheld and the level of deprivation.

    If aversive stimulation is to be used, describe the parameters (intensity, frequency, duration, total number of presentations and sessions) and state whether or not the animal can avoid or escape stimulation.

    Describe the nature and parameters of other potentially stressful procedures such as prolonged restraint, extreme environmental conditions, or aggressive encounters.

    Describe any surgery or other invasive procedures in lay terms, and state what measures you take to minimize the animals' discomfort before, during, and after surgery.
    _____
    _____
    _____
    _____

Signature of Instructor _____ Date _____
Submit this proposal to the Chair of the Department's Committee on Animal Care and Use at least ten days before you propose to use animals in your course.

APA Guidelines for Ethical Conduct in the Care and Use of Animals*

Psychology encompasses a broad range of areas of research and applied endeavors. Important parts of these endeavors are teaching and research on the behavior of nonhuman animals, which contribute to the understanding of basic principles underlying behavior and to advancing the welfare of both human and nonhuman animals. Clearly, psychologists should conduct their teaching and research in a manner consonant with relevant laws and regulations. In addition, the conscience of the individual psychologist critically contributes to establishing and implementing the humane use of animals. Ethical concerns mandate that psychologists should weigh the probable costs and benefits of procedures involving animals.

The following Guidelines were developed by the American Psychological Association for use by psychologists working with nonhuman animals (vertebrates). They are based upon and are in conformity with Principle 10, "Care and Use of Animals" of the *Ethical Principles of Psychologists* of APA:

An investigator of animal behavior strives to advance understanding of basic behavioral principles and/or to contribute to the improvement of human health and welfare. In seeking these ends, the investigator ensures the welfare of animals and treats them humanely. Laws and regulations notwithstanding, an animal's immediate protection depends upon the scientist's own conscience.

These Guidelines are incorporated by reference in the *Ethical Principles of Psychologists* of APA. Individuals publishing in APA journals shall attest to the fact that animal research was conducted in accordance with these Guidelines.

I. General

A. In the ordinary course of events, the acquisition, care, housing, use, and disposition of animals should be in compliance with relevant federal, state, local, and institutional laws and regulations and with international conventions to which the United States is a party. In accordance with Principle 3 (d) of the *Ethical Principles of Psychologists* of APA, when federal, state, provincial, organizational, or institutional laws, regulations, or practices are in conflict with Association Guidelines, psychologists should make known their commitment to Association Guidelines and, whenever possible, work toward resolution of the conflict.

B. Psychologists and students working with animals should be familiar with these Guidelines, which should be conspicuously posted in every laboratory, teaching facility, or other setting in which animals are maintained and used by psychologists and their students.

C. Violations of these Guidelines should be reported to the facility supervisor whose name is appended at the end of this document. If not resolved at the local level, allegations of violations of these Guidelines should be referred to the APA Committee on Ethics, which is empowered to impose sanctions. No psychologist should take action of any kind against individuals making, in good faith, a report of a violation of these Guidelines.

D. Individuals with questions concerning these Guidelines should consult with the Committee on Animal Research and Experimentation.

E. Psychologists are strongly encouraged to become familiar with the ethical principles of animal research. To facilitate this, the Committee on Animal Research and Experimentation will maintain a list of appropriate references.

II. Personnel

A. A supervisor, experienced in the care and use of laboratory animals, should closely monitor the health, comfort, and humane treatment of all animals within the particular facility.

B. Psychologists should ensure that personnel involved in their research with animals be familiar with these Guidelines.

---

* These guidelines will soon be revised to reflect anticipated changes in Federal regulations during 1990.

(*Continued on next page*)

C. It is the responsibility of the supervisor of the facility to ensure that records of the accession, utilization, and disposition of animals are maintained.

D. A veterinarian should be available for consultation regarding: housing, nutrition, animal-care procedures, health, and medical attention. The veterinarian should conduct inspections of the facility at least twice a year.

E. Psychologists should ensure that all individuals who use animals under their supervision receive explicit instruction in experimental methods and in the care, maintenance, and handling of the species being studied. Responsibilities and activities of all individuals dealing with animals should be consistent with their respective competencies, training, and experience in either the laboratory or the field setting.

F. It is the responsibility of the psychologist to ensure that appropriate records are kept of procedures with animals.

G. It is the responsibility of the psychologist to be cognizant of all federal, state, local, and institutional laws and regulations pertaining to the acquisition, care, use, and disposal of animals. Psychologists should also be fully familiar with the *NIH Guide for the Care and Use of Laboratory Animals*.

III. Facilities

A. The facilities housing animals should be designed to conform to specifications in the *NIH Guide for the Care and Use of Laboratory Animals*.

B. Psychologists are encouraged to work toward upgrading the facilities in which their animals are housed.

C. Procedures carried out on animals are to be reviewed by a local institutional animal care and use committee to ensure that the procedures are appropriate and humane. The committee should have representation from within the institution and from the local community. If no representative from the local community is willing to serve, there should be at least one representative on the committee from a non-science department. In the event that it is not possible to constitute an appropriate local institutional animal care and use committee, psychologists should submit their proposals to the corresponding committee of a cooperative institution.

IV. Acquisition of Animals

A. When appropriate, animals intended for use in the laboratory should be bred for that purpose.

B. Animals not bred in the psychologist's facility are to be acquired lawfully. The U.S. Department of Agriculture (USDA) may be consulted for information regarding suppliers.

C. Psychologists should make every effort to ensure that those responsible for transporting the animals to the facility provide adequate food, water, ventilation, and space, and impose no unnecessary stress upon the animals.

D. Animals taken from the wild should be trapped in a humane manner.

E. Endangered species or taxa should be utilized only with full attention to required permits and ethical concerns. Information can be obtained from the Office of Endangered Species, U.S. Department of the Interior, Fish and Wildlife Service, Washington, D.C., 20240. Similar caution should be used in work with threatened species or taxa.

V. Care and Housing Animals

Responsibility for the conditions under which animals are kept, both within and outside of the context of active experimentation or teaching, rests jointly upon the psychologist and those individuals appointed by the institution to administer animal care. Animals should be provided with humane care and healthful conditions during their stay in the facility. Psychologists are encouraged to consider enriching the environments of their laboratory animals, where appropriate.

(*Continued on next page*)

VI. Justification of the Research

A. Research should be undertaken with a clear scientific purpose. There should be a reasonable expectation that the research will a) increase knowledge of the processes underlying the evolution, development, maintenance, alteration, control or biological significance of behavior, b) increase understanding of the species under study, or c) provide results that benefit the health or welfare of humans or other animals.

B. The scientific purpose of the research should be of sufficient potential significance as to outweigh any harm or distress to the animals used. In this regard, psychologists should act on the assumption that procedures that would produce pain in humans will also do so in other animals.

C. The psychologist should always consider the possibility of using alternatives to animals in research and should be familiar with the appropriate literature.

D. Research on animals may not be conducted until the protocol has been reviewed by the institutional animal care and use committee to ensure that the procedures are appropriate and humane.

E. The psychologist should monitor the research and the animals' welfare throughout the course of an investigation to ensure continued justification for the research.

VII. Experimental Design

Humane considerations should constitute one of the major sets of factors that enter into the design of research. Two particularly relevant considerations should be noted:

1. The species chosen for study should be well-suited to answer the question(s) posed. When the research paradigm permits a choice among species, the psychologist should employ that species which appears likely to suffer least.

2. The number of animals utilized in a study should be sufficient to provide a clear answer to the question(s) posed. Care should be exercised to use the minimum number of animals consistent with sound experimental design, especially where the procedures might cause pain or discomfort to the animals.

VIII. Experimental Procedures

Humane consideration for the well-being of the animal should be incorporated into the design and conduct of all procedures involving animals. *The conduct of all procedures is governed by Guideline VI.*

A. Procedures which involve no pain or distress to the animal, or in which the animal is anesthetized and insensitive to pain throughout the procedure and is euthanized before regaining consciousness, are generally acceptable.

B. Procedures involving more than momentary or slight pain not relieved by medication or other acceptable methods should be undertaken only when the objectives of the research cannot be achieved by other methods.

C. Procedures involving severe distress or pain that is not alleviated require strong justification. An animal observed to be in a state of severe distress or chronic pain that cannot be alleviated and that is not essential to the purposes of the research, should be euthanized immediately.

D. When aversive or appetitive procedures appear to be equivalent for the purposes of the research, then appetitive procedures should be used. When using aversive stimuli, psychologists should adjust the parameters of stimulation to levels that appear minimal, though compatible with the aims of the research. Psychologists are encouraged to test painful stimuli on themselves whenever reasonable. Whenever consistent with the goals of the research, consideration should be given to providing the animal with control of painful stimulation.

E. Procedures involving extensive food or water deprivation should be used only when minimal deprivation procedures are inappropriate to the design and purpose of the research.

(*Continued on next page*)

    F. Prolonged physical restraint should be used only if less stressful procedures are inadequate to the purposes of the study. Convenience to the psychologist is not a justification for prolonged restraint.

    G. Procedures that entail extreme environmental conditions, such as high or low temperatures, high humidity, modified atmospheric pressure, etc. should be undertaken only with particularly strong justification.

    H. Studies entailing experimentally-induced prey killing or intensive aggressive interactions among animals should be fully justified and conducted in a manner that minimizes the extent and duration of pain.

    I. Procedures entailing the deliberate infliction of trauma should be restricted and used only with very strong justification. Whenever possible, without defeating the goals of the research, animals used in such research should be anesthetized.

    J. Procedures involving the use of paralytic agents without reduction in pain sensation require particular prudence and humane concern. Utilization of muscle relaxants or paralytics alone during surgery, without general anesthesia, is unacceptable and shall not be used.

    K. Surgical procedures, because of their intrusive nature, require close supervision and attention to humane considerations by the psychologist.

       1. All surgical procedures and anesthetization should be conducted under the direct supervision of a scientist who is competent in the use of the procedure.

       2. If the surgical procedure is likely to cause greater discomfort than that attending anesthetization, and unless there is specific justification for acting otherwise, animals should be maintained under anesthesia until the procedure is ended.

       3. Sound post-operative monitoring and care should be provided to minimize discomfort and to prevent infection and other untoward consequences of the procedure.

       4. As a general rule, animals should not be subjected to successive surgical procedures unless these are required by the nature of the research, the nature of the surgery, or for the well-being of the animal. However, there may be occasions when it is preferable to carry out more than one procedure on a few animals rather than to carry out a single procedure on many animals. For instance, there may be experimental protocols where it would be appropriate to carry out acute terminal surgical procedures on animals scheduled for euthanasia as part of another protocol rather than to utilize additional animals.

IX. Field Research

    A. Psychologists conducting field research should disturb their populations as little as possible. Every effort should be made to minimize potential harmful effects of the study on the population and on other plant and animal species in the area.

    B. Research conducted in populated areas should be done with respect for the property and privacy of the inhabitants of the area.

    C. Particular justification is required for the study of endangered species. Such research should not be conducted unless all requisite permits are obtained.

X. Educational Use of Animals

    A. For educational purposes, as for research purposes, consideration should always be given to the possibility of using nonanimal alternatives. When animals are used solely for educational rather than research purposes, the consideration of possible benefits accruing from their use vs. the cost in terms of animal distress should take into account the fact that some procedures which can be justified for research purposes cannot be justified for educational purposes. Similarly, certain procedures, appropriate in advanced courses, may not be appropriate in introductory courses.

(*Continued on next page*)

B. Classroom demonstrations involving animals should be used only when instructional objectives cannot effectively be achieved through the use of videotapes, films, or other alternatives. Careful consideration should be given to the question of whether the type of demonstration is warranted by the anticipated instructional gains.

C. Animals should be used for educational purposes only after review by a departmental committee or by the local institutional animal care and use committee.

D. Psychologists are encouraged to include instruction and discussion of the ethics and values of animal research in courses, both introductory and advanced, which involve or discuss the use of animals.

E. Student projects involving pain or distress to animals should be undertaken judiciously and only when the training objectives cannot be achieved in any other way.

F. Demonstrations of scientific knowledge in such contexts as exhibits, conferences, or seminars do not justify the use of painful procedures or surgical interventions. Audiovisual alternatives should be considered.

XI. Disposition of Animals

A. When the use of an animal is no longer required by an experimental protocol or procedure, alternatives to euthanasia should be considered.

   1. Animals may be distributed to colleagues who can utilize them. Care should be taken that such an action does not expose the animal to excessive surgical or other invasive or painful procedures. The psychologist transferring animals should be assured that the proposed use by the recipient colleague has the approval of, or will be evaluated by, the appropriate institutional animal care and use committee and that humane treatment will be contined.

   2. It may sometimes be feasible to return wild-trapped animals to the field. This should be done only when there is reasonable assurance that such release will not detrimentally affect the fauna and environment of the area and when the ability of the animal to survive in nature is not impaired. Unless conservation efforts dictate otherwise, release should normally occur within the same area from which animals were originally trapped. Animals reared in the laboratory generally should not be released because, in most cases, they cannot survive or they may survive but disrupt the natural ecology.

B. When euthanasia appears to be the appropriate alternative, either as a requirement of the research, or because it constitutes the most humane form of disposition of an animal at the conclusion of the research:

   1. Euthanasia shall be accomplished in a humane manner, appropriate for the species, under anesthesia, or in such a way as to ensure immediate death, and in accordance with procedures approved by the institutional animal care and use committee.

   2. No animal shall be discarded until its death is verified.

   3. Disposal of euthanized animals should be accomplished in a manner that is in accord with all relevant legislation, consistent with health, environmental, and aesthetic concerns, and approved by the institutional animal care and use committee.

These Guidelines have been approved by the American Psychological Association Council of Representatives on August 22, 1985, and were developed by the Committee on Animal Research and Experimentation of the Board of Scientific Affairs, 1200 17th Street, N.W., Washington, D.C. 20036 (202) 955-7755.

81 THE (UN)ETHICS OF THE THROWAWAY SOCIETY

C. Sue Lamb

University of North Carolina at Wilmington

Although this activity can be adapted for use in any undergraduate or high school psychology class that includes a section on ethics and values and their relevance in human relationships, it is particularly suited to courses on psychology of adjustment, introductory applied psychology, and general psychology. The materials required are readily available, and no previous background in psychology is required. The background lecture on the relation between ethics or values and resulting behavior sets the stage for the "throwing away" and the class discussion that follows.

CONCEPT

Courses in psychology of adjustment and psychology applied to human life, as well as general psychology, frequently address values and their relation to everyday life. This topic is common in texts for these courses (e.g., Weiten, 1986). Bringing the abstract concepts alive and making them meaningful for students, particularly freshmen, can be difficult. This exercise involves students in the relationships among values, attitudes, and behavior by showing how our "throwaway" attitudes toward things reflect our basic value judgments and system of ethics, which in turn affect our attitudes toward people and relationships. It demonstrates how our behavior has long-term as well as short-term consequences. The context is a topic of current social concern, the consequences of our throwing away so many things.

The exercise is based on Chapter 4 in Toffler's (1971) *Future Shock* in which he points out that from birth, people in our society are embedded in a throwaway society. The values, attitudes, and behaviors that stem from our using things briefly, then throwing them out and replacing them, has extended to how we value relationships and other people.

MATERIALS NEEDED

You will need a copy of *Future Shock*, disposable plastic grocery bags, and a variety of trash, some commonly seen, some unusual. Examples include soft-drink and beer cans, plastic fast-food containers, disposable diapers, half-eaten candy bars, old makeup cases, tampon containers, and condom envelopes. Particularly useful are examples of things that until recently were not considered throwaway items, such as disposable contact lenses and cameras. You will also need more personal items indicative of a relationship with another person. (e.g., Mother's Day and birthday cards, photographs of relatives, personal letters from parents or children, gifts from former students); a large, sturdy trash can; overhead transparencies of polluted and destroyed environments (e.g., garbage-covered beaches and roadsides, garbage dumps, smog-covered cities, destroyed environments such as clear-cut rain forests); and overhead transparencies of people thrown away by our society (e.g., teenage prostitutes and runaways, abandoned children, homeless families, elderly people, deinstitutionalized mentally ill and retarded people).

Read Chapter 4 in Toffler (1971) on throwaway society and material on the relationships among values, attitudes, and behavior. Put the trash and personal items in a disposable grocery bag, with the personal items at the bottom.

In the classroom, discuss the general psychological concept of relationships among values, attitudes, and behavior and in turn the relationship of those to a general system of ethics that guides a society's actions. Present the main theme from Toffler concerning the relationship between people and things in an affluent society. Discuss the adverse effects that living in an affluent society has on values, attitudes, and behavior. Relate them to the general concept of ethics and "unethics."

Pick up a grocery bag and pull out the impersonal trash items, one by one, and literally throw them away into the trash can. As you throw each away, say something about it, such as, "Who needs that old drink can?", "I'm tired of that shirt; I want to get the latest fashion," and so on. Gradually shift to more personal items, throwing them away one by one, saying something such as, "Who needs this card? I'll probably get another one next year anyway."

Show the overhead transparencies that show that the things that we throw away generally really do not go away but return to pollute our environment, kill wildlife, and generally make our world a worse place in which to live. Show the overheads that show people whom our society throws away, discussing the personal tragedies resulting from our society's values and actions.

Discuss ethics and the consequences of living in a society of economic and personal transience in which we throw away not only things but people. Relate back to particular items thrown away. Ask students what specific things society as a whole and we as individuals could do to help solve problems of the throwaway society.

DISCUSSION Students are very curious about the (full) disposable garbage bag when I put it on the desk at the beginning of the class period. I do not refer to it at all for the first part of the class, letting them wonder what it is. After the background lecture, when I start to throw the regular trash away, students generally laugh and join in, saying "throw it away" with me as I throw away each item. As might be expected, items such as tampon containers and condom envelopes evoke loud, if somewhat embarrassed, laughter. When I start throwing away old Mother's Day cards and gifts from family and former students, most students become more serious and questioning. As I show the overheads of the environment and people, students become visibly moved. Discussion is generally lively and thought provoking.

REFERENCES Toffler, A. (1971). *Future shock.* New York: Bantam Books.
Weiten, W. (1986). *Psychology applied to modern life* (2nd ed.). Monterey, CA: Brooks/Cole.

CHAPTER X
GENDER ROLES
AND STEREOTYPING

This section on sex roles appears for the first time in this volume of the *Activities Handbook*. Gender issues and male–female roles have become central issues of debate and discussion in the classroom; these activities will allow your students to explore their own attitudes on these matters in an enjoyable, nonthreatening way. With one exception, all of the activities are suitable for students with no prior knowledge of psychology, and most require minimal preparation.

Activity 82 is an out-of-class exercise centering on sexism in the toy store. In Activity 87 a game is used to test for sex role stereotyping among students. Such stereotyping is discussed from a more theoretical standpoint in Activity 88.

In three of these activities popular media are used as a basis for discussion: The film *Tootsie* is used in Activity 85 in a discussion of men's and women's places in society. In Activity 83 the focus is on the portrayal of the sexes on television shows. A rating system for sexism in music videos is outlined in Activity 90.

Basic statistics are used in Activity 84 to study sex differences, and a model for sex-fair methodology is provided in Activity 89. In Activity 91 a discussion of how language affects perceptions about sex roles is presented. Activity 86 involves a series of games and exercises that cover different aspects of male sex roles, includes highly sensitive areas such as homosexuality and father–son relationships, and is best suited for advanced undergraduate classes.

82 Gender-Role Stereotyping in Toys: An Out-of-Class Project

Margaret A. Lloyd
Georgia Southern College

■——■

This activity requires students to visit a toy department and summarize their observations in a written report. Other than instruction sheets outlining the assignment, there are no materials needed and any size class can participate, from high school through undergraduate. A class discussion is recommended once students have turned in their papers.

■——■

CONCEPT   The purpose of this project is to make students aware of an important aspect of gender-role socialization, namely, the presence of gender-role stereotyping in children's toys. Children's play constitutes an important arena in which beliefs are developed at a very young age about the appropriateness of certain behaviors for the two sexes.

MATERIALS NEEDED   Students will need a handout to complete this out-of-class project. You can easily construct one by combining useful portions of the Concept and Instructions sections.

INSTRUCTIONS   Ask students to visit a toy store (or the toy section in a department store) that has a relatively wide range of toys. Once in the store, they are to survey the toys and make observations that will enable them to respond to the following questions: (a) Was it common that boys' and girls' toys were related to adult roles (and, therefore, serve as vehicles of gender-role stereotyping?) (b) Was there subtle gender-role stereotyping apparent in the placement of toys (e.g., were tea sets placed near dolls and microscopes near trucks)? (c) Did gender-role stereotyping occur more often in toys for a particular age range? (d) Were there many gender-neutral toys relative to the number of boys' and girls' toys? (e) What were the two most common themes among boys' toys? (f) What were the two most common themes among girls' toys?

After students have completed their general observations, they should select three toys that they believe exemplify *each* of the following categories: girls' toys, boys' toys, and gender-neutral toys (nine toys altogether).

As each of the nine toys is selected, students should note the specific features of the toys that caught their eye and motivated them to list the toy in one of the three categories.

Students should be instructed to pay particular attention to toys in packages because they are likely to have pictures, labels, or advertising messages that can be analyzed for gender-role stereotyping. For example, does a chemistry set or doctor kit have a picture of a boy on the front and either no girl or a girl in the background looking at another microscope?

Students should summarize their observations in writing in the following format:

GENDER ROLES AND STEREOTYPING   ■ **293**

Introduction. Briefly explain the purpose of the project and what you attempted to do in it (¼–½ page).

Method. Briefly describe the steps you used in conducting the project, including a brief description of the toy department (½ page).

Results. Describe examples of three toys in each of the three categories. The following page layout is suggested (see the sample layout). Divide the page into three columns. In the left-hand column, list three girls', three boys', and three gender-neutral toys. In the middle column, briefly describe the advertising features of each toy. In the right-hand column, state the explicit and implicit implications of the advertising messages for the (prospective) buyers–users (2–3 pages).

Girls' Toys	Description of Package and Advertising Features	Implications of Advertising for Buyers–Users
1. Doll	Girl (only) on package with doll; use of pastel colors; has "For the little mother in every girl" written on it.	This toy is for girls only; only girls are interested in babies.

Conclusion. (a) Comment on your observations of toys as reported in the Results section; (b) comment on your general observations using the questions outlined in the Instructions section; and (c) evaluate this project in terms of its educational value to you.

DISCUSSION

After students have turned in their papers, it is easy to generate a lively discussion about the similarities and differences in their observations and on their views of the implications of their observations.

SUGGESTED READING

Fein, G., Johnson, D., Kosson, N., Stork, L., & Wasserman, L. (1975). Sex stereotypes and preferences in the toy choices of 20-month-old boys and girls. *Developmental Psychology, 11,* 527–528.

Fling, S., & Mansovitz, M. (1972). Sex-typing in nursery school children's play interests. *Developmental Psychology, 7,* 146–152.

Pogrebin, L. C. (1974, December). Gifts for children. *Ms.,* pp. 63–68, 76–79.

83 PORTRAYAL OF THE SEXES ON TV

David L. Watson
University of Hawaii at Manoa

This activity can be used with classes of virtually any size, from high school through undergraduate. No prior knowledge is necessary. The instructor must reproduce the observation sheet, and I recommend written instructions as well. The reports can be written or oral, but in-class discussion is also useful. This activity could be used in a social psychology unit in the discussion of sex roles, stereotypes, or persuasion. By specifying types of commercials to observe, the instructor can incorporate the activity into discussions of methodology.

CONCEPT

In a famous TV commercial for a detergent, a couple is shown with a third person, who points out a ring of dirt around the man's shirt collar and teasingly chants, "Ring around the collar!" The man is embarrassed and angry, and glowers at his wife. The purpose of the commercial, of course, is to get people to buy the product. But a second message is being sent. A wife is responsible for her husband's laundry and must not shirk that responsibility.

In 1971 McArthur and Resko observed 199 commercials and found considerable sex role stereotyping. I adapted this activity from their study. The activity allows students to observe sex role stereotyping in TV commercials and teaches them how to use observational schedules, dealing with coding and reliability issues. Today is there as much stereotyping as in 1971? Most students will expect that there is not, but the results can be surprising.

MATERIALS NEEDED

Copy the Instructions section and the TV Commercial Rating Sheet (see the end of this activity) for each student. Ask them to make several copies of the rating sheet. If your students cannot easily do this, you may want to make the copies for them.

INSTRUCTIONS

Ask students to watch 20 commercials with another person. (This can be reduced, but 20 is not an onerous amount.) They will use a separate rating sheet for each commercial. Suppose, for example, that they watch a detergent commercial depicting a woman at home doing her laundry while her children run around in the background. She is saying, "I always use Morning Fresh because that way I never have to worry about my kids smelling clean." This commercial would be coded as female, product user, parent and homemaker, at home, nonscientific argument, home-type product. (Go over an example similar to this with the students.) The categories of observation here are the same ones used in the original study.

Students carry out their observations with another person, who does not have to be from the class. They should not comment about the scoring while doing it. Partners should agree exactly when they will start and stop; for example, start with the first commercial, skip the second, do the third, and so on. Only every other commercial that comes on is scored so that partners can score one commercial while another is showing.

Eliminate commercials with more than two central figures—to avoid confusion—and do not use cartoon figures. If there is a narrator, that person counts as one central figure.

Working with a partner allows the students to evaluate the reliability of their observations. This teaches the need for discussion and clear definitions in analysis. Reliability can be expressed simply as the percentage of agreement for each observational category. The two must be in perfect agreement about the central figures in the commercial. Reliability of agreement on the central figures' roles does not have to be perfect, but it should be 85% or greater. It should be reported for each category. For example, percent agreement for both spouse and parent is 90%, and so on. Reliability will be increased if the students do a few practice observations together before beginning and discuss discrepancies and definitions of the categories with each other.

Students can sample different channels and different viewing times. They could compare daytime and prime-time commercials or commercials aired during women's versus men's programs.

In their report they should present the percentage of men and women in each of the coding categories. For example, the central figure is male 65% of the time and female 35% of the time; the central figure is the narrator 40% of the time, the product user 40% of the time, and so forth. The report can follow this outline: what they did, their reliability, their findings, and their discussion.

DISCUSSION

McArthur and Resco (1975) found that the sexes were treated very differently. More men than women were shown, and men were more frequently the central figure. Men were more often shown as experts, whereas women were shown as product users. Even when the product was part of the stereotyped woman's role (e.g., laundry detergent) the expert was likely to be a man and the product user a woman.

Women were more likely to be shown in the role of homemaker, spouse, parent, or girlfriend. Men were more likely to be shown as celebrities, workers, or professionals. Women were more often shown in the home. Men were more likely to give scientific arguments. A high proportion of the women gave no argument at all, merely showing the product in one way or another. Finally, women were more likely to be shown endorsing home products.

I have used this assignment about a dozen times, and the results always parallel those found in 1971 by McArthur and Resco. This usually surprises the students, who will have expected great changes. "Wow," one said, "this is mind-blowing."

REFERENCES

McArthur, L. Z., & Resco, B. G. (1975). The portrayal of men and women in American television commercials. *Journal of Social Psychology, 97,* 209–220.

TV Commercial Coding Sheet

Name of product   Date and time

1. Central figure: Male   Female

    Do not use a commercial that has more than two central figures. The narrator counts as one. Score below for each figure.

                 Central figure is: narrator
                                   product user
                                   authority

            Central figure's role is:
                           spouse
                           parent
                           homemaker
                           boyfriend or girlfriend
                           interviewer or narrator
                           worker
                           celebrity
                           professional

2. Location of the scene: home
                                   office
                                   store
                                   other

3. Type of arguments given by each central figure:
                           scientific (facts)
                           nonscientific (opinions or testimonials)
                           none

4. Type of product: home
                                   food
                                   body
                                   other

84 SEX DIFFERENCES AND THE VARIABILITY HYPOTHESIS

Michael Wertheimer
University of Colorado

In this in-class activity, sex differences are investigated using the students as subjects and some simple statistics to measure variability. A few readily available materials are needed for this task depending on what kinds of lists of variables the instructor decides to have the class generate and measure. Other than gathering the minimal materials, the instructor does not need any advance preparation. Best suited for medium to large classes, this activity can be adapted for high school as well as undergraduate students. The activity fits well with a discussion of statistics or group differences and what they mean.

CONCEPT

Late in the 19th and early during the 20th century, it was widely believed that the *variability hypothesis* accounted for major differences that were assumed to characterize the sexes. Mental retardation, genius, social disability, and creative production were more frequently observed among males than among females, it was hypothesized, because females are inherently more homogeneous (i.e., less variable) than males. A pioneer American woman psychologist, Leta Stetter Hollingworth, during the teens of the 20th century, undertook extensive measurements of the two sexes and in fact found no dimensions on which males clearly demonstrated more variability than females, thereby dealing a death blow to the variability hypothesis.

MATERIALS NEEDED

Materials needed can be minimal. Encourage the class to generate its own set of variables on which individual differences can be readily measured without the need for complex apparatuses. Among the kinds of activities that can be used are asking all participants to write down as many words as they can think of in 2 minutes that start with the letter *b* (and counting that number for each student); reading a set of 15 nonsense syllables to the class and asking each participant to write down as many as that participant can recall immediately after the teacher has finished reading the list (and counting the number of syllables recalled correctly by each student); or requiring each participant to throw 20 pennies successively at a wastebasket from 10 feet away (and recording the number of coins that end up in the basket for each student). Some less behavioral and more anatomical measurements might also be included, such as the length of the middle finger from the valley between the middle and the ring finger to the middle finger's tip, or the distance around the waist, determined by a tape measure, or each student's height or foot length from the heel to the end of the big toe. The materials needed can thus be minimal: a watch with a second hand, a ruler, a tape measure, a set of coins, and so forth.

INSTRUCTIONS

A single number is recorded for each participant for each variable measured. Separate the numbers into those characterizing the female and male participants. At issue is not the average performance of the two sexes, but each sex's *variability*. Thus, what is required is a measure of the variability of the distribution generated by the males on each variable and the variability of the distribution generated by the females on that variable. An older and perfectly appropriate measure of variability for this purpose is the *average deviation*. To calculate it, you first need to determine the mean of each of the two distributions and then to specify for each participant how much that participant's performance differed (in absolute numbers, that is, disregarding the sign of the difference) from the mean of that participant's sex distribution. For example, if 7 females scored 3, 5, 5, 6, 7, 7, and 9, then the mean of the distribution would be 6 (42 ÷ 7), and the respective deviations would be 3, 1, 1, 0, 1, 1, and 3. Now take the *average* of these deviations (in this case it would be 1.43, 10 ÷ 7). Do the same for the males. Say their scores were 4, 6, 6, 7, 7, 8, 8, and 10. Their mean would be 7 (56 ÷ 8); therefore the deviation scores would be 3, 1, 1, 0, 0, 1, 1, and 3, and the average deviation would be 1.25 (10 ÷ 8). If the variability hypothesis were correct, then the average deviation of the males' scores should be greater on most dimensions than the average deviation of the females' scores. It probably will not be.

Alternatively, with a more sophisticated class, or as a next step with any class, you might calculate the *standard deviation (SD)* of each sex's distribution of scores on each dimension you measured. The standard deviation is a far more widely used measure of variability or dispersion than the average deviation, because it has a variety of desirable statistical properties. Calculation of the standard deviation again requires the determination of the mean of the distribution (within each sex in this case). Each student's score is then subtracted from the mean of that student's sex distribution, all of these differences (within each distribution) are *squared*, and the sum of the squares is obtained and divided by the number of cases in the distribution. This mean squared deviation from the mean is the *variance*; its square root is the standard deviation, often also written as the Greek letter σ. Again, if the variability hypothesis were tenable, then the standard deviation of the distribution of males' performances should be substantially greater than that of the females' performances; that is, the dispersion or variability of males' scores should exceed that of females' scores. It probably will not.

DISCUSSION   Differences in social expectations for the two sexes around the turn of the century were much greater than they are now, but they have by no means been eradicated. In earlier days the variability hypothesis served to justify and explain why there were far more famous male than female composers, business tycoons, inventors, painters, and political leaders, as well as convicted criminals, inmates of mental institutions, and juvenile delinquents. If greater inherent dispersion (more variability) among males is not a tenable hypothesis for explaining the preponderance of males who are at the extremes of both positive and negative ends of distributions in the population at large (i.e., who are characterized as being socially highly valued or socially censured), what alternative explanation might there be for the underrepresentation of females at the extremes of many distributions of individual differences? What role could social expectations play? What might happen if there were to be genuine equality for the two sexes in terms of educational opportunity, access to a wide variety of occupational and career goals, and the erosion of widely held social stereotypes about "male" and "female" roles? Might not the sex differences in recognized achievement (and in the imposition of social sanctions) be substantially reduced, or even totally eradicated?

SUGGESTED READING

Hollingworth, L. S. (1916). Phi Beta Kappa and women students. *School and Society, 4*, 932–933.

Montague, H., & Hollingworth, L. S. (1914). The comparative variability of the sexes at birth. *American Journal of Sociology, 20*, 335–370.

Shields, S. A. (1975). Ms. Pilgrim's progress: The contributions of Leta Stetter Hollingworth to the psychology of women. *American Psychologist, 30*, 852–857.

85 TOOTSIE AND GENDER ROLES

Barbara C. Jessen
University of Evansville

In this activity, although many students will have seen the movie Tootsie, *they will have the opportunity to view it with new eyes when they are instructed to look for examples of gender differences. Other than the video equipment needed to show the film, no preparation or materials is needed. This activity is suitable for high school and undergraduate classes of any size. Because of the length of the film, special arrangements will be necessary, perhaps an out-of-class viewing followed by in-class discussion.*

CONCEPT
In this activity, the film *Tootsie* is used to illustrate aspects of gender roles and differences. The film can be used in a psychology of women course or in courses that have sections on gender differences or roles, such as introductory psychology.

MATERIALS NEEDED
You will need a videotape of the film *Tootsie* and equipment to show it.

INSTRUCTIONS
Before showing the film, instruct students to look for examples of specific concepts, with or without a written description of the concepts.

DISCUSSION
The film lends itself to a discussion of sex differences in behavior, men and women as viewed by the opposite sex, and the concept of androgyny. In the discussion of sex differences in behavior, students can be asked to give examples of the differences in the behavior of Dustin Hoffman as "Michael" and as "Dorothy." Especially noticeable are differences in smiling, eye contact, gestures, stance, and walk. Differences in the language used by Michael and Dorothy can also be discussed. The scene in the bar in which Dorothy comments on the waiter's "lovely mauve shirt" is an example.

The film is very useful for discussing the concept of androgyny, as Michael discovers more feminine aspects in his personality while playing the role of Dorothy. His relationship to the baby in the movie is one example of this. At first he is awkward and uncomfortable. Later he can be nurturing and loving.

The relationship between men and women and the view men and women have of the opposite sex can also be discussed using the film as the basis. Michael's closing lines to Julie—"I was a better man with you, as Dorothy"—is one example that can be pointed out; the line would have been better written as "I was a better *person* with you, as Dorothy." Another example is Michael's explanation of how he gets along with the domineering male director of the soap opera: "He tells me what to do. I do what I want to. He gets angry. I apologize."

Many additional examples of concepts and aspects of the psychology of women and of gender differences can be found through a careful viewing of this film.

SUGGESTED READING
Cook, E. P. (1985). *Psychological androgyny.* New York: Pergamon Press.
Hoyenga, K. B., & Hoyenga, K. T. (1979). *The question of sex differences: Psychological, cultural, and biological issues.* Boston: Little, Brown.

Lakoff, R. (1975). *Language and woman's place*. New York: Harper & Row.

Tavris, C., & Wade, C. (1984). *The longest war: Sex differences in perspective* (2nd ed.). San Diego, CA: Harcourt Brace Jovanovich.

Williams, J. (1983). *Psychology of women: Behavior in a biosocial context* (2nd ed.). New York: Norton.

86 TEACHING MEN'S ROLES: FIVE CLASSROOM EXERCISES

Martin S. Fiebert
California State University, Long Beach

This activity contains five experiential exercises designed to increase students' awareness of their attitudes and feelings about men's roles, increase empathy toward and understanding of others, and explore alternative perspectives and responses. The exercises can be used in undergraduate and graduate classes of 10–30 students. No advance preparation or materials are needed.

For the past 3 years I have been teaching a course on male roles in which students, both men and women, examine their relationships with men in terms of their interactions at work, at play, and in family life. In addition to traditional lectures and student reports, I have incorporated an experiential component into the course. These exercises permit students to directly examine their sex role attitudes and perspectives and encourage experimentation with change. In student evaluations, the experiential component has consistently been rated as one of the most valuable facets of the course.

The framework I use to present experiential exercises is the view of the classroom as a community in which individuals learn to interact with increasing openness with each other. The goals are to increase awareness of one's attitudes and feelings, expand empathic capacity to understand others, and experiment with alternative perspectives and responses. My guidelines stress that all exercises be made explicit to students before they participate and that participation be voluntary. If the student chooses not to engage in a particular exercise, an alternate assignment is developed to cover the subject matter. I present five experiential exercises that I have found very useful in the male roles class.

EXERCISE 1   SEX ROLE STEREOTYPES

Concept. This exercise provides students with an opportunity to confront their own perceptions of sex-appropriate roles and to discuss gender-based stereotyping.

Materials needed. No materials are needed. The class should be divided into groups of about 10 each, with an equal number of men and women.

Instructions. Early in the semester, divide the class into groups of about 10 students with as close to an equal number of men and women as possible. In this and the following exercises, have one student trained as a group facilitator, with the primary task of reviewing directions for the activity and monitoring time so that each participant has an opportunity to communicate.

Begin the exercise with each person giving one response to the phrase, "A man is _____." Have each student present a cultural stereotype in either an adjective or phrase (e.g., a man is a breadwinner, competitive, mechanical, unemotional, brave, and so on). The stereotypes presented should be both positive and negative and should not necessarily conform to the participants' personal beliefs. After learning each other's names, participants sit in a circle and present their statements sequentially without pause or discussion.

As the group immerses itself in this activity, there are occasional bursts of humor as well as novel and creative responses. When repetition begins to occur, or participants have trouble producing responses, the facilitator may ask for additions from the whole group before the activity ends. Now repeat the exercise, producing stereotypes for women. (The order of presenting stereotypes for men and women is optional.)

Discussion. Question each person for about 5 minutes to ascertain how closely each individual matches the cultural stereotype of his or her sex role. Other members of the group should participate in the interviewing. Questions will either examine how much individuals conform to their cultural roles (e.g., competition for men, emotionality for women) or break the stereotype. If rapport in the group is high and defensiveness is low, I usually suggest that each person interviewed close his or her eyes and that the group vote on a scale of 1–10 on how that individual conforms to the stereotype. In my experience, despite some lack of clarity in the criteria, the reliability of ratings is pretty high and the feedback is welcomed. To complete this activity with a group of 10 takes about 90 minutes.

SEX ROLE EMPATHY

Concept. This activity has discussion as an integral element. It requires the participants to adopt the opposite sex's perspective on relationships and to express to one another the insights they gain from this.

Materials needed. No materials are needed. The class should be divided into groups of about 10 each, with an equal number of men and women.

Instructions. The facilitator asks the men, or the women, to form an inner circle with the other sex seated in an outer circle around them. The inner circle is asked to imagine that they are a group of members of the opposite sex discussing their relationships. For example, men are asked to pretend that they are women talking about their relationships with men. The discussion will focus on what they really want from men: in what ways are they both frustrated and satisfied.

After about 20 minutes, the facilitator asks the inner circle to turn around and listen to the comments of the outer, observing group. Feedback from the observers is structured to focus on how empathic the discussants were with the needs and experiences of (in this example) women. If crucial areas were neglected, these should now be addressed.

After about 10 minutes the groups change places and repeat the exercise. I have found that both sexes are quite empathic with the needs of each other and that the exercise breaks down some of the barriers between men and women. Total time for the exercise is about 1 hour.

Discussion. After the class has finished the exercise, certain questions will provide for continued discussion. For example, how did each group adapt to viewing things from the perspective of the other sex? On what did they base their ideas of how the other sex thinks: from experience, common sense, close friendships with members of the opposite sex, from having read about or studied human relationships? Did they feel uncomfortable adopting these new roles? What did they learn about the way they behave in their own relationships and did they feel they learned how to communicate better within those relationships?

A CONVERSATION WITH ONE'S FATHER

Concept. This exercise is a modification of a Gestalt therapy approach to exploring relationships that I have developed in my counseling course.

Materials needed. No materials are needed. Divide students into groups of about six. The sex ratio does not need to be strictly balanced, although it is helpful if both sexes are represented in each group.

Instructions. Each participant takes a turn having a "conversation" with his or her father. (Because the course is a study of male roles, I chose fathers; the same task can be quite valuable applied with mothers.)

The individual sits facing an empty chair and imagines his or her father seated there. The individual then tells his or her father some important positive things about their relationship or events recalled as pleasant childhood interactions. The person then changes chairs. Now he or she imagines being the father and responds to the "child."

The participant now returns to the original chair and speaks of the negative aspects of the relationship, again giving the father a chance to respond. The third phase of the exercise requires the student to express his or her present needs and desires from the father and, again, the father's response to these requests. While the dialogue is taking place, group members sit silently and support and encourage interaction and risk taking.

Discussion. With encouragement to honestly and freely express their feelings, individuals will typically gain insight into their pattern of relating to their expectations for change and in some cases become aware of their own similarities to their father's behaviors and attitudes.

Because there are often similarities in how fathers and children interact, much shared learning and insight can take place. With each individual "working" for about 15 minutes, the total time for this exercise is about 90 minutes.

ROLE REVERSAL DATING

Concept. I was originally introduced to this fourth exercise at a workshop presented by Warren Farrell, an innovator in exploring and modifying sex role behavior. Farrell identified one of the traditional roles of women in relationships with men as that of "sex object," whereas the corresponding role of men is that of a "success object." This activity allows both sexes to trade these roles in order to gain a deeper understanding of each other.

Materials needed. No materials are needed. Students will need access to a cafeteria or student lounge.

Instructions. Have the men leave the room while the women remain. Have each man reenter the class one at a time and pretend that he is a beauty contest applicant. Each man is observed and interviewed by the women for about 1 minute. Although the interactions are playful and punctuated with humor, the lesson is a serious one. Very few men are aware of the intense experience of being evaluated continually on the basis of physical appearance and superficial characteristics.

Tell the men that they are going to be asked out on a date by a woman in the class. Tell the class that the women are to play the traditional masculine role of being assertive, decisive, and worldly-wise and that the men are to be traditionally feminine: passive, supportive, and somewhat "helpless." Each individual is told to play the role to the best of his or her ability. As a prelude to the initiation of the date, the women in the class present themselves as success objects by sharing a 15-second profile of themselves that emphasizes their financial, material, and intellectual achievements. The women are encouraged to exaggerate their achievements and project a profile of success consistent with their goals. The men are then asked out, couples leave in pairs and are told to return within a half hour. The boundaries for the exercise is the university campus, with most couples going to the lounge and eating area in the student union. If there is an unequal number of men and women, the "date" can be in triads, with each individual playing the traditional role of the opposite sex.

Discussion. When the class returns, have them discuss their experiences and the psychological impact of attempting to operate within the framework of the opposite-sex role. Ask the men if they understand the discomfort women feel at being judged simply as sex objects, and ask the women if they understand men's frustrations at being considered "catches" on the basis of their outside achievements.

It will be interesting to find out how the participants reacted to the shift in role. How did the women feel to have that kind of power, of control—did they enjoy it? Did they feel they might abuse it? Did the men feel at a loss by not being in control, or was it a relief to let someone else make the decisions? Ask students if the exercise revealed any ways in which the roles of the two sexes could be more evenly balanced. The exercise takes about 90 minutes.

EXERCISE 5 EXPLORING HOMOPHOBIA

Concept. This activity helps to break down stereotypical reactions toward homosexuality, to explore heterosexist prejudice, and to increase awareness and understanding of the psychological framework of gay men and lesbians.

Because of the controversial and delicate subject matter involved, this activity is probably more suitable for a college-level course than a high school one.

Materials needed. You will need a film or videotape in which gay men and lesbians discuss their concerns, difficulties, and daily lives, to be shown at the start of the exercise.

Instructions. After a brief discussion of the film, divide the class into groups of 10 with at least 2 members of the other sex in each group. The group's task is to imagine that they are all gay or lesbian and have come together to discuss issues and problems of common concern.

Each individual is asked to empathize with the perspectives of gay men and lesbians and to make up or share some major facet of their personal history. For example, individuals may talk about the psychological impact of finding out they were gays and lesbians. After each person shares a significant facet of his or her life as a gay person, general issues and concerns of gay people in a straight society are explored.

Discussion. Because of the intense stigmatizing of gay people and entrenched heterosexism in American society, this exercise is the most challenging of the five. I intentionally place it at the end of the series, at a point when students have become familiar with experiential work, are trusting of their classmates, and are relatively comfortable expressing their feelings and interacting with others.

Focus the discussion on the feelings experienced by the participants when they "adopted" a gay perspective. Did they feel a sense of isolation, of fear? How did they, from this new viewpoint, see their futures? Did they imagine telling their parents and friends for the first time, either by "remembering" having done so, or trying to decide how it would be handled at some future time? Did they imagine being in a relationship, perhaps translating their current concerns with a relationship into this new context?

A few students (in my experience, about 10%) may choose not to participate in this activity. Half of those are often willing to observe and the remainder write a short paper on the topic of homophobia. The majority who work with this topic are surprised by the high degree of empathy that the group displays toward gays and have reported significant changes in their personal attitudes. This exercise takes about 75 minutes.

SUGGESTED READING

Doyle, J. (1989). *The male experience* (2nd ed.) Dubuque, IA: Wm. C. Brown.

Farrell, W. (1986). *Why men are the way they are.* New York: McGraw-Hill.

Lazarus, M. (Producer), & Wunderlich, R. (Director). (1982). *Pink triangles: A study of prejudice against lesbians and gay men.* Cambridge, MA: Cambridge Documentary Films.

□87 THE SECRETARY GAME

W. E. Scoville

University of Wisconsin—Oshkosh

Students will be surprised when they learn the purpose this activity, particularly if the outcome is as predicted: open discussion about sex role stereotyping. No materials are needed, and any size class can participate as long as neither males nor females are less than 25% of the total students. This activity is appropriate for social psychology classes in discussions of prejudice, group dynamics, or leadership.

CONCEPT

This activity demonstrates the stereotype of role, showing how people tend to assign particular roles to people according to their sex. Typically, men are assigned those positions that concern decision making and managing, whereas women are seen as fitting into certain limited roles that involve little decision making or independent contributions. This activity will make students more aware of their own gender-related biases.

MATERIALS NEEDED

No extra materials are needed. Class should be a coed group, with a minimum of about 25% of each sex.

INSTRUCTIONS

Arbitrarily divide the class into groups of 4–6 members. Each group should include at least 1 member of each sex, but do not make this an obvious part of the process as you form the groups.

Instruct each group to select a "leader–chair" who is responsible for making sure that all members of the group get a chance to participate and a "secretary–recorder" who is responsible for writing down a list of the group members and a summary of the main points and ideas developed in the group discussion.

The groups are then given 20 minutes or less to discuss a topic that is relevant to the course. For the purpose of this demonstration the topic does not matter, but you might as well provide a topic that has further use within your course structure. After the time is up, each secretary–recorder is asked to provide the class with a brief informal report on the group discussion. If time is short, you might prefer to defer the reports until the following class period or to simply ask that the notes be handed in.

DISCUSSION

The tabulation of numbers and proportion of leaders and secretaries by sex is the whole point of this activity. It has been my experience that college students tend to select (in one fashion or another) a male leader and a female secretary. There are few things as enlightening and liberating as the moment when the housewife or secretary who has returned to college on a part-time basis ends up finding herself still in the secretarial role. You can generate some very interesting discussions through getting each group to tell the class how they selected those persons, what the various considerations were, and to explain sex bias that seems to exist. When the conventional roles are reversed, you can ask the following question: Was this tokenism deliberate or was sex not considered?

People who have just found themselves guilty of sex stereotyping are apt to be open to a discussion of this problem and to be more ready to consider the possibilities for a change.

SUGGESTED READING

Frieze, I. H., Parsons, J. E., Johnson, P. B., Ruble, D. N., & Zellman, G. L. (1978). *Women and sex roles: A social psychological perspective.* New York: Norton.

Kanowitz, L. (1973). *Sex roles in law and society: Cases and materials.* Albuquerque: University of New Mexico Press.

Williams, J. H. (1977). *Psychology of women: Behavior in a biosocial context.* New York: Norton.

88 SEX ROLE STEREOTYPING IN CHILDREN'S BOOKS

Lita Linzer Schwartz
Pennsylvania State University

This activity is a good companion piece to "Sex Role Stereotyping in Toys: An Out-of-Class Project" (Activity 83 in this volume). Both activities can be used in conjunction with discussions of developmental psychology. Students will need access to the children's book section in a library. No other materials are needed, although written questions or observation–recording forms would help structure the observations. Any size high school or undergraduate class can participate. Several variations on this activity, using textbooks, magazines, or TV, are also discussed.

CONCEPT

Stereotypes are oversimplified generalizations about people in a particular category. This activity focuses on stereotyping by gender. Different cultures define masculinity and femininity in different ways, ascribing roles and behaviors to each. These presumably gender-appropriate roles are taught to children in varied ways, from direct instruction to modeling.

If females are constantly taught that they have fewer skills than males, or that they are limited to certain adult roles, then girls will grow up with lowered self-esteem and aspirations. If boys are constantly taught that they need to be aggressive and competitive to prove their masculinity or that they must not show emotional reactions or both, they are likely to grow up with lowered sensitivity to the needs of others. If children are shown, through parental modeling, through books, or through television stories, that adventure and curiosity are the exclusive province of boys and passivity is the role for girls, the potential negative effects will be seen in personality, academic performance, adult behavior, and other areas as the children mature. Conflict is also created if either the boy or girl prefers behavior or roles ascribed to the other gender. Does the individual try to impress others as being an "ideal" or "typical" male or female regardless of his or her personal traits or preferences?

MATERIALS NEEDED

No extra equipment or materials are needed. Students should have access to a local library that has a children's book section.

INSTRUCTIONS

Ask students to choose 10 books at random from the picture book section (e.g., the Golden Books series). Have them look at both the illustrations and the text in each book and answer the following questions: (a) Who are the leading characters in the story? (b) How do you know? (c) What are the leading characters doing in the story? (d) Are the characters doing things that are typical of one gender more than the other? (Are boys being active in sports or girls seen in the kitchen, playing with dolls, etc.)? (e) If women are shown, are they in stereotypical roles (e.g., housewife, teacher, nurse, secretary)? Students may wish to look for books published at different times, such as in the 1950s or 1960s as well as in the 1980s.

Several questions can be raised during the discussion, such as the following: (a) What messages do the characters and the story line convey to boys and girls about gender roles in American society? (b) Do these reflect contemporary reality or traditional stereotyping? (c) Are there differences between the earlier and more recently published books with regard to gender stereotypes?

Supplementary activities. A similar survey may be made of history texts used in elementary and secondary schools, allowing students to compare the apparent versus the real role of women in history.

Students could also survey Saturday morning children's cartoons or after-school features, sitcoms, and magazine advertising for indications of gender-role stereotyping. (If the TV option is chosen, refer students to a series of articles in the *Journal of Broadcasting,* beginning about 1978).

If students compare books from different decades, they are likely to find that there was a move away from rigid stereotyping beginning in the mid-1970s, although some continues to exist. If they survey history texts, they are likely to find that there is still limited references to women or to women's contributions, except perhaps in a token way. If they work with the television activity, they will probably find a wide variety of perspectives, although the sitcoms appear to derive at least some of their "humor" from stereotyping and from inept attempts to overcome it.

At the very least, students should come away from this activity with a greater awareness of and sensitivity to gender stereotyping. Some students may perceive the general injustice of stereotyping. Others may become aware of alternative behaviors and goals that they had previously thought closed to them because of their gender. Still others may become alert to the effects of modeling and other forms of socialization on the personal, social, and intellectual development of children.

Suggested Reading

Archer, C. (1984). Children's attitudes toward sex-role division in adult occupational roles. *Sex Roles, 10,* 1–10.

Basow, S. A. (1986). *Gender stereotypes: Traditions and alternatives* (2nd ed.) Monterey, CA: Brooks/Cole.

Davis, A. (1984). Sex-differentiated behaviors in nonsexist picture books. *Sex Roles, 11,* 1–16.

Franken, M. (1983). Sex role expectations in children's vocational aspirations and perceptions of occupations. *Psychology of Women Quarterly, 8,* 59–68.

Gardner, J. (1970). Sesame Street and sex role stereotypes. *Women, 1,* 42.

Key, M. (1975). The role of male and female in children's books: Dispelling all doubt. In R. Unger & F. Denmark (Eds.), *Woman* (pp. 56–70). New York: Psychological Dimensions.

Kolbe, R., & LaVole, J. (1981). Sex-role stereotyping in preschool children's picture books. *Social Psychology Quarterly, 44,* 369–374.

U.S. Commission on Civil Rights. (1980). *Characters in textbooks: A review of the literature.* Washington, DC: U.S. Government Printing Office.

89 FEMINIST AND SEX-FAIR METHODOLOGY

Michele A. Paludi
Hunter College of the City University of New York

Charles Epstein
Burke Marketing Research

This activity is designed to acquaint students with library resources on the psychology of women and to show how sex bias enters the research process. Undergraduate classes of any size can be used. Advance preparation is required.

CONCEPT
The general purpose of this activity is to acquaint students with the library resources on the psychology of women.

A considerable amount of research has indicated that males and, by extension, "masculine" activities, occupations, and personality characteristics are perceived as normative; the female and what is "feminine" is a deviation from the norm. Perhaps the best example of the "male as normative" theme in psychology is the sex bias in the psychological research process. The hypotheses tested by a researcher are shaped by a theoretical model and by gender-role stereotypes. Stereotypes about women have influenced the kinds of questions researchers have investigated scientifically. In addition, there appears to be good evidence that sexism exists in selecting participants for research. Boys and men are used more frequently as participants than are girls and women. In fact, some entire areas of research have been developed using males only (e.g., moral development or achievement motivation in their early years). Thus, sexism has typically existed in the field of psychology inasmuch as that it has led to a psychology of male behavior, not human behavior. Furthermore, there may be a tendency for research conducted by women scholars to be considered less authoritative than reports by men.

Biases may therefore exist at every stage of the research process and include conceptual biases, experimenter effects, observer effects, bias in interpretation of results, and male norming in test construction. In recent years, a constructive alternative to sexist research methodology has been offered: feminist methodology. The feminist alternative suggests that researchers avoid thinking in terms of simple causal statements and focus on interactive relationships. Feminists also devote specific research attention to the special concerns of women. Feminist methodology has provided answers to a set of research questions that were not asked, let alone answered, in the sexist paradigm (e.g., androgyny, rape, sexism in psychotherapy). Therefore, feminist researchers have counteracted the neglect and misrepresentation of women in psychology and other disciplines. Feminist scholarship has helped shift viewing the world as revolving around only men to viewing it as revolving around both men and women.

MATERIALS
NEEDED You will need copies of *Psychology of Women Quarterly* and *Sex Roles*, which are available in libraries or in a private collection. The *Psychology of Women Quarterly* is published by Division 35 of the American Psychological Association and can be ordered from Cambridge University Press, 32 East 57th Street, New York, NY 10022. *Sex Roles* is published by Plenum Publishing Corporation, 233 Spring Street, New York, NY 10013.

INSTRUCTIONS

Ask students to browse through the latest issues of *Psychology of Women Quarterly* and *Sex Roles* and answer the following questions about each issue they read: (a) Who is the general editor of this journal? (b) Who publishes the journal? (c) What type of articles does the journal publish (e.g., reviews, reports on research, theoretical articles)?

Now have the students select one research article from each journal and answer the following questions: (a) Which volume of the journal did you select? (b) What is the full citation (in American Psychological Association house style) of the article? (c) What question, problem, or hypotheses did the author want to investigate? (d) Why do you believe this topic is important? How does the author say the topic relates to what has been previously published? (e) Where was the study conducted? (f) What instruments and techniques were used? (g) Who was studied and why? (h) How did the author summarize the findings? (i) Did the findings turn out as the author had anticipated? Why or why not? (j) Pretend that you have been asked to do a follow-up study to the one you have read. What would you do? Why? (k) Look for evidence of feminist methodology in the article and your follow-up study. (l) Check for sources of sex bias in the studies: conceptual biases, biases in selection of research participants, experimenter effects, observer effects, statistical biases, biases in reporting results, biases in interpreting results, and male norming in test construction.

DISCUSSION

This exercise will help explain to students how psychologists do research and some of the points at which bias may enter the research process. Generally, the research process includes the following steps: conceptualization of the problem, finding out about previous research, formulating hypotheses, designing experiments, collecting data, summarizing data, analyzing data, explaining results, sharing results, and conceptualization of additional problems.

Students should become aware of this process and of the ways in which sexist bias may enter. Center the discussion around any biases they found in the articles relating to the stages of the research process. For example, in the conceptualization of the problem, perhaps the model was biased and only certain questions were asked. When reviewing previous research, perhaps students found that journals and studies were used according to the scientist's bias. Perhaps in formulating hypotheses the researcher portrayed men and women in a stereotypical way. Or in designing experiments, the researcher selected only certain participants or used male norming in test construction. Maybe in collecting data there were observer or experimenter effects. Other examples include the following: "file drawer" and effect size problems can emerge in data analysis; results can be interpreted in a biased fashion; in presenting results, only significant results are published, journals are used selectively, or female scientists are considered to be less authoritative; and in conceptualization of additional problems, the model may be biased.

Have the students address feminist alternatives to these biases. Discuss the ways in which the authors of the selected articles have used feminist methodology. Ask the class the following questions: (a) Did the researchers observe the participants in their natural environment and try to determine how they experience their everyday lives? (b) Did the researcher devote specific attention to the special concerns of women? (c) Did the researcher control for sex of experimenter effects? (d) Did the researcher suggest a complex, interactive relation among the variables studies instead of simple cause–effect relation? (e) Were adequate control groups used? (f) Is there an emphasis on gender similarities as well as differences? (g) Can the results be generalized to include women of different ethnic groups?

You may wish to organize a "Feminist Methodology Conference" in which students may display their own designed experiments.

SUGGESTED READING

Unger, R. K. (1983). Through the looking glass: No wonderland yet! *Psychology of Women Quarterly, 8,* 9–32.

Unger, R. K. (1981). Sex as a social reality: Field and laboratory research. *Psychology of Women Quarterly, 5,* 645–653.

Wallston, B. S. (1981). What are the questions in the psychology of women? A feminist approach to research. *Psychology of Women Quarterly, 5,* 597–617.

Wallston, B. S., & Grady, K. E. (1985). Integrating the feminist critique and the crisis in social psychology: Another look at research methods. In V. E. O'Leary, R. K. Unger, & B. S. Wallston (Eds.), *Women, gender, and social psychology* (pp. 7–33). Hillsdale, NJ: Erlbaum.

90 MUSIC VIDEOS AND THE PORTRAYAL OF MEN AND WOMEN

Michele A. Paludi
Hunter College of the City University of New York

Bradley M. Waite
Wright State University

For this activity the instructor will need to order the Bem Sex-Role Inventory and the Attitudes Toward Women Scale and to have access to a VCR and monitor for showing videos to the class. Students rate four or five rock videos using the scales provided them and then compare their ratings. This activity is suitable for any size high school or undergraduate class. The recommended discussion and background reading make this activity most appropriate in conjunction with topics in social or developmental psychology.

CONCEPT

The purpose of this activity is to acquaint students with the media's antiwoman message, especially as it is expressed in music videos.

According to *Action for Children's Television* (1978), children under 5 years of age watch an average of more than 25 hours of television each week. This translates into more than 15,000 hours by the time the child completes high school. A considerable amount of research has been devoted to the way in which children and adolescents are exposed to stereotyped representations of men and women on television. For example, males and females perform different activities on television: the men are more likely to be shown at work while women are typically shown at home. In addition, male humans and animals are more than three times as common as females on children's television programs. Furthermore, men are typically described using terms that reflect rationality, assertiveness, and competence (or objectivity, self-confidence, and independence). Occupations stereotyped as "male appropriate" include attorney, police officer, physician, and office manager. Women are shown to be emotional, submissive, and subjective. Traditional "female-appropriate" occupations include elementary school teacher, typist, librarian, and nurse. Both the masculine personality characteristics and the roles in which men appear are rated by both men and women as being more desirable, important, and prestigious.

Thus, on television, women are relatively invisible, inaudible, and stereotyped in terms of their personality characteristics and occupations. Women of color are especially represented in a particularly biased manner. Research has indicated that this biased representation of men and women in the media influences reality. Children and adolescents who view stereotypic portrayals on TV become more stereotyped in their attitudes toward men's and women's roles and abilities.

MATERIALS NEEDED

You will need to find a TV channel (such as MTV on cable) that shows rock music videos. You may also want to videotape some videos to show in class as an in-class exercise. The short form of the Bem Sex-Role Inventory (BSRI) is available from Consulting Psychologists Press, Inc., 577 College Avenue, P.O. Box 11636, Palo

Alto, CA 94306. The short form of the Attitudes Toward Women Scale (AWS) is available from its senior author, Janet T. Spence, Department of Psychology, University of Texas, Austin, TX 78712.

INSTRUCTIONS Describe the impact of gender role stereotypes in the media and how they contribute to gender differences in real life. References summarized in the Background Section of this article would be helpful in this regard.

Discuss advertisements that are demeaning to girls and women. It would be helpful to view the film *Killing Us Softly*, which describes the misogyny in classic advertisements for women's clothes, perfume, cars, and so on. This film may be rented from Cambridge Documentary Films, P.O. Box 385, Cambridge MA, (617)-354-3677.

Ask students to watch four or five rock music videos and complete the BSRI for the main male and female characters in each video. Students will rate the characters on a series of adjectives (10 each of masculine, feminine, and neutral). The scale can be completed in about 5 minutes per character.

Ask students to complete the AWS for each video according to how they believe the director of the video would answer the items. Students will answer 25 statements about the attitudes toward the rights and roles of women in contemporary society. Areas assessed include vocation, behavior, sexual behavior, dating, and independence.

DISCUSSION Have students discuss whether the videos they watched were violent, sexist, or both. Ask them to consider how the videos perpetuate gender-role stereotypes. What kinds of activities are the women in the videos engaged in and how does it relate to what the men are doing? Some of the videos may seem to show women in a favorable light (portraying them as beautiful, desirable, talented), but have the students ask themselves if these women are being prized for anything more than their physical attributes or if there is any indication that the woman has an identity separate from the man she is associated with.

Ask students to compare their ratings on the BSRI and AWS with other classmates. Look for gender differences in responses to the items. You may also address ethnic and racial differences. Is there a difference between the way Black men (or men from other minorities) and White men are portrayed? What about the women? Discuss the reasons why these stereotypes continue to be presented in the videos and what could be done about it.

REFERENCES Action for Children's Television newsletter (1978, Spring). [Entire issue], 7(3).

SUGGESTED READING
Beere, C. A. (1979). *Women and women's issues: A handbook of tests and measures.* San Francisco: Jossey-Bass.

Bem, S. L. (1974). The measurement of psychological androgyny. *Journal of Consulting and Clinical Psychology, 42,* 155–162.

Bem, S. L. (1975). Sex role adaptability: One consequence of psychological androgyny. *Journal of Personality and Social Psychology, 31,* 634–643.

Bem, S. L. (1975, April). Androgyny vs. the tight little lives of fluffy women and chesty men. *Psychology Today,* pp. 58–59.

Cassata, M. (1983). The more things change, the more they are the same: An analysis of soap operas from radio to television. In M. Cassata & T. Skill (Eds.), *Life on daytime television: Tuning-in-American serial drama* (pp. 85–100). Norwood, NJ: Ablex.

Courtney, A. E., & Whipple, T. W. (1983). *Sex stereotyping in advertising*. Lexington, MA: Lexington Books.

Kane, E. (Director). *Misogyny in rock* [Video]. New York: Women Against Pornography.

Lull, J., Mulac, A., & Rosen, S. L. (1983). Feminism as a predictor of mass media use. *Sex Roles, 9*, 165–177.

Reid, P. T. (1979). Racial stereotyping on television: A comparison of the behavior of both black and white television characters. *Journal of Applied Psychology, 64*, 465–471.

Ross, L., Anderson, D. R., & Wisocki, P. A. (1982). Television viewing and adult sex-role attitudes. *Sex Roles, 8*, 589–592.

Spence, J. T., & Helmreich, R. L. (1972). The Attitudes Toward Women Scale: An objective instrument to measure attitudes toward the rights and roles of women in contemporary society. *Journal Supplement Abstract Service Catalog of Selected Documents in Psychology*, Volume 2, 66.

Spence, J. T., Helmreich, R. L., & Stapp, J. (1973). A short version of the Attitudes Toward Women Scale (AWS). *Bulletin of the Psychonomic Society, 2*, 219–220.

Women's Action Alliance. (1981). *The radio and television commercials monitoring project: Summary report*. New York: Author.

91 NONSEXIST LANGUAGE USAGE

Michele A. Paludi
Hunter College of the City University of New York

This activity can be used with classes of up to 60 and can be modified for even larger groups by using a written format. No prior knowledge on the part of students is necessary, and instructor preparation is minimal. This topic is most likely to be relevant in discussions of social psychology but could be incorporated into sections on perceptual set, impression formation, or self-concept.

CONCEPT

This exercise can help students become aware of the attitudes toward generic masculine and sex-neutral terms.

The generic masculine is the use of masculine pronouns and nouns to refer to all human beings, female and male, instead of males alone. Examples include man, he/his/him, businessman, chairman, forefathers, and mankind. Although it has been asserted that whenever people see or hear masculine pronouns they think of both males and females, research has indicated that generic masculine terms are not really sex neutral. In fact, generic masculine terms are more likely than sex-neutral terms (e.g., "he or she," "they") to produce thoughts that are oriented around males and masculinity. For example, potential illustrators for a book were more likely to select all-male photos when the chapter titles were Industrial Man or Social Man rather than Industrial Life or Society. Furthermore, Briere and Lanktree (1983) found that students who saw the generic masculine version rated a career in psychology as being less attractive for women than did students who saw sex-neutral versions.

Because of these findings, psychologists have been working on ways to eliminate generic masculine usage. For example, the American Psychological Association (1983) has provided information about how sex-biased language can be avoided in the third edition of the *Publication Manual*. It has been extremely difficult to eliminate sex-biased language, however, because many individuals do not think that generic masculine terms are sexist (Matlin, 1983). Clearly, though, this verbal exclusion of women from "mankind" is undesirable; the generic masculine can be eliminated, and this activity will help students to at least gain a greater awareness of the problem.

MATERIALS NEEDED

You can use a list of terms containing items such as the following: sportsmanship, stewardess, chairman, businessman, mankind, manhole cover, policeman, fireman, to man (as in to man a booth at a carnival), brotherly (as in brotherly love), and bachelor's degree.

INSTRUCTIONS

Distribute a list of terms similar to the one just listed. Ask students to break up into smaller groups and assign a recorder for each group. Each group will generate nonsexist alternatives to the terms, and the recorder will present the findings to the rest of the class.

Provide the class with the following sexist sentences: (a) Julie is such a little tomboy. (b) The men's basketball team and the girl's basketball team won last night.

(c) I like the dancers and male dancers too. (d) We have slimnastics here for girls and body building for boys. (e) Let's have four-man teams.

Ask the students to write a nonsexist alternative to each sentence and to share their responses with the entire class. Discuss the implications of nonsexist language in textbooks and children's readers.

REFERENCES

American Psychological Association. (1983). *Publication manual of the American Psychological Association* (3rd ed.). Washington, DC: Author.

Briere, J., & Lanktree, C. (1983). Sex-role related effects of sex bias in language. *Sex Roles, 9,* 625–632.

Matlin, M. (1983, April). *Attitudes toward masculine-generic and gender-neutral language.* Paper presented at the meeting of the Eastern Psychological Association, Philadelphia, PA.

SUGGESTED READING

Schneider, J. W., & Hacker, S. L. (1973). Sex role imagery and use of the generic "man" in introductory texts: A case in the sociology of sociology. *American Sociologist, 8,* 12–18.

Stericker, A. (1981). Does this "her or she" business really make a difference? The effects of masculine pronouns as generic on job attitudes. *Sex Roles, 7,* 627–642.

APPENDIXES

APPENDIX A

Chapter Summaries From *Activities Handbook for the Teaching of Psychology, Volumes 1 and 2*

Volume 1

METHODOLOGY

The activities in this chapter cover the experimental method and systematic observation as strategies in behavioral science. Nine of the eleven activities are designed for in-class use. Two activities deal specifically with observational methods: Activity 1 focuses on the problems of interobserver agreement using a standardized experience for all observers, and Activity 2 demonstrates the accuracy of observation. Similarly, Activities 3 and 4 illustrate the investigations employing the experimental method; both emphasize appropriate control procedures. Activity 5 is designed to provide examples of sampling procedures and the nature of probability. Hypothesis formation and testing are stressed in Activities 6 and 7, which also illustrate components of the experimental method. The final four activities in this chapter emphasize factors that can lead to erroneous conclusions in observation and experimentation. Activity 8 deals with the issues of randomization, particularly the random assignment of subjects to differing conditions. Activity 9 demonstrates the relation between experimenter expectancy and subject performance. Activity 10 allows students to experience errors in measurements, and Activity 11 illustrates a large number of factors that, if left uncontrolled, can bias experimental results.

SENSORY PROCESSES AND PERCEPTION

The 11 activities in this chapter, all of which are designed for in-class use, cover a range of sensory and perceptual phenomena. These exercises focus on individual sensory systems, as well as on the interaction of two or more of these systems. The first three activities deal with taste, smell, and tactile perception. Activity 12, a study of taste preferences, looks at the influence of smell and sight. Activity 13 measures cutaneous sensitivity by means of the classic two-point threshold technique. Seven basic smells are studied in Activity 14, which relates to the stereochemical theory of odor. The next four activities illustrate various visual phenomena: Activity 15 deals with blue-blindness or tritanopia, Activity 16 is about the process of accommodation, Activity 17 uses the Pulfrich pendulum effect to discuss information transmission from the eye, and Activity 18 concerns the retinal blind spot. Two activities demonstrate interactions with the visual system. Activity 19 uses the size-weight illusion to study the relation between vision and touch. Activity 20 investigates the role played by vision in the maintenance of a person's equilibrium. Activity 21 shows the effects of delayed auditory feedback on speech, and Activity 22 illustrates the nature of perceptual adaptation to displaced vision.

LEARNING AND CONDITIONING

All but one of the nine activities described in this chapter are designed for use within the classroom. The first four exercises describe different methods for illustrating operant conditioning in humans. Activity 23 requires very little class time, whereas Activities 24, 25 and 26 are more elaborate and employ shaping procedures in which the instructor serves as the source of reinforcement. Activity 25 describes a procedure that uses all of the students in the class in an operant-conditioning demonstration. That exercise also uses a verbal punishment procedure that can be compared with the use of reinforcement. Activity 26 demonstrates an extinction procedure. Activity 27 describes a recording procedure that can serve as a form of self-modification and discusses ways in which individuals can use operant-conditioning techniques to modify their own behavior. Three activities deal with the relation between learning and performance and show factors that affect both. Activity 28 illustrates the importance of knowledge of results by using groups of subjects given either no knowledge, full knowledge, or partial knowledge. Activity 29 uses the Stroop Color Word Test to show how irrelevant stimuli can interrupt attention and thus affect performance. The effects of practice and negative transfer on performance are demonstrated in Activity 30. Activity 31 describes a procedure for generating a number of learning curves for a variety of motor and cognitive tasks.

MEMORY AND COGNITION

The 16 activities in this chapter are designed for use in the classroom. All but one of the activities involve the entire class simultaneously. Memory, language, problem solving, transfer, and creativity are among the topics covered by demonstrations and experiments in this chapter. Activity 32 illustrates a number of memory phenomena, including forgetting curves, the serial position effect, and the effects of emphasis, repetition, and meaningfulness on retention. Activity 33 looks at memory storage and the reconstructive nature of memory that becomes apparent when missing details are added in recall. Activity 34 contrasts the most commonly used methods for measuring retention—recall and recognition. Four activities stress the importance of meaningfulness for memory: Activity 35 demonstrates the enhancement of recall, Activity 36 shows the importance of context for interpreting and recalling material, Activity 37 illustrates the role of association value in memorization, and Activity 38 demonstrates how emphasis can make nonmeaningful material impossible to forget. Retroactive and proactive inhibition are components of Activity 39, which looks at interference in learning and retention. Activity 40 illustrates transfer in a mirror-tracing task and leads to discussion of transfer in other forms of learning. Three activities describe problem-solving demonstrations: Activity 41 investigates the effectiveness of problem solving by individuals versus groups, Activity 42 looks at set as an aid and a hindrance to problem solving, and Activity 43 provides an example of the Zeigarnik effect relating memory to success and failure in a problem-solving situation. The final four activities focus on other phenomena within the field of cognition. Concept-learning using Greek-letter trigrams is described in Activity 44. Activity 45 illustrates the meaning of the word language and its role in communication. Various aspects of creativity are explored in Activity 46, which is designed to enhance student creativity. Activity 47 uses a semantic clustering technique to demonstrate the role of unconscious processes in categorization in a recall task.

DEVELOPMENTAL PSYCHOLOGY

The activities in this chapter span human development from infancy through the aging process and even include an exercise on development in subhuman animals. Five of the nine activities are proposed for classroom use. Two activities involve investigations with human infants; Activity 48 examines object permanency in infants between 2 and 12 months old, and Activity 49 looks at sensory stimulation in infants around 8 months old. If access to human infants is not available, Activity 50 involves the students in observing a litter of rat pups from birth to 4 weeks. Following the work of Jean Piaget, Activity 51 describes a procedure to assess conservation ability in preschool children. Three exercises focus on general issues across the span of development. Activity 52 illustrates the distinction between developmental changes and those due strictly to maturation. Activity 53 looks at life-span development in an exercise based on Erik Erikson's eight stages of development. The topic of life-span development is also the emphasis of Activity 54, which has students associate tasks, behaviors, attitudes, and so forth with various ages by decade. Activity 55 is a demonstration of attitudes toward and beliefs about old age, and Activity 56 is an exercise on death and dying related to the theory of dying proposed by Elisabeth Kübler-Ross.

SOCIAL PSYCHOLOGY

This chapter contains 14 exercises, 4 of which are designed for projects outside of class. Four activities deal with the concept of stereotyping, each focusing on different aspects of that process. Activity 57 looks at the relation of sex role stereotypes and judgments of good mental health. Activity 58 examines stereotypes in a decision task and contrasts individuals and groups as decision makers. Activities 59 and 60 illustrate the prevalence of ethnic stereotypes. (A statement of caution is warranted in regard to the latter two activities. Both require that students either exhibit ethnic stereotyped attitudes or be able to role-play those attitudes. Such activities may prove discomforting for students and instructors unless the participation and explanations are handled with a great deal of sensitivity.) Obedience to authority is demonstrated in two exercises. Activity 61 shows obedience to the instructor, and Activity 62 illustrates cooperation with perceived authority in the completion of a public opinion poll. The other activities span the diverse phenomena of social psychology: the psychology of humor (Activity 63); sexism as it occurs in the classroom (Activity 64); an analysis of advertising appeals and how they produce changes in attitudes (Activity 65); co-operation and competition in daily activity (Activity 66); smiling as a response to social stimuli (Activity 67); the effects of group interactions on the maintenance of self-concept (Activity 68); body language as nonverbal communication (Activity 69); and assigned roles as they influence group dynamics in a problem-solving situation (Activity 70).

PERSONALITY The seven activities described in this chapter are all designed for classroom use. Activities 71 and 72 illustrate the generalities frequently found in personality descriptions and how easy it is to assume the validity of those descriptions. Activity 73 covers cognitive styles such as field dependence-independence and global versus detailed perception. Suggestibility and susceptibility to set are dealt with in Activity 74. Activity 75 is a role-playing exercise that familiarizes students with defense mechanisms. Factors affecting level of aspiration in a perceptual-motor task are the subject of Activity 76, and impression formation is covered in Activity 77.

MISCELLANEOUS As the title implies, this chapter is a collection of activities that do not fit readily into one of the other chapter headings but that range the gamut of the psychological enterprise. Activity 78 involves observation of animal behavior in a natural habitat. Activity 79 is an analysis of crisis and conflict resolution. Data on sleep and dreaming are collected and analyzed in Activity 80. Activity 81 demonstrates the ease with which people attribute "mental illness" to other people based on observation of their behavior. Activity 82 relates creativity to artistic ability. Activities 83 and 84 are studies of reaction time; the latter activity uses a chain reaction procedure. Activity 85 demonstrates neural transmission, using students as neurons. The next two activities are studies of human emotion: Activity 86 attempts to label the dimensions of emotion, and Activity 87 examines facial expressions in emotion, based on the work of Paul Ekman. Finally, Activity 88 uses ethograms in the observation and recording of animal behavior.

Volume 2

METHODOLOGY The first four activities in this chapter emphasize the observational method. None require that the students have prior knowledge in psychology, and they can all be adapted to any class size. Activity 1 contains four separate exercises that demonstrate the distinction between observable behavior and inferences and provide an opportunity to consider individual differences in observations that can create difficulties in the simplest research endeavors. Activity 2 explores the impact of interobserver agreement and is best used when students have access to a group of preschool children or a videotape of children at play. Operational definitions are presented in Activity 2 and continued in Activity 3, in which observational methods are applied to the written word. A card game is used to simulate a scientific investigation in Activity 4, in which once again the pivotal issue is the systematic observation of phenomena.

Students must have some understanding of positive and negative correlation coefficients before engaging in Activity 5, which illustrates the difference between experimental and correlational research.

Activity 6 provides an amusing illustration of the hazards of hypothetical questions in survey research and lends itself to use in discussions of other topics, such as conformity, social norms, and so on, as well as methodology. Activity 7 describes an approach to teaching research methods at the introductory level and requires outside reading and paper assignments. Students can experience firsthand the stages involved in test construction and analysis in Activity 8, an exercise best suited for presentation in an upper-level undergraduate tests and measurements course.

SENSORY PROCESSES AND PERCEPTION The nine activities in this chapter require no prior knowledge of psychology, can be adapted to classes of any size (with the possible of exception of Activity 14, which is limited by number of pinpoint lights available), and can all be done in class.

Activity 9 presents three separate exercises that examine different aspects of the "split brain" phenomenon and raise questions about gender differences in lateralization. A modification of students' hand-eye systems provides insights into the role of past experiences and the importance of conscious effort in sustaining manual control in Activity 10. You can elicit students' interest in vision further by doing the inverted retinal image demonstration in Activity 11. The author of Activity 12, in which subtle color perception demonstrations are done with inexpensive homemade equipment, reports that students both enjoy it and learn significantly about color mixing.

The study of sensation and perception through direct experience is continued in Activities 13, 14, and 15. Activity 13 illustrates the principles of size perception as well as other features of visual perception. In Activity 14, students look at the homogeneous viewing surface of a simply constructed Ganzfeld and thus experience receptor adaptation, which helps them see that sensory systems require varied stimulation to function properly. Activity 15, which is based on the old children's game of identifying the number of fingers held to a person's back, discusses sensitivity to touch and demonstrates the spatial map of the body skin surface.

The demonstration in Activity 16 suggests strongly that sensations can be measured. Activity 17 illustrates the influence of expectancy on the perception of language and sets the stage for a more general discussion of the subjectivity of perception.

LEARNING AND MEMORY

The nine activities in this chapter are all appropriate for beginning psychology students. Activity 21 can be used at both the introductory and the advanced level. Although it is best suited for classes of 25 to 35 students, the other eight activities are suitable for classes of any size. With the exception of Activities 21 and 26, which require take-home assignments, all are in-class exercises.

Activity 18 demonstrates the accomplishment of a simple learning task and could be used as an activity associated with statistics as well as learning and memory. Activity 19 is a clever and humorous way to introduce students to the concept of classical conditioning. Human operant conditioning is illustrated by a simple learning task in Activity 20, which introduces the concepts of shaping, successive approximations, and extinction.

Activities 21, 22, 23, 25, and 26 work well together as a unit on "learning to learn." Activity 21 turns to experiential learning theory and offers students the opportunity to gain understanding about their individual learning styles. This activity could be adapted for discussions about group dynamics or group processes as well. Although Activity 22 demonstrates to students the importance of studying actively and examines techniques that enhance recall, it can also be used to illustrate research methods or experimental design. Activity 23 reveals the distinction between the storage of long-term and short-term memory and continues the theme of study improvement through an understanding of the learning process. The fourth in this "learning to learn" unit, Activity 25, extends the concepts presented in Activity 23 and demonstrates how students can learn and retain new material efficiently.

Activity 26 demonstrates the serial position effect, which is relevant to students because they are frequently called on to remember lists such as terms, dates, or facts in class.

Activity 24, which will help a large percentage of students in the class experience a déjà vu episode, is designed to explain this type of experience within the bounds of empirical psychology.

DEVELOPMENTAL PSYCHOLOGY

The activities in this chapter offer students a number of ways to directly examine the developmental process: by recalling their own experiences; by interviewing children, their peers, and middle-aged adults; and by analyzing role models as presented by the television media.

Activity 27 offers a formal way to integrate students' own childhood experiences when the class is studying the topic of developmental psychology by having each student present a part of his or her childhood to the class.

Two simple classroom demonstrations for introducing the Piagetian concepts of assimilation, accommodation, and equilibration are described in Activity 28, which encourages students to discover firsthand the basic cognitive processes that underlie intellectual development.

You will need to conduct a thorough discussion of ethical guidelines for research with human participants before introducing Activities 29, 32, and 33—activities that focus on childhood, middle age, and the elderly. The cognitive-structural approach to artistic development in children is demonstrated in Activity 29, which requires that each student obtain a drawing of a "person" from a child of a specified age. The class then categorizes the drawings, graphs the results, and plots the proportion of different types of drawings as a function of the child's age. In Activity 32, students investigate the attitudes of their peers toward older adults and attain hands-on experience in research methodology. To do Activity 33, you need to present a discussion of ethical guidelines as well as interview methodology so that studnets are prepared to conduct an out-of-class interview with a middle-aged adult. These activities are suited for classes of any size.

Activity 30 presents an informal research project that encourages students to critically examine the images of current television shows. Students evaluate their own views about the impact media models have on children as well as practice the observational technique. For Activity 31, the class must read *The Catcher in the Rye* before they do analyses in writing or in discussion groups. Activity 34 presents an approach to teaching a course on human development.

SOCIAL PSYCHOLOGY

Of the ten activities in this chapter, only one requires that the students have prior knowledge in psychology. Two activities suggest that students read the text material on persuasion before introducing the activities. Five of the activities rely on handouts, and one activity requires that the students write a term paper.

Activity 35 illustrates that the right circumstances can elicit antisocial, highly inappropriate behavior in most people. Students are surprised to learn that their responses differ little from responses gathered from prisoners. Activity 36 is an effective illustration of the surprising potential and complex character of social influence. That you don't get a second chance to make a first impression is shown by the illustration of the primacy effect in Activity 38. Activity 39 demonstrates that people consistently tend to blame the "person" and overlook the "situation."

Activity 37 allows students to consensually define aggression by having each student anonymously complete a copy of a questionnaire containing 25 diverse statements that span the gamut of issues relevant to the consideration of aggression. This activity could be used in an introductory course as well as any course that will cover the topic of aggression.

The major determinants of interpersonal attraction are explored in the context of a "scavenger hunt" in Activity 40, which actually contains four separate exercises. Activities 41 and 42 are apt to generate lively discussion from students eager to share their analyses of the persuasion techniques employed by television commercials. Activity 42 expands on Activity 41 by using a student paper in the format. Activity 43 helps students understand the development of gender stereotypes and how stereotypes influence behavior and attitudes.

Activity 44 is designed to illustrate intergroup conflict. You should be cautioned that real hostility is often generated in the participants, so it is absolutely necessary to plan time for the conflict resolution phase of the activity at the end of the class.

PERSONALITY, ABNORMAL, AND CLINICAL PSYCHOLOGY

Of the nine activities in this chapter, six require no prior knowledge in psychology on the part of students, eight are suitable for classes of any size, four extend over several class periods, and all require only minimal preparation by the teacher.

Activity 45 succeeds in making basic concepts and ideas practical and personally relevant by teaching specific techniques that can be employed by students to develop their own stress management programs.

Activity 46 is designed to create a situation in which manipulative behavior is elicited in a game in which three students participate while the class observes.

Activities 47 and 48 concern personality, tapping an area familiar to students and of great interest to them. Both activities demand that students review carefully the Ethical Guidelines of Research with Human Participants before engaging in the exercises. These activities could be used in the context of methodology as well. Activity 47 requires out-of-class assignments, and Activity 48 extends over two class periods. Activity 49, a good companion piece to Activity 47, can be used as an opener for a discussion personality testing.

Two of the activities are designed to sensitize students to persons who are considered abnormal. Students have the chance to engage in some harmless deviant behavior in Activity 50 and then write about the experience in a report. Activity 51 involves administering a bogus personality test to students and preparing bogus feedback. Because it can be discomforting to students when they receive scores indicating they are marginally adjusted, it is important that sufficient debriefing take place before the class period is concluded.

Activity 52 introduces personality theories with an exercise based on clustering the psychological concepts embraced by the five major approaches to personality. Designed to be used in a personality theories course, Activity 53 is composed of a pretest and a posttest. This activity assists in augmenting students' awareness of their own theoretical perspectives and the degree to which those perspectives change during the course.

STATISTICS

The eleven activities in this chapter demonstrate ways you can engagingly present some basic statistical concepts by making the content personally relevant to the students. All can be adapted for any size class.

Activity 54 presents a clear and simple introduction to descriptive statistics and would be suitable for a discussion of statistics in an introductory course. Activity 55 makes a simple statistical analysis relevant to students by using data related to a current topic of interest, in this case a Greyhound bus drivers' strike. Similarly, in Activity 56 the class joins in on ESP experiments by determining whether parapsychological phenomena have actually taken place via plotting frequency distributions and calculating measures of central tendency.

The concept of sampling fluctuation is empirically illustrated in Activity 57, and Activity 58 describes classroom demonstrations of the regression effect that are concrete and psychological in content. Students usually become interested in Activity 59 when the instructor poses the question, "How closely can I predict your performance on the final exam from your earlier exam scores?" Another question of perennial interest to students is whether those who complete exams early score better—a topic that lends itself to statistical analyses that can be put on the blackboard for all the class to see in Activity 60. Activity 61 accomplishes the necessary posttest review with data highly relevant to the students by using their actual exam scores to illustrate the principles covered on the statistics exam itself.

Activity 62 presents a Piagetian approach to understanding statistics. You can use Activity 63 to demonstrate that people do not generally produce truly random sequences (even when instructed to do so), and in making this point help students to grasp some basic statistical concepts. To review statistical material, Activity 64 presents a series of poems that are intended to engender memory-enhancing images.

MOTIVATION AND EMOTION

The five activities in this chapter require no prior knowledge of psychology and can be adapted to classes of any size. Little or no preparation is necessary on your part.

Activity 65 demonstrates how level of aspiration varies with a person's experience of success and failure. Activity 66 contains an exercise that evokes a wide range of emotional responses in students, which can be used as a forum for discussion of motivation and emotion. Activity 67 employs Maslow's hierarchy of needs and a fictional character to explore motives for behaviors. The Worries Survey presented in Activity 68 was designed as both a research instrument and as a pedagogical device to promote student self-analysis and stimulate classroom discussion of worries. The semantic differential method detailed in Activity 69 fits into discussions of emotion, self-esteem, or psychological measurement, among others.

COMPUTERS IN TEACHING

The five activities in this chapter all require computer equipment. If you have access to computers, you can use the novel approaches to presenting psychological concepts presented here. None require that students have prior knowledge in psychology.

Does mood affect dreams? Are the dreams of men and women different? Do bad dreams occur more frequently than good dreams? These are some of the questions raised by Activity 70, which engages students in an extensive computer project on the topic of dreams. Activity 71 presents a computer program that teaches students to judge emotions from facial expressions.

The use of computers in the classroom has many advantages, not the least of which include dispensing with costly laboratory facilities and the inherent ethical considerations. Activity 72 uses a computerized laboratory to allow students to conduct animated simulations of known laboratory phenomena in place of demonstrations using live animals. A computerized testing situation is simulated for students in Activity 74, which is designed to teach students about psychological testing while minimizing ethical problems. Activity 73 describes a method to present material to the class using an electronic blackboard that is connected to a personal computer.

SPECIAL TOPICS   This chapter contains 11 activities that are not neatly assigned to any one topic area. With the exception of Activity 78, these activities can be adapted to any size class and require no prior knowledge in psychology on the part of students.

Activity 75 illustrates simply and dramatically how psychology can promote understanding of as well as tolerance and appreciation for individual differences. It's a good icebreaker for the first day of class.

Activities 76 and 77 concern stress management and help students become aware of how they experience tension and relaxation. Activity 78 continues the theme of having students focus on their own experience by illustrating the role the autonomic nervous system plays in emotional response.

The four separate exercises contained in Activity 79 illustrate some common examples of human variation and lend themselves to use in many different psychology courses.

Activities 80 and 81 work well together as a unit on assertiveness, a topic that has become immensely popular in recent years.

There are almost as many variations of Activities 82 and 83 as there are high school psychology teachers. Students who participate in these activities should gain an appreciation of some of the responsibilities inherent in parenting.

The last two activities in the book, 84 and 85, detail approaches to teaching rather than actual exercises. Activity 84 presents a method of classroom testing that enhances the learning process. Activity 85, designed for teachers who require that their students prepare papers according to APA style, provides checklists that ease the grading task.

APPENDIX B

Basic Statistical Methods

Charles M. Stoup

This appendix is designed to provide a basic understanding of a few of the statistical techniques commonly used to analyze data from psychological experiments. While it is not intended as a complete introduction to statistical analysis, the techniques it presents should enable you to analyze and interpret the data from most of the activities described in this handbook. Any techniques not described here may be found in most introductory statistics texts, several of which are listed at the end of this appendix.

Measurement

For information about a subject or group of subjects to be useful as data, it must be reducible to numerical form. This process of assigning numbers to observations is called *measurement.* Measurement is of concern to psychologists because the ways in which numbers are assigned to observations vary a great deal depending on the variable being observed. Thus, the psychologist (indeed, all behavioral scientists) must consider the *level of measurement* that corresponds to a particular dependent variable—where level of measurement indicates the degree of correspondence between the numbers assigned to the observations and the actual characteristics of the subjects being observed. That is, the level of measurement describes the *nature* of the information produced by the operations that define the dependent variable. Four broad classes or levels of measurement may be identified: nominal-, ordinal-, interval-, and ratio-level measurements.

Nominal-level measurement. A nominal variable is one that assigns labels to observations such that each observation receives one label or another but never more than one. That is, nominal-level measurement allows us only to state whether one observation is the *same as* or *different from* another observation with respect to the characteristic being measured. For example, individuals may be classified according to their eye color, with the colors being coded as brown = 1, blue = 2, green = 3, and other = 4. Similarly, the football jerseys worn by the players on a team are marked with conspicuous numbers, which serve only to identify different players. Both of these examples constitute nominal-level measurement, since in each case only one label may be assigned to the different units of observation (i.e., subjects), and the labels serve only to distinguish equivalent or different observations without allowing any statements concerning the magnitude of the characteristic being measured. Thus, it makes no sense to say that an individual with eye color coded as "3" has more of any characteristic than an individual with eye color coded as "1"—the measurement only specifies that the individuals differ with respect to this characteristic.

Ordinal-level measurement. An ordinal variable has all the characteristics of a nominal variable and, in addition, assigns labels to observations in such a way that the observations can meaningfully be placed in rank order. If we observe a group of individuals and classify each of them as being short = 1, medium = 2, or tall = 3, we have performed ordinal-level measurement on the height variable, since the three categories can be rank ordered with respect to the "amount" of height observed. Another example of ordinal-level measurement is the classification system used to denote a person's "rank" in college. Individuals are classified as freshmen = 1, sophomores = 2, juniors = 3, or seniors = 4, with the class designation signifying the amount of progress made by the student toward a college degree.

Ordinal-level measurement is quite common in psychology, since it is often impossible to make absolute quantitative measurements of psychological attributes. The major drawback of ordinal-level measurement is that the differences between adjacent classes in the rank ordering are not necessarily equal. This deficiency limits the kinds of statistical analyses possible with ordinal-level data.

Interval-level measurement. An interval-level variable meets the requirements of ordinal-level measurement and also has equal distances between adjacent measurement classes. Interval-level measurement implies the use of a *unit* of measurement: Each measurement category is the same distance from the categories above and below it.

The most commonly cited example of interval-level measurement is the Fahrenheit temperature scale. The scale is clearly both nominal and ordinal and, in addition, has equal intervals between adjacent classes. Thus, the temperature difference between 40°F and 50°F is the same as the difference between 60°F and 70°F. This fact allows us to apply more powerful and sophisticated statistical techniques to data resulting from interval-level measurement than to ordinal- or nominal-level data. The only limitation of interval-level measurement is that the scales resulting from it do not possess an absolute zero point that signifies the complete absence of the attribute being measured. While the Fahrenheit temperature scale has a point labeled 0°, that point is arbitrarily defined and does not indicate the complete absence of temperature. This limitation prevents us from meaningfully using interval-level data to form *ratios* of measurements. That is, it would *not* be valid for us to say that a temperature of 100°F is twice as "hot" as a temperature of 50°F, since both temperatures are referenced to a completely arbitrary zero point.

Ratio-level measurement. This level of measurement is said to be the highest level of measurement, since ratio-level scales have all the characteristics of the other measurement levels and also possess a zero point that represents the absolute absence of the variable being measured. Ratio-level measurement is common in the physical sciences, as represented by measurements of length, mass, voltage, velocity, and pressure. One of the more commonly used ratio-level scales in psychology is the measurement of time, as in the measurement of reaction time or the time required to complete a task. In ratio-level measurement it is meaningful to compare the magnitude of measurements in ratio form: 6 inches is twice as long as 3 inches, and 2 hours is twice as long a time as 1 hour.

When analyzing the data from a psychological experiment or demonstration, a good place to begin is with a determination of the level of measurement that corresponds to your dependent variable. As we shall see, the level of the dependent variable used can have an important impact on the types of statistical analyses that are appropriate for use with the data from a particular experiment.

Computational Notation

To make effective use of the formulae for the various statistical techniques presented in this appendix, it is necessary that the reader have a basic understanding of the notation used in them. Two basic concepts must be understood in order to use most statistical formulae: subscripting of variables and summation notation.

Subscripting of variables. Subscripting enables us to refer to a set of numbers (e.g., data) without actually writing all of them down every time we

need them in a computation. This is accomplished by first choosing an arbitrary letter (usually X or Y) to stand for the variable that we have measured and then adding a subscript (usually i or j) to the variable symbol. This gives us a subscripted variable, X_i (read X sub i), where X indicates the value of a variable, and i indicates which particular observation we are referring to. We can refer to any observation in a set by allowing the subscript i to take on any value from 1 to n, where n is the number of observations in the set. For example, if we were to randomly select 3 students from a psychology class, we could let the numbers 1, 2, and 3 represent the students; in this case n = 3. Now if we let X stand for the ages of the students, we might obtain the following data: $X_1 = 18$, $X_2 = 17$, $X_3 = 18$. Since we can represent these observations by the subscripted variable X_i, with i varying from 1 to 3, we have a convenient shorthand for representing this set of data. In general, if we have a group of n observations, we may denote them by the symbols X_1, X_2, . . . X_n, with X_1 denoting the ith observation.

Summation notation. In many of the statistical procedures presented below, it is necessary to add up a set of scores as a part of the necessary computations. Summation notation provides us with a convenient shorthand way of representing this "adding-up" process. In summation notation, the symbol Σ (the Greek capital letter sigma) stands for the process of summation (adding up). For example,

$$\sum_{i=1}^{n} X_i$$

instructs us to add up all the values of X_i as i varies from 1 to n. That is,

$$\sum_{i=1}^{n} X_i = X_1 + X_2 + X_3 + \cdots + X_n.$$

Summation notation provides us with an increase in precision and economy, thus increasing the readability of our computational formulae.

As an example of the use of summation notation, consider the three psychology students described above and their corresponding ages, $X_1 = 18$, $X_2 = 17$, $X_3 = 18$. To compute the average age of these students, it is necessary to find the sum of their respective ages. We could write this sum as

$$X_1 + X_2 + X_3 = 17 + 18 + 18 = 53,$$

or, using summation notation, as

$$\sum_{i=1}^{n} X_i = 53.$$

If we consider a set of scores with 20 observations (i.e., n = 20), the economy of summation notation becomes quite obvious.

Measures of Central Tendency

It is often necessary (or at least convenient) to be able to characterize an entire set of scores or measurements by just a few statistics. One category of such descriptive statistics is called *measures of central tendency*; these measures produce single numbers that can be thought of as the "typical" or "most likely" observation. We will be concerned with the three most common measures of central tendency: the *mode*, the *median*, and the *arithmetic mean*.

Mode. The mode is the simplest measure of central tendency to obtain, since it requires no actual computations to be performed on the data. The mode is defined as the most frequently occurring value of the variable. That is, for a given set of scores, the mode is that score value that occurs more often than any other score. For example, if the scores for 10 individuals on a 10-point quiz were 2, 4, 5, 6, 6, 7, 7, 7, 9, 9, the mode for this set of scores would be 7, since 7 occurs more often than any other value.

The mode is easy to "compute," but its usefulness is limited by the fact that its value is unaffected by the distribution of any scores other than the modal value. Consider the following set of scores: 1, 1, 2, 2, 3, 3, 4, 7, 7, 7. Here, as in the previous example, the modal value is 7. Note that the values of the mode for these two sets of scores do not in any way reflect the radically different shapes of the two distributions. This clearly shows that the mode uses very little of the information present in a distribution. Thus the mode is generally not the preferred measure of central tendency when it is possible to compute one of the other measures.

Because of its simplicity, the mode can be determined for data at any level of measurement. However, if the data represent nominal-level measurement, the mode is the *only* appropriate measure of central tendency.

Median. The median is defined as that value on the measurement scale above which half of the observations fall and below which half of the observations fall. To find the median of a set of scores, it is necessary to rank order the scores from smallest to largest and then find the middle value—the one with an equal number of scores above and below it. If there are an even number of scores in the set, the median is the average of the middle *pair* of observations.

Since the median is obtained by rank ordering the observations, it cannot be computed unless the data can be meaningfully placed in an order. Thus, computation of the median requires that the observations be at the ordinal, interval, or ratio level of measurement. By definition, the median cannot be computed for nominal-level data. The median

makes use of more of the information in the data than does the mode, since the median is based on the rank order of the observations. The median does not, however, reflect the actual *value* of every observation in the set. This characteristic makes the median useful with very asymmetric distributions, which are commonly found in measures such as annual income or in tasks involving speeded responses (such as reaction times). However, if one wishes the measure of central tendency to reflect the value of each observation, the median is not the measure to use.

Mean. The arithmetic mean is the most widely used measure of central tendency, largely because of its logical appeal and the precise way in which it is defined. Symbolically, the mean is defined as

$$M = \frac{\sum_{i=1}^{n} X_i}{n},$$

where n is the number of observations, X_i represents the variable that was measured, and M is the conventional symbol used for the mean. To find the mean, simply add up the values of the measured variable and then divide this sum by the number of observations. For the data from the first example given earlier, the mean, M, would be

$$M = \frac{2 + 4 + 5 + 6 + 6 + 7 + 7 + 7 + 9 + 9}{10}$$

$$= \frac{62}{10} = 6.2.$$

By definition, every value in the set of observations contributes to the value of the mean. Because of this, the mean is sensitive to the presence of a few very high or very low values in the set of scores. This characteristic limits the usefulness of the mean for describing the central tendency of very asymmetric distributions; in such cases the median is the measure of choice.

The appropriate use of the mean requires that the data represent either interval- or ratio-level measurement, since the actual values of the observations are used in its computation. The mean cannot be meaningfully computed on nominal- or ordinal-level measurements.

Describing the Variability of Data

The measure of central tendency obtained from a set of data provides us with an estimate of the "most typical" value in the set. While this measure provides useful information about the characteristics of the data, it does not give us a complete description of all of the attributes of the data that we might consider important. In addition to a measure of central tendency, it is often necessary for us to be able to describe the *variability* of a set of data, where by variability we mean the extent to which the scores in a set of data differ among themselves.

The most common measures of variability are the *standard deviation* and the related statistic, the *variance*. The variance and the standard deviation are computed using the same steps, with the standard deviation defined as the square root of the variance. Computation of these two statistics is as follows:

$$\text{variance} = SD^2 = \frac{\sum\limits_{i=1}^{n} X_i^2 - \left(\frac{\sum\limits_{i=1}^{n} X_i}{n}\right)^2}{n - 1},$$

where

$$\sum_{i=1}^{n} X_i^2 = X_1^2 + X_2^2 + X_3^2 + \cdots + X_n^2,$$

$$\left(\sum_{i=1}^{n} X_i\right)^2 = (X_1 + X_2 + X_3 + \cdots + X_n)^2,$$

and n = number of observations;

standard deviation = $SD = \sqrt{SD^2}$.

As a computational example, consider the data we used earlier to illustrate the computation of the mean. For our computations, we require the following sums:

$$\sum_{i=1}^{n} X_i = 2 + 4 + 5 + 6 + 6 + 7 + 7 + 7 + 9 + 9$$

$$= 62$$

$$\sum_{i=1}^{n} X_i^2 = 2^2 + 4^2 + \cdots + 9^2 = 426$$

$$n = 10.$$

Thus,

$$SD^2 = \frac{426 - \frac{(62)^2}{10}}{9}$$

$$= \frac{426 - \frac{3844}{10}}{9}$$

$$= \frac{426 - 384.4}{9}$$

$$= \frac{41.6}{9}$$

$$= 4.62$$

and the standard deviation is given by

$$SD = \sqrt{SD^2}$$

$$= \sqrt{4.62}$$

$$= 2.15.$$

(Note: The formula given here for computing the variance and standard deviation is not the formula commonly used to *define* these two statistics. The definitional formula for the variance is

$$SD^2 = \frac{\sum\limits_{i=1}^{n} (X_i - M)^2}{n - 1}.$$

The formula given earlier is a more convenient computational form of this definitional formula.)

Both the variance and standard deviation provide us with useful information concerning the variability (dispersion) of a set of observations. The variance, however, is not particularly useful as a *descriptive* statistic of variability, since it is expressed in terms of squared units of measurement (i.e., if one were measuring height in terms of inches, the variance would be expressed in inches²). (As we shall see later in this appendix, this drawback does not prevent the variance from being extremely important in the derivation of other statistics.) The standard deviation does not share this limitation, since it is expressed in terms of the original units of measurement and thus can be interpreted directly as a measure of the variability exhibited by a set of data.

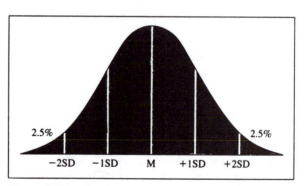

Normal Distribution

The standard deviation is particularly useful in relation to variables that produce what are called *normal distributions*. When graphed, normally distributed variables produce the familiar symmetric, bell-shaped curves often obtained when large numbers of observations are made on a single variable. The measurement of many of the physical characteristics of humans produce normal (or approximately normal) distributions; height, weight, and hat size are just a few examples. In addition, many other variables, such as scores on standardized aptitude tests (e.g., the Scholastic Aptitude Test—SAT), are scaled so as to produce normal distributions. Knowing that a variable is normally distributed enables us to make some fairly precise statements concerning the distribution of the values of that variable. For a normally distributed variable, 68.3% of the observations fall within the interval ranging from 1 standard deviation below the mean to 1 standard deviation above the mean (i.e., ±1 standard deviation unit around the mean). Similarly, 95.4% of the observations fall within ±2 standard deviation units around the mean. Finally, 99.7% of the observations fall within ±3 standard deviation units around the mean. These values hold for any normally distributed variable and provide us with a great deal of information about the characteristics of that variable. For example, the SAT scores are scaled to have a mean of 500 and a standard deviation of 100. (These values have changed somewhat in recent years but will suffice for the sake of illustration.) This means that 68.3% of all persons taking the SAT obtain scores between 400 and 600 (±1 standard deviation unit), and 95.4% obtain scores between 300 and 700 (±2 standard deviation units). Knowing the mean and standard deviation of any normally distributed variable enables us to make these kinds of statements concerning the actual distribution of the scores.

Correlation

Up to this point we have been concerned with descriptive statistics of groups of data, such as the mean and standard deviation. All of these statistics involve only one variable or dimension and are concerned with summarizing large amounts of data. However, we often are interested in determining whether there is a *relationship* between two variables—that is, whether two variables tend to "go together" in any manner. The statistic developed for this purpose is called the *coefficient of correlation*, and it is commonly used in psychological research.

Suppose we consider the (somewhat trivial) question of determining whether there is a relationship between people's heights and weights. To answer this question we could measure a group of students on both variables and obtain a distribution of heights (call this variable X) and a distribution of weights (variable Y). We can get a rough idea of the relationship between these two variables by constructing what is called a scatter diagram. To make a scatter diagram, one constructs a graph with variable X on the abscissa (horizontal axis) and variable Y on the ordinate (vertical axis). Since each person measured yields two scores, we take a person's

score on variable X and first draw an imaginary line up from that point on the abscissa, and then draw another imaginary line across from the point on the ordinate corresponding to that person's score on variable Y. Where these two lines cross we draw a point, and this point represents *one person's* scores on both variables. If we followed these steps for all of the students measured, we would obtain a complete scatter diagram.

Inspection of scatter diagrams can provide us with some approximate information regarding both the direction and the strength of the relationship. A direct or *positive* relationship is shown by a scatter diagram that points upward to the right. (This assumes that the graph follows the convention of having the zero point of each variable at the origin, with increasing values of X to the right on the abscissa and increasing values of Y upward on the ordinate.) If the points fall into no discernible pattern, that is, if they form a more or less circular shape, there is probably no relationship present. If the pattern points upward to the left, a *negative* relationship is shown. The strength of the relationship is shown by how closely the pattern approximates a straight line. If the points fall on a straight line pointing upward to the right, then a perfect positive relationship is present. A straight line pointing upward to the left signifies a perfect negative relationship.

Looking at scatter diagrams provides only an approximate estimate of the direction and strength of a relationship, but the coefficient of correlation gives an exact answer. A convenient computational formula for the correlation coefficient is as follows:

$$r_{xy} = \frac{\Sigma\, X_i Y_i - \dfrac{(\Sigma\, X_i)(\Sigma\, Y_i)}{n}}{\sqrt{\left(\Sigma\, X_i^2 - \dfrac{(\Sigma\, X_i)^2}{n}\right) \cdot \left(\Sigma\, Y_i^2 - \dfrac{(\Sigma\, Y_i)^2}{n}\right)}},$$

where all summations are over $i = 1$ to n; $\Sigma\, X_i Y_i = (X_1 \cdot Y_1) + (X_2 \cdot Y_2) + \cdots + (X_n \cdot Y_n)$; all other summations are as described in previous sections; and r_{xy} is the conventional symbol for the correlation coefficient.

As an example of the computation of the correlation coefficient, consider the following hypothetical scores obtained by 10 students on an English test (X) and a math test (Y), each with 10 points possible.

Student	X	Y
1	4	6
2	7	9
3	9	8
4	4	4

Student	X	Y
5	3	2
6	6	7
7	7	7
8	5	6
9	8	10
10	4	4

The necessary sums are $\Sigma X_i = 57$, $\Sigma X_i^2 = 361$, $\Sigma Y_i = 63$, $\Sigma Y_i^2 = 451$, and $\Sigma X_i Y_i = 398$. Using these values in the formula, we obtain

$$r_{xy} = \frac{398 - \dfrac{(57)(63)}{10}}{\sqrt{\left(361 - \dfrac{(57)^2}{10}\right)\left(451 - \dfrac{(63)^2}{10}\right)}}$$

$$= \frac{398 - 359.1}{\sqrt{361 - 324.9)(451 - 396.9)}}$$

$$= \frac{38.9}{\sqrt{(36.1)(54.1)}}$$

$$= \frac{38.9}{\sqrt{1953.01}} = \frac{38.9}{44.2}$$

$$= +.88.$$

Thus, the value of the correlation coefficient for the hypothetical test data is +.88, which indicates a strong positive relationship between the scores on the two tests.

The value obtained for the correlation coefficient provides information concerning both the direction and the relative strength of the relationship between the two variables. The direction of the relationship is indicated by the sign (+ or −) attached to the correlation coefficient. A positive relationship (positive value of r_{xy}) signifies that as the values of one variable increase, the values of the other variable tend to increase as well. A negative relationship (negative value of r_{xy}) can be interpreted to mean that as the values of one variable increase, the values of the other variable tend to decrease; that is, the relationship between the two variables is an inverse one. The relative strength of the relationship between the two variables is indicated by the absolute value of the correlation coefficient. That is, the fact that one correlation coefficient is positive and one is negative *does not* mean that the positive correlation signifies a stronger relationship. A correlation of −.65 implies a stronger relationship than one of +.40, since the absolute value (ignoring the sign) of −.65 is greater than that of +.45.

Several other characteristics of the correlation coefficient should be mentioned. First, the values of the correlation coefficient can only range from −1.0 to +1.0 (that is, $-1.0 \leq r_{xy} \leq +1.0$). Any computed values of r_{xy} that fall outside of this range indicate that a computational error has occurred. Second, a value for r_{xy} of +.60 does not indicate twice as strong a relationship as an r_{xy} of +.30. Correlation coefficients cannot be used to form meaningful ratios of the strength of relationships. Finally, obtaining a large value of the correlation coefficient does not imply that the two variables are causally related, that is, that the change in the values of one variable *caused* the values of the other variable to change. A nonzero correlation implies only that there is a relationship between the two variables, not that the change in the value of one variable caused a change in the other variable.

Tests on Means

A common problem in psychological research is deciding whether the means from two groups in an experiment are sufficiently different in value to warrant the conclusion that the experimental treatment given to one of the groups produced a "significant" effect. In such situations, we are concerned with testing the hypothesis (termed the *null hypothesis*, H_0) that the difference between the two means is zero:

$$H_0 : \mu_1 - \mu_2 = 0.$$

Note that this is just another way of saying that the two means μ_1 and μ_2 (μ is the lower-case Greek letter mu) are equal. We wish to test this null hypothesis against the *alternative hypothesis*,

$$H_1 : \mu_1 - \mu_2 \neq 0.$$

Hypotheses of this form are tested by using what is called a *t* test on the means. These *t* tests have two basic forms: the *independent samples* test and the *dependent samples* test.

Independent samples test. The independent samples *t* test is used whenever the subjects in the two groups (experimental group vs. control group; Treatment 1 vs. Treatment 2, etc.) are assigned completely at random and the observations made on the subjects in the two groups are independent of each other. The formula for the independent samples *t* test is

$$t = \frac{M_1 - M_2}{\sqrt{SD_p^2 \left(\dfrac{1}{n_1} + \dfrac{1}{n_2}\right)}}$$

$$SD_p^2 = \frac{(n_1 - 1)SD_1^2 + (n_2 - 1)SD_2^2}{n_1 + n_2 - 2}$$

where M_1 = mean of the first group, M_2 = mean of the second group, and $n_1 + n_2 - 2$ is called the degrees of freedom (*df*) associated with this particular test. Computation of the independent samples *t* test requires that we know the mean and variance for Group 1 and the mean and variance for Group 2.

To complete the test, the obtained value of t is compared to a value of the t distribution for the appropriate degrees of freedom obtained from a table of t values. An abbreviated list of the t values corresponding to the .05 level of significance is presented in Table 1. Assuming that H_0 is true, we would expect to obtain a computed value of t equal to (or greater than) the value listed in Table 1 for the correct degrees of freedom only 5% of the time by random or chance variation alone. Thus, if we obtain a value of t greater than the corresponding value from the table, we can feel safe in rejecting H_0 and concluding that the means of the two groups are significantly different at the .05 level of significance; we are inferring that something other than chance factors produced that large a difference.

As an example, consider the following situation. An experimenter wishes to compare the effectiveness of two methods of teaching vocabulary words in a foreign language. A total of 20 students are randomly divided into two equal groups, with each group taught according to one of the methods for a 2-week period. At the end of this 2-week learning period, the students in both groups are given a standardized vocabulary test that yields the following results:

$$M_1 = 70 \qquad\qquad M_2 = 60$$
$$SD_1^2 = 80 \qquad\qquad SD_1^2 = 75$$
$$n_1 = 10 \qquad\qquad n_2 = 10.$$

The computation of t is as follows:

$$SD_p^2 = \frac{(10-1)80 + (10-1)75}{10 + 10 - 2}$$
$$= \frac{(9)80 + (9)75}{18}$$
$$= 77.5$$
$$t = \frac{70 - 60}{\sqrt{77.5\left(\frac{1}{10} + \frac{1}{10}\right)}}$$
$$= \frac{10}{\sqrt{15.5}}$$
$$= \frac{10}{3.937}$$
$$= 2.54.$$

This value of t is then compared to the value obtained from the table for $df = 10 + 10 - 2 = 18$, which yields a table value of 2.101. Since our obtained t value of 2.54 is *greater* than the value of 2.101 obtained from the table, we reject $H_0; \mu_1 - \mu_2 = 0$ and conclude that the alternative hypothesis, $H_1 : \mu_1 - \mu_2 = 0$, is supported by the data. That is, we would conclude that Method 1 of teaching foreign language vocabulary is more effective than Method 2.

Dependent samples test. The dependent samples test is used when some degree of dependency exists between the two groups; subjects are *not* assigned to the two groups in a completely random manner. For example, in the independent samples experiment described above, the teacher could have given the 20 students a test of their ability in the foreign language prior to the beginning of the experiment and then grouped the students into pairs according to their scores on the test; the two students scoring highest would be Pair 1, the next two students Pair 2, and so forth. Then the teacher could have randomly selected one member of Pair 1 to receive the first teaching method and continued this procedure until one member from each pair had been selected for Method 1 and the other

Table 1. *Critical Values of Student's* t *Distribution for Level of Significance (α) of .05 for Two-Tailed Test*

df	t_c
1	12.706
2	4.303
3	3.182
4	2.776
5	2.571
6	2.447
7	2.365
8	2.306
9	2.262
10	2.228
11	2.201
12	2.179
13	2.160
14	2.145
15	2.131
16	2.120
17	2.110
18	2.101
19	2.093
20	2.086
22	2.074
24	2.064
26	2.056
28	2.048
30	2.042
40	2.021
60	2.000
120	1.980
∞	1.960

member of each pair for Method 2. This procedure would tend to reduce the variability between the groups, since each member of the Method 1 group would have a counterpart in the Method 2 group who scored similarly on the initial test.

A very common way of introducing a dependency between the two groups is to have each subject in the experiment serve in both treatment conditions. This is called a *repeated-measures* design, and the data from a study conducted in this manner could be analyzed using the dependent sample *t* test. (Note: To avoid sequence effects in the repeated-measures design, half of the subjects should receive Treatment 1 followed by Treatment 2, with the other half of the subjects receiving the treatments in the reverse order.)

The data from a dependent samples test may be analyzed by using the *direct-differences method*. In this method, a difference score, d_i, is obtained for each *pair* of observations:

$$d_1 = X_1 - X_2 \text{ for Pair 1}$$

$$d_2 = X_1 - X_2 \text{ for Pair 2} \ldots$$

$$d_n = X_1 - X_2 \text{ for Pair } n$$

The value of *t* is then obtained by

$$t_{n-1} = \frac{M_d}{SD_d/\sqrt{n}},$$

where M_d is the mean of the difference scores,

$$M_d = \frac{\sum\limits_{i=1}^{n} d_i}{n},$$

SD_d is the standard deviation of the difference score,

$$SD_d = \sqrt{\frac{\sum d_i^2 - \frac{(\sum d_i)^2}{n}}{n-1}}$$

n = number of *pairs* of observations, and $df = n - 1$.

The value of *t* obtained by the direct-differences method is then compared to the values of *t* from Table 1 in the same manner as in the independent samples case described above, except that the degrees of freedom for this test are given by $n - 1$ (one fewer than the number of pairs). The logic of the test and the hypotheses tested are basically the same as those described above.

As an example, consider the following data obtained in a repeated-measures experiment that used 8 subjects:

Subject	1	2	3	4	5	6	7	8
Condition A	12	31	17	17	8	14	25	4
Condition B	8	17	12	19	5	6	20	3
d_i	4	14	5	−2	3	8	5	1

The necessary sums are

$$\sum_{i=1}^{n} d_i = 38$$

and

$$\sum_{i=1}^{n} d_i^2 = 340.$$

The mean difference score is

$$M_d = \frac{\sum d_i}{n} = \frac{38}{8} = 4.75.$$

The standard deviation of the difference scores, SD_d, is

$$SD_d = \sqrt{\frac{340 - \frac{38^2}{8}}{8 - 1}}$$

$$= \sqrt{\frac{340 - 180.5}{7}}$$

$$= 4.77.$$

The value of *t* is given by

$$t = \frac{4.75}{4.77/\sqrt{8}}$$

$$= \frac{4.75}{1.68}$$

$$= 2.81.$$

with $df = 8 - 1 = 7$.

To test the hypothesis that the means of the two conditions are the same, $H_0 : \mu_1 - \mu_2 = 0$, we compare our obtained *t* value to the value of *t* from Table 1 when $df = 7$. Since our obtained value of 2.81 is greater than the table value of 2.365, we reject the null hypothesis and conclude that there is a significant difference between the means of the two conditions at the .05 level of significance. Had our computed value been less than the value from the table, we would have been forced to conclude that the present data provided no evidence that there was a difference in effectiveness between our two treatment conditions.

Analysis of Frequency Data

A common procedure in psychological experimentation involves making observations that permit nominal measurement of each observational unit (person, animal, etc.) with respect to two variables. For example, students can be classified both with respect to sex (male or female) and academic major. For data of this type, the *frequencies* of the various combinations of levels of the two variables may be tabulated in a *contingency table*. With data of this form, we are generally concerned with testing the null hypothesis which states that the two classification variables are *independent*, against the alternative hypothesis that they are not independent.

We will consider only the simplest kind of test of independence: the chi-square (χ^2) test of independence for a 2×2 contingency table. (More general procedures for tests of independence for larger contingency tables can be found in any of the suggested readings listed at the end of this appendix.) To compute the chi square test of independence, we represent the cell and marginal frequencies with the following notation:

A	*B*	*A + B*
C	*D*	*C + D*
A + C	*B + D*	*N*

Chi-square is then calculated as follows:

$$\chi^2 = \frac{N(AD - BC)^2}{(A + B)(C + D)(A + C)(B + D)}$$

As an example of the computation of the chi square test of independence, consider the following hypothetical data from 100 patients in a psychiatric institution:

	Treatment method		
Evaluation	Therapy A	Therapy B	
Improvement	20	40	60
No improvement	25	15	40
	45	55	100

We want to test whether there is an association between treatment method and subsequent evaluation. Computation of chi square is as follows:

$$\chi^2 = \frac{100(20 \cdot 15 - 40 \cdot 25)^2}{(60 \cdot 40 \cdot 45 \cdot 55)}$$
$$= 8.25.$$

This value of chi square is then compared to a tabled value of chi square for the appropriate degrees of freedom and level of significance. For a 2×2 contingency table, the degrees of freedom are always equal to 1. Thus, the tabled value of chi square for $df = 1$ at the .05 level of significance is 3.84. Since our obtained value of chi square, 8.25, exceeds the tabled value of 3.84, we reject the hypothesis that the two classification variables are independent and conclude that an association does exist between the treatment method used and subsequent psychological evaluation. If our obtained value had been less than 3.84, we would have been led to conclude that no evidence existed in the present data which indicated an association existed between the two variables.

A caution concerning the chi square test of independence is in order: The test given above should not be used for cases in which the cell frequencies are small (less than 10). A test of independence is still possible in such cases, but the computational procedure is somewhat different. The appropriate formula may be found in the references listed at the end of this appendix.

Suggested Reading

Coladarci, A., & Coladarci, T. *Elementary descriptive statistics: For those who think they can't.* Belmont, CA: Wadsworth, 1980. Provides a straightforward, clear introduction to descriptive statistics. This book would be especially useful as a review and extension of the material presented in Sections 1–5 of this appendix.

Ferguson, G. A. *Statistical analysis in psychology and education* (5th ed.). New York: McGraw-Hill, 1981. Provides a comprehensive treatment of statistical analysis of variance techniques appropriate for experiments employing more than two treatment conditions.

Weinberg, S. L., & Goldberg, K. P. *Basic statistics for education and the behavioral sciences.* Boston: Houghton Mifflin, 1979. Provides a clear, thorough introduction to statistical analysis.

APPENDIX C

A Bibliography of Do-It-Yourself
Laboratory and Classroom Apparatuses

Animal Apparatuses

A. Activity

Christiano, J. M. Setting up a high school psychology laboratory. *Behavioral and Social Science Teacher*, 1975, 2(2), 34–37. A general description of the problems and advantages of setting up a high school psychology laboratory. Describes how a lab may be started from scratch and how equipment may be built. Discusses the need for well-trained student lab assistants.

Pfister, H. P., Mudge, R. R., & Harcombe, A. O. A multipurpose activity platform utilized in the open-field setting. *Behavior Research Methods and Instrumentation*, 1978, 10(1), 21–22. Describes an automated multipurpose activity platform (MAP) that can be used to measure activity in the horizontal plane. The MPA has no built-in data storage facility and needs to be interfaced with a recording system. The system has been used successfully in measuring open-field activity of rats.

Stong, C. L. An apparatus for simulating high altitudes and testing their effects on small animals. *Scientific American*, 1965, 213(3), 239–254. A complete review of the procedure and results on testing the physiological effects of high altitudes on white rats, with a detailed description of the experimental apparatus involved (diagrams).

Weiss, C. S. An inexpensive animal laboratory course. *Teaching of Psychology*, 1980, 7, 103. This article describes an animal laboratory course that is both inexpensive and compact (easily stores on a bookshelf), yet permits students to conduct a wide variety of behavioral investigations comparable to those performed with rodents.

B. Feeding

Bostwick, A. D., & Porter, J. J. An efficient, inexpensive food hopper for monitoring feeding habits of rats. *Behavior Research Methods and Instrumentation*, 1977, 9(5), 471–472. Describes a food hopper designed for the constant monitoring of home-cage free-feeding patterns of rats. The apparatus is inexpensive and is designed to attach to standard rat housing cages.

Stong, C. L. An amateur asks: Does a hummingbird find its way to nectar through its sense of smell? *Scientific American*, 1960, 202(2), 157–166. A brief introduction to the olfactory sense phenomenon in birds, incorporated in a discussion of instinct vs. learned behavior. Gives a complete description of an experiment used to test the sense of smell in wild hummingbirds, including method, procedure, and results.

C. Learning

Abplanalp, P. Stabilized construction of a Hebb-Williams maze. *Behavior Research Methods and Instrumentation*, 1972, 4(3), 174. Describes a method of constructing a Hebb-Williams maze which enables the internal walls to be conveniently moved about to construct different pathways from startbox to goal. The arrangement is cheaper and less cumbersome than building a separate maze for each problem.

Abramson, C. I., Collier, D. M., & Marcucella, H. An aversive conditioning unit for ants. *Behavior Research Methods and Instrumentation*, 1977, 9(6), 505–507. Describes an apparatus for studying aversive conditioning in ants. The aversive stimulus is mechanically produced vibration, and responses are recorded automatically by an infrared photocell system. Preliminary data on the acquisition and extinction of escape responses in three ants are presented.

Etscorn, F. A home tank aquatic shuttlebox. *Behavior Research Methods and Instrumentation*, 1974, 6(1), 77. Annotation not available.

Hay, D. A., & Crossley, S. A. The design of mazes to study *Drosophila* behavior. *Behavior Genetics*, 1977, 7(5), 389–402. Although mazes have been widely used in studying phototaxis, geotaxis, and more recently, learning in *Drosophila*, there is no uniformity in maze design, and little is known about the effects such apparatus differences may have on behavior. The new maze design described here is based on T-junctions molded individually in acrylic and provides an inexpensive and standardized means of building mazes to any desired specification. The need for uniformity in maze design is demonstrated with an experiment on 3 variables at the start of a maze that affect the subsequent response of 4 strains of *D. melanogaster* in different ways. Some applications for future *Drosophila* research using mazes are considered (25 references included).

Katz, A. N. An inexpensive animal learning exercise for huge introductory laboratory classes. *Teaching of Psychology*, 1978, 5, 91. Describes how barriers of expense, space, and maintenance were overcome by employing planaria as experimental subjects and building a cheap yet effective learning chamber.

Londo, N. A runway for the cockroach. *Behavior Research Methods and Instrumentation*, 1970, 2(3), 118–119. Describes a runway and training procedure that minimizes handling. Acquisition and extinction trials are presented to illustrate the technique.

Millar, R. D., & Malott, R. W. An inexpensive discrimination apparatus for classroom use with pigeons. *Psychological Record*, 1968, 18(3), 369–372. Presents an apparatus for classroom use with pigeons which is similar in function to the Wisconsin General Test apparatus.

Plant, L. The gerbil jar: A basic home experience in operant conditioning. *Teaching of Psychology*, 1980, 7, 109. Describes a homemade operant chamber for use with gerbils and includes several appropriate conditioning tasks.

Potts, A., & Bitterman, M. E. A runway for the fish. *Behavior Research Methods and Instrumentation*, 1968, 1(1), 26–27. Describes a runway and a training procedure. Acquisition and extinction curves for 12 goldfish trained in space trials are plotted in terms of 3 measures.

Stong, C. L. A simple analogue computer that simulates Pavlov's dogs. *Scientific American*, 1963, 208(6), 159–166. An introduction to Pavlov's research on classical conditioning, with an explanation of his original experiment. Includes a description of the function of the analogue laboratory and instructions for implementing a collection of basic experiments in classical conditioning (graphs and illustrative diagrams included).

Stong, C. L. How to study learning in the sow bug and photographing live crustaceans. *Scientific American*, 1967, 216(5), 142–148. Detailed description of two experiments. The first involves maze learning in the sow bug, an invertebrate that must avoid direct light in order to prevent evaporation of its body fluids. The second describes procedures for recording the anatomical details of live crustaceans by high-speed photomicrography.

Stong, C. L. The color vision of pigeons is tested in a Skinner box. *Scientific American*, 1970, 223(4), 124–129. A guide to constructing a Skinner box in which pigeons can learn to reward themselves for pecking at light of a predetermined color. Gives a detailed description of the apparatus and circuitry, with illustrations. Also describes simple experiments and their results.

Stong, C. L. The voiceprints of birdsongs and cockroaches in a maze. *Scientific American*, 1974, 230(2), 110–115. A two-part article. Part 1 describes how a young scientist tape-records birdsongs and reproduces them on an electrocardiograph. Part 2 discusses the effects of temperature change on the retention of learning in cockroaches. Detailed directions for building apparatus for both experiments are given.

Stong, C. L. How to build and work with a Skinner box for the training of small animals. *Scientific American*, 1975, 233(5), 128–134. A class activity. Describes in detail how to build a Skinner box (or where to buy a kit for building one). Explains how to train and care for the animals and how to analyze and graph data from simple experiments.

Wise, L. M., & Pope, M. S. An inexpensive discriminative Y-maze. *Psychological Record*, 1969, 19(1), 93–94. Describes a Y-shaped maze designed to minimize the handling of subjects and to increase operating efficiency. Construction is simple and inexpensive.

Zych, K. A., Raymond, B., McHale, M. W., & Allen, H. A new runway for goldfish. *Psychological Record*, 1972, 22(1), 121–123. Describes the development of a betta tank with a built-in runway. The apparatus permits housing goldfish in the same water that circulates in the runway. Subjects need not be removed from the runway for the duration of study.

D. Observation

Stong, C. L. How to collect and preserve the delicate webs of spiders. *Scientific American*, 1963, *208*(2), 159–166. A description of the webs that different spiders spin and where to look for them. Includes illustrations and directions for spraying the webs with lacquer and mounting them.

Stong, C. L. The joys of culturing spiders and investigating their webs. *Scientific American*, 1972, *227*(6), 108–111. A class activity in which students catch spiders, build boxes to house them, observe patterns of web-building, and conduct simple experiments. A detailed how-to guide to the study of spider behavior.

Stong, C. L. The pleasures and problems of raising snails in the home. *Scientific American*, 1975, *232*(2), 104–107. A do-it-yourself guide to raising snails and experimenting with their behavior. Tells where to obtain the snails, how to build them a home, and what to feed them. Gives a detailed diagram of snail anatomy and suggestions for observing snail behavior.

E. Taste Studies

Marks, H. E. A simple, inexpensive apparatus to measure taste preference behavior in mice. *Journal of Biological Psychology*, 1977, *19*(2), 20–21. Describes a preference-testing apparatus consisting of a plastic cage, 2 plastic pipes, 2 small specimen bottles, and 2 rubber stoppers. Only 1 animal out of 80 failed to adapt to the preference cages within the 6 days allotted for adaptation.

General Apparatuses

A. Graphic Recorder

Stong, C. L. An inexpensive machine to record observational data automatically. *Scientific American*, 1966, *215*(1), 114–118. A detailed description of how to build a simple graphic recorder for use in recording observational data, including an explanation of how each component functions (illustrative diagrams).

B. Observation Windows

Burton, R. V. An inexpensive and portable means for one-way observation. *Child Development*, 1971, *42*(3), 959–962. Annotation not available.

Horowitz, H. Observation room windows. *American Psychologist*, 1969, *24*(3), 304–308. Presents general criteria for observation-room windows. Various glazing materials available for proper lighting and the typical transmission and reflection characteristics of each, acoustical factors relating to sound control, and general design considerations are discussed.

Lott, D. F., & Woll, R. J. A device permitting one-way vision without a mirror image. *Perceptual and Motor Skills*, 1966, *23*(2), 533–534. Describes a device that makes it possible for the experimenter to observe subjects while subjects see neither the experimenter nor reflections of themselves. The basic optical principles and several suggested applications are presented.

Passman, R. H. The smoked plastic screen: An alternative to the one-way mirror. *Journal of Experimental Child Psychology*, 1974, *17*(2), 374–376. Describes a double-thickness, smoked-plastic screen as an alternative to the one-way mirror. Relative to the glass mirror, the use of the plastic screen provides a safe, nondistracting, durable, lightweight, and inexpensive method for unobserved viewing without an appreciable loss in light transmission.

C. Slide Transparencies

Bushell, D., Jr. A rapid method for making inexpensive slide projector transparencies. *Journal of the Experimental Analysis of Behavior*, 1968, *11*(23), 172. Methods and materials are described. In contrast to R. D. Petre's method, this method "eliminates the need to handle 3 sheets of material and special coloring materials for each slide."

D. Stimulus Control

Cox, V. C., & Smith, R. G. A concentric bipolar electrode for use in small animals. *Perceptual and Motor Skills*, 1967, *24*(1), 205–206. A description is provided of a rigid bipolar concentric electrode suitable for recording and stimulation with small animals. Details concerning construction materials and fabrication technique are also provided.

E. Scoring Exams

Tauber, Robert T. An efficient and effective handscoring system for tests, the Quick-Key exam scoring system, consists of a scoring stencil and student answer sheets. The stencil can accommodate up to 100 multiple-choice or true–false questions, with up to 5 responses (*a, b, c, d, e*) available for each question. Quick-Key scoring stencils are $0.35 each; Quick-Key answer sheets are $11 per ream of 500. Both scoring stencils and student answer sheets are available from TTK Communication Products, 3892 Gay Road, Erie, PA 16510.

Apparatuses for Research With Humans

A. Activity

Kohn, A., & Brill, M. An introductory demonstration laboratory produced entirely by undergraduates. *Teaching of Psychology*, 1981, 8, 133. A detailed description of the planning and production of an Introductory Demonstration Laboratory (IDL) by undergraduate students at Oakland University.

B. Auditory Perception

Huggins, A. W. Accurate delays for auditory feedback experiments. *Quarterly Journal of Experimental Psychology*, 1967, 19(1), 78–80. Describes a way of modifying a tape recorder for producing accurately controllable delays for experiments with delayed auditory feedback. Any value of dealy from 80 msec to 1.2 sec can be obtained to the nearest msec, and the range can be extended by some minor changes. The delay is continuously monitored on a digital electronic timer.

C. Biofeedback

Heisel, D. M. *The biofeedback guide: Affiliating with excellence.* New York: Gordon & Breach, 1977, 269 pp. Describes a variety of devices and techniques that can be used to experience biofeedback. Biofeedback hardware, such as alpha brain wave monitors, and biofeedback software strategies for individuals and groups are discussed.

D. Learning

Goldstein, S. R. A simple variable-interval, variable-ratio generation for student use. *Teaching of Psychology Newsletter*, May 1973, p. 14. Describes an easily constructed Roulette-like device which signals the delivery of random events appropriate to any variable schedule desired.

Munro, D. An inexpensive automatic material reward dispenser for use with children. *Bulletin of the British Psychological Society*, 1970, 23(80), 194. Describes the mechanism and operation of an inexpensive device that can deliver small rewards such as sweets and peanuts in material-reward experiments.

E. Psychophysiology

Klostrehalfen, W. Teaching of psychophysiology: Student apparatus for monitoring skin conductance. *Teaching of Psychology*, 1981, 8, 243. Describes the construction of inexpensive, battery-driven apparatus that can be used in monitoring skin conductance.

F. Visual Perception

Benjamin, L. T., Jr. Perceptual demonstrations—Or, what to do with an equipment budget of $75. *Teaching of Psychology*, 1976, 3(1), 37–39. A collection of ideas for equipment and visual materials to be used in a course in perception, including displacement goggles, visual cliff, Pulfrich apparatus, distorted room and trapezoidal window, Muller-Lyer apparatus, and overhead transparencies and slides. Also includes additional references that can be used to further experimentation and/or class demonstration.

Cowan, T. M. Creating illusions of movement by an overhead projector. *Teaching of Psychology*, 1974, 1(2), 80–82. Describes various ways in which an overhead projector can be used with simple constructions to produce different visual effects for a classroom demonstration. Includes eight different types of visual effects: the phi phenomenon, Michotte's perceptual causality, the Fujii and Johnson illusions, the cycloid illusion, and three complex constructions. Also included are illustrative figures for utilizing the visual effects.

Fried, R. A simple additive color mixer for exploration of the color solid. *Bulletin of the Psychonomic Society*, 1975, 5(4), 325–326. Describes a simple additive color mixer requiring only 3 degrees of mechanical translation and permitting manipulation of hue, saturation, and intensity of 3 primary light sources.

Jankowicz, A. Z., & Heffernan, D. An inexpensive unit for demonstrations of the phi and autokinetic phenomena. *Perceptual and Motor Skills*, 1977, 45(1), 69–70. Describes a small apparatus for demonstrating the phi phenomenon and the autokinetic effect. Circuit diagrams for construction of the device are included.

Larson, J. H. The Pulfrich illusion—A twist for the simple pendulum. *Journal of College*

Science Teaching, 1979, *9*, 89–90. Describes simple instructions for a laboratory activity—the Pulfrich illusion. Includes a basic explanation of the Pulfrich illusion plus some other possible hypotheses developed by students.

Mansueto, C. S., & Adevia, G. Development and evaluation of a portable rod and frame test. *Journal of Psychosomatic Research*, 1967, *11*(2), 207–211. Describes a miniaturized rod-and-frame apparatus developed and tested on 50 subjects. Although ranks on the two tests correlated highly ($P = .91$), there was a systematic difference between the mean scores on the two tests. The miniaturized test seemed to be consistently easier for the subjects—there was a mean difference of approximately 1.6 degrees, significant at the .01 level, between the two tests. After the apparatus was altered, this difference disappeared. Ranks of scores on the test were shown to approximate those of error scores obtained on Witkin's standard rod-and-frame test ($P = .97$).

Morris, J. B. The rod-and-frame box: A portable version of the rod-and-frame test. *Perceptual and Motor Skills*, 1967, *25*(1), 152. Annotation not available.

Oltman, P. K. A portable rod-and-frame apparatus. *Perceptual and Motor Skills*, 1968, *26*(2), 503–506. Subjects were 83 female and 80 male college students. Scores on the portable apparatus test correlated .89 with scores obtained on Witkin's original rod-and-frame test.

Parrott, G. L. Techniques of teaching perception and social processes. *High School Behavioral Science*, 1976, *3*(2), 80–82. Details classroom and home experiments with M. Sherrifs' autokinetic phenomenon which use easily available equipment. Ways of building a tachistoscope with a slide projector and a folding camera are presented, along with a schematic design.

Rodgers, W. A., Mayhew, J. E., & Frisby, J. P. A simple apparatus for measuring visual illusions of orientation. *Perception*, 1975, *4*(4), 475–476. Describes a small, economical, and portable device that can be used to study both simultaneous and successive orientation illusions in a systematic fashion (e.g., allowing psychophysical functions to be plotted relating size of illusion to orientation of an inducing figure). The device is suitable for teaching as well as research, and its all-purpose nature allows students to carry out projects of their own design.

Rouse, R. O., & Tarpy, R. M. A simple tachistoscope for student labs. *Behavior Research Methods and Instrumentation*, 1969, *1*(4), 156–157. Describes an inexpensive tachistoscope that utilizes a camera shutter to control exposure duration and a potentiometer to vary light intensity. Stimuli can be drawn or typed on 3×5 inch index cards.

Stong, C. L. Moiré patterns provide both recreation and some analogues for solving problems. *Scientific American*, 1964, *211*(5), 134–142. Includes (a) numerous instructions for creating different types of moiré patterns, (b) some of the visual effects produced, (c) an address for ordering kits containing more precise patterns for more interesting experiments, and (d) some illustrative examples of moiré patterns.

Stong, C. L. Generating visual illusions with two kinds of apparatus. *Scientific American*, 1971, *224*(3), 110–114. Two simple illustrations of optical illusions. Directions are also given for building two instruments with which students can investigate time-related phenomena in the sense of vision that account for illusions such as motion pictures and television.

Walker, J. L. Visual illusions that can be achieved by putting a dark filter over one eye. *Scientific American*, 1978, *238*(3), 142–143; 146; 148–153. Includes instructions for setting up a demonstration of the Pulfrich illusion and suggestions for variations of the illusion. Discusses how visual adaptation plays a major role in the illusion and describes other experiments dealing with visual latency (diagrams and graphs).

APPENDIX D

Invertebrates in the Classroom
Charles I. Abramson

Laboratory courses in animal behavior offer university and high school students a unique educational experience. While attempting to maintain or increase the quality of such experiences, instructors can choose among several low-cost programs using gerbils (Hunt & Shields, 1978; Plant, 1980), chickens (Ackil & Ward, 1982; Rowland, Jordan, & Orson, 1984), or fishes (Weiss, 1980).

This appendix presents an inexpensive program using invertebrates in the classroom.

Although invertebrates are standard subjects in many biology courses, their potential value for psychology courses is not well-known. To familiarize psychology instructors with the many uses of invertebrates in conditioning experiments, the invertebrate program is presented in tabular form. The reader will need to consult the relevant references to obtain details for any demonstration. The invertebrates chosen for this program are ants, earthworms, honeybees, and planarians. They were selected on the basis of laboratory adaptability, availability of apparatus, and unequivocal demonstrations of learning ability.

Invertebrates offer several advantages over more traditional laboratory animals. First, they are inexpensive to procure and maintain. Cockroaches, for example, can survive without food and water for 30 days (Longo, 1970). They can be ordered from commercial suppliers or brought from home. Second, students can train their own subjects in a variety of mazes, runways, shuttle boxes, and operant chambers that cost a few dollars rather than hundreds of dollars. The apparatus can often be manufactured from plastic tubes and connectors. Third, invertebrates can easily be used under the proper conditions (McConnell, 1967a; Ratner, 1967) to demonstrate principles of the comparative analysis of learning, the biochemistry of learning, behavioral pharmacology, physiological psychology, and economics. Fourth, students can take part in some of the classic controversies in animal behavior such as the relative importance of stimulus–stimulus (SS) versus stimulus–response (SR) associations, the learning of planarians, taste-aversion

learning, RNA transfer experiments, and the role of genetic versus environmental factors in learning.

To assist the instructor in preparing demonstrations, this article is divided into four sections: (a) review articles, (b) procuring and maintaining subjects, (c) apparatus, and (d) demonstrations. For convenience, tables accompany each of these sections.

Review Articles
The most comprehensive series of reviews about invertebrate learning appear in Corning, Dyal, and Willows (1973, 1975). Volume 1 of this three-volume set includes chapters on protozoans, planarians, and earthworms. The learning of crabs, snails, bees, ants, and roaches is covered in Volume 2. The final volume contains discussions of octopus and plant learning. Other reviews include the chemical changes associated with invertebrate learning (Corning & Ratner, 1967; Thorpe & Davenport, 1964), foraging behavior (Hassell & Southwood, 1978), and statements regarding the importance of invertebrate learning in behavior theory (Farley & Alkon, 1985; Quinn, 1984; Sahley, 1984). Instructors interested in neuroanatomy and physiology can find much material in Bullock and Horridge (1965) and, to a lesser extent, in Corning et al. (1973, 1975). Instructors are encouraged to consult Table 1 to obtain reviews on specific invertebrates. All of the reviews contain information on learning; many also include suggestions on how to ensure stable performance.

Procuring and Maintaining Subjects
When invertebrates are purchased from commercial suppliers, instructions on feeding and maintenance typically accompany each order. If additional information is required (e.g., materials for nest construction), it can be found in Lutz, Welch, Galtsoff, and Needham (1937/1959) and in R. L. Best (1978). Commercially constructed nests for ants, bees, earthworms, and fruitflies are available from Connecticut Valley Biological Supply Company. Table 2 presents a list of suppliers and their ad-

Table 1. *Review Articles*

Animal	Source
Ant, roach	Alloway (1973)
Bee	Wells (1973); Menzel & Bitterman (1983)
Earthworm	Ratner (1967); Dyal (1973)
Fruitfly	McGuire (1984); Tully (1984)
Housefly	McGuire (1984)
Planarian	McConnell (1967b); Corning & Kelly (1973); Corning & Riccio (1970)

dresses as well as some of the invertebrates that can be purchased.

Apparatus

There is a rich variety of apparatus available for the study of invertebrate behavior. Descriptions of this equipment can be found in published reports. Most apparatus can be constructed from inexpensive materials; however, some can be purchased commercially. For example, a planarian maze/classical conditioning arena, which eliminates handling, is available from Connecticut Valley Biological Supply Company, as is a fruitfly conditioning chamber suitable for genetic analysis. The type of apparatus reported in the literature ranges from simple runways and mazes to automated shuttle boxes and operant chambers (see Table 3). A major advantage of an automated apparatus is that it minimizes handling and, depending on the type of invertebrate used, minimizes the emotional reactions associated with using "bugs" in the classroom. Nevertheless, an automated apparatus is more difficult to construct. When using an apparatus, it is often desirable to program contingencies automatically. To demonstrate the philosophy of an invertebrate pro-

Table 2. *Commercial Suppliers of Invertebrate Material*

Animal	Source
Bee, fruitfly, housefly	Carolina Biological Supply Company Burlington, NC 27215
Ant, earthworm, planarian	Connecticut Valley Biological Supply Company Southampton, MA 01073
Ant	Uncle Milton Industries 10459 West Jefferson Boulevard Culver City, CA 90230

Table 3. *Instrumentation Used in the Study of Invertebrate Behavior*

Type	Source
Unautomated	
Runway	
Ant	Abramson, Miler, & Mann (1982)
Earthworm	Reynierse & Ratner (1964)
Roach	Longo (1970)
Maze	
Ant	Schneirla (1933), Vowles (1964)
Bee	Menzel & Erber (1972)
Earthworm	Datta (1962)
Fruitfly	Dudai (1977), Drudge & Platt (1979)
Roach	Longo (1964)
Planarian	J. B. Best & Rubinstein (1962), Corning (1964)
Free-flying situation (bee)	Couvillon & Bitterman (1980), Abramson (1986)
Automated	
Operant chamber	
Ant	Abramson, Collier, & Marcucella (1977)
Bee	Sigurdson (1981a, 1981b)
Planarian	Crawford & Skeen (1967)
Roach	Rubadeau & Conrad (1963)
Shuttle box	
Ant	Abramson et al. (1977, 1982)
Bee	Abramson (1986)
Housefly	Leeming & Little (1977)
Running wheel	
Earthworm	Marian & Abramson (1982)
Fruitfly	DeJianne, McGuire, & Pruzan-Hotchkiss (1985)
Housefly	Miller, Bruner, & Fukuto (1971)
Roach	Ball (1972)
Programming equipment	
Calculator	Robinson (1979)
Computer	Nicholls & Potter (1982)
Integrated circuit	Wolach (1979)

gram being low in cost and flexible, several references to inexpensive programmers are included in Table 3.

Demonstrations

Table 4 cites references that will enable an instructor to produce demonstrations of classical, instrumental, and avoidance conditioning. There is also a

Table 4. *Demonstrations of Invertebrate Learning Suitable for the Classroom*

Animal	Initial Demonstration	Manipulation
	Classical Conditioning	
Bee	Sigurdson (1981a); Bitterman, Menzel, Fietz, & Schäfer (1983); Abramson (1986)	CS preexposure: Bitterman et al. (1983); Abramson & Bitterman (1986). Compound conditioning: Couvillon & Bitterman (1982); Couvillon, Klosterhalfen, & Bitterman (1983). Second-order conditioning: Bitterman et al. (1983).
Earthworm	Ratner & Miller (1959a); Peeke, Herz, & Wyers (1967)	CS–US interval: Ratner & Miller (1959b); Wyers, Peeke, & Herz (1964); Herz, Peeke, & Wyers (1967). Intertrial interval: Ratner & Miller (1959b); Ratner & Stein (1965). Reinforcement probability: Wyers et al. (1964).
Planarian	Thompson & McConnell (1955); Griffard (1963); Fantl & Nevin (1965); Block & McConnell (1967); Corning & Freed (1968)	
	Instrumental Conditioning	
Ant	Schneirla (1943); Vowles (1964); Martinsen & Kimeldorf (1972); Stratton & Coleman (1972); Abramson (1981a); Morgan (1981); Abramson (1981b)	Partial reinforcement: Fleer & Wyers (1963); Ramos (1966). Reinforcement probability: Simmel & Ramos (1965); Fleer (1972). Time allocation: DeCarlo & Abramson (1989).
Bee	Couvillon & Bitterman (1980); Sigurdson (1981a)	Contrast: Couvillon & Bitterman (1984); Sigurdson (1981a). Delay of reinforcement: Couvillon & Bitterman (1980). Partial reinforcement: Robacker & Ambrose (1978); Sigurdson (1981a, 1981b). Probability learning, reversal learning: Sigurdson (1981a).
Earthworm	Datta (1962); Zellner (1966)	Intertrial interval, reversal learning: Datta (1962).
Fruitfly	Quinn, Harris, & Benzer (1974); Dudai (1977); Booker & Quinn (1981); Hewitt, Fulker, & Hewitt (1983); DeJianne, McGuire, & Pruzan-Hotchkiss (1985)	US intensity: Dudai (1977)
Roach	Szymanski (1912); Ebeling, Wagner, & Reierson (1966); Ebeling, Reierson, & Wagner (1968); Freckleton & Wahlsten (1968); Longo (1970); Pritchatt (1970)	

(Table 4 continued on next page)

(Table 4: Demonstrations—*continued from previous page*)

Animal	Initial Demonstration	Manipulation
Signalled Avoidance		
Ant	Abramson (1983)	
Bee	Abramson (1986)	
Earthworm	Ray (1968)	
Roach	Chen, Aranda, & Luco (1970)	
Unsignalled Avoidance		
Bee	Abramson (1986)	
Roach	Longo (1964)	
Special Topics		
Drugs		
Ant	Kostowski, Beck, & Meszaros (1965); Kostowski & Tarchalska (1972)	
Earthworm	Arbit (1964)	
Genetic analysis (fruitfly)	Quinn et al. (1974); Dudai (1977); Booker & Quinn (1981); Hewitt et al. (1983)	
Lesions		
Ant	Vowles (1964, 1967)	
Earthworm	Ratner & Miller (1959b); Ratner & Stein (1965); Zellner (1966)	

section of that table, labeled *Special Topics*, that cites experiments concerned with physiological and genetic manipulations. An attempt was made to select experiments that could be performed in a two-hour laboratory period, although this was not always possible. Where possible, experiments that use controls were selected; however, some uncontrolled experiments were intentionally included. It has been my experience that students obtain a stronger foundation in experimental design when they are asked to interpret a poorly controlled experiment than when they are simply told to follow the instructions of one that is well-controlled. Of course, nothing prevents the instructor from improving a deficient design. For convenience, the experiments are listed under general headings. If more detailed information is required, such as class of reinforcer (i.e., appetitive or aversive), simply consult the reference list.

Conclusion

Over the past several years, I have used invertebrates as a supplement to rodent programs, as a source for independent student projects, and for lecture demonstrations. Invertebrates are well-suited for lecture demonstrations because they are easily transported and can be placed on an overhead projector for mass viewing. The choice behav-

ior of an ant, for instance, can be demonstrated to a large audience by placing a T-maze on the projector.

In a laboratory course, the ability to supplement rodent experiments with invertebrates adds flexibility. Students can explore a problem, such as reversal learning, across the evolutionary scale or can study a series of problems with one class of organism. Especially appealing is the ability to conduct classical conditioning experiments without being limited to conditioned suppression or the general activity conditioning of rats confined in student-operant conditioning chambers. Invertebrate experiments are also a wonderful source for independent student projects and provide a data base to test the generality of the results and interpretations of vertebrate experiments.

Although I have only informal data supporting the benefits of using invertebrates, there is no reason to believe that the intellectual rewards of an experimental animal course or animal demonstration depend on vertebrates. In fact, some of the most difficult experiments in psychology, such as those involving lesions, cannibalistic transfer, and genetic variations, can be performed inexpensively only with invertebrates.

The material cited enables an instructor or student to acquire background information, to maintain various invertebrates, and to create automated or manual demonstrations on a wide range of topics with minimal expense. A laboratory course based entirely on invertebrates may be a bit too radical, although, with a severely limited budget, there is no reasonable alternative that permits as much flexibility.

References

Abramson, C. I. (1981a). Passive avoidance in the California harvester ant *Pogonmyremex californicus. Journal of General Psychology, 104,* 29–40.

Abramson, C. I. (1981b, April). *Resistance to extinction as a function of reinforcement magnitude and punishment in the harvester ant.* Paper presented at the meeting of the Eastern Psychological Association, New York.

Abramson, C. I. (1986). *Aversive conditioning in honeybees (Apis mellifera). Journal of Comparative Psychology, 100,* 108–116.

Abramson, C. I., & Bitterman, M. E. (1986). *Latent inhibition in honeybees (Apis mellifera). Animal Learning and Behavior, 14,* 184–189.

Abramson, C. I., Collier, D. M., & Marcucella, H. (1977). An aversive conditioning unit for ants. *Behavior Research Methods and Instrumentation, 9,* 505–507.

Abramson, C. I., Miler, J., & Mann, D. W. (1982). An olfactory shuttlebox and runway for insects. *Journal of Mind and Behavior, 3,* 151–159.

Abramson, C. I. (1983, April). *Demonstration of discretetrial signaled avoidance learning in the carpenter ant (Componotus herculeanus).* Paper presented at the meeting of the Eastern Psychological Association, Philadelphia, PA.

Ackil, J. E., & Ward, E. F. (1982). Chickens in the classroom: Introductory laboratory courses in experimental psychology. *Teaching of Psychology, 9,* 107–108.

Alloway, T. M. (1973). Learning in insects except apoidea. In W. C. Corning, J. A. Dyal, & A. O. D. Willows (Eds.), *Invertebrate learning: Vol 2. Arthropods and gastrioid mollusks* (pp. 131–171). New York: Plenum Press.

Arbit, J. (1964). Learning in annelids and attempts at the chemical modification of this behavior. *Animal Behaviour, 13* (Suppl. 1), 83–87.

Ball, H. J. (1972). A system for recording activity of small insects. *Journal of Economic Entomology, 65,* 129–132.

Best, J. B., & Rubinstein, I. (1962). Maze learning and associated behavior in planaria. *Journal of Comparative and Physiological Psychology, 55,* 560–566.

Best, R. L. (1978). *Living anthropods in the classroom.* Burlington, NC: Carolina Biological Supply Company.

Bitterman, M. E., Menzel, R., Fietz, A., & Schäfer, S. (1983). Classical conditioning of proboscis extension in honeybees (Apis mellifera). *Journal of Comparative Psychology, 97,* 107–119.

Block, R. A., & McConnell, J. V. (1967). Classically conditioned discrimination in the planarian, *Dugesia dorotocephala. Nature, 215,* 1465–1466.

Booker, R., & Quinn, W. G. (1981). Conditioning of leg position in normal and mutant Drosophila. *Proceedings of the National Academy of Sciences of the United States of America, 78,* 3940–3944.

Bullock, T. H., & Horridge, G. A. (1965). *Structure and function of the nervous systems of invertebrates* (Vols. 1–2). San Francisco: Freeman.

Chen, W. Y., Aranda, L. C., & Luco, J. V. (1970). Learning and long- and short-term memory in cockroaches. *Animal Behaviour, 18,* 725–732.

Corning, W. C. (1964). Evidence of right–left discrimination in planarians. *Journal of Psychology, 58,* 131–139.

Corning, W. C., Dyal, J. A., & Willows, A. O. D. (1973). *Invertebrate learning* (Vols. 1–2). New York: Plenum Press.

Corning, W. C., Dyal, J. A., & Willows, A. O. D. (1975). *Invertebrate learning* (Vol. 3). New York: Plenum Press.

Corning, W. C., & Freed, S. (1968). Planarian behavior and biochemistry. *Nature, 219,* 1227–1229.

Corning, W. C., & Kelly, S. (1973). Platyhelminthes: The turbularians. In W. C. Corning, J. A. Dyal, & A. O. D. Willows (Eds.), *Invertebrate learning: Vol 1. Protozoans through annelids* (pp. 171–224). New York: Plenum Press.

Corning, W. C., & Ratner, S. C. (Eds.). (1967). *Chemistry of learning.* New York: Plenum Press.

Corning, W. C., & Riccio, D. (1970). The planarian controversy. In W. Byrne, (Eds.), *Molecular approaches to learning and memory* (pp. 107–150). New York: Academic Press.

Couvillon, P. A., & Bitterman, M. E. (1980). Some phenomena of associate learning in honeybees. *Journal of Comparative and Physiological Psychology, 94,* 878–885.

Couvillon, P. A., & Bitterman, M. E. (1982). Compound conditioning in honeybees. *Journal of Comparative and Physiological Psychology, 96,* 192–199.

Couvillon, P. A., & Bitterman, M. E. (1984). The overlearning-extinction effect and successive negative contrast in honeybees (Apis mellifera). *Journal of Comparative Psychology, 98,* 100–109.

Couvillon, P. A., Klosterhalfen, S., & Bitterman, M. E. (1983). Analysis of overshadowing in honeybees. *Journal of Comparative Psychology,* 97, 154–166.

Crawford, F. T., & Skeen, L. C. (1967). Operant responding in the planarian: A replication study. *Psychological Reports,* 20, 1023–1027.

Datta, L. G. (1962). Learning in the earthworm *Lumbricus terrestris. American Journal of Psychology,* 75, 531–553.

DeCarlo, L. T., & Abramson, C. I. (1989). *Time allocation in carpenter ants. Journal of Comparative Psychology,* 103, 389–400.

DeJianne, D., McGuire, T. R., & Pruzan-Hotchkiss, A. (1985). Conditioned suppression of proboscis extension in *Drosophilia melanogaster. Journal of Comparative Psychology,* 99, 74–80.

Drudge, O. W., & Platt, S. A. (1979). A versatile maze for learning and geotaxic selection in *Drosophila melanogaster. Behavior Research Methods and Instrumentation,* 11, 503–506.

Dudai, Y. (1977). Properties of learning and memory in *Drosophila melanogaster. Journal of Comparative Physiology,* 114, 69–89.

Dyal, J. A. (1973). Behavior modification in annelids. In W. C. Corning, J. A. Dyal, & A. O. D. Willows (Eds.), *Invertebrate learning: Vol. 1. Protozoans through annelids* (pp. 225–290). New York: Plenum Press.

Ebeling, W., Reierson, D. A., & Wagner, R. E. (1968). Influence of repellency on the efficacy of blatticides: IV. Comparison of four cockroach species. *Journal of Economic Entomology,* 61, 1213–1219.

Ebeling, W., Wagner, R. E., & Reierson, D. A. (1966). Influence of repellency on the efficacy of blatticides: I. Learned modification of behavior of the German cockroach. *Journal of Economic Entomology,* 59, 1374–1388.

Fantl, S., & Nevin, J. A. (1965). Classical discriminations in planarians. *Worm Runner's Digest,* 7, 32–34.

Farley, J., & Alkon, D. L. (1985). Cellular mechanisms of learning, memory, and information storage. *Annual Review of Psychology,* 36, 419–494.

Fleer, R. (1972). Some behavioral observations on the ant *P. californicus,* with special reference to habit-reversal learning. *Dissertation Abstracts International,* 33, 2730. (University Microfilms No. 72-30, 477)

Fleer, R. E., & Wyers, E. J. (1963). Partial reinforcement in the ant *Pogonomymex californicus. American Psychologist,* 18, 444.

Freckleton, W. C., Jr., & Wahlsten, D. (1968). Carbon dioxide induced amnesia in the cockroach *Periplaneta americana. Psychonomic Science,* 12, 179–180.

Griffard, C. D. (1963). Classical conditioning of the planarian *Phagocata gracilis* to water flow.

Journal of Comparative and Physiological Psychology, 56, 597–600.

Hassell, M. P., & Southwood, T. R. E. (1978). Foraging strategies of insects. *Annual Review of Ecology and Systematics,* 9, 75–98.

Herz, M. J., Peeke, H. V. S., & Wyers, E. J. (1967). Classical conditioning of the extension response in the earthworm. *Physiology and Behavior,* 2, 409–411.

Hewitt, J. K., Fulker, D. W., & Hewitt, C. A. (1983). Genetic architecture of olfactory discriminative avoidance conditioning in *Drosophila melanogaster. Journal of Comparative Psychology,* 97, 52–58.

Hunt, K., & Shields, R. (1978). Using gerbils in the undergraduate operant laboratory. *Teaching of Psychology,* 5, 210–211.

Kostowski, W., Beck, J., & Meszaros, J. (1965). Drugs affecting the behaviour and spontaneous bioelectric activity of the central nervous system in the ant, *Formica rufa. Journal of Pharmacy and Pharmacology,* 17, 253–255.

Kostowski, W., & Tarchalska, B. (1972). The effects of some drugs affecting brain 5-HT on the aggressive behaviour and spontaneous electrical activity of the central nervous system of the ant, *Formica rufa. Brain Research,* 38, 143–149.

Leeming, F. C., & Little, G. L. (1977). Escape learning in houseflies (*Musca domestica*). *Journal of Comparative and Physiological Psychology,* 91, 260–269.

Longo, N. (1964). Probability learning and habit reversal in the cockroach. *American Journal of Psychology,* 77, 29–41.

Longo, N. (1970). A runway for the cockroach. *Behavior Research Methods and Instrumentation,* 2, 118–119.

Lutz, F. E., Welch, P. S., Galtsoff, P. S., & Needham, J. G. (Eds.). (1959). *Culture methods for invertebrate animals.* New York: Dover. (Original work published in 1937)

Marian, R. W., & Abramson, C. I. (1982). Earthworm behavior in a modified running wheel. *Journal of Mind and Behavior,* 3, 67–74.

Martinsen, D. L., & Kimeldorf, D. J. (1972). Conditioned spatial avoidance behavior of ants induced by X-rays. *Psychological Record,* 22, 225–232.

McConnell, J. V. (Ed.). (1967a). *A manual of psychological experiments on planarians.* Ann Arbor, MI: Journal of Biological Psychology.

McConnell, J. V. (1967b). Specific factors influencing planarian behavior. In W. C. Corning & S. C. Ratner (Eds.), *Chemistry of learning* (pp. 217–233). New York: Plenum Press.

McGuire, T. R. (1984). Learning in three species of Diptera: The blow fly *Phormia regina,* the fruit fly *Drosophila melanogaster*, and the housefly *Musca domestica. Behavior Genetics, 14,* 479–526.

Menzel, R., & Bitterman, M. E. (1983). Learning by honeybees in an unnatural situation. In F. Huber & L. Markl (Eds.), *Behavioral physiology and neuroethology* (pp. 206–215). Heidelberg, West Germany: Springer-Verlag.

Menzel, R., & Erber, J. (1972). The influence of the quantity of reward on the learning performance in honeybees. *Behaviour, 41,* 27–42.

Miller, T., Bruner, L. J., & Fukuto, T. R. (1971). The effects of light, temperature, and DDT poisoning on housefly locomotion and flight muscle activity. *Pesticide Biochemistry and Physiology, 1,* 483–491.

Morgan, R. F. (1981). Learning in submerged *Formica rufa. Psychological Reports, 49,* 63–69.

Nicholls, R. J., & Potter, R. M. (1982). An inexpensive computer and interface for research in the behavioral sciences. *Behavior Research Methods and Instrumentation, 14,* 532–533.

Peeke, H. V. S., Herz, M. J., & Wyers, E. J. (1967). Forward conditioning, backward conditioning, and pseudoconditioning sensitization in the earthworm (*Lumbricus terrestris*). *Journal of Comparative and Physiological Psychology, 64,* 534–536.

Plant, L. (1980). The gerbil jar: A basic home experience in operant conditioning. *Teaching of Psychology, 7,* 109.

Pritchatt, D. (1970). Further studies on the avoidance behaviour of *Periplaneta americana* to electric shock. *Animal Behaviour, 18,* 485–492.

Quinn, W. G. (1984). Work in invertebrates on the mechanisms underlying learning. In P. Marler & H. R. Terrace (Eds.), *The biology of learning* (pp. 197–246). Berlin: Springer-Verlag.

Quinn, W. G., Harris, W. A., & Benzer, S. (1974). Conditioned behavior in *Drosophila melanogaster. Proceedings of the National Academy of Sciences of the United States of America, 71,* 708–712.

Ramos, F. (1966). *Rate of extinction as a function of varying schedule of reinforcement in the harvester ant P. californicus.* Unpublished master's thesis, California College, Los Angeles.

Ratner, S. C. (1967). Annelids and learning: A critical review. In W. C. Corning & S. C. Ratner (Eds.), *Chemistry of learning* (pp. 391–406). New York: Plenum Press.

Ratner, S. C., & Miller, K. R. (1959a). Classical conditioning in earthworms, *Lumbricus terrestris. Journal of Comparative and Physiological Psychology, 52,* 102–105.

Ratner, S. C., & Miller, K. R. (1959b). Effects of spacing of training and ganglia removal on con-

ditioning in earthworms. *Journal of Comparative and Physiological Psychology, 52,* 667–672.

Ratner, S. C., & Stein, D. G. (1965). Responses of worms to light as a function of intertrial interval and ganglion removal. *Journal of Comparative and Physiological Psychology, 59,* 301–305.

Ray, A. J. (1968). Instrumental light avoidance by the earthworm. *Communications in Behavioral Biology, 1,* 205–208.

Reynierse, J. H., & Ratner, S. C. (1964). Acquisition and extinction in the earthworm, *Lumbricus terrestris. Psychological Record, 14,* 383–387.

Robacker, D. C., & Ambrose, J. T. (1978). Random partial reinforcement in the honeybee: Effect on asymptomatic performance and resistance to extinction. *Journal of Apiculture Research, 17,* 182–187.

Robinson, G. H. (1979). Programming experiments with pocket programmable calculators. *Behavior Research Methods and Instrumentation, 11,* 61–63.

Rowland, D. L., Jordan, E. K., & Orson, M. (1984). On the use of chicks as experimental laboratory subjects. *Teaching of Psychology, 11,* 45–46.

Rubadeau, D. O., & Conrad, K. A. (1963). An apparatus to demonstrate and measure operant behavior of arthropoda. *Journal of the Experimental Analysis of Behavior, 6,* 429–430.

Sahley, C. L. (1984). Behavior theory and invertebrate learning. In P. Marler & H. S. Terrace (Eds.), *The biology of learning* (pp. 181–196). Berlin: Springer-Verlag.

Schneirla, T. C. (1933). Motivation and efficiency in ant learning. *Journal of Comparative Psychology, 15,* 243–266.

Schneirla, T. C. (1943). The nature of ant learning: II. The intermediate stage of segmental maze adjustment. *Journal of Comparative Psychology, 35,* 149–176.

Sigurdson, J. E. (1981a). Automated discrete-trials techniques of appetitive conditioning in honeybees. *Behavior Research Methods and Instrumentation, 13,* 1–10.

Sigurdson, J. E. (1981b). Measurement of consummatory behavior in honeybees. *Behavior Research Methods and Instrumentation, 13,* 308–310.

Simmel, E. C., & Ramos, F. (1965). Spatial-probability learning in ants. *American Zoologist, 153,* 228.

Stratton, L. O., & Coleman, W. P. (1972). Maze learning and orientation in the fire ant (*Solenopsis saevissima*). *Journal of Comparative and Physiological Psychology, 83,* 7–12.

Szymanski, J. S. (1912). Modification of the innate

behavior of cockroaches. *Journal of Animal Behavior, 2,* 81–90.

Thompson, R., & McConnell, J. V. (1955). Classical conditioning in the planarian, *Dugesia dorotocephala. Journal of Comparative and Physiological Psychology, 48,* 65–68.

Thorpe, W. H., & Davenport, D. (Eds.). (1964). *Learning and associated phenomena in invertebrates. Animal Behavior, 13* (Suppl. 1).

Tully, T. (1984). Drosophila learning: Behavior and biochemistry. *Behavior Genetics, 14,* 527–557.

Vowles, D. M. (1964). Olfactory learning and brain lesions in the wood ant (*Formica rufa*). *Journal of Comparative and Physiological Psychology, 58,* 105–111.

Vowles, D. M. (1967). Interocular transfer, brain lesions, and maze learning in the wood ant (*Formica rufa*). In W. C. Corning & S. C. Ratner (Eds.), *Chemistry of learning* (pp. 425–447). New York: Plenum Press.

Weiss, C. S. (1980). An inexpensive animal laboratory course. *Teaching of Psychology, 7,* 193–195.

Wells, P. H. (1973). Honey bees. In W. C. Corning, J. A. Dyal, & A. O. D. Willows (Eds.), *Invertebrate learning: Vol. 2. Anthropods and gastropod mollusks* (pp. 173–185). New York: Plenum Press.

Wolach, A. H. (1979). *Programming schedules of reinforcement with integrated circuits.* Chicago: K.D.V.H.E.

Wyers, E. J., Peeke, H. V. S., & Herz, M. J. (1964). Partial reinforcement and resistance to extinction in the earthworm. *Journal of Comparative and Physiological Psychology, 57,* 113–116.

Zellner, D. K. (1966). Effects of removal and regeneration of the suprapharyngeal ganglion on learning, retention, extinction, and negative movements in the earthworm *Lumbricus terrestris* L. *Physiology and Behavior, 1,* 151–159.

APPENDIX E

Suggested Readings by Topic Area on Ethical Principles of Psychologists

Thomas V. McGovern

APA Documents and Texts

Ad Hoc Committee on Ethical Standards in Psychological Research. (1973). *Ethical principles in the conduct of research with human participants.* Washington, DC: American Psychological Association.

American Psychological Association. (1952). Discussion on ethics. *American Psychologist, 7,* 425–455.

American Psychological Association. (1953). *Ethical standards of psychologists.* Washington, DC: Author.

American Psychological Association. (1959). Ethical standards of psychologists. *American Psychologist, 14,* 279–282.

American Psychological Association. (1963). Ethical standards of psychologists. *American Psychologist, 18,* 56–60.

American Psychological Association. (1973). Ethical principles in the conduct of research with human participants. *American Psychologist, 28,* 79–80.

American Psychological Association. (1974). *Casebook in ethical standards of psychologists.* Washington, DC: Author.

American Psychological Association. (1981). Ethical standards of psychologists. *American Psychologist, 36,* 633–638.

American Psychological Association. (1983). *Ethical principles in the conduct of research with human participants.* Washington, DC: Author.

American Psychological Association. (1985). *Duty to protect: Legislative alert.* Washington, DC: Author.

American Psychological Association, American Educational Research Association, National Council on Management in Education. (1985). *Standards for educational and psychological testing.* Washington, DC: Author.

Ethics Committee of the American Psychological Association. (1985). Rules and procedures. *American Psychologist, 40,* 685–694.

Ethics Committee of the American Psychological Association. (1986). Report of the Ethics Committee: 1985. *American Psychologist, 41,* 694–697.

Ethics Committee of the American Psychological Association. (1987). Report of the Ethics Committee: 1986. *American Psychologist, 42,* 730–734.

Hall, J., & Hare-Mustin, R. (1983). Sanctions and the diversity of complaints against psychologists. *American Psychologist, 38,* 714–729.

Hare-Mustin, R., & Hall, J. (1981). Procedures for responding to ethics complaints against psychologists. *American Psychologist, 36,* 1494–1505.

Hobbs, N. (1948). The development of a code of ethical standards for psychology. *American Psychologist, 3,* 80–84.

Mills, D. (1984). Ethics education and adjudication within psychology. *American Psychologist, 39,* 669–675.

Sanders, J. R. (1979). Complaints against psychologists adjudicated informally by APA's committee on scientific and professional ethics and conduct. *American Psychologist, 34,* 1139–1144.

Sanders, J. R., & Keith-Spiegel, P. (1980). Formal and informal adjudication of ethics complaints against psychologists. *American Psychologist, 35,* 1096–1105.

Principle 1: Responsibility

Abramowitz, C., & Dokecki, P. (1977). The politics of clinical judgment: Early empirical returns. *Psychological Bulletin, 84,* 460–476.

Albee, G. W. (1977). Does including psychotherapy in health insurance represent a subsidy to the rich from the poor? *American Psychologist, 32,* 719–721.

Albee, G. W. (1986). Toward a just society: Lessons from observations on the primary prevention of psychopathology. *American Psychologist, 41,* 891–898.

Anderson, J. K., Parente, F. J., & Gordon, D. (1981). A forecast of the future for the mental health profession. *American Psychologist, 36,* 848–855.

DeLeon, P. H., O'Keefe, A. M., VandenBos, G. R., & Kraut, A. G. (1982). How to influence public policy: A blueprint for activism. *American Psychologist, 37,* 476–485.

Edwards, D. W., Greene, L. R., Abramowitz, S. I., & Davidson, C. V. (1979). National health insurance, psychotherapy, and the poor. *American Psychologist, 34,* 411–419.

Good, P., Simon, G. C., & Coursey, R. D. (1981). Public interest activities of APA members. *American Psychologist, 36,* 963–971.

Goodstein, L., & Sandler, I. (1978). Using psychology to promote human welfare: A conceptual analysis of the role of community psychology. *American Psychologist, 33,* 882–892.

Jahoda, M. (1981). Work, employment, and unemployment: Values, theories, and approaches in social research. *American Psychologist, 36,* 184–191.

Morawski, J. G., & Goldstein, S. E. (1985). Psychology and nuclear war: A chapter in our legacy of social responsibility. *American Psychologist, 40,* 276–284.

Parloff, M. B. (1979). Can psychotherapy research guide the policymaker? A little knowledge may be a dangerous thing. *American Psychologist, 34,* 296–306.

Payton, C. R. (1984). Who must do the hard things? *American Psychologist, 39,* 391–397.

Robinson, D. N. (1984). Ethics and advocacy. *American Psychologist, 39,* 787–793.

Sarason, S. B. (1986). And what is the public interest? *American Psychologist, 41,* 899–905.

Sobel, S., & Cummings, N. (1981). The role of professional psychologists in promoting equality. *Professional Psychology, 12,* 171–179.

Weiss, J., & Weiss, C. (1981). Social scientists and decision makers look at the usefulness of mental health research. *American Psychologist, 36,* 837–847.

Principle 2: Competence

American Psychological Association. (1981). Specialty guidelines for the delivery of services by clinical psychologists. *American Psychologist, 36,* 640–651.

American Psychological Association. (1981). Specialty guidelines for the delivery of services by counseling psychologists. *American Psychologist, 36,* 652–663.

American Psychological Association. (1981). Specialty guidelines for the delivery of services by industrial/organizational psychologists. *American Psychologist, 36,* 664–669.

American Psychological Association. (1981). Specialty guidelines for the delivery of services by school psychologists. *American Psychologist, 36,* 670–681.

American Psychological Association, Committee on Professional Standards. (1981). Casebook for providers of psychological services. *American Psychologist, 36,* 682–685.

American Psychological Association, Committee on Professional Standards. (1982). Casebook for providers of psychological services. *American Psychologist, 37,* 698–701.

American Psychological Association, Committee on Professional Standards. (1983). Casebook for providers of psychological services. *American Psychologist, 38,* 708–713.

American Psychological Association, Committee on Professional Standards. (1984). Casebook for providers of psychological services. *American Psychologist, 39,* 663–668.

American Psychological Association, Committee on Professional Standards. (1985). Casebook for providers of psychological services. *American Psychologist, 40,* 678–684.

American Psychological Association, Committee on Professional Standards. (1986). Casebook for providers of psychological services. *American Psychologist, 41,* 688–693.

American Psychological Association, Committee on Professional Standards. (1987). Casebook for providers of psychological services. *American Psychologist, 42,* 704–711.

Board of Professional Affairs, Committee on Professional Standards. (1987). General guidelines for providers of psychological services. *American Psychologist, 42,* 712–773.

Laliotis, D. A., & Grayson, J. H. (1985). Psychologist, heal thyself: What is available for the impaired psychologist? *American Psychologist, 40,* 84–96.

Matarazzo, J. D. (1977). Higher education, professional accreditation, and licensure. *American Psychologist, 32,* 856–859.

Matarazzo, J. D. (1987). There is only one psychology, no specialties, but many applications. *American Psychologist, 42*, 893–903.

Peterson, D. (1976). Is psychology a profession? *American Psychologist, 31*, 572–581.

Licensure

Danish, S. J., & Smyer, M. A. (1981). Unintended consequences of requiring a license to help. *American Psychologist, 36*, 13–21.

Gross, S. J. (1978). The myth of professional licensing. *American Psychologist, 33*, 1009–1016.

Herbsleb, J. D., Sales, B. D., & Overcast, T. D. (1985). Challenging licensure and certification. *American Psychologist, 40*, 1165–1178.

Howard, A., & Lowman, R. L. (1985). Should industrial/organizational psychologists be licensed? *American Psychologist, 40*, 40–47.

Kane, M. (1982). The validity of licensure examinations. *American Psychologist, 37*, 911–918.

Phillips, B. (1982). Regulation and control in psychology: Implications for certification and licensure. *American Psychologist, 37*, 919–926.

Shimberg, B. (1981). Testing for licensure and certification. *American Psychologist, 10*, 1138–1146.

Van Hoose, W., & Kottler, J. (1977). Professional and legal regulation. In *Ethical and legal issues in and psychotherapy* (pp. 101–126). San Francisco: Jossey-Bass.

Principle 3: Moral and Legal Standards

Anderton, P., Staulcup, V., & Grisso, T. (1980). On being ethical in legal places. *Professional Psychology, 11*, 764–773.

Baldick, T. (1980). Ethical discrimination ability of intern psychologists: A function of training in ethics. *Professional Psychology, 11*, 276–282.

Claiborn, W. L. (1982). The problem of professional incompetence. *Professional Psychology, 13*, 153–158.

Keith-Spiegel, P. (1977). Violations of ethical principles due to ignorance or poor professional judgment versus willful disregard. *Professional Psychology, 8*, 288–296.

Knapp, S. (1980). A primer on malpractice for psychologists. *Professional Psychology, 11*, 606–612.

Pope, K. S., Tabachnick, B. G., & Keith-Spiegel, P. (1987). Ethics of practice: The beliefs and behaviors of psychologists as therapists. *American Psychologist, 42*, 993–1006.

Welfel, E. R., & Lipsitz, N. E. (1984). The ethical behavior of professional psychologists: A critical analysis of the research. *The Counseling Psychologist, 12*, 31–42.

Wright, R. (1981). What to do until the malpractice lawyer comes: A survivor's manual. *American Psychologist, 36*, 1535–1541.

Principle 4: Public Statements

Larson, C. (1981, December). Media psychology: New roles and new responsibilities. *APA Monitor*, pp. 3, 7.

McCall, R., & Stocking, S. H. (1982). Between scientists and the public: Communicating psychological research through the mass media. *American Psychologist, 37*, 985–995.

Weigel, R., & Pappas, J. (1981). Social science and the press: A case study and its implications. *American Psychologist, 36*, 480–487.

Principle 5: Confidentiality

Bersoff, D. (1976). Therapist as protector and policeman: New roles as a result of Tarasoff? *Professional Psychology, 7*, 267–273.

DeKraai, M. B., & Sales, B. D. (1982). Privileged communications of psychologists. *Professional Psychology, 13*, 372–388.

Denkowski, K., & Denkowski, G. (1982). Client-counselor confidentiality: An update of rationale, legal status, and implications. *Personnel and Guidance Journal, 60*, 371–375.

Eberlein, L. (1980). Confidentiality of industrial psychological test. *Professional Psychology, 11*, 749–754.

Everstine, L., Everstine, D. S., Heymann, G. M., True, R. H., Frey, D. H., Johnson, H. G., & Seiden, R. H. (1980). Privacy and confidentiality in psychotherapy. *American Psychologist, 35*, 828–840.

Knapp, S., & Vandercreek, L. (1982). Tarasoff: Five years later. *Professional Psychology, 13*, 511–516.

Meyer, R., & Smith, S. (1977). A crisis in group therapy. *American Psychologist, 32*, 638–643.

Siegel, M. (1979). Privacy, ethics, and confidentiality. *Professional Psychology, 10*, 249–258.

Woods, K., & McNamara, J. (1980). Confidentiality: Its effect on interviewee behavior. *Professional Psychology, 11*, 714–721.

Principle 6: Welfare of the Consumer

Berger, M. (1982). Ethics and the therapeutic relationship: Patient rights and therapist responsibilities. In M. Rosenbaum (Ed.),

Ethics and values in psychotherapy: A guidebook. New York: Free Press.

Brickman, P., Rabinowitz, V., Karuza, J., Coates, D., Cohn, E., & Kidder, L. (1982). Models of helping and coping. *American Psychologist, 37,* 368–384.

Buck, J. A., & Hirschman, R. (1980). Economics and mental health services: Enhancing the power of the consumer. *American Psychologist, 35,* 653–661.

Coe, W. C., & Ryken, K. (1979). Hypnosis and risks to human subjects. *American Psychologist, 34,* 673–681.

Faustman, W. O. (1982). Legal and ethical issues in debt collection strategies of professional psychologists. *Professional Psychology, 13,* 208–214.

Hare-Mustin, R. T., Marecek, J., Kaplan, A. G., & Liss-Levinson, N. (1979). Rights of clients, responsibilities of therapists. *American Psychologist, 34,* 3–16.

Holroyd, J. D., & Brodsky, A. M. (1977). Psychologists' attitudes and practices regarding erotic and nonerotic physical contact with patients. *American Psychologist, 32,* 843–849.

Katz, J. H. (1985). The sociopolitical nature of counseling. *The Counseling Psychologist, 13,* 615–624.

Martorano, J. (1982). Ethics and psychopharmacology: Revolution or war? In M. Rosenbaum (Ed.), *Ethics and values in psychotherapy: A guidebook* (pp. 328–359). New York: Free Press.

Masters, W., Johnson, V., Kolodny, R., & Weems, S. (Eds.). (1980). *Ethical issues in sex therapy and research* (Vol. 2). Boston: Little, Brown.

Pope, K. S., Keith-Spiegel, P., & Tabachnick, B. G. (1986). Sexual attraction to clients: The human therapist and the (sometimes) inhuman training system. *American Psychologist, 41,* 147–158.

Van Hoose, W., & Kottler, J. (1977). Issues in behavior therapy. In *Ethical and legal issues in counseling and psychotherapy* (pp. 146–159). San Francisco: Jossey-Bass.

White, M. D., & White, C. A. (1981). Involuntarily committed patients' constitutional right to refuse treatment: A challenge to psychology. *American Psychologist, 36,* 953–962.

Widiger, T. A., & Rorer, L. G. (1984). The responsible psychotherapist. *American Psychologist, 39,* 503–515.

Principle 7: Professional Relationships

American Association of Marriage and Family Counselors. (1975). *Code of professional ethics.* Claremont, CA: Author.

American Medical Association. (1981). *Principles of medical ethics.* Chicago: Author.

American Psychiatric Association. (1981). The principles of medical ethics with annotations especially applicable to psychiatry. Chicago: American Medical Association.

American Psychological Association. (1952). Psychology and its relationships with other professions: Ad hoc committee on relations between psychology and the medical profession. *American Psychologist, 7,* 145–152.

Glaser, R. D., & Thorpe, J. S. (1986). Unethical intimacy: A survey of sexual contact and advances between psychology educators and female graduate students. *American Psychologist, 41,* 43–51.

Landis, B. (1927). *Professional codes.* New York: Teachers College, Columbia University.

National Association of Social Workers. (1980). *Code of ethics.* Washington, DC: Author.

Pope, K. S., Levenson, H., & Schover, L. R. (1979). Sexual intimacy in psychology training: Results and implications of a national survey. *American Psychologist, 34,* 682–684.

Roberts, A. (1982). Ethical guidelines for group leaders. *Journal for Specialists in Group Work, 7,* 174–181.

Principle 8: Assessment Techniques

Bersoff, D. N. (1981). Testing and the law. *American Psychologist, 36,* 1047–1056.

Gordon, E., & Terrell, M. (1981). The changed social context of testing. *American Psychologist, 36,* 1167–1171.

Korchin, S., & Schuldberg, D. (1981). The future of clinical assessment. *American Psychologist, 36,* 1147–1158.

London, M., & Bray, D. W. (1980). Ethical issues in testing and evaluation for personnel decisions. *American Psychologist, 35,* 890–901.

Matarazzo, J. D. (1986). Computerized clinical psychological test interpretations. Unvalidated plus all mean and no sigma. *American Psychologist, 41,* 14–24.

Messick, S. (1980). Test validity and the ethics of assessment. *American Psychologist, 35,* 1012–1027.

Novick, M. (1981). Federal guidelines and professional standards. *American Psychologist, 36,* 1035–1046.

Principle 9: Research With Human Participants

Adair, J. G., Dushenko, T. W., & Lindsay, R. C. L. (1985). Ethical regulations and their impact on research practice. *American Psychologist, 40,* 59–72.

Baumrind, D. (1971). Principles of ethical conduct in the treatment of subjects: Reaction to the draft report of the Committee on Ethical Standards in Psychological Research. *American Psychologist, 26,* 887–896.

Baumrind, D. (1985). Research using intentional deception: Ethical issues revisited. *American Psychologist, 40,* 165–174.

Ceci, S. J., Peters, D., & Plotkin, J. (1985). Human subjects review, personal values, and the regulation of social science research. *American Psychologist, 40,* 994–1002.

Holden, C. (1979, November 2). Ethics in social science research. *Science,* pp. 537–540.

Lindsey, R. T. (1984). Informed consent and deception in psychotherapy research: An ethical analysis. *The Counseling Psychologist, 12,* 79–86.

Loftus, E., & Monahan, J. (1980). Trial by data: Psychological research as legal evidence. *American Psychologist, 35,* 270–283.

McHugh, M. C., Koeske, R. D., & Frieze, I. H. (1986). Issues to consider in conducting nonsexist psychological research. A guide for researchers. *American Psychologist, 41,* 879–890.

O'Leary, D. K., & Borkovec, T. D. (1978). Conceptual, methodological, and ethical problems of placebo groups and psychotherapy research. *American Psychologist, 33,* 821–830.

Rosenthal, R. (1978). How often are our numbers wrong? *American Psychologist, 33,* 1005–1008.

Schlenker, B., & Forsyth, D. (1977). On the ethics of psychological research. *Journal of Experimental Social Psychology, 13,* 369–396.

Smith, D. (1981). Unfinished business with informed consent procedures. *American Psychologist, 36,* 22–26.

Stanley, B., Sieber, J. E., & Melton, G. B. (1987). Empirical studies of ethical issues in research. *American Psychologist, 42,* 735–741.

West, S. G., & Gunn, S. P. (1978). Some issues of ethics and social psychology. *American Psychologist, 33,* 30–38.

Wilson, D. W., & Donnerstein, E. (1976). Legal and ethical aspects of nonreactive social psychological research: An excursion into the public mind. *American Psychologist, 31,* 765–773.

Principle 10: Care and Use of Animals

American Psychological Association. (1981). Guidelines for the use of animals in school science behavior projects. *American Psychologist, 36,* 685.

Gallistel, C. R. (1981). Bell, Magendie, and the proposals to restrict the use of animals in neurobehavioral research. *American Psychologist, 36,* 357–360.

Gallup, G. G., & Suarez, S. D. (1985). Alternatives to the use of animals in psychological research. *American Psychologist, 40,* 1104–1111.

Rollin, B. E. (1985). The moral status of research animals in psychology. *American Psychologist, 40,* 920–926.

Minorities/Cross-Cultural Sensitivities

Bernal, M., & Padilla, R. (1982). Status of minority curricula and training in clinical psychology. *American Psychologist, 37,* 780–787.

Bronstein, P. (1986). Self-disclosure, paranoia, and unaware racism: Another look at the black client and the white therapist. *American Psychologist, 41,* 225–227.

Carney, C. G., & Kahn, K. B. (1984). Building competencies for effective cross-cultural counseling: A developmental review. *The Counseling Psychologist, 12,* 111–119.

Hicks, L. H., & Ridley, S. E. (1979). Black studies in psychology. *American Psychologist, 34,* 597–602.

Isaac, P. (1985). Recruitment of minority students into graduate programs in psychology. *American Psychologist, 40,* 472–475.

Jones, A., & Seagull, A. A. (1977). Dimensions of the relationship between the Black client and the White therapist. *American Psychologist, 32,* 850–855.

Jones, J. M. (1981). The concept of racism and its changing reality. In B. Bowser & R. Hunt (Eds.), *Impacts of racism on White Americans* (pp. 27–49). Beverly Hills, CA: Sage.

Korchin, S. (1980). Clinical psychology and minority problems. *American Psychologist, 35,* 262–269.

Leong, F. T. (1986). Counseling and psychotherapy with Asian-Americans: Review of the literature. *Journal of Counseling Psychology, 33,* 196–206.

Lonner, W. J. (1985). Issues in testing and assessment in cross-cultural counseling. *The Counseling Psychologist, 13,* 599–614.

Malgady, R. G., Rogler, L. H., & Constantino, G. (1987). Ethnocultural and linguistic bias in mental health evaluation of Hispanics. *American Psychologist, 42,* 228–234.

Morin, S. F. (1977). Heterosexual bias in psychological research on lesbianism and male homosexuality. *American Psychologist, 32,* 629–637.

Rogler, L. H., Malgady, R. G., Constantino, G., & Blumenthal, R. (1987). What do culturally sensitive mental health services mean? The case of Hispanics. *American Psychologist, 42,* 565–570.

Russo, N., Olmedo, E., Stapp, J., & Fulcher, R. (1981). Women and minorities in psychology. *American Psychologist, 36,* 1315–1363.

Smith, E. M. J. (1985). Ethnic minorities: Life stress, social support, and mental health issues. *The Counseling Psychologist, 13,* 537–579.

Sue, D. W., Bernier, J. E., Durran, A., Feinberg, L., Pederson, P., Smith, E. J., & Vasquez-Nutall, E. (1982). Position paper: Cross-cultural counseling competencies. *The Counseling Psychologist, 10,* 45–52.

Sue, S. (1977). Community mental health services to minority groups: Some optimism, some pessimism. *American Psychologist, 32,* 616–624.

Sue, S. (1983). Ethnic minority issues in psychology: A reexamination. *American Psychologist, 38,* 583–592.

Sue, S., & Zane, M. (1987). The role of culture and cultural techniques in psychotherapy: A critique and reformulation. *American Psychologist, 42,* 37–45.

Suinn, R., & Witt, J. (1982). Survey on ethnic minority faculty recruitment and retention. *American Psychologist, 37,* 1239–1244.

Women

Emmons, C. (1982). A longitudinal study of the careers of a cohort of assistant professors in psychology. *American Psychologist, 37,* 1228–1238.

Hare-Mustin, R. T. (1938). An appraisal of the relationship between women and psychotherapy. *American Psychologist, 38,* 593–601.

Huston, K. (1984). Ethical decisions in treating battered women. *Professional Psychology: Research and Practice, 15,* 822–832.

Kaplan, M. (1983). A woman's view of DSM-III. *American Psychologist, 38,* 786–792.

Lott, B. (1985). The potential enrichment of social/personality psychology through feminist research and vice versa. *American Psychologist, 40,* 155–164.

Solmon, L. (1978). Attracting women to psychology: Effects of university behavior and the labor market. *American Psychologist, 33,* 990–999.

Stricker, G. (1977). Implications of research for psychotherapeutic treatment of women. *American Psychologist, 32,* 14–22.

Task Force on Sex Bias and Sex Role Stereotyping in Psychotherapeutic Practice. (1978). Guidelines for therapy with women. *American Psychologist, 33,* 1122–1123.

Williams, J. B. W., & Spitzer, R. L. (1983). The issue of sex bias in DSM-III. *American Psychologist, 38,* 793–798.

Academia

Adair, J. G., Lindsay, R. C. L., & Carlopio, J. (1983). Social artifact research and ethical regulations: Their impact on the teaching of experimental methods. *Teaching of Psychology, 10,* 159–162.

Bridgwater, C. A., Bornstein, P. H., & Walkenbach, J. (1981). Ethical issues and the assignment of publication credit. *American Psychologist, 36,* 524–525.

Britton, B. K., Richardson, D., Smith, S. S., & Hamilton, T. (1983). Ethical aspects of participating in psychology experiments: Effects of anonymity on evaluation and complaints of distressed subjects. *Teaching of Psychology, 10,* 146–149.

Deutsch, M. (1979). Education and distributive justice: Some reflections on grading systems. *American Psychologist, 34,* 391–401.

Fishman, D. B., & Neigher, W. D. (1982). American psychology in the eighties: Who will buy. *American Psychologist, 37,* 533–546.

Goodstein, L. (1981). Ethics are for academics too! *Professional Psychology, 2,* 191–193.

Kimble, G. A. (1987). The scientific value of undergraduate research participation. *American Psychologist, 42,* 267–278.

Handelsman, M. M., Rosen, J., & Arguello, A. (1987). Informed consent of students: How much information is enough? *Teaching of Psychology, 14,* 107–109.

Wachtel, P. L. (1980). Investigation and its discontents: Some constraints on progress in psychological research. *American Psychologist, 35,* 399–408.

Consultation and Program Evaluation

Gorry, G., & Goodrich, T. (1978). On the roles of values in program evaluation. *Evaluation Quarterly, 2,* 561–572.

Guba, E. (1975). Problems in utilizing the results of evaluation. *Journal of Research and Development in Education, 8,* 42–54.

Mirvis, P. H., & Seashore, S. E. (1979). Being ethical in organizational research. *American Psychologist, 34,* 766–780.

Robinson, S. E., & Grass, D. R. (1985). Ethics of consultation: The Canterville ghosts. *The Counseling Psychologist, 13,* 444–465.

Scheinfeld, S., & Lord, G. (1981). The ethics of evaluation researchers. *Evaluation Review, 5,* 377–391.

Child, Marriage, Family Therapy

Glenn, C. (1980). Ethical issues in the practice of child psychotherapy. *Professional Psychology, 11,* 613–619.

Kosinski, F. (1982). Standards, accreditation, and licensure in marital and family therapy. *Personnel and Guidance Journal, 60,* 350–352.

Margolin, G. (1982). Ethical and legal considerations in marital and family therapy. *American Psychologist, 37,* 788–801.

Melton, G. B. (1983). Toward "personhood" for adolescents: Autonomy and privacy as values in public policy. *American Psychologist, 38,* 99–103.

Muehlman, T., & Kimmons, C. (1981). Psychologists' views on child abuse reporting, confidentiality, life and the law: An exploratory study. *Professional Psychology, 12,* 631–638.

Theoretical Papers and Texts

Boyd, D. (1984). The principle of principles. In W. Kurtines & J. Gewirtz, *Morality, moral behavior, and moral development.* New York: Wiley.

Callahan, D. (1980). Goals in the teaching of ethics. In D. Callahan & S. Bok (Eds.), *Ethics teaching in higher education.* New York: Plenum Press.

Drane, J. (1982). Ethics and psychotherapy: A philosophical perspective. In M. Rosenbaum (Ed.), *Ethics and values in psychotherapy* (pp. 15–50). New York: Free Press.

Flanagan, S., & Liberman, R. (1982). Ethical issues in the practice of behavior therapy. In M. Rosenbaum (Ed.), *Ethics and values in psychotherapy: A guidebook* (pp. 207–236). New York: Free Press.

Forsyth, D. (1980). A taxonomy of ethical ideologies. *Journal of Personality and Social Psychology, 39,* 175–184.

Gibbs, J. C., & Schnell, S. V. (1985). Moral development "versus" socialization: A critique. *American Psychologist, 40,* 1071–1080.

Gilligan, D. (1982). *In a different voice: Psychological theory and women's development.* Cambridge, MA: Harvard University Press.

Haan, N. (1982). Can research on morality be "scientific"? *American Psychologist, 37,* 1086–11804.

Hogan, R. (1973). Moral conduct and moral character: A psychological perspective. *Psychological Bulletin, 79,* 217–232.

Kaminsky, H. (1984). Moral development in historical perspective. In W. Kurtines & J. Gewirtz (Eds.), *Morality, moral behavior, and moral development* (pp. 400–413). New York: Wiley.

Kimble, G. (1984). Psychology's two cultures. *American Psychologist, 39,* 833–839.

Kimmel, A. (Ed.). (1981). *Ethics of human subject research: New directions for methodology of social and behavioral science.* San Francisco: Jossey-Bass.

Kitchener, K. S. (1984). Intuition, critical evaluation, and ethical principles: The foundation for ethical decisions in counseling psychology. *The Counseling Psychologist, 12,* 43–55.

Kohlberg, L. (1976). Moral stages and moralization: The cognitive–developmental approach. In T. Lickona (Ed.), *Moral development and behavior* (pp. 31–53). New York: Holt, Rinehart & Winston.

Kurtines, W., & Gewirtz, J. (1984). Certainty and morality: Objectivistic versus relativistic approaches. In W. Kurtines & J. Gewirtz (Eds.), *Morality, moral behavior, and moral development* (pp. 3–23). New York: Wiley.

Lickona, T. (1976). Critical issues in the study of moral development and behavior. In T. Lickona (Ed.), *Moral development and behavior* (pp. 3–27). New York: Holt, Rinehard & Winston.

Lickona, T. (1980). What does moral psychology have to say to the teacher of ethics? In D. Callahan & S. Bok (Eds.), *Ethics teaching in higher education* (pp. 105–132). New York: Plenum Press.

May, W. (1980). Professional ethics: Setting, terrain, and teacher. In D. Callahan & S.

Bok (Eds.), *Ethics teaching in higher education*. New York: Plenum Press.

Morawski, J. (1982). Assessing psychology's moral heritage through our neglected utopias. *American Psychologist, 37,* 1082–1095.

Morrill, R. (1980). *Teaching values in college.* San Francisco: Jossey-Bass.

Raphael, D. (1981). *Moral philosophy.* New York: Oxford University Press.

Reese, H., & Fremouw, W. (1984). Normal and normative ethics in behavioral sciences. *American Psychologist, 39,* 863–876.

Rest, J. R. (1984). Research on moral development: Implications for training counseling psychologists. *The Counseling Psychologist, 12,* 19–29.

Rosenbaum, M. (Ed.). (1982). *Ethics and values in psychotherapy: A guidebook.* New York: Free Press.

Schuler, H. (1982). *Ethical problems in psychological research.* New York: Academic Press.

Schwitzgebel, R. L., & Schwitzgebel, R. K. (1980). *Law and psychological practice.* New York: Wiley.

APPENDIX F

A Selected Computer Resource List
for Teachers of Psychology

The sources listed here may help you obtain the information you need about the use of computers in teaching psychology. This is not intended to be an exhaustive list, and neither does the inclusion of an item on this list imply endorsement by APA.

Organizations

CONDUIT. CONDUIT is a nonprofit organization that distributes inexpensive software for higher education, including several packages of programs for psychology. Contact: CONDUIT, University of Iowa, Oakdale Campus, Iowa City, IA 52242.

Microcomputer Applications in Education. This is a special interest group of the American Educational Research Association that promotes the sharing of information with and about microcomputers as well as the use of microcomputers. Contact: Dennis Deck, Northwest Regional Educational Laboratory, 300SW 6th Avenue, Portland, OR 97204; 503/248-6800.

Society for Computers in Psychology. The society is an adjunct to the Psychonomic Society and has a "special goal of aiding psychologists in using microcomputers in their teaching and research." Contact: David A. Eckerman, Secretary-Treasurer, Department of Psychology, University of North Carolina, Chapel Hill, NC 27514; 919/962-5084.

Publications

Behavioral Research Methods, Instruments and Computers. This is a professional journal that focuses on instructional and research applications of the computer in psychology. It is published by the Psychonomic Society, Department of Psychology, University of Minnesota, Minneapolis, MN 55455.

"Computers and Technology." This column appears three times a year in a newsletter called *Network: The Newsletter for Psychology Teachers at Two-Year Colleges*, which examines the technology and applications of computers to the classroom. To subscribe to *Network*, write to the High School and Undergraduate Program, Office of Educational Affairs, American Psychological Association, 1200 17th Street, N.W., Washington, DC 20036.

Computers in Psychiatry and Psychology. The *CPP* newsletter addresses issues mainly of a clinical nature in psychology. Contact: Marc D. Schwartz, *Computers in Psychiatry and Psychology*, 26 Trumbull Street, New Haven, CT 06511; 203/562-9873.

Computer Use in Social Services Network. The *CUSS Network* newsletter is devoted to linking people who want to exchange resources, information, and ideas about using computers in the social services. Contact: Dick Schoech, University of Texas at Arlington, P.O. Box 19129, Arlington, TX 76019.

Computer Use in Psychology: A Directory of Software, Second Edition. Edited by Michael L. Stoloff and James V. Couch. Designed to assist psychologists in identifying those software packages that best fit their needs, the *Directory* provides impartial, nonevaluative summaries of over 800 software packages, allowing academics and clinicians to choose the software they need. The volume is divided into four sections: Academic Software, for use in psychology instruction; Psychological Testing Software, for use in testing; Other Clinical Software, for use in clinical practice; and Statistics and Research Software, for data analysis and presentation. Available from the American Psychological Association, Order Department, P.O. Box 2710, Hyattsville, MD 20784.

Computing in Undergraduate Psychology: Proceedings and *Computing in Undergraduate Psychology: Software Guide.* These two publications are from the Gettysburg Conference. The *Proceedings* lists the presentations on computer uses. The *Software*

Guide lists numerous commercial and noncommercial computer programs, including cost and contacts. They are available for $6 each from Dick Wood, Academic Computing Center, Gettysburg College, Gettysburg, PA 17325-1486.

Micro-Psych Network. The *Micro-Psych Network* newsletter is by and for psychologists interested in using microcomputers. "It is intended as an informal forum of communication, including articles about ongoing projects, software, hardware description and reviews, questions for and replies from readers," and so on. *Micro-Psych Network* is published by Professional Resource Exchange, 635 S. Orange Avenue, Suites 4 and 5, Sarasota, FL 33577.

Using Computers in Clinical Practice: Mental Health. Written by Marc D. Schwartz, this new book (1985) is published by Haworth Press, 28 East 22nd Street, New York, NY 10010.

Meetings

The Society for Computers in Psychology has an annual meeting that is held in the same location as, and on the day before, the annual meeting of the Psychonomic Society. Traditionally, proceedings of the meetings have been published in the April issue of *Behavior Research Methods, Instruments, and Computers.*

Many national and regional conventions now include symposia on computers. For example, the 1984 Annual Meeting of the American Psychological Association included a workshop called "Microcomputer Applications for the Anxious User." The Mid-America Conference for Teachers of Psychology includes a "Computers in the Teaching of Psychology" presentation. Contact Joe Palladino for details about upcoming Mid-America Conferences for Teachers of Psychology at 812/464-1719.

Awards

EDUCOM/NCRIPTAL. EDUCOM (a consortium of 450 colleges and universities committed to the quality of academic computing) and NCRIPTAL (National Center for Research to Improve Postsecondary Teaching and Learning) at the University of Michigan are jointly sponsoring with disciplinary associations, foundations, and corporations a program to promote excellence in the development and application of educational computer software. Awards are given annually in two divisions, one for the application of software to solve educational problems and the other for the development of high-quality software. Awards are limited to software and applications addressed to undergraduate education. For more information, contact Robert B. Kozma, Program Director, NCRIPTAL, Suite 2400, School of Education Building, University of Michigan, Ann Arbor, Michigan 48109-1259; 313/936-2741.

APPENDIX G

Where to Go for More Information: Selected APA Offices

Office of Educational Affairs

Identifies and analyzes developments in education and public policy affecting the education and training of psychologists. This office provides direct services to APA's high school teacher affiliates and monitors and coordinates activities related to the teaching of psychology at the undergraduate and graduate levels. It publishes two newsletters: *High School Psychology Teacher*, for psychology instructors in secondary schools, and *Network*, for teachers of psychology at 2-year colleges. For more information call (202) 955-7721.

Undergraduate Consultant Service. This service provides consultants for curriculum evaluations, departmental self-assessments, planning of laboratory and teaching facilities, advising issues, and general personnel issues such as promoting faculty development. The Office of Educational Affairs can suggest the names of potential consultants for departments, all of whom have been approved by the Committee on Undergraduate Education. The requesting department is responsible for contacting these individuals to refine the consultation questions, to discuss availability time and the issues of honorarium and expenses, to ascertain what types of materials might be sent to the consultant prior to the visit to enhance the outcome of the consultation, and to agree on the form in which feedback would be delivered.

Office of Ethics

Educates the public and the profession on appropriate scientific and professional ethics and conduct as well as investigates alleged infractions of APA's *Ethical Principles of Psychologists* by APA members and determines appropriate actions. Among its concerns is the use of human participants in experiments. Copies of *Ethical Principles of Psychologists* or of Rules and Procedures of the Ethics Committee are given out only in conjunction with a filed claim; bulk copies may be ordered from the APA's Order Department.

Office of Ethnic Minority Affairs

Works to increase scientific understanding of how psychology pertains to culture and ethnicity, pro-

motes the quality and number of educational and training opportunities for ethnic minority persons in psychology, and works to increase the delivery of appropriate psychological services to ethnic minority communities. The APA publication *Preparing for Graduate Study in Psychology: NOT for Seniors Only!* has an excellent chapter on educational resources for minority students. There are chapters pertinent to ethnic minority students in *Is Psychology the Major for You?* and chapters for advisers in *Is Psychology for Them? A Guide to Undergraduate Advising.* All three publications are available from the APA Order Department. To contact the Office of Ethnic Minority Affairs, call (202) 955-7763.

Office of Women's Programs

Coordinates APA's efforts to ensure equal opportunity for women psychologists as practitioners, educators, and scientists. Strives to eliminate gender bias in education and training, research, and diagnosis. Monitors the welfare of women as consumers of psychological services and promotes the development and application of psychological knowledge to improve the status of women throughout society. Among its publications are *Understanding the Manuscript Review Process: Increasing the Participation of Women* and *Graduate Faculty Interested in the Psychology of Women,* both available through the APA Order Department. To contact the office call (202) 955-7767.

Special Publications

In addition to a wide variety of books and pamphlets, APA publishes special editions of APA journals. These and other APA publications are available from the APA Order Department.

Casebook on Ethical Principles of Psychologists. Presents conflicts and dilemmas that reflect the ongoing search for a balance between two opposing forces—changing societal values and the responsibilities of the profession.

The G. Stanley Hall Lecture Series. A series of volumes covering subjects usually addressed in introductory psychology courses. Each lecture was originally presented by a leading psychologist as an invited lecturer at the APA Annual Convention. The 1989 volume includes chapters by Michael Mahoney on sport psychology, Carroll Izzard on the role of emotions, and Martin Seligman on depression.

The Gifted and Talented: Developmental Perspectives. Leading psychologists discuss the nature of giftedness and the role of society in preparing gifted and talented children for a productive life. 1985, 478 pages.

Standards for Educational and Psychological Testing. Developed for use by a wide audience including students, test developers, publishers, and users, this book includes standards for testing in particular environments such as schools and employment settings. A joint project of the American Educational Research Association, APA, and the National Council of Measurement in Education. 1985, 96 pages.

Teaching a Psychology of People: Resources for Gender and Sociocultural Awareness. Scholars from a variety of cultural and ethnic backgrounds review the deficiencies in psychological theory and research on cultural, ethnic, and gender issues; present recent theory and research; and discuss approaches and obstacles to teaching about these groups.

Other Services

Membership/Affiliation. To apply for membership in APA, contact the Membership Office, APA, 1200 17th Street NW, Washington, DC 20036. The minimum standard for election to Member status is receipt of the doctoral degree based in part on a psychological dissertation or based on other evidence of proficiency in psychological scholarship. Those who do not qualify for membership status may become Associate Members, and high school teachers may become High School Teacher Affiliates. High School Teacher Affiliates receive a subscription to *High School Psychology Teacher* as well as to the *APA Monitor* and are entitled to the same discounts on publications enjoyed by members. Undergraduate and graduate students of psychology may become Student Affiliates; they must be endorsed by a member of the Association. For details, contact the Membership Office.

CONTRIBUTORS

Charles Abramson, Department of Biochemistry, Health Science Center, State University of New York at Brooklyn, 450 Clarkson Avenue, Box 8, Brooklyn, NY 11203-2098.

Drew C. Appleby, Psychology Department, Marlan College, 3200 Cold Spring Road, Indianapolis, IN 46222.

J. David Arnold, Psychology Department, St. Lawrence University, Canton, NY 13617.

Eileen C. Astor-Stetson, Psychology Department, Bloomsburg University, Bloomsburg, PA 17815.

George Banziger, Psychology Department, Marietta College, Marietta, OH 45750-3031.

Kathy Barsz, Department of Psychology, State University of New York at Geneseo, Geneseo, NY 14454.

Angela H. Becker, Emporia State University, 1200 Commercial, Emporia, KS 66801-5087.

Peter H. Bohling, Department of Psychology, Bloomsburg University, Bloomsburg, PA 17815.

Thomas F. Brothen, General College, University of Minnesota, 128 Pleasant Street, SE, Minneapolis, MN 55455.

Robert T. Brown, Psychology Department, University of North Carolina at Wilmington, Wilmington, NC 28403.

Peter R. Burzynski, 8688 Hillside Drive, Newburgh, IN 47630.

Bernardo J. Carducci, Division of Social Science, Indiana University Southeast, New Albany, IN 47150.

Ronda J. Carpenter, Psychology Department, Roanoke College, Salem, VA 24153.

Alan L. Carsrud, Bridge Hall, Room 6, University Park, University of Southern California, Los Angeles, CA 90089-1421.

J. R. Corey, Psychology Department, Long Island University, C. W. Post Campus, Brookvale, NY 11548.

Michael T. Crovello, Department of Psychology, University of Notre Dame, Notre Dame, IN 46556.

Stephen F. Davis, Psychology Department, Emporia State University, Emporia, KS 66801-5087.

George M. Diekhoff, Division of Social and Behavioral Sciences, Midwestern State University, 3400 Taft Boulevard, Wichita Falls, TX 76308.

Stephen J. Dollinger, Psychology Department, Southern Illinois University, Carbondale, IL 62901.

Paul K. Dunay, Department of Psychology, University of Notre Dame, Notre Dame, IN 46556.

Jean L. Engelhardt, Department of Psychology, University of Notre Dame, Notre Dame, IN 46556.

Charles Epstein, Burke Marketing Research, 800 Broadway, Cincinnati, OH 45202.

Cynthia A. Erickson, Psychology Department, Emporia State University, 1200 Commercial, Emporia, KS 66801-5087.

Charles Denton Fernald, Department of Psychology, University of North Carolina, Charlotte, NC 28223.

L. Dodge Fernald, Harvard University, Garden Street, Cambridge, MA 02138.

Peter S. Fernald, 160 Rockland Street, Portsmouth, NH 03801.

Sue Sampen Fernald, Division TEACCH, University of North Carolina at Chapel Hill, Chapel Hill, NC 27514.

Martin S. Fiebert, Psychology Department, California State University, Long Beach, CA 90840.

G. Alfred Forsyth, Provost and Vice President, Millersville University of Pennsylvania, Millersville, PA 17551-0302.

Cathy A. Grover, Emporia State University, 1200 Commercial, Emporia, KS 66801-5087.

Gregory F. Harper, 9 Holmes Place, Fredonia, NY 14063.

Frank Hollingsworth, 2440 Creekview Drive, Lancaster, PA 17602.

George S. Howard, Psychology Department, University of Notre Dame, Notre Dame, IN 46556.

William J. Hunter, Education Tower, 1134, University of Calgary, 2500 University Drive, NW, Calgary, Alberta T2N 1N4, Canada.

Jane A. Jegerski, 8915 West 104th Street, Palos Hills, IL 60465.

Barbara C. Jessen, University of Evansville, 1800 Lincoln Avenue, Evansville, IN 47714.

Alan R. P. Journet, Psychology Department, Southeast Missouri State University, Cape Girardeau, MO 63701.

Ernest D. Kemble, Division of Social Sciences, University of Minnesota, Morris, MN 56267.

Allen H. Keniston, Department of Psychology, University of Wisconsin—Eau Claire, Eau Claire, WI 54702-4004.

Darlene Kennedy, Beaver College, Glenside, PA 19038-3295.

Jeffrey S. Kixmiller, Emporia State University, 1200 Commercial, Emporia, KS 66801-5087.

Bruce G. Klonsky, Psychology Department, SUNY —Fredonia College, Fredonia, NY 14063.

Paul G. Konstanty, Department of Psychology, University of Notre Dame, Notre Dame, IN 46556.

C. Sue Lamb, Psychology Department, University of North Carolina, Wilmington, NC 28403-3297.

Linda Leal, Psychology Department, Eastern Illinois University, Charleston, IL 61920.

Thomas L. Lestina, 725 East Bauer Road, Naperville, IL 60540.

Margaret A. Lloyd, 39 Gannett Pasture Lane, Scituate, MA 02066.

Salvador Macias III, Division of Humanities, Social Sciences, and Education, University of South Carolina, 200 Miller Road, Sumter, SC 29150-2498.

Margaret S. Martin, 160 Valley Road, Greenwood, SC 29646.

Bernard Mausner, Psychology Department, Beaver College, Glenside, PA 19038.

Richard B. May, University of Victoria, Victoria, British Columbia V8W 2Y2, Canada.

Thomas V. McGovern, Office of the Provost, Virginia Commonwealth University, 901 West Franklin Street, Richmond, VA 23284.

Janet M. Morahan-Martin, 17 Fuller Brook Road, Wellesley, MA 02181.

James P. Motiff, 73 West 21st Street, Holland, MI 49423.

Fred L. Nesbit, Sauk Valley Community College, 173 IL Route 2, Dixon, IL 61021-9110.

Epp P. Ogden, Salem College, Salem, WV 28036.

Kenneth W. Olm, University of Texas at Austin, Austin, TX 78712.

Michele A. Paludi, Women's Studies, Hunter College, City University of New York, New York, NY 10021.

Blaine F. Peden, Psychology Department, University of Wisconsin—Eau Claire, Eau Claire, WI 54702-4004.

Antonio E. Puente, Psychology Department, University of North Carolina, Wilmington, NC 28406.

Ellen P. Reese, Route 1, Box 82, Oskaloosa, KS 66066.

Thomas R. Rocklin, Division of Psychological and Quantitative Foundations, College of Education, University of Iowa, 374 Lindquist Center, Iowa City, IA 52242.

Kurt Salzinger, 161 West 75th, Apt. 7-D, New York, NY 10023.

Connie Schick, 827 Light Street Road, Bloomsburg, PA 17815.

Lita Linzer Schwartz, Cedar Brook Hill Apts. C-PH-13, Wyncote, PA 19095.

Wilber E. Scoville, Psychology Department, University of Wisconsin—Oshkosh, Oshkosh, WI 54901.

Barbara K. Sholley, Psychology Department, University of Richmond, Richmond, VA 23173.

Joan E. Sieber, Psychology Department, California State University, Hayward, CA 94542.

Melinda A. Sletten, University of Minnesota: Morris, Morris, MN 56267.

Joan Young Smith, 613 Glencoe Road, SE, Huntsville, AL 35802.

Charles M. Stoup, Office of the Dean, College of Liberal Arts, Texas A & M University, College Station, TX 77843.

S. J. Tatz, Psychology Department, Long Island University, C. W. Post College, Brookvale, NY 11548.

Robert T. Tauber, Humanities and Social Sciences Division, The Behrend College of Penn State, Erie, PA 16563.

Thomas J. Thieman, Psychology Department, College of St. Catherine, St. Paul, MN 55105.

Ashton D. Trice, Psychology Department, Mary Baldwin College, Staunton, VA 24401.

O. Ashton Trice, Mary Baldwin College, Staunton, VA 24401.

Mary Moore Vandendorpe, 1913 Coach Drive, Naperville, IL 60565.

Walter F. Wagor, Psychology Department, Indiana University East, 2325 Chester Boulevard, Richmond, IN 47374.

Bradley M. Waite, Department of Psychology, Wright State University, Fairborn, OH 45324.

David L. Watson, Psychology Department, University of Hawaii, Honolulu, HI 96882.

Michael Wertheimer, Psychology Department, Box 345, University of Colorado, Boulder, CO 80309.

Walter A. Woods, 389 Smyrna Church Road, Carrollton, GA 30117.

Fred L. Yaffe, Psychology Deparment, Eastern Illinois University, Charleston, IL 61920.

David H. Young, Psychology Department, Purdue University, 2101 Coliseum Boulevard East, Ft. Wayne, IN 46805.

INDEX